Marines Dodging Death

Marines Dodging Death

Sixty-Two Accounts of Close Calls in World War II, Korea, Vietnam, Lebanon, Iraq and Afghanistan

Edited by ROBERT A. SIMONSEN

McFarland & Company, Inc., Publishers
Jefferson, North Carolina, and London

Maps by C. Douglas Anderson.

Excerpts in Chapter 18 from the *Korean War: Pusan to Chosin; An Oral History*, copyright © 1985 by Donald Knox, are reprinted by permission of Harcourt, Inc.

LIBRARY OF CONGRESS CATALOGUING-IN-PUBLICATION DATA

Marines dodging death : sixty-two accounts of close calls in World War II, Korea, Vietnam, Lebanon, Iraq and Afghanistan / edited by Robert A. Simonsen.
  p.   cm.
Includes bibliographical references and index.

ISBN 978-0-7864-3821-1
softcover : 50# alkaline paper ∞

1. Marines — United States — Biography — Anecdotes.
2. United States. Marine Corps — Biography.   3. World War, 1939–1945 — Personal narratives, American.   4. Korean War, 1950–1953 — Personal narratives, American.   5. Vietnam War, 1961–1975 — Personal narratives, American.   6. United States Marine Compound Bombing, Beirut, Lebanon, 1983 — Personal narratives.   7. Afghan War, 2001 — Personal narratives, American.   8. Iraq War, 2003 — Personal narratives, American.
9. United States — History, Military — 20th century — Anecdotes.
10. United States — History, Military — 21st century — Anecdotes.
I. Simonsen, Robert A.
VE24.M375 2009
359.9'6092273 — dc22   2008049017

British Library cataloguing data are available

©2009 Robert A. Simonsen. All rights reserved

No part of this book may be reproduced or transmitted in any form or by any means, electronic or mechanical, including photocopying or recording, or by any information storage and retrieval system, without permission in writing from the publisher.

Cover photographs ©2008 Shutterstock

Manufactured in the United States of America

McFarland & Company, Inc., Publishers
  Box 611, Jefferson, North Carolina 28640
    www.mcfarlandpub.com

Marines Dodging Death

Sixty-Two Accounts of Close Calls in World War II, Korea, Vietnam, Lebanon, Iraq and Afghanistan

Edited by ROBERT A. SIMONSEN

McFarland & Company, Inc., Publishers
Jefferson, North Carolina, and London

Maps by C. Douglas Anderson.

Excerpts in Chapter 18 from the *Korean War: Pusan to Chosin; An Oral History*, copyright © 1985 by Donald Knox, are reprinted by permission of Harcourt, Inc.

LIBRARY OF CONGRESS CATALOGUING-IN-PUBLICATION DATA

Marines dodging death : sixty-two accounts of close calls in World War II, Korea, Vietnam, Lebanon, Iraq and Afghanistan / edited by Robert A. Simonsen.
    p.   cm.
Includes bibliographical references and index.

ISBN 978-0-7864-3821-1
softcover : 50# alkaline paper ∞

1. Marines — United States — Biography — Anecdotes.
2. United States. Marine Corps — Biography. 3. World War, 1939–1945 — Personal narratives, American. 4. Korean War, 1950–1953 — Personal narratives, American. 5. Vietnam War, 1961–1975 — Personal narratives, American. 6. United States Marine Compound Bombing, Beirut, Lebanon, 1983 — Personal narratives. 7. Afghan War, 2001 — Personal narratives, American. 8. Iraq War, 2003 — Personal narratives, American. 9. United States — History, Military — 20th century — Anecdotes. 10. United States — History, Military — 21st century — Anecdotes. I. Simonsen, Robert A.
VE24.M375   2009
359.9'6092273 — dc22   2008049017

British Library cataloguing data are available

©2009 Robert A. Simonsen. All rights reserved

No part of this book may be reproduced or transmitted in any form or by any means, electronic or mechanical, including photocopying or recording, or by any information storage and retrieval system, without permission in writing from the publisher.

Cover photographs ©2008 Shutterstock

Manufactured in the United States of America

McFarland & Company, Inc., Publishers
  Box 611, Jefferson, North Carolina 28640
     www.mcfarlandpub.com

To the BNO Marines and their spouses.

and

The memory and families of

Private First Class Jason Hanson,
who lost his life in Iraq on 29 July 2006 (chapter 46).

Navy Corpsman Chadwick Kenyon,
who was killed in action in Iraq on 20 August 2006 (chapter 46).

Private First Class Dewayne Williams,
who was killed in action in Vietnam on 19 September 1968 (chapter 37).

World War II veteran of Iwo Jima George Smyth,
who passed away on 26 February 1986 (chapter 15).

World War II veteran of Saipan and Tinian Earl Dunlap,
who passed away on 27 November 2006 (chapter 5).

Korean War veteran John Bastian,
who recently passed away (chapter 25).

Korean War veteran Arthur Wilson, editor/publisher of
Korean Vignettes and *Red Dragon*,
who recently passed away.

and

to the hopeful recovery of

Corporal John McClellan,
*who was seriously wounded in Iraq (his third
Purple Heart) on 26 September 2006 (chapter 42).*

World War II veteran of Peleliu Beryl Bonacher,
who suffered a stroke on 24 February 2007 (chapter 8).

Korean War veteran of the Pusan Perimeter Herbert Luster,
who now suffers from Lewy Body Dementia (chapter 18).

Acknowledgments

First and foremost, thank you to all the Marines and Navy Corpsmen who provided me with their war experiences and, in most cases, shared their personal background information. I was pleasantly surprised and especially honored by the number of 80 year olds from World War II and the 70-year-old Korean War veterans who trusted me with their stories. I feel especially lucky to have made contacts with these men since many are now dying, at a rate of over 1,000 a day.

Next, I want to offer thanks to my wife of 37 years, Nan, who provided initial editing help, as did my sister, Karen C. Simonsen Jones, and my friend, Jeanette Gregor.

As always, special thanks goes to my friend of many years, Doug Anderson, who produced the maps, as he did in my first book, *Every Marine.*

I want to especially express my appreciation to former Marines and Vietnam veteran friends, Andy Boyko and Terry Rigney, for providing me with suggestions, insight and research. I thank them for allowing me to hash out my stories with them over three-way phone calls and e-mails from time to time.

Gratitude is extended to Eileen Judd, whose father George Smyth's story is related in chapter 15. She provided me with a tremendous amount of information that the Smyth family had collected over many years. Also to Diane Kuebler, the daughter of a World War II Seabee, who put me in contact with two Marines, whose stories appear within the book.

Tremendous appreciation is given to Norman Stickbine, the sole surviving editor, self-publisher and photographer of *Korean Vignettes: Faces of War* and *Red Dragon: Faces of War II,* for allowing me to use stories and quotes from these two books. Also, to Al Zdon, writer, editor and self-publisher of *War Stories: Accounts of Minnesotans Who Defended Their Nation,* for permitting me to use portions of some of his stories from his book and from the Minnesota American Legion Web site "War Stories" link.

Other source and quoted material was acquired at little or no copyright permission cost from the following: *Stars and Stripes, Military* magazine, *Military History* magazine, *Depoe Bay Beacon, Body Armor News* and numerous government and military publications, especially from the Marine Corps Newsroom. Thank you all.

In addition, appreciation is extended to the many military magazines and newsletters that provided free space for me to help publicize my request for "close call" stories, including, but not limited to: *Leatherneck* magazine, *Old Breed News, Caltrap, Follow Me, Military* magazine and *Sgt. Grit's Newsletter*. I am also indebted to dozens of military Web sites that allowed my messages on their guest books.

Contents

Acknowledgments	vii
List of Maps	xi
Preface	1

PART ONE: WORLD WAR II

1 — USMC Sergeant John Egan	7
2 — USMC Lieutenant Bob Johnson	14
3 — USMC Private First Class Harry Drendall	18
4 — USMC Private First Class Jack Porter	27
5 — USMC Corporal Earl Dunlap	33
6 — USMC Corporal Andrew Samo	38
7 — USMC Private James Seidler	43
8 — USN Hospital Corpsman First Class Beryl Bonacker	50
9 — USMC Sergeant George Peto	56
10 — USMC Corporal Jim Anderson	64
11 — USN Hospital Corpsman Second Class Benton Corry	68
12 — USMC Private First Class Charles Nichols	78
13 — USMC Private First Class Kenneth Stevens	82
14 — USMC Warrant Officer-1 George Green	92
15 — USMC Private George Smyth	103
16 — USMC Private First Class William Byrd	113
17 — USMC Private First Class Lee Bergee (Part 1 of 2)	118

PART TWO: KOREA

18 — USMC Private First Class Herbert Luster	125
19 — USMC Sergeant Kermit Wilhelm	136
20 — USMC Staff Sergeant Lee Bergee (Part 2 of 2)	144

21 — USMC Sergeant Joe Ohman	149
22 — USMC Corporal Renald Valkenburg	153
23 — USMC Private First Class John Bastian	160
24 — Korea: "Hell Fire Valley"	165
25 — USMC Sergeant Elbert Koonce	170
26 — USMC Sergeant Forest Heistermann	172
27 — USMC Sergeant William Palizzolo	177
28 — USMC Private First Class Richard Aiple	180
29 — USMC Private John Graham	182
30 — USMC Acting Sergeant James Larkin	185
31 — Korea: "Calls of Nature"	195

PART THREE: VIETNAM

32 — USMC Private First Class Bruce Horton	203
33 — USMC Captain John McLaughlin	212
34 — USMC Corporal Robert Simonsen	218
35 — USMC Lance Corporal Arthur Riordan	226
36 — USMC Corporal John Wear II	232
37 — USMC Corporal Jay Vincens	238
38 — USMC Private First Class Mike Stagner	245
39 — USMC Sergeant Ralph Bohannon	250

PART FOUR: THE WARS AGAINST TERRORISM

40 — Beirut: Bombing of the Marine Barracks	259
41 — Iraq: Female Search Force	266
42 — Afghanistan: "The Nightfighters"	272
43 — USMC Gunnery Sergeant Michael Burghardt	280
44 — Iraq: Combat Train One	286
45 — Iraq: Kevlar Helmet Headshots	291
46 — Iraq: Body Armor Shots	297
47 — Iraq: Combat Photographers	303

Chapter Notes	309
Bibliography	319
Index	325

Contents

Acknowledgments	vii
List of Maps	xi
Preface	1

Part One: World War II

1 — USMC Sergeant John Egan	7
2 — USMC Lieutenant Bob Johnson	14
3 — USMC Private First Class Harry Drendall	18
4 — USMC Private First Class Jack Porter	27
5 — USMC Corporal Earl Dunlap	33
6 — USMC Corporal Andrew Samo	38
7 — USMC Private James Seidler	43
8 — USN Hospital Corpsman First Class Beryl Bonacker	50
9 — USMC Sergeant George Peto	56
10 — USMC Corporal Jim Anderson	64
11 — USN Hospital Corpsman Second Class Benton Corry	68
12 — USMC Private First Class Charles Nichols	78
13 — USMC Private First Class Kenneth Stevens	82
14 — USMC Warrant Officer-1 George Green	92
15 — USMC Private George Smyth	103
16 — USMC Private First Class William Byrd	113
17 — USMC Private First Class Lee Bergee (Part 1 of 2)	118

Part Two: Korea

18 — USMC Private First Class Herbert Luster	125
19 — USMC Sergeant Kermit Wilhelm	136
20 — USMC Staff Sergeant Lee Bergee (Part 2 of 2)	144

21 — USMC Sergeant Joe Ohman	149
22 — USMC Corporal Renald Valkenburg	153
23 — USMC Private First Class John Bastian	160
24 — Korea: "Hell Fire Valley"	165
25 — USMC Sergeant Elbert Koonce	170
26 — USMC Sergeant Forest Heistermann	172
27 — USMC Sergeant William Palizzolo	177
28 — USMC Private First Class Richard Aiple	180
29 — USMC Private John Graham	182
30 — USMC Acting Sergeant James Larkin	185
31 — Korea: "Calls of Nature"	195

PART THREE: VIETNAM

32 — USMC Private First Class Bruce Horton	203
33 — USMC Captain John McLaughlin	212
34 — USMC Corporal Robert Simonsen	218
35 — USMC Lance Corporal Arthur Riordan	226
36 — USMC Corporal John Wear II	232
37 — USMC Corporal Jay Vincens	238
38 — USMC Private First Class Mike Stagner	245
39 — USMC Sergeant Ralph Bohannon	250

PART FOUR: THE WARS AGAINST TERRORISM

40 — Beirut: Bombing of the Marine Barracks	259
41 — Iraq: Female Search Force	266
42 — Afghanistan: "The Nightfighters"	272
43 — USMC Gunnery Sergeant Michael Burghardt	280
44 — Iraq: Combat Train One	286
45 — Iraq: Kevlar Helmet Headshots	291
46 — Iraq: Body Armor Shots	297
47 — Iraq: Combat Photographers	303

Chapter Notes	309
Bibliography	319
Index	325

List of Maps

PART ONE: WORLD WAR II

1. World War II Pacific Theater — 6
2. 1st and 2nd Naval Battles of Guadalcanal — 10
3. Betio, Tarawa Atoll — 22
4. Battles for the Mariana Islands — 24
5. Peleliu, Palau Island Group — 46
6. Okinawa — 59
7. Iwo Jima — 85
8. Philippines — 120

PART TWO: KOREA

9. Overall Map of Korea — 126
10. First Battle of the Naktong Bulge at Pusan Perimeter — 130
11. Inchon to Seoul — 139
12. Chosin Reservoir Campaign Area — 142
13. The Western Korean Front & COP Vegas — 187

PART THREE: VIETNAM

14. South Vietnam and the I Corps — 204
15. Vietnam DMZ Area — 206

PART FOUR: THE WARS AGAINST TERRORISM

16. Lebanon — 261
17. Beirut—Marine Barracks Bombings — 263
18. Iraq — 268
19. Afghanistan — 274

Preface

Nearly every military person who has been in combat has, at one or more times, experienced an extremely close call where he or she has escaped death by just a matter of inches, seconds or a quick physical or mental decision. Whether it could be called luck, chance, fate, good fortune, destiny or divine intervention, thousands of combat warriors have eluded their probable deaths while others died. There is probably no real explanation of why one person dies and another one lives in similar situations. Can one really say that an individual lived so he could extol peace, make a difference in the world, or father a genius who creates a life-saving medicine? Perhaps, but I think not. Regardless, many people have gone through similar life-threatening close-call experiences and lived to talk about it. These events have quite often been life-changing occurrences, which have had a prolonged effect upon the individual, both good and bad.

My own personal close-call combat experience occurred in Vietnam in May 1968. Two Marines, within a few yards on either side of me, were killed while I had a bullet go through my helmet, which knocked me out but caused only relatively minor head shrapnel wounds. Why was I so fortunate? This question has followed and hounded me for over 39 years now. It was the budding impetus for beginning my research on this book. Another Marine, fighting in Iraq in April 2006, had a similar situation: a bullet sliced through his helmet and cut a picture of his wife in half where it had been placed. He, too, was only slightly injured. Who can forget the stirring image in Stephen Spielberg's World War Two (World War II) movie, *Saving Private Ryan*, when in the early battle on D-Day, an American soldier was shot in the head? He took his helmet off and looked at the bullet holes in stunned silence, while another man said, "Jesus, lucky bastard!" However, this infantryman's luck immediately ran out as he took another head shot, killing him instantly. As Brett Harte once said, "The only sure thing about luck is that it will change."

This book is intended to show the American fighting spirit of men and women in all wars, who share the common factor of living through a unique, close combat near-death experience. Most of the stories include first person narrations by the "close call" individuals. I have taken certain liberties in changing some wording, punctuation and spelling, but their narrative intent has been retained. It is also true that time may have eroded complete story accuracy but the essence of each incident described is true, for all these men and women have repeatedly relived these events in their minds. For the sake of privacy, I have changed, eliminated or used nicknames for references to many of the secondary individuals mentioned in the stories.

My initial intent was to include only stories that were very unusual or unique for, as I have previously stated, nearly every person who has had combat experience has had one or more close encounters with death. I then expanded my criteria by permitting stories where an individual had several close calls in a short time frame. Perhaps none of the incidents would qualify on their own, but the fact that death was escaped numerous times seemed to be unusual enough to be included in the book. I also found myself looking for stories which reflected the different island battles during World War II, the major separate battles in Korea, and the different aspects of other wars in order to tell more than just a close-call story. I wanted to relate a history of the wars as they evolved.

Some stories that had similar or linked incidents have been combined into one chapter. I have utilized the symbols * * * * to distinguish the change from one story, incident, date or individual to the next.

Most of the book's information was obtained by placing "requests for information" in various military publications and from leaving messages on military website guest books. I received numerous personal phone calls, e-mails, letters and even entire memoirs from interested parties who wanted to share their experiences. Some of the stories, especially the ones from Part Four (The Wars against Terrorism), were discovered from online news, newspapers and magazine sources. In these instances, I then searched for as much information as possible to supplement the story. It would seem that either the younger generation of warriors are not reading the military publications in which I advertised, or are not quite ready to recount their sometimes very horrific, yet lucky experiences.

Readers will be taken into combat and hear from an 84-year-old former Sea Duty Marine who was at Pearl Harbor on that fateful day of 7 December 1941, as well as from a 19-year-old fighting in Iraq. They will also read dozens of other stories from World War II, Korea, Vietnam, Beirut, Afghanistan and Iraq. Besides Marines, a few stories involve Navy Corpsmen, who have always been with Marines, providing them with medical aid whenever and wherever needed on the battlefields.

When possible, I have added a prelude and postlude section to each chapter which describes the individual's personal background prior to and after his close-call incidents. I wanted to provide a more human view of the Marines and Corpsmen who were describing their war experiences. Several people, although willing to talk about their narrow escapes, were not as receptive to providing their personal information and I fully honored their privacy.

I have also researched the battles where the events occurred, along with military unit histories, to add historically accurate information surrounding the personal narratives. Most books on wars focus on stories of brave deeds by heroes who saved lives and earned numerous medals for valor. Although I truly believe that every person who has stood and fought in war is a hero, my stories, for the most part, reflect common Marines and Corpsmen who were just doing their jobs to the best of their abilities and who experienced some well-deserved good luck.

Throughout the book, the exact words of Marines are in a different typeface and are set off with a vertical rule at the left.

I have included a small section of personal remarks at the conclusion of each chapter, citing my oral and written communication with the primary individual and explaining how I first came into contact with him or his story. I have also occasionally added personal comments about the Marine or Corpsman.

The Chapter Notes specify the location and identify the source of the information utilized for each of the 47 chapters.

Throughout the book, and especially at the beginning of every part and chapter, I have included epigraphs of quotations concerning fate, luck, and so on from the famous, the not so famous and ancient proverbs.

Helpful Information for the Non-Military Reader

Military terminology makes extensive use of letter and number abbreviations. Although I have attempted to minimize these as much as possible, one simply cannot escape them all. I have tried to spell out all of them on first occurrence and then place their abbreviations directly following, in parentheses. For example, "There were 25 Marines killed in action (KIA)." Conversely, if a person's narrations include an abbreviation, I immediately placed the identifying words in parentheses.

A common word use for Marine Corps units, which may be confusing, is to substitute the word Marines for the word Regiment. It is also customary to replace a spelled number for the actual number. Hence, the First Marine Regiment is primarily shown as the 1st Marines. A battalion in a specific regiment is usually written as follows: 2nd Battalion, 1st Marines or further abbreviated as 2/1.

The breakdown composition of Marine Corps units may frustrate a regular non-military reader. Although the configuration and size of the core unit components have changed at various times from the Second World War to the present, the following basic hierarchy is provided, with the largest entity listed on top:

> Division
> Regiment
> Battalion
> Company
> Platoon
> Squad
> Fire-team

The size of military ammunition and ordnance is usually identified by the words caliber or millimeters. A .45-caliber pistol or a .30-caliber machine gun is shown with the decimal point before the number, and quite often the word caliber is eliminated in a sentence. A person might say, "I shot him with my .45 pistol," or even further simplified, "I shot him with my .45." A 7.62-millimeter bullet or a 60-millimeter mortar round is commonly abbreviated using mm for millimeter, such as 60mm mortar round.

I have also used the 24-hour military time clock system to indicate the time of an event. Hence, 6:00 A.M. is 0600 and 6:00 P.M. is 1800. In addition, unlike normal civilian usage, dates are listed by day, month and year; for example, 16 May 1968, instead of May 16, 1968.

> He either fears his fate too much,
> Or his deserts are small,
> That dares not put it to the touch
> To gain or lose it all.
> — James Graham

Semper Fidelis,
Robert A. Simonsen
Veteran Marine Sergeant (1966–1969)

Part One: World War II

Fate has carried me
'Mid the thick arrows:
I will keep my stand
Not shrink and let the shaft pass by my breast
To pierce another.
— George Eliot (pseudonym for Mary Ann Evans Cross)

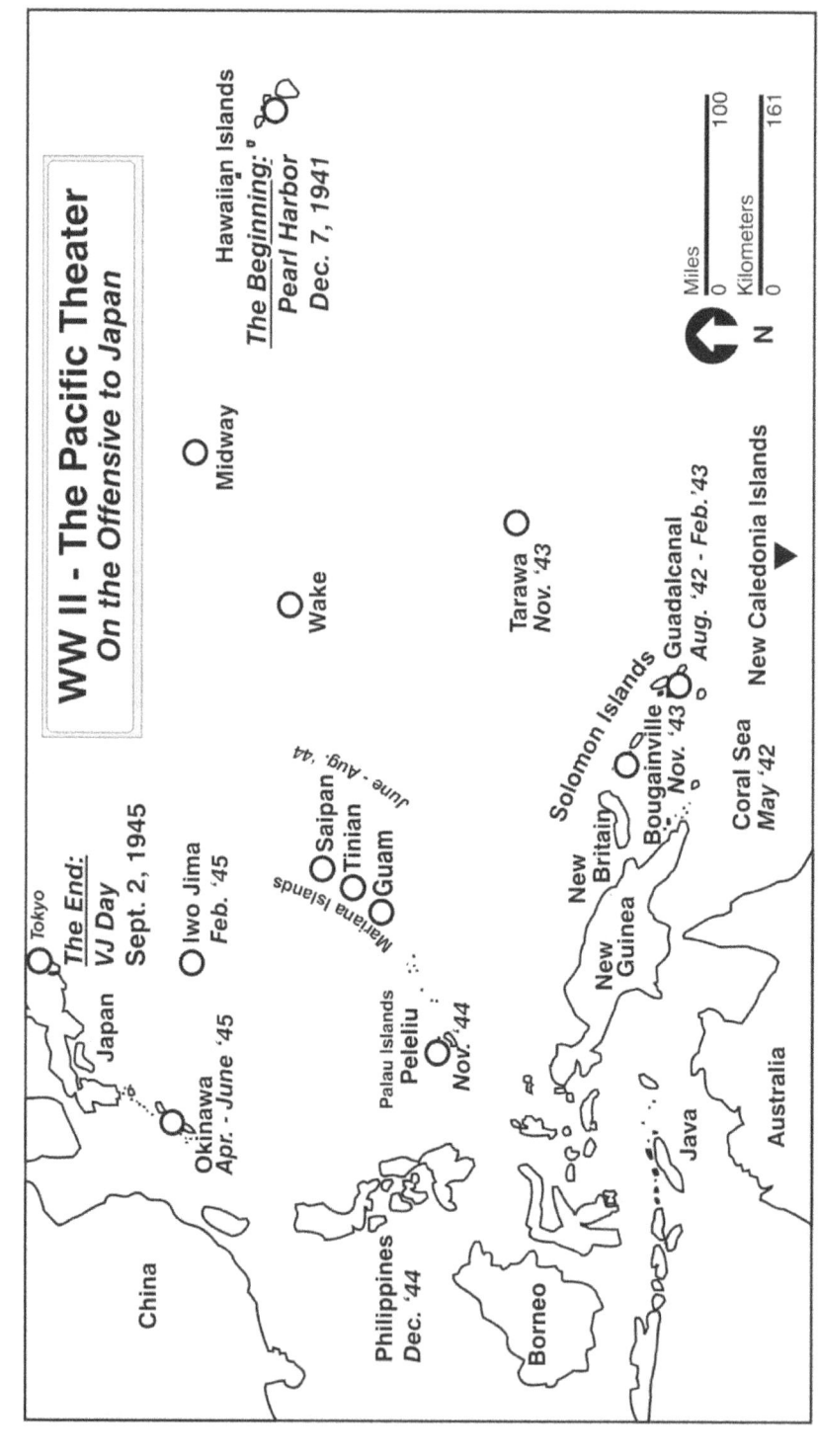

1

USMC Sergeant John Egan

> Wherever you go and whatever you do,
> may the luck of the Irish be there with you.
> — Irish blessing

Prelude

John Egan was born on 2 October 1922 in Hammond, Indiana. John was one of two sons and a daughter raised in a predominantly Irish-Catholic neighborhood in Chicago, Illinois. His father was a small, feisty Irishman, twice awarded the Purple Heart during the First World War in Germany. His diminutive mother, a combination of French and Spanish, met his father during the war in France. They married there and later settled in Chicago.

By the time John was nine, he had been in and out of trouble with the nuns and priests of his parents' parish and had his fair share of scrapes with the local cop on the beat. He was disruptive and always questioned authority, which eventually led to his removal from Catholic school. He joined the Marine Corps Reserve in 1938 with the blessing of the Catholic Diocese, his juvenile officer and the local police. Being under the legal age, John asked his father to sign for him after he had already enlisted. "You're a chip off the old block. The Marines will be good for you," his dad remarked as he signed the consent form. At the time, John was 5'9" tall, lithe and wiry with sparkling green eyes. He was happy to get out of Chicago and the Corps even promised him two pairs of shoes and three square meals a day! However, he would soon miss his mother's French and Spanish gourmet cooking. He attended boot camp at Camp Pendleton, California. He was called to active duty in January 1940 and was later assigned as a "seagoing" Marine aboard the USS *San Francisco* (CA-38) in May of 1940.[1]

The USS *San Francisco* was launched on 9 May 1933 and was commissioned at the Mare Island Yard in Vallejo, California. She was a 10,000-ton Treaty Cruiser, mainly providing neutrality patrols prior to the outbreak of the war. On 7 December 1941, the *San Francisco* was undergoing overhaul at the Pearl Harbor Navy Yard in the early morning hours. The ship escaped damage during the extensive Japanese raid and would soon go on to play important roles in the Battles of Midway and Cape Esperance.[2]

0755 on 7 December 1941 (The "Day of Infamy")
USS San Francisco
Pearl Harbor, Hawaii

I was serving as Sergeant of the Guard and was "making colors" on the fantail of the ship with a 5-man Marine Color Guard, Field Music [bugler], along with a sailor whose job was to cast out the flag at the appointed 0800 hour. We had to rush the flag raising just as the Japanese attack started.

Fortunately, all of the ship's ammo (8", 5" and 3" shells) had been off-loaded since we were dry-docked the day before. The attack caused a delay in the planned complete removal of all of our ammo that had been stacked on the dock next to our ship. There were still two boxcars loaded with our high explosive ammo. Luckily, the shipyard worker operating the crane at the time of the attack drove his large machine over the boxcars. The crane took a direct hit from a bomb and his action prevented both the USS *New Orleans* and us from being blasted out of the water.[3]

August–November 1942
Guadalcanal, Solomon Islands

By July 1942, Japan's juggernaut had invaded many countries in the Far East. They had also worked feverishly occupying and building airfields on several strategic islands across the Pacific Ocean. The airfield on Guadalcanal was their last and most important. It was to be used as the final island hop prior to their planned invasion of Australia.

U.S. Marines landed on Guadalcanal on 7 August 1942. They quickly captured and secured the Japanese-built airfield, renamed Henderson Field by the Marines, and then fought for the next several months to maintain its control.

Japanese Vice Admiral Hiroaki Abe was dispatched to bombard and land troops on Guadalcanal. His strike force consisted of two battleships, one cruiser, fourteen destroyers and eleven transports carrying 14,000 troops. His two battleships, the *Hiei* and the *Kirishima*, were capable of firing nearly 24,000 pounds of bombardment salvos every three minutes, continuously for three hours.

Rear Admiral (RADM) Daniel J. Callaghan, on board his flagship the USS *San Francisco*, was directed to intercept the Japanese naval strike force with his thirteen ships, consisting of five cruisers and eight destroyers. On 12 November 1942, near Guadalcanal, a damaged enemy plane crashed into the *San Francisco*, destroying the aft control station, killing and wounding 51 men.[4]

I saw the face of the pilot of the Japanese torpedo bomber as he circled our ship with flames coming out of his cockpit. I knew he was probably wounded, but he bravely came back at us under intense anti-aircraft fire and slammed into our aft section. I have never seen a braver man than he was, doing his duty for his country. It was heroic yet very sad at the same time.[5]

With a crippled flagship, RADM Callaghan prepared his task force for an imminent battle. Overheard on the bridge was the comment, "But this is suicide." RADM Callaghan, cool, calm and resolute, replied, "Yes I know, but we've got to do it!"[6]

0148 on 13 November 1942 (Friday the 13th)
Iron Bottom Sound
Between Guadalcanal, Florida and Savo Islands

At 0148 on 13 November 1942, the two task forces suddenly clashed in an all-out naval battle in the pitch-black early morning hours. Hundreds of salvos rained down upon both sides as blazing ships became easy targets. Men tried to escape their sinking ships and swam for their lives in the blackened seas. Many were killed in the water by the spinning propellers of ships that were twisting and turning to avoid collisions. Circling sharks killed many more!

The USS *San Francisco* advanced on the battleship *Hiei* and the ships exchanged fire. The *Hiei*'s first salvo was type 3 shells, which were high explosive and not designed to penetrate armor, and as a result did little ship damage. Most of the crew on the deck, however, was killed. The third salvo hit the bridge, killing Admiral Callahan and most of the bridge crew. While damage crews worked on repairing the ship, Lieutenant Commander Bruce McCandless turned the ship to rejoin the battle, knowing that if the flagship *San Francisco* left, the rest of the force might follow.[7]

Marine Platoon Sergeant Klatt was "gun captain" on gun mount one while I was in charge of mount two. As gun captains we were located on an elevated platform with only a thin metal handrail for protection. The

5-man gun crews at least had a steel shield "gun tub" for safety. We had no body armor in those days.

A passing enemy destroyer sprayed our ship, grievously wounding Sergeant Klatt and others. My mount two was totally knocked out of action. After administering to the most seriously wounded Marines, including Klatt, who died in my arms, I reassigned an experienced corporal to gun mount one. I then ordered the remaining Marines to follow me down below to the gun deck where I hoped some 5" guns might still be operational, although I knew their crews were probably all wounded. On the way down the ladders, several decks below, another "broadside" hit us and I do not remember much after that. I was badly wounded in 13 different places. It was Friday the 13th, we had 13 U.S. ships and I was hit 13 times, yet I still survived. I think it was the luck of the Irish! So then, what exactly was my close call?

Years later, I attended a USS *San Francisco* reunion and a couple of sailors from the ship said, "Hey, Marine, you owe us a drink or more!" It seems, and it was verified by a former Marine officer in attendance, that these two were one of several pairs delegated to throw corpses over the side from the pile that had accumulated on the forward deck after being thrown down from the decks above. These "burial crews" would pick up a body, one by the legs and the other by its arms, and then dash to either

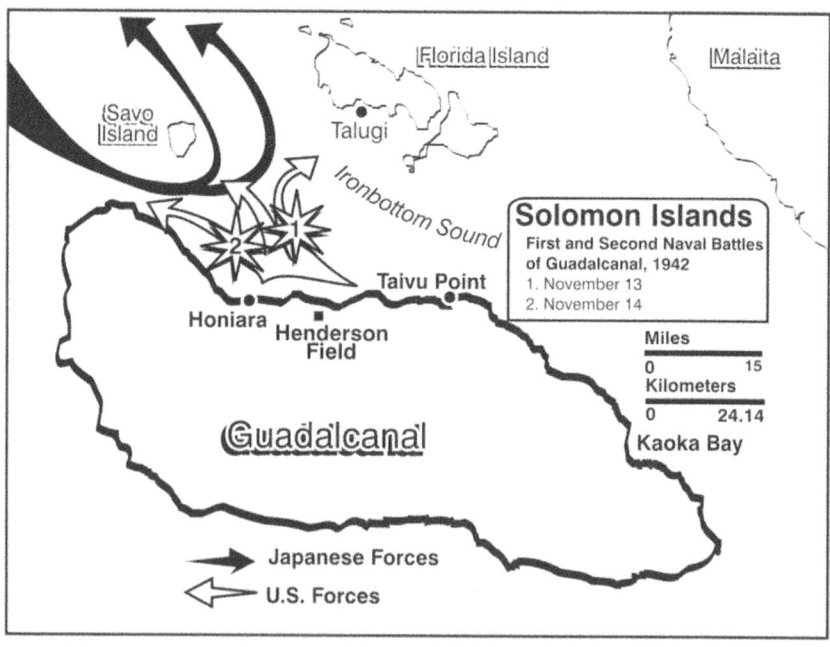

port or starboard. They were trying to avoid the ship's zigzagging movement in an attempt to prevent the dead from being caught up in the screws [propellers] which might impede its movement. They claimed that I was tossed down from above, possibly from the Signal Bridge, onto the pile of bodies and as they grabbed me to fling me into the sea, one yelled above the racket of the sea battle, "This is Sergeant Egan! I feel some life! Let's haul his ass to the hangar." The hangar was being used for casualties since the sick bay had been knocked out with all doctors and corpsmen killed or wounded. The on-ship hangar was normally used for the four Scout Observation Curtis (SOC) seaplanes assigned to the ship.

I did not regain consciousness until the next day when the USS *Juneau* exploded and sank. This was the ship that the famous five Sullivan brothers were killed on. When the action died down, I was transferred to another ship by crane and eventually taken to an Army hospital in Fiji. Obviously, I owe my life to my sailor buddies because they felt a little movement before they were going to toss me into the Pacific as shark food![8]

The *San Francisco* reportedly was hit 45 times and had nearly 25 fires on board during the engagement. RADM Daniel J. Callaghan and the ship's captain, Cassin Young, were both killed along with another 75 men. No fewer than 105 more were wounded in action. Four men from the ship were awarded the Medal of Honor, more than any other ship would receive in a single battle. The men on the ship were also honored with a Presidential Unit Citation.[9]

More than 6,000 men on both sides were killed or wounded during the First Naval Battle of Guadalcanal. Two U.S. cruisers, four U.S. destroyers and two Japanese destroyers were sunk. At dawn the next day, the battleship *Hiei*, aflame, floundering and dead in the water, was abandoned and sunk. During the next few days, other Japanese ships were chased down and sunk, including the battleship *Kirishima*.

The USS *San Francisco*, severely damaged and crippled, limped home at Christmas time to receive a new bridge and other repairs at the Mare Island Naval Shipyard. She then returned to sea to give battle and bombardment support for landings and occupations in the Pacific. At Okinawa, she earned the last of her 17 battle stars.[10]

Postlude

John spent 15 months in Army and Navy hospitals, including a month on Fiji, nearly a year at the Oak Knoll Navy Hospital in California, and ended his recovery at the Ahwahnee Hotel in Yosemite, which was used as a Navy convalescent home during the war. His most serious wounds were to his head and leg, which was nearly amputated. Doctors even resorted to the use of maggots on his gangrenous leg to eat away the dead flesh. He was very fortunate to have several expert specialty doctors for both his head and leg wounds. He was discharged from the Marines in February 1944, prior to the end of the war. He received 75 percent disability for his wounds and has recurring headaches to this day from the shrapnel, which had shattered the top of his head. One of his legs is also slightly shorter than the other as a result of several operations.

A few Marines took him out for a night on the town just prior to his discharge. He remembers the others leaving early while he continued to drink late into the evening. He later found himself on a street curb, crying his eyes out. It was the only time that he remembers crying in his entire life, even in his childhood. It was extremely hard for him to be forced out of the Marines while the war was still being fought. According to John, "The Marines gave me the opportunity to know how I would hold up under combat and other dangerous situations. I reached manhood, not by my size, but rather how I conducted myself."[11]

John moved around the country working in a variety of jobs, never staying in one place too long. Finally, with the encouragement of a Marine friend, he decided to go back to school. John had never finished high school, but under the G.I. Bill of Rights, he took a comprehensive college-level test and passed with ease. He then received his bachelor of arts degree from the American University in Mexico City at the age of 32.

Through the Department of Disabled American Veterans, John learned that teachers were needed to fill positions at U.S. military bases around the world. Thus encouraged, he went back to school and obtained his teaching credentials. He met his first wife in England; they had four sons, each born in a different country. John continued taking courses and by age 40, he was appointed principal of the high school teaching program for children of American servicemen in Europe. Eventually, however, John and his wife divorced and parted as friends.

John later met a lovely English widow in England and swept her off her feet. He married Pat and now has two complete sets of children and grandchildren. They currently divide their time between the United States and England visiting their families. He retired in 1983.[12]

John still maintains an active participant in many veteran groups including: 1st Marine Division Association, Pearl Harbor Survivors, Marine Corps League, Purple Heart Society, and Disabled American Veterans, and of course attends reunions for the USS *San Francisco* (CA-38). He has many Marine and Navy friends, though time is reducing the ranks as the years go by.[13]

I received a long letter from Mr. Egan, dated 26 April 2006, in response to an ad that I had placed in the 1st Marine Division Association's magazine (*Old Breed*

News, April/May 2006) where he described his close call incident. He was 83½ years old and still vividly remembered quite a bit about his experiences. He also sent me a printed general description of the 13 November 1942 battle produced by the USS *San Francisco* Memorial Foundation, which I utilized as background material.

On May 6, 2006, I received another letter from Mr. Egan in response to my questionnaire for personal information. Along with his responses, he sent me an eight-page short biography titled "John," written by his friend, Mickey Gold (now deceased), dated 2 February 1992. Also included in the package was another treasure. He sent an oral history tape on which he was interviewed about his experiences in and out of the service. To hear him describe events in his own voice was very valuable and the interviewer did a great job in drawing out good stories and anecdotes. It was a great source for my chapter on John. WO-1 John Garvey from the California Center for Military History conducted the interview on 19 May 2003 in Concord, California. John also told me to keep everything that he had sent me.

2

USMC Lieutenant Bob Johnson

> Luck has a peculiar habit of favoring
> those who don't depend on it.
> — Unknown author

Prelude

Bob Johnson grew up on a farm outside of Anoka, Minnesota. He entered the University of Minnesota in the 1930s and played as a defensive tackle on the varsity football team, which participated in a national championship and two Big Ten titles. Farm life and football hardened this young man, who would soon find himself in America's first land battle of the Second World War. After earning a business degree, Johnson found himself unemployable during the depression years. "The only job I could find was as a grease monkey at the local Standard station. I decided to look for something else."

He decided to enter the University of Minnesota Law School. When the war broke out, even though he had a high draft number, he decided to leave school and join the war effort. "If I was going to fight, I wanted to be with an outfit that knew how to fight, so I joined the Marines." Johnson went to Quantico, Virginia, and trained to become a Marine officer. Upon graduation, he traveled across country and continued training at Camp Elliot in San Diego, California. He was assigned as the executive officer in an artillery battery with the 10th Marine Regiment, 2nd Marine Division. His outfit soon boarded the commercial liner *Matsoman* and headed off unescorted for New Zealand, where they trained and prepared for war. His battery had four 75mm cannons that could be disassembled and moved by hard work from place to place, even in a jungle environment.[1]

A Brief History of the 2nd Marine Division

The Division was initially activated on 1 July 1936 as the 2nd Marine Brigade, Fleet Marine Force. It was deployed in 1937 to Shanghai, China, and later relocated to San Diego in 1938. On 1 February 1941, it was re-designated as the 2nd Marine Division. After a short stint in Iceland, it entered the War in the Pacific and participated in the campaigns for Guadalcanal, Tarawa, Saipan, Tinian and Okinawa. After the war, the Division was sent to Japan for occupation duty until 1946, when it was then relocated to Camp Lejeune, North Carolina.

Following the war years, elements of the 2nd Marine Division participated in the landing in Lebanon (1958), the Cuban Missile Crisis (1962), the intervention in the Dominican Republic (1965), the multi-national peacekeeping force in Lebanon (1982–1984), the landing in Grenada (1983), Operation Just Cause in Panama (1989–1990) and Operations Desert Shield and Desert Storm (1990–1991).

The Division is now engaged in the war in Iraq (Operation Iraqi Freedom), where its personnel continue to uphold its highest traditions.[2]

August 1942
Guadalcanal, Solomon Islands

The first American ground offensive of the war began on 7 August 1942 when the 1st Marine Division, led by Major General Alexander Vandergrift, landed on Guadalcanal in the Solomon Islands. The 19,000 Marine forces landed unopposed and quickly took the critically important airfield without significant opposition. The 90-by-35-mile island was defended by the Japanese army, which was constantly augmented by additional troop landings during the next several months. Many battles for the airfield were fought, mainly in desperate, banzai frontal attacks. The Japanese were not used to losing or having an enemy stand and fight them toe to toe. They had never lost a battle since the beginning of the war. The jungle environment and the constant fighting with little resupply support due to the naval battles surrounding the island left the 1st Marine Division depleted and completely exhausted by December 1942.[3]

By December 1942, the 2nd Marine Division and two Army divisions had replaced the 1st Marine Division, who had fought valiantly for five months under terrible conditions. No amount of training can prepare a man for a banzai attack, which happened to Johnson three times in his Marine career, including one dark night on Guadalcanal. "The Japanese would get all sakied up as the night went on. Then they would charge en masse, yelling 'Banzai,' and screaming like you've never heard before." The attack came at 0300 and Johnson's battery leveled their howitzers and fired canister shot pointblank into the 300-man Japanese attack. "The resourcefulness of our men was incredible. I didn't have to give one order. They knew what to do. The fuses were set for the minimum and we just kept firing. I don't know how many rounds we fired, but the enemy was stopped."

As an artillery battery, his outfit did not have to face many of the same dangers of the infantry, but life was still not easy. "I remember it was very hot and it rained all of the time. I don't think we ever got mail."

Johnson's closest brush with death on Guadalcanal came one day when he was on a simple jeep ride down to the sea and back to camp. "We watched an enemy plane, which we had all nicknamed 'Pistol Pete,' drop a couple bombs that hit nearby, with the second one closer than the first. I said to the driver, 'You know the next one could be pretty close.' I didn't even get the words out before it hit right next to the jeep. I'll never know if I dove out of the jeep or if I was blown out of it. I woke up on the ground and my first thought was, 'I'm still alive.' I wasn't injured except my eardrum was blown out. I was worried about the driver and it turned out he was cut up pretty badly. The jeep was destroyed."

One of the last things Johnson and his comrades did before departing Guadalcanal in early February was to take part in a memorial service for the thousand-plus men who had died on the island.[4]

Saipan, Mariana Island Group
June 1945

After fighting in the Tarawa battle, Bob's next island landing was on Saipan. He considered the Saipan attack his worst landing during the war and perhaps his closest call. The amtrac (amphibious tractor) he was riding in was hit on its way to the beach and he was severely wounded. "There was blood all over the place. It was just spurting out of my arm. It must have hit an artery. When we got to shore, I told the men to get out, but they were hesitating. I got to the front and dove out and as I dove, a hand grenade went right over my head and into the amtrac. I landed right on top of the Jap who had thrown the grenade. I had to get rid of him; that's all I knew. And so I did it. I never talked about that at all until a few years ago."

Johnson was transferred to a ship offshore where his arm was treated. The doctors also found a piece of shrapnel lodged against his cranial nerve in his neck. He was patched up and would rejoin his outfit a few days later. After Saipan, he also participated in the fight for the island of Tinian, just to the south of Saipan.[5]

Postlude

Following the end of the war, Johnson was sent to Kyushu, Japan, and went from town to town, accepting the surrender from local militia. When he eventually made it back to the United States, he took up his life again and graduated from law school. He married, had a family, and eventually became a municipal judge in 1948. He later served as the Anoka County Attorney. As of 2002, the 81-year-old Johnson was still practicing law in a partnership with his son with no plans of retiring. "I just come to work every day. I enjoy it."[6]

On 24 October 2007, I came across some online close call stories of from a newsletter link on the Minnesota American Legion website. I was able to locate the editor, Al Zdon, who writes "War Stories" for the website and also produced a book, titled *War Stories: Accounts of Minnesotans Who Defended Their Nation*. I immediately purchased his book, which the Legion used as a fundraiser to build a World War II memorial. I sent Mr. Zdon a letter at Moonlit Eagle Productions, requesting permission to use parts of his stories for my book and he e-mailed me back on 14 November 2007, granting me permission to use portions of two stories on the website and two from his book, including this one about Bob Johnson.

3

USMC Private First Class Harry Drendall

> Fate laughs at probabilities.
> — E.G. Bulwer-Lytton

Prelude

Harry Drendall was born on 5 September 1920 in Mountaintop, Pennsylvania. The Great Depression hit in 1929 and his father, like many Americans, lost his job. Fortunately, his family had a large garden and kept a flock of chickens. "There was not much cash for our seven family members, but at least we ate well. We were far luckier than most." In addition to garden and chicken chores, Harry collected coal from the railroad tracks nearly every day for several years. As a preteen, he also sold magazines around the tiny village, delivered morning newspapers for four years and was active in Boy Scouts and the Methodist Church.

From an early age, he spent considerable time listening to light classics on a wind-up Victrola and began a lifetime interest in music. At the age of eight, his siblings bought a piano and a church organist friend came from the city to give him lessons for 25 cents.

His school was very small and only had a graduating class of 28. He was a cheerleader and president of his senior class. Although he had virtually no money, his teacher friends convinced him to try for college. He decided to become a music teacher, and worked and borrowed his way to a bachelor's degree in music education at the small liberal arts Lebanon Valley College. In college, besides the piano, he learned to play the bassoon, clarinet, saxophone, French horn, trombone and the baritone.

During the middle of his college senior year, the Japanese bombed Pearl Harbor. Upon graduating, he knew that he would have to join the service, so on 29 July 1942 he decided to enlist and make his contribution. "A good musician buddy had joined the Marine Corps, so I signed up for the best too." He attended boot camp at Parris Island, South Carolina. Upon graduation, he was assigned to radar school, but his friend was able to get him assigned to the post band and he began his service as a Marine Corps musician.[1]

A Brief History of Marine Corps Bands

On 11 July 1798, President John Adams signed an act of Congress establishing the United States Marine Band. The original 32 drummers and fifers assisted in recruiting and entertaining residents. The Marine Band presented its first public concert in Washington, in August 1800, on a hill overlooking the Potomac River. Early settlers thronged to hear the Marine Band. The Band made its White House debut in the unfinished executive mansion at a New Year's Day reception in 1801. On 4 March 1801, the Marine Band performed for Thomas Jefferson's inauguration. Jefferson, an avid music lover and amateur violinist, gave the Marine Band the title of the "President's Own." Since that time, the band has played for every presidential inauguration.

On 1 October 1880, 25-year-old John Phillip Sousa was appointed the band leader, a post he held for 12 years. During this time, the Band made its first concert tour, premiered many of Sousa's most famous marches, and produced some of the first phonograph recordings ever made.[2]

Music is deeply rooted in the history and ceremony of the Marine Corps. It is an integral part of the Marine experience. Today, Marine Corps bands are assigned to field commands throughout the world. They provide music to support military ceremonies, official and community activities, including scores of parades. The most notable is the Rose Bowl Parade in Pasadena, California, on New Year's Day. In addition, there is the USMC Drum and Bugle Corps and the elite band that serves the Commandant of the Marine Corps.

Today, there are typically fifty musicians and one band officer for each of the twelve regular bands. There is a total complement of 700–800 Marine band musicians serving around the world.

Each band member is required to complete normal recruit and advanced combat training. During the Second World War, band members served as litter bearers, runners and ammunition carriers during the Pacific island campaigns. Even in Vietnam, three band musicians were killed in action.[3]

Going Overseas

I was in the Post Band a few weeks before being assigned to an 18-piece band, which soon left for San Diego by train. From there, we boarded an old World War I troopship and sailed, unescorted, to New Caledonia and then on to New Zealand to join the 18th Defense Battalion coming off Guadalcanal. After about seven months, I developed a bad case of boils around my waist and butt. A Navy Corpsman sent me to the base hospital in Wellington, from which I was discharged and then assigned to the 72-member 2nd Marine Division Band. I played the French horn, trombone, saxophone and the piano in a dance band in New Zealand. The Red Cross canteen paid us a pound [$3.30] a night to perform. Soon the Division sailed to Pearl Harbor for exercises, in the preparation for the attack on Tarawa. We all realized that during battle, the band members in our Division were usually assigned as litter bearers. In between combat operations, we functioned as bands, playing for field parades, boxing matches and ceremonies of all kinds.[4]

November 1943
Tarawa, Gilbert Islands

In order to set up forward air bases capable of supporting operations across the mid–Pacific, in the Philippines and into mainland Japan, the United States needed to take the Mariana Islands. These islands were heavily defended, and in order for attacks against them to succeed, land-based bombers would have to soften up the defenses. However, the closest islands capable of supporting such an effort were the Marshall Islands, northwest of Guadalcanal. Taking the Marshall Islands would provide the base needed to launch an offensive on the Marianas, but the Marshalls were cut off from direct communications from Hawaii by a garrison on the small island of Betio, on the western side of the Tarawa Atoll in the Gilbert Islands. Therefore, to capture the Marianas, the battles had to start far to the east, at Tarawa.

The Japanese forces were well aware of the Gilberts' strategic location and had invested considerable time and effort fortifying the islands. The garrison, under the command of Rear Admiral (RADM) Shibaski Keiji, consisted of 2,600 elite Imperial Japanese marines. To help bolster the island defenses, 1,000 Japanese civilians and 1,200 Korean workers were brought in to build 500 pillboxes and trenches that connected all points on the island. They also constructed an airfield along the high point on the island. Fourteen coastal defense guns, including 8-inch guns taken from Singapore and forty other artillery pieces, were scattered throughout the small island. RADM Keiji boasted, "It would take one million men one hundred years to conquer Tarawa." The Marines would do it in four very bloody days!

The American invasion force, under the command of Marine General Julian Smith, consisted of 35,000 men of the 2nd Marine Division and elements of the Army's 27th Infantry Division. The naval forces, including 17 aircraft carriers, 12 battleships, 8 heavy and 4 light cruisers, 66 destroyers and

36 transports, opened fire on 20 November 1943, shelling continually for over an hour and a half, stopping only briefly to allow dive-bombers to operate against the fixed positions. The island, at the most just a few hundred yards wide, soon looked like a moonscape and the majority of the larger Japanese guns were knocked out.[5]

0900 on 20 November 1943
Betio Island, Tarawa Atoll

Betio was roughly shaped like a long thin triangle with a lagoon lying to the north and east of the atoll. The attack had to come through the lagoon, which offered the only reasonable landing areas. The Japanese had constructed a coconut log wall along this lagoon, just in from the high-water mark, behind which they had placed a series of machine gun posts and pillboxes that could fire on anyone trying to move over the wall.

The Marines started their attack at 0900, later than expected, and most of the landing craft found themselves stuck on a reef some 500 yards offshore. They had no other choice than to disembark and head for shore by foot under tremendous fire from the Japanese, who had quickly manned their positions after the naval bombardment stopped. A few amphibious tractors were able to breach the reef and make it ashore, but over half of them were knocked out of action.[6]

Tarawa was my first close call. Due to faulty calculations of the tides and sandbars, the ship-to-shore Higgins boats in our sector had to dump us off several hundred yards from the beach. We waded ashore amid all of the considerable firepower that the Japs could throw at us. An alarming number of Marines never made it ashore. I was one of the lucky ones, reaching the beach, unharmed. I was told that I hit the beach just 30 minutes after the first Marine made it.

I found my buddy, Charlie, and we tried to make sense of the confusion. Our beach was about four or five yards wide, ending against a coconut retaining wall, which gave us some protection from the Jap fire. Shortly, an upper NCO [noncommissioned officer] friend of Charlie offered us his foxhole, as he was moving on. Before he left, he advised us to stay away from the foot end of the hole and to use only the head end when getting in and out because a Jap sniper had it zeroed in. While Charlie was out bringing in some wounded, another NCO showed up and asked me if Charlie had made it ashore. I said, "Yes, but please come up to this end to talk. There's a sniper zeroed in here." "We got that sniper by now," he said, and was then shot dead, right where he stood.[7]

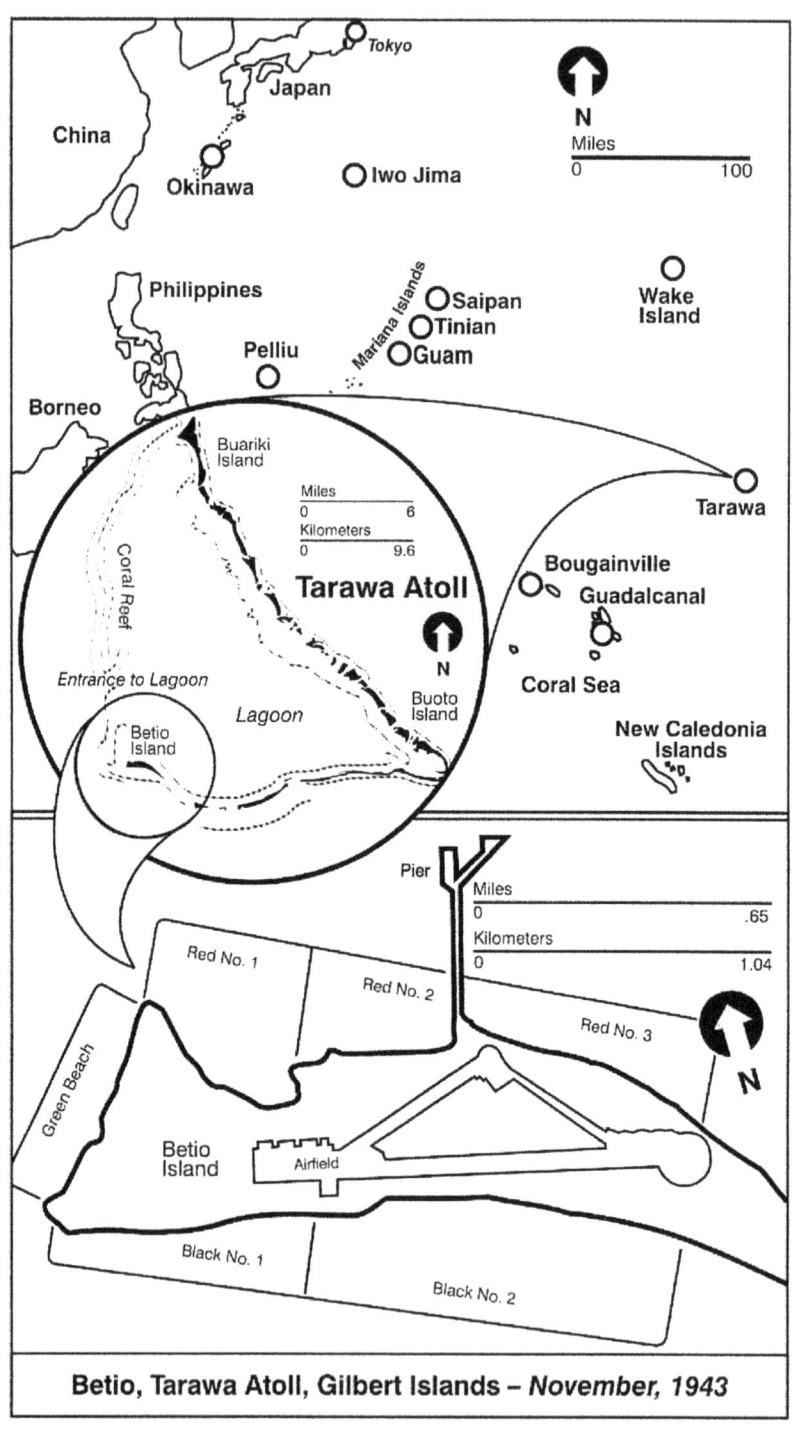

Betio, Tarawa Atoll, Gilbert Islands – *November, 1943*

The Japanese resistance ended about 0500 on 23 November after their third banzai attack in the last two days had failed. The Japanese lost 3,583 killed and only 17 surrendered. The Korean laborers suffered 1,169 deaths and just 129 were found alive and freed. American losses were 1,009 killed and 2,101 wounded. These heavy casualties sparked a storm of protest in the United States, where the high losses could not be understood for such a tiny and seemingly unimportant island.[8]

16 June 1944 (D-Day + 1)
Saipan, Marianas Island Group

I was now a sergeant. My third and fourth close call incidents were on Saipan. My group went ashore during the early evening of the second day. Another buddy and I dug a two-man hole, filled sandbags for the head end and proceeded to stand a 50–50 watch, with mortars exploding in the general area. During the night, a shell exploded a yard or two in front of our hole. My buddy, a broad-shouldered trombone player from Texas, took shrapnel in a shoulder and was evacuated. The blast shredded our sandbags, dented my helmet, scored my face with flying sand and pebbles, and gave me a bleeding, ruptured eardrum.

Several days later, our group had another incident of unusually high casualties. We litter bearers went out singly with stretchers and would recruit buddies of the wounded to help bring them back to the Navy Corpsmen's station. My assignment sent me to an area where a wounded man was down in a small overgrown bowl of terrain. I asked a group of men in front of me for a volunteer on the stretcher. A Marine behind me said, "OK, Sarge, I know where the injured man is, let's go." He picked up one end of the stretcher and led off. Halfway down the bowl, he took a fatal shot in the stomach, which I would have taken had I been leading. It was on Saipan that I was awarded the Bronze Star for going out beyond front lines to bring in wounded men, so I guess I was lucky then, too.[9]

Postlude

Sergeant Drendall would later participate in the battles on Tinian and Okinawa, where he had other narrow escapes, especially from Japanese kamikaze pilots off the shores of Okinawa. Returning to Guam, he served as the Assistant Division Bandmaster. After his overseas requirements had been met, he returned from the Pacific for a few weeks of orientation at San Diego.

**Battles for the Mariana Islands
June–August 1944**

Before heading back east to complete his enlistment, he went to San Francisco to marry Ethel, his high school sweetheart, who came down from her job in Seattle. The Japanese surrendered the next day. Ethel returned to Seattle to quit her job and settle her affairs while Harry managed to hop a flight back east. After a 30-day leave, he was briefly stationed at the Philadelphia Navy Detention barracks, where he made a failed attempt to form a band among the few prisoners. Next, he was sent to Camp Lejeune to await his discharge, which finally came on 12 October 1945.

Harry attended the University of Pennsylvania for a year to earn his master's degree in music education. He began teaching high school music and had a 38-year career teaching instrument music, including 19 years of high school bands. Since teaching pay was meager, he did many extra jobs such as working in a gas station, a farm market, a post office, a fancy food gift store, an ice cream factory, and at summer resorts and as a door-to-door salesman. He also taught instruments part-time at the Overbrook School for the Blind for four years.

He and Ethel had three children, all teachers at one time or another. One son later put himself through law school and another became a computer programmer. He and his first wife divorced after 27 years of marriage and he would later marry Lois. After 10 years, he divorced again, but he considered it a failed divorce, since he and Lois remarried in 2003 and now remain very happy in their twilight years.

Harry continues to read, play the piano, do cryptograms and tend to his yard and garden. For thirty years, he played bassoon in a woodwind quintet and would teach music pupils from time to time. He belongs to the 2nd Marine Division Association and the American Legion. Harry is quite upset with the "current avoidable mess our country and military are in with the war in Iraq." He also has had an ongoing concern for the welfare of women, children and minorities.[10]

Postscript

As of mid–2005, no fewer than four Marine Corps Bands have served in Iraq. These bands provide a dual role: playing morale-building music when the situation permits and providing security when it doesn't. Several of the bands are on their third deployment to the war zone. One picture in the October 2005 *Leatherneck* magazine is unique because it shows the band playing music with their rifles slung over their shoulders. These Marines man perimeter lines in the evening and several have been under fire while standing guard duty at various outposts. Several of the band members have received combat action ribbons while performing their duties under combat conditions. They have continued the tradition that every Marine is first and foremost a basic rifleman.[11]

I received a letter, dated 11 August 2006, from Harry in response to an ad that I had previously placed in the 2nd Marine Division Association's newsletter (*Follow Me*). The uniqueness of his story was that he was a band member with the 2nd Marine Division who had fought at Tarawa, amongst other island campaigns. In another letter, dated 22 August 2006, he sent me answers to a questionnaire that I had sent him.

4

USMC Private First Class Jack Porter

> Men at some time are the masters of their fates.
> — William Shakespeare

Prelude

Jack Porter was born on 8 October 1925 in Clinton, Kentucky. His father was a traveling salesman who was promoted and constantly moved by the Shell Oil Company up and down the Mississippi River. He attended 16 public schools in Kentucky, Tennessee, Illinois and Arkansas. His father died when he was just twelve and he spent the first three years of high school living with his grandmother. At the age of sixteen, he quit school and joined the Marine Corps. His grandmother, as his legal guardian, signed his enlistment papers, on which he had lied that his age was seventeen. This was considered a fraudulent enlistment, but before he got out of the Marines, years later, he would straighten everything out and would receive an honorable discharge.

I was sworn in on 2 June 1942 in Nashville, Tennessee, and was sent to Recruit Depot, Marine Corps Base at San Diego, California. I never considered service with any other U.S. force. Why did I join? Adventure! Romance! I was hardly yet a man, but I wanted to be one. I have never had a single regret for the decision. It was a magic time for the kid I was. I still feel a thrill when I contemplate MCB [Marine Corps Base] San Diego. One of the greatest months of my life was serving, after finishing boot camp, in the NCO mess of the main base and enjoying the pleasures of liberty in the gem of Southern California, "Dago."

After finishing my stint at MCB San Diego, I was assigned up in the hills of Camp Elliot to the 10th Marines [2nd Division Artillery Regiment] and placed in the Headquarters and Service Battery as a "chairborne paragraph trooper" [clerk typist]. Taking typing in 1941–1942 was one of the best things I ever did. It landed me good and interesting duty in the Corps and would later help me through eight years of college. Word processing is now one of the most useful skills I have. In September 1942, the 2nd Marine Division landed on Guadalcanal. A few of us "Johnnie-come-latelies," as members of the rear echelon, would have the good fortune of sailing down to New Zealand in October. We began preparing for the gaunt, malaria-stricken veterans of Guadalcanal, once that stinking island was secured. After several months helping to prepare Camp Pahatanui for the return of the 10th Marines from the "Canal," this lowly private was selected to join the Military Police [MP] Company stationed in the capital city of Wellington. There ensued one of the finest years of my life. After several months of various MP duties, I answered the call for someone who could type and became the company clerk. I remained in this position for the duration of my time in the 2nd Marine Division. The role of company clerk left me behind when the Division went off to Tarawa. Then after a six-month stint in Hawaii, all members of the Company, including me, went off to Saipan.[1]

June 1944
Saipan, Mariana Island Group

In the campaigns of 1943 and the first half of 1944, the Allies had captured the Solomon Islands, the Gilbert Islands, the Marshall Islands and the Papuan peninsula of New Guinea. This brought the Allies up against the main Japanese defense line in the Pacific: the Caroline Islands, the Palau Islands and the Mariana Islands, all occupied by the Japanese since the end of the First World War and all heavily fortified. The Allies embarked on two campaigns to break this line. General Douglas MacArthur's Southwest Pacific Command advanced through New Guinea and Morotai towards the Philippines. Admiral Chester Nimitz's Central Pacific Command attacked the Mariana Islands. The selection of the Marianas as a target was influenced by the introduction of the B-29 Superfortress long-range bomber, which would be well within range of Tokyo from this Island group.

Lieutenant General Yoshitsugu Saito led the 31,000-strong Japanese defense forces of the 43rd Division of the Imperial Japanese Army on the island of Saipan. His counterpart was Marine Lieutenant General Holland Smith, who had 71,000 troops from the 2nd and 4th Marine Division, along with the U.S. Army's 27th Infantry Division. Bombing and bombardment of Saipan began on 13 June 1944. Fifteen battleships were involved and 165,000 shells were fired.[2]

15 June 1944 (D-Day)
Saipan, Mariana Island Group

The landings began at 0700 on 15 June 1944. More than 300 LVTs [landing vehicles, tracked], also known as amtracs, landed 8,000 Marines on the west coast of Saipan by 0900. Careful Japanese preparation allowed them to destroy about 20 of the amphibious tanks, but by nightfall, the two Marine divisions had a beachhead about 10 kilometers wide and 1 kilometer deep. The Japanese counterattacked at night, but were repulsed with heavy losses. On 16 June, units of the Army's 27th Infantry Division landed and advanced on the Aslito airfield. The invasion location surprised the Japanese, who had been expecting an attack further north.[3]

It was now D-Day + 1 and our time to go in. We were the headquarters detachment of the Military Police Company, 2nd Marine Division. The rest of our company was already ashore, divided and assigned to the invading infantry divisions. The landing was reminiscent of our previous action the year before at Tarawa, in that we had a coral reef to go over. We went from the transports onto LCVPs [landing craft, vehicle and personnel], more commonly referred to as Higgins boats, to a rendezvous midway to the beach where we loaded onto amtracs [amphibious tractors].

An amtrac [LVT] had a small cockpit into which a very small number of Marines had to be wedged. It moved through the water to the edge of the reef, which may lie about three to five feet below the surface, and would then let a wave push it up onto the reef where it lumbered to the beach.

When it was halfway up on the sandy beach, Marines had to extricate themselves by clambering over the gunwales on each side and drop down about six or seven feet to the sand. I jumped and landed right at the water's edge and, heavily laden with the usual equipment of rifle, knapsack, plus additional maps and equipment cases, I fell straight backward into the surf. I believe someone helped me get up.

The front lines had advanced well beyond the rail line that ran several hundred yards inland from and parallel to the beach between the sugar factory at Charan Kanoa to the city of Garapan. We moved to the railroad to dig in and established a site for our internment and POW stockade. I was very intimidated by the fact that within fifteen feet from my foxhole lay an unexploded 16-inch navy shell that had been fired by one of our battleships and had slithered along the ground, coming to rest within our perimeter. For several days, before it was removed, we all gave the shell a wide berth, both day and night. I was extremely leery of its inconvenient position. On top of that fear, we were also in the middle of our 10th Marine Battery of 75mm howitzers, which fired all day and night long. This made us a prime target for a Japanese artillery piece, which we labeled as "Pistol Pete," that was situated on Mount Tapotchau (Mount Tapioca to us). It remained hidden in a cave during the day, but its gunners had well marked our gun batteries and were able to zero in on us at night.

I cannot imagine more shooting and racket going on that first night; small arms, intermittent chattering of machine gun fire, grenade and mortar explosions and both Japanese and our own battery artillery fire. The sound that etched into me, however, was friendly naval gunfire, presumably coming from one of our destroyers. It sent three simultaneous shells overhead every few minutes, all night long, in support of our frontline troops. Their sharp crack seemed to pierce every inch of my body.

At the height of our first evening's bombardment, as we trembled in our foxholes, our First Sergeant stuck his head up and yelled, "Porter, Colt!" We peered over the edge and responded, "Yeah, Top." We were both astounded when he said, "Move back to the beach and keep an eye on that Jap ammo dump. They're gonna come back in there tonight." Things never looked more dismal to me. The barrage was still going on. Even if we made it to the beach, the one thing the Japs knew for sure was where their own ammunition dump was. They were sure to zero in on it.

Colt and I took off, dodging and weaving through the intense fire, down the road we had just come up that afternoon. Along the way, we saw our first dead Marines. We had seen them earlier trying to bed down and now we saw them lying on their ponchos, which were smoking where little pieces of shrapnel had hit them. The Marines, who seemed to be sleeping, were actually sleeping the "long sleep." Once we reached the ammo dump and began to dig in, I felt very despondent and knew this could be my last night on earth. How we ever made it to the dump unscathed, I'll never know.

A few Japanese did infiltrate into our area in the dark, but Colt and I never confronted them. They were killed by others around us. Despite the furor throughout the night, we ended up being safer than our mates back at the railroad track. They were actually on the front lines for a time and helped repulse a banzai and tank counterattack of that second night of the battle for Saipan. I still feel extremely lucky to have survived my first night on the island.

By D-Day + 2, the front moved up to Mount Tapioca. Though little groups of Japanese infiltrated back into our area several nights, they were disposed of by day and we began to receive our internees.[4]

Without resupply, the battle on Saipan was hopeless for its defenders; however, the Japanese were determined to fight to the last man. General Saito organized his troops into a line anchored at Mount Tapotchau in the defensible mountainous terrain of central Saipan. The Japanese used the many caves in the volcanic landscape to delay the attackers by hiding in the day and making small sorties at night. The Americans gradually developed tactics for clearing out the caves by using flamethrower teams supported by artillery and machine guns.

The operation was marred by inter-service rivalry and controversy when Marine General Holland Smith, unsatisfied with the performance of the Army's 27th Division, relieved its commander, General Ralph Smith.

Navajo code talkers played a key role in directing naval gunfire onto the Japanese positions during the fighting. By 7 July, the Japanese had nowhere to retreat, so General Saito ordered his 3,000 remaining able-bodied troops to make a last effort banzai charge, while he committed hara-kari. Thousands of Japanese troops and civilians also committed suicide by jumping off cliffs to their deaths because they feared that the Americans would torture them. The battle officially ended on 9 July 1944. Japanese losses were 24,000 killed, 5,000 suicides and 921 prisoners. Forty-six soldiers did hide out in the mountains until December of the following year (1945). Americans suffered 3,426 killed and 13,160 wounded.

As a result of this defeat, Hideki Tojo, the Japanese prime minister, fell from power. He was relieved as head of the Japanese Army and on 18 July his entire cabinet resigned. Saipan quickly became an important base for further operations in the Marianas (Tinian and Guam), and then for the invasion of Okinawa in October 1944. B-29 bombers could now attack the Philippines, the Ryukyu Islands and the Japanese homeland.[5]

Postlude

With the securing of Saipan, the Corps instituted a rotation-back-to-the-States policy for most of us with twenty-four months overseas. Upon sailing under the Golden Gate Bridge, I had logged in twenty-six months. We were housed and classified in the familiar Recruit Depot, MCB San Diego. I was pleased and subsequently gratified to be classified again as a clerk typist. We were given a choice of duty on either the east or west coast and since I had been thrilled by Southern California, I indicated "west" as my choice. The Marine Corps thought otherwise and after a thirty-day leave, I was ordered to report to Marine Barracks, Naval Operating Base, Norfolk, Virginia. How different my life might have been if I had stayed "west." As it was, I had exceedingly good duty in the Sergeant Major's office for the remaining year of my enlistment, where I was also promoted to the NCO ranks of both Corporal and Sergeant. I also met and courted my future wife and have been supremely happy living on the east coast for sixty-one years now.

Within a month after discharge, I married the love of my life on 2 December 1945 and have lived happily ever after! Three days after our marriage, we went over the mountains to Peabody College in Nashville, Tennessee, and I became a college student. Upon my graduation in May 1949, we returned to Norfolk, where we both taught high school for a year. That was too long! I enrolled at the University of North Carolina, earned a master of arts degree, and then taught for three years at Armstrong College in Savannah, Georgia. We made a brief move to Furman University to teach and then later left for North Carolina State University. Continuing there for nine years in my field of communication arts, I also acquired a Ph.D. Thus, the high school dropout became a doctor!

In July 1965, I was tapped to become a managing director of the statewide public education television system, which was just beginning. Having played a significant role in its development and implementation, I took early retirement in January 1983. As an active and faithful church member and participant in Baptist affairs, I believe retirement must be considered "liberation for service."

My wife and I had three children: Philip, Anne and Mary. We also have four grandchildren. Golf has been very dear to me, but I think I have played my last round. I have spent much time sweating and bleeding in building additions and making overall improvements to five or six houses, both my own and my children's. I have enjoyed writing and received great pleasure in writing my memoirs several years ago.

Being a member of the 2nd Marine Division Association and its Carolinas Chapter has given me much pleasure, especially attending the division's birthday observance at Camp Lejeune, which is only two and a half hours away. I have also attended annual meetings when they were in interesting places.[6]

I received a letter, dated 24 August 2006, from Jack in response to my request for information that I had placed in the 2nd Marine Division's newsletter. He sent me his story on his first day on Saipan (D-Day +1). I sent him a questionnaire to gather more info and to request a copy of an article that he wrote for the *Follow Me* newsletter in the March–April 2005 issue. I received a very comprehensive letter dated 2 September 2006, answering my questions in the most thorough and erudite manner that I could have ever expected. He also included a copy of the previously mentioned article. Jack, a high school dropout at the age of 16, would later earn a Ph.D. and thoroughly enjoys writing, as evident from his narrations.

5

USMC Corporal Earl Dunlap

Luck is what you have left over after you give 100 percent.
— Langston Coleman

Prelude

Earl Dunlap was born on 5 July 1925 and raised in the small New England town of Auburn, Massachusetts. He enjoyed playing tennis and even though he was quite small, he played one year of high school football. He claims his one moment of glory was intercepting a pass and running for a touchdown against a rival high school. He left high school early because he wanted to fight for his country and joined the Marines in Boston, Massachusetts, on 7 September 1942 at the age of 17. Some 50 years later, his former high school awarded diplomas to all of its World War II veterans who left for the war prior to graduation. Earl went to Marine Corps boot camp at Parris Island, South Carolina, and after graduating, he was assigned to Company L, 3rd Battalion, 25th Marines, 4th Marine Division as a rifleman.[1]

The East Coast echelon of the 4th Marine Division was located at Camp Lejeune, North Carolina. In July and August 1943, the 25th Marines left for Camp Pendleton, California, where the entire 4th Division officially formed up on 14 August 1943. After intensive training, the Division shipped out from California on 13 January 1944 and became the first division of Marines to go directly into battle from the United States. They attacked the dual islands of Roi-Namur in the Kwajelein Atoll of the Marshall Islands on 1 February 1944 after an 18-day sea voyage. After the islands were taken, the Division licked its wounds and set off for their next objective, Saipan in the Mariana Islands, where they fought from 15 June through 9 July 1944.[2]

Earl participated in both of these island campaigns. Of the battles he participated in, Earl considers Saipan the worst experience. "Saipan still bothers me to this day. I lost almost all of my friends the first few days of the battle. Only my squad leader survived. It made a loner out of me. I was afraid to make new friends because they would probably be killed. Even today, I am the same way."[3]

A Brief History of the 4th Marine Division

The 4th Marine Division, known as the "Fighting Fourth," had its roots in the shifting and redesignation of several other smaller units. The 23rd Marines began as infantry detached from the 3rd Division in February 1943. This was the same month that an artillery battalion became the genesis of the 14th Marines, and engineer elements of the 19th Marines formed the start of the 20th Marines. The 24th Marines was organized in March, and by May, it was split in two to supply the men for the 25th Marines. This wartime shuffling provided the building blocks for the newly formed 4th Marine Division. By 14 August 1943, all Division units were united at Camp Pendleton, California.

During the war, the Division fought on Roi-Namur, Saipan, Tinian and Iwo Jima. Twelve members of the Division earned Medals of Honor and the Division was awarded two Presidential Unit Citations. They suffered a total casualty loss of 17,000 Marines and sailors. It was the first Marine division to return to the United States after the war and was later deactivated on 28 November 1945.

The 4th Marine Division was reactivated as the lead division in the Marine Corps Reserves on 16 February 1966. Several of its reserve units have been put on active status during times of need and fought in Desert Storm in the 1990s and the current Wars against Terrorism in Iraq and Afghanistan.[4]

July 1944
Tinian, Mariana Islands

Tinian was one of the three larger principal islands in the Mariana Island group. It was situated between Saipan and Guam and was only 3½ miles south of Saipan, which had been seized by the Marines on 9 July 1944. On 21 July, the 3rd Marine Division was engaged in battle on Guam and the 4th and 2nd Marine Divisions were preparing for their attack on Tinian. General Harry Schmidt commanded the Marines, while Colonel Kiyochi Ogata oversaw a force of 4,700 soldiers and 4,110 Japanese marines on Tinian.[5]

Tinian's terrain was much flatter than the mountains found on Saipan. The Japanese knew that Tinian was going to be one of the next targets for the American forces and had begun their defensives in earnest. They worked at night and hid out during daylight hours. Observation planes were never able to see the enemy or the civilians, who spent the days in caves, tunnels and underground complexes.

The obvious wide landing beaches were on the southwestern part of the island near Tinian Town, and this is where the Japanese made their sturdier defenses and located the vast majority of the troops. Marines, knowing this, planned a surprise move by selecting two very small beachheads on the northwestern end, named White Beach 1 and 2. These beaches were only 65 and 130 yards wide and no one believed that the Marines would even consider landing two divisions in one day at these locations. Besides surprise, these beaches also had the advantage of being very close to American artillery situated on the southwestern area of Saipan.[6]

Admiral "Terrible" Turner vetoed the landings on White Beach 1 and 2. He wanted to land in the vicinity of Tinian Town. In an exchange, the Admiral told Marine General "Howling Mad" Smith, "You are not going to land on the White Beaches. I won't land you there." Smith replied, "Oh yes you will. You'll land me any God-damned place I tell you to." If we had landed at Tinian Town, it would have been another Tarawa. Prior to landing on Tinian, we received a few replacements and brought our equipment up to date. Our battalion was still under strength, down about 35 percent to just 565 men. I was now a fire team leader corporal.[7]

24 July 1944 (Jig-Day)
Company L, 3rd Battalion, 25th Marines
White Beach 1 and 2, Tinian Island

At 0557 on 24 July 1944, the Marines feigned an attack near the beaches at Tinian Town, adding to the confusion for the Japanese defenders. The Japanese responded by coming out of their holes and began shelling the offshore ships. "The Japanese gunners scored 22 hits on the USS *Colorado* and six on the USS *Scott*, killing 62, including 10 Marines. An additional 31 Marines were wounded aboard these two ships."

At approximately 0830, the 2nd Battalion on the right flank and the 3rd Battalion on the left, headed for White Beach 2. We lost our company commander shortly after the landing. We were receiving mortar and anti-tank fire along with automatic weapon fire from pillboxes and caves. All of a sudden, a six-foot-tall Japanese marine came flying out of a spider hole about ten feet in front of me. He had a Nambu machine gun with a 16-inch bayonet. He fired two rounds at me before his gun jammed, catching me in the left side with probably the first round. I tried to shoot him, but I had a faulty round in the chamber. He was now on top of me and his bayonet sliced my left wrist. Fortunately, we had been trained in jiujitsu and I somehow took his legs out from under him. I came down right on top of him and I was able to work a fresh round in the chamber. I then moved my muzzle under his chin and squeezed one off, blowing the top of his head off. For some reason, I was mad as hell and chewed everybody out. I guess I was just scared as hell. I knew I had been very lucky.[8]

The landings at the White Beaches totally surprised the Japanese and the resistance was considered very light, with the bulk of the defenders remaining in the south. By the end of Jig-Day 1, the Marine beachhead was 4,000 yards wide and 2,000 yards deep. Only fifteen Marines had been killed and another 150 wounded. That first night, the Japanese, as expected, counterattacked. By the next morning, over 2,000 Japanese lay dead, which broke the enemy's back. Dazed and weak resistance followed until 1 August 1944, when the island was declared secure.[9]

There were 8,010 Japanese killed and 313 captured. The remaining enemy hid out underground until the end of the war, surrendering on 4 September 1945. The Marine losses were considered light at 389 killed and 1,816 wounded. On 14 August, the Division boarded ships and headed for Maui in the Hawaiian Islands.[10]

Postlude

Tinian was the first battle that saw the use of napalm in war. Of the 120 tanks dropped during the operation, 25 contained the napalm mixture and the remainder an oil-gasoline mixture. Carried by P-47 Thunderbolts, the "fire bombs" burned away foliage that concealed enemy installations. After the battle, Tinian became an important base for further Allied operations in the Pacific Campaigns. Camps were built for 50,000 troops, and 15,000 Navy Seabees turned the island into the busiest airfield in the war, with six runways for attacks by B-29 Superfortress bombers on targets in the Philippines, the Ryukyu Islands and mainland Japan.[11]

On 9 May 1945, a new, secretive organization began arriving at the island's North Field Airbase, manned by the 1,767-man 509th Composite Group headed by Colonel Paul W. Tibbets Jr. On 26 July 1945, the USS *Indianapolis* (CA-35), a Portland-class heavy cruiser, delivered the component parts and the uranium projectile of the first atomic bomb, "Little Boy," to Tinian Island. Finally, on 6 August, Tibbets's B-29 *Enola Gay* left runway 1 at the North Field and dropped the atomic bomb on the city of Hiroshima, Japan, in a matter of seconds destroying 62,000 buildings and killing nearly 80,000 people. Three days later on 9 August, Major Charles W. Sweeney, flying from Tinian in his B-29 *Bock's Car*, dropped the second atomic bomb, "Fat Man," on Nagasaki. His original target had been Kokura, but bad weather forced the bomber plane to fly to its alternate target. On August 14, President Harry S. Truman announced Japan's unconditional surrender, which ended the Second World War.[12]

In a disturbing side note, the USS *Indianapolis* was sunk by a Japanese submarine (I-58) on 30 July 1945. Only 317 of 1,199 crewmembers survived five days of floating in shark-infested waters before their rescue.[13]

Corporal Dunlap recovered from his wounds, but failed to make the last 4th Marine Division World War II campaign at Iwo Jima. He decided to remain in the Marine Corps and retired as a master sergeant in September 1962.

When he retired, he worked in the driving school business for a few years and then operated his own water bottle company until finally retiring for good in 1981. He is currently married to his second wife and has one daughter (a second daughter passed away a few years ago), a stepson and stepdaughter, eight grandchildren and five great-grandchildren.[14]

Postscript

On 2 September 2007, Earl's stepson contacted me by phone to report that Earl had passed away on 27 November 2006, the day before Thanksgiving.

Earl Dunlap called me in early July 2006 in response to my ad in the July issue of *Military Magazine* and briefly told me about his narrow escape on Tinian during World War II. I sent him off a questionnaire, which he promptly returned along with his written incident narration on 26 July 2006.

6

USMC Corporal Andrew Samo

> A man's greatest good luck is to die at the right time.
> — Eric Hoffer

Prelude

On 4 August 1922, Andrew Samo was born in San Antonio, Texas. His father, a World War I veteran, was a carpenter and his mother, a homemaker. He also had two younger sisters. Andrew did not care for school, but did enjoy playing baseball with his buddies. Although the depression years were very lean, Andrew was a very enterprising young man. He started to work at the age of eleven in a local drug store as both a delivery boy and soda jerk. When he was sixteen, he traded a bicycle for a Whippet car. Unfortunately, this turned out to be a bad deal since the car kept him broke all of the time. Later, he worked with the National Youth Administration, a government program, and helped to rebuild an historic site in San Antonio. In high school, he belonged to the Reserve Officer Training Corps (ROTC) and later served for a short time in the Texas National Guard.

In early 1940, there was talk about starting up the national draft and Andrew began thinking about joining the service. His father had once told him stories about the "Devil Dogs," the legendary Marines who had fought in Europe during the First World War. The Marines had earned this nickname from the Germans whom they fought in the bloody battle of Belleau Wood. These stories generated his interest in the Marine Corps and at the age of 18, in September 1940, he enlisted. He attended boot camp at San Diego, California, and was eventually assigned to Company K of the 3rd Battalion, 21st Marines (3/21), 3rd Marine Division in 1942.[1]

A Brief History of the 3rd Marine Division

The 3rd Marine Division was activated on 16 September 1942 at Camp Elliot, California. In early 1943, the unit deployed to New Zealand and later participated in the Pacific campaigns of Bougainville, Northern Solomons,

Guam and Iwo Jima. The Division was deactivated after World War II on 28 December 1945. They were reactivated during the Korean War but deployed to Japan and Okinawa and did not engage in combat.

By May 1965, the 3rd Marine Division was once again committed to war during the Vietnam conflict. Its units operated out of Quang Tri, Quang Nam and the Thua Thien Provinces until November 1969 when they were redeployed to Okinawa. Elements later participated in the evacuation operations in Vietnam and Cambodia in 1975.

The Division was awarded numerous unit citations for its war efforts during both World War II and Vietnam. In the 1990s and 2000s, the Division participated in the wars in Iraq and Afghanistan.[2]

February 1943
Company K, 3rd Battalion, 21st Marines

By February 1943, 3/21 found itself in Auckland, New Zealand, preparing for island combat. In New Zealand, Andrew attended Malaria Control School and, because he had previously used the M-1 rifle in the National Guard, he helped to train his fellow Company K Marines in the familiarization with the M-1, which had replaced the Marines' '03 Springfield rifles.[3]

"We landed on Guadalcanal in August 1943, after the main fighting was over," Andrew said. "We did our jungle warfare training there and went out on several patrols looking for stray Japs. From there, our first major campaign was Bougainville."[4] The 3rd Marine Division landed on Bougainville on 1 November 1943. It would fight stiff and heavy enemy resistance for nearly two months. On 16 January 1944, the Army took control of the island and the Division returned to Guadalcanal. "Back on Guadalcanal, we regrouped, got replacements and started training for the invasion of Guam."[5]

The 3/21 left Guadalcanal on 3 June 1945 and initially sailed for Kwajalein in the Marshall Island Group, en route to Guam in the Mariana Island Group. It remained afloat off Saipan, also in the Marianas, from 15 to 28 June 1944 as part of a reserve force for the ongoing battle. "We were at sea for several weeks because the Marines were having a hard time securing Saipan, and we were kept on standby."[6]

20 July 1944
Landing Ship, Tank (LST) 117
Enroute to Guam

LSTs were used extensively throughout the Pacific and European theaters of war. Over 300 feet in length and capable of carrying 2,100 tons of tanks, vehicles and men, the craft could approach land with their loaded front draft of 5 to 8 feet, enabling fast off-loading during heavy fighting. They were capable of carrying nearly 300 men, including an entire Marine company and their beach landing crafts.[7]

Our convoy consisted of ships as far as you could see. Battleships, cruisers, destroyers, LSTs and LCIs [Landing Craft, Infantry] were everywhere. Overhead, the sky was crowded with our planes protecting the convoy. On the eve of invasion day, a group of us K Company Marines was up on the bow talking. Just to our port side was a smaller LCI.[8]

LCIs were 158 feet long and were designed for beaching, allowing fighting troops to disembark at a rapid rate. Capable of holding 200 men, but no vehicles, these craft were also used as rocket launchers, gun ships, mortar ships, and demolition ships, and for smoke laying and mine hunting. They were nicknamed "water-bugs" by an admiral who looked down on them from his battleship, watched the LCIs down below scurrying back and forth, and commented that they looked like a bunch of water-bugs. The name stuck.[9]

"At just about sundown and all of a sudden, a Japanese torpedo bomber, flying low, appeared to our front and headed right for our LST 117."[10] By the Marianas Campaign the Japanese torpedo bomber, the Nakajima B5N, had been replaced by the Nakajima B6N Tenzan (Heavenly Mountain). This bomber was a three-seater and could be both carrier or land based. The two rear crewmembers manned 7.7mm machine guns, while the pilot dropped the torpedo bombs. It was capable of carrying one 800-kilogram (kg) torpedo or six 100-kg bombs under its fuselage. Towards the end of the war, some Tenzans were equipped with radar for night torpedo attacks on Allied shipping. Additionally, many Jills (the Allied reporting name) were utilized in kamikaze attacks on the United States fleet, especially during the Okinawa Campaign in April and May 1945.[11]

At approximately 1,000 yards, the bomber dropped his torpedo, which was aimed straight for our ship. The plane then banked off to the left and got away, while every ship in the convoy was shooting at it. We were on the bow of our ship and had nowhere to go. We just kept staring at the torpedo, knowing we would surely be injured or killed. I then observed the LCI on our port immediately take off to intercept the torpedo. After nearly 30 seconds had passed since the bomb had been dropped, I saw the little LCI's bow raised as he deliberately rammed his ship into the torpedo. It was only about 500 yards away from our ship when this action took place. The captain of the LCI sacrificed his ship to save our larger ship and probably numerous lives, including my own.[12]

The LCI's bow broke off and sank when the torpedo hit. The remaining part of the ship was later towed away and sunk by gunfire. I still do not know if the captain or how many crewmembers were killed, but I am sure there were some survivors. I often wonder if that captain was given a citation for his heroic act. The Marines all around me were sure that we had just had a very close call."[13]

Postlude

The battle for Guam began the next day on 21 July 1944 and lasted until 10 August 1944. Guam was the largest of the Marianas. It had been a United States possession since 1898 until it had been captured by the Japanese early in the war. Guam was chosen as a target because its large size made it suitable as a supporting base, preparing for attacks against the Philippines and the Ryukyu Islands. It had a deep harbor and two airfields capable of supporting the B-29 bombers.

Although Guam did not have as many fortifications as Saipan did, the Japanese had a strength of 18,500 men under Generals Takeshi Takashima and Hideyoshi Obata. The Americans had two divisions under the command of Marine General Roy S. Geiger. His forces consisted of the 3rd Marine Division, the 1st Provisional Marine Brigade and the Army's 77th Infantry Division.[14]

From my perspective, as I ran ashore, it appeared that we were on the first landing craft to hit the beach. To our surprise, the landing was lightly defended. Not long afterwards, however, the fighting became very fierce. I was promoted to sergeant on Guam and after about seven days, I was shot through the right arm and eventually sent back to the States. I was very fortunate because my wounds kept me from the battle on Iwo Jima.[15]

Eventually, the Americans were able to isolate the Japanese when their line collapsed on 4 August. As in other Pacific island battles, most of the Japanese refused to surrender. Over 18,000 were killed and just 485 were captured. American losses were 3,000 killed and 7,122 wounded. A few Japanese held out and hid in the jungle. Over a year after the battle was over, a few stray Japanese ambushed and killed three Marines. On 24 January 1972, some hunters discovered a Sergeant Shoichi Yokoi, still hiding out in the jungle. He had lived alone in a cave for 27 years and would later receive quite a bit of publicity for never surrendering after all those years.[16]

Andrew got out of the Marines in November 1946. He went to photography school and started up his own business. Unfortunately, this business was unsuccessful and he went to work for Hunt-Wesson Foods. He remained with this company for 35 years and retired in 1988. Andrew married and had four children.

Now 84 years old, he currently lives on Padre Island in Corpus Christi, Texas, where he enjoys boating and fishing. He is a member of the Coast Guard Auxiliary and the 3rd Marine Division. He last attended 3rd Marine Division reunions in 1959 and 1960 in Washington, D.C.[17]

On 8 July 2006, I received an e-mail from 83-year-old Andrew Samo in response to my request for info in the 3rd Marine Division newsletter (*Caltrap*). He briefly told me about his close call incident. I replied with a series of questions to obtain additional information and he responded on 15 July 2006 with his competed answers.

7

USMC Private James Seidler

> Death and life have their determined appointments.
> — Confucius

Prelude

James Seidler was born in Milwaukee, Wisconsin, on 24 July 1926. His parents, Ethel and Walter, gave him great positive direction, and although they were not churchgoers, they were Christians. As a child, James loved to draw, swim and play ball with two or three good friends. They also constructed a diving helmet made out of a hot water tank, a garden hose and a bicycle pump for air. They would search the surrounding lakes for motors, tackle and other salvageable objects.[1]

> I was a stupid 17-year-old kid who had never been out of Wisconsin when I joined the Marines in October 1943. I enlisted because I was afraid the war would be over if I waited until I graduated. I picked the Marines because I thought, and still do, that they were the best.[2]

By the summer of 1944 victories in the Southwest and Central Pacific had brought the war even closer to Japan, with American bombers now able to strike at the Japanese homeland itself. The continued strategy for the war was debated between General Douglas MacArthur and Admiral Chester Nimitz. MacArthur wanted to take the Philippine Islands, while Nimitz wanted to bypass them. President Franklin D. Roosevelt traveled to Pearl Harbor and met both commanders to settle the dispute. The President chose MacArthur's strategy. However, before the Philippines could be taken, the Palau Islands, specifically Peleliu, had to be neutralized to protect the right flank. The 1st Marine Division led by General William H. Rupertus and the Army's 81st Division under General Paul Mueller were selected to go against the approximately 11,000 Japanese troops of the Reinforced Infantry Regiment, 14th Division, under the command of Colonel Kunio Nakagawa. Most importantly, the coral atoll, Peleliu, held a strategic enemy airstrip.[3]

A Brief History of the 1st Marine Division

The 1st Marine Division is the oldest and most decorated division in the Marine Corps. Known as the "Old Breed," the Division's motto is "No Better Friend, No Worse Enemy." The 1st Marine Regiment was formed in 1911 at Guantanamo Bay, Cuba. The Division participated in 15 major engagements during World War I, including Belleau Wood, Chateau Thierry and St. Mihiel.

After being deactivated between wars, the Division was brought back on 1 February 1941 in anticipation of American involvement in the Second World War. The Division fought admirably in the battles for Guadalcanal, Peleliu and Okinawa. It earned three Presidential Unit Citations (PUCs) during the War.

During the Korean War, the Old Breed participated in the assault at Inchon, the Chosin Reservoir battle against the overwhelming Chinese Army, and several other major battles. It earned an additional three PUCs during the war and its Marines suffered 4,004 dead and 25,864 wounded.

From 1965 through 1971, the Division fought in Vietnam, operating mainly in the southern I Corps region. They would be presented with two more PUCs for their outstanding performances. In 1971, the Division relocated to their home base at Camp Pendleton, California.

In the early 1990s, they participated in Operation Desert Shield and Desert Storm in Saudi Arabia, Kuwait and Iraq. They also helped with relief efforts in Bangladesh, the Philippines and Somalia. In the 2000s, the Division has been engaged in the war in Iraq.[4]

June 1944
1st Marine Division
Pavuvu, Russell Islands

During the planning stages of the assault of Peleliu, in what would be called "Stalemate II," the 1st Marine Division was positioned on the island of Pavuvu, an extremely small bit of land in the Russell Islands. Pavuvu was intended as a place for rest, retraining and reorganization for the tired Division; however, there was little opportunity for any such activity. The Division was forced to build its own camps on the barren island, losing valuable time for combat training. The Marines were also re-equipped piecemeal, with new weapons and machinery coming in day-by-day, even right up to their departure for the long sea voyage to Peleliu.[5]

I ended up being part of a replacement group that joined the 1st Marine Division at Pavuvu in the Russell Island group on 1 June 1944.

At Pavuvu, I was assigned to the 1st Pioneer Battalion where our primary duties were to unload supplies and move them to where they were needed. I never kept a diary because if you were killed, the enemy would know what outfit you were in. "Tokyo Rose" knew where we were going before we did! Therefore, I do not know the exact dates of my five close calls that all occurred on Peleliu in September and October 1944, but I swear by all that is holy that they are true.[6]

The convoy of Navy ships arrived several days ahead of the planned D-Day of 15 September 1944. On the 12th, a massive naval bombardment began against the six-square-mile Island. All buildings and Japanese planes were destroyed, but the enemy refused to return any fire, thus not revealing their positions. They remained hidden in caves, bunkers, trenches and pillboxes and lost very few men and equipment prior to the beach assaults.[7]

0832 on 15 September 1944
1st Marine Division
Peleliu, Palau Islands

The Marines landed on the beaches on the southwest side of the island on 15 September 1944 and by the next day took the airfield away from the Japanese. It was not, however, until 24 September that friendly aircraft were able to use the airstrip. By the 19th and 20th, the Division had moved to the base of higher ground, called the Umurbrogal Mountains, in the middle of the island, where they met the main enemy resistance and the fighting became ferocious. The elevation rose to nearly 500 feet above sea level. The Army took the northern islands of the Palau Island group with little or no resistance. Later, after the Marines had taken heavy losses, the Army landed their troops on Peleliu north of the Marine positions, with the 321st Infantry hitting the beaches on 23 September and the 323rd Infantry on 15 October.[8]

My squad leader and I stopped to ask a bulldozer operator for some directions. His name was Kenneth White and, in the course of our conversation, we learned that we went to the same school in Milwaukee [Benjamin Franklin School]. He was clearing an area for a command post just off White Beach. After our chat, we said, "So long, catch you later." We had gone maybe 75 to 100 yards away from Kenny, when there was a tremendous explosion that lifted us both off the ground and temporarily took away our hearing. We hurried back to where Kenny had been working and found a huge crater in the ground. Kenny had run over an aerial bomb that had been buried in the ground. The dozer was blown

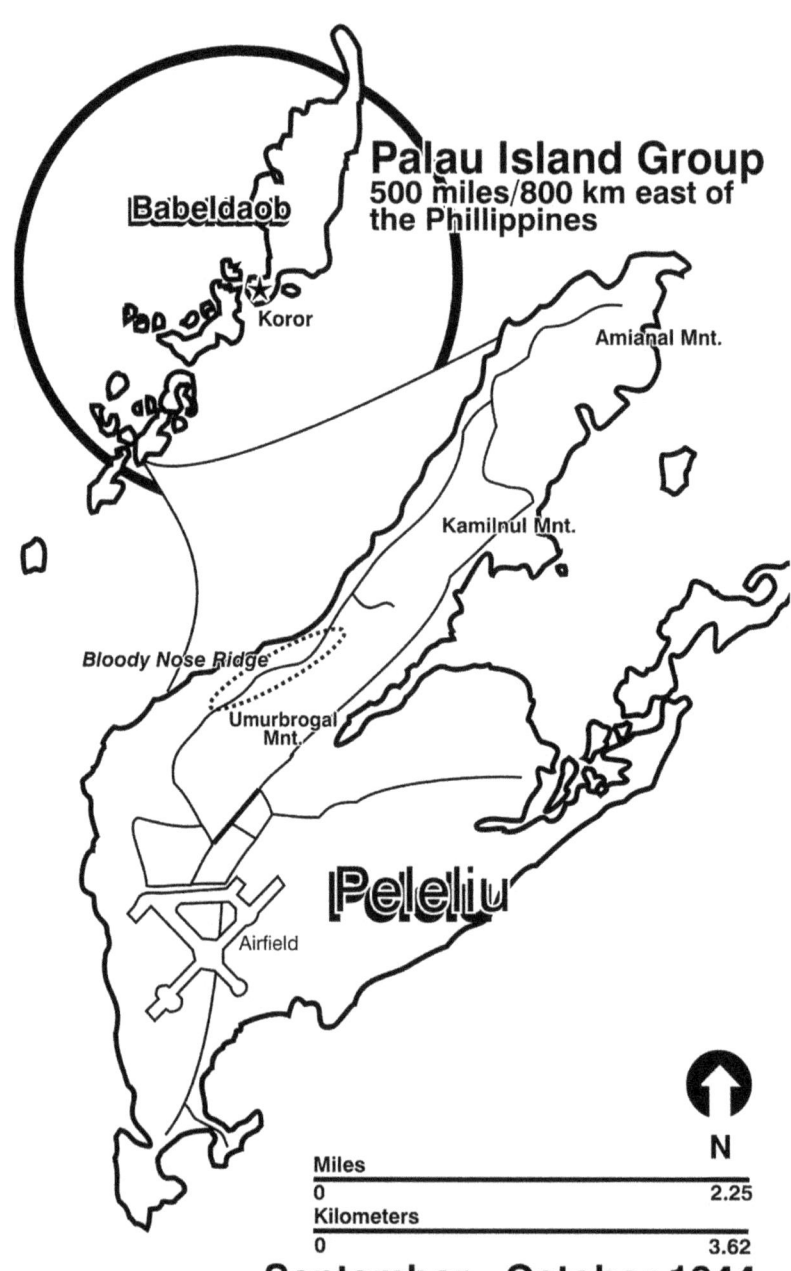

into the ocean! Kenny was seriously injured and was taken to the hospital ship where he later died. If we had walked a little slower, we might have been on that hospital ship too.[9]

* * * *

At night, we unrolled our shelter-halves on the ground and went to sleep listening to the sound of big artillery shells whooshing overhead. One morning when I awoke, I saw an enemy mortar round on the ground about 10–15 yards from where I had been sleeping! Stupid kid that I was, I walked over and picked it up. A live Japanese round had landed on its shoulder instead of on the detonator. I unscrewed the bottom, dumped out the explosive, unscrewed the detonator and pounded the primer with a piece of coral. That mortar round still sits on my desk to this day with its Japanese markings clearly visible.[10]

* * * *

Sometime around the end of September, on a very dark night, my lieutenant told me to go to the beachmaster to arrange for amtracs to assist the wounded coming off the front lines. I headed off in the dark, stumbling along for about 15 minutes when I heard a voice, "Halt! Who goes there? What's the password?" I cried out, "January, January!" I then heard several clicks and then saw a shadowy figure about six feet in front of me. It was one scared kid, even more so than I was. He told me that I should be dead as he had his carbine aimed at my chest and the clicks that I had heard was him pulling the trigger. The reason his weapon didn't fire was he had forgot to chamber a round! I found the beachmaster without further problems and returned to my bivouac area. My guardian angel was sure working overtime![11]

* * * *

During the first week of October, our Company was sent out to assist the decimated ranks of the 2nd Battalion, 7th Marines (2/7), who had suffered as much as 70 percent casualties. They took every available Marine on the island to act as replacements. It was at that time that water was first available near the front lines. A 10,000-gallon trailer was dragged up to where our lines were. In addition, everyone was issued one can of ABC [Aztec Brewing Company] beer, one pair of socks and one pack of Ramses cigarettes. No one had had a bath since the landing on that chunk of coral, so I got a 5-gallon water can, set it up on a fallen log after filling my helmet and pulled off my clothes. My socks were almost non-existent and my feet had jungle rot as I started to wash. As I bent over to wash my feet, I heard a "twang!" A piece of shrapnel had hit my water can dead center! If I had been standing up, it would have hit me in the groin. Needless to say, I quickly finished my bath.[12]

* * * *

Once the Marines were into the Umurbrogal Mountains, they came upon a large coral ridgeline called Bloody Nose Ridge, which overlooked the airfield. In the 8-day battle for the ridge, Marines suffered nearly 50 percent casualties.[13]

My fifth and last close call experience came on the night of either the 14th or 15th of October. Our outfit was on top of the China Wall part of Bloody Nose Ridge. It was the last remaining pocket of Japanese holdouts. The coral was too hard to dig a foxhole, so we piled chunks of coral in a circle large enough for the four of us: Coy, Doug, Tennessee (the only name I knew) and me. Coy was a veteran of Guadalcanal and New Guinea, while the rest of us were recent replacements. During the night, we did two-hour watches. On this particular night, Tennessee and I were asleep when there was a tremendous explosion and then screams from the wounded. Coy was on top of me crying, "Oh my God! I'm dying!" I was all wet and sticky with blood and I didn't know if it was mine or someone else's. Doug's arm was all shredded and Tennessee must have been wounded too, as all three were evacuated. I was told to "hang in there" as the Army would relieve me in the morning. That mortar round had landed in our foxhole, but once again I was uninjured. I made sure that I would be alive in the morning by utilizing four cases of hand grenades during the rest of the night! Coy was sent to Australia and eventually to the United States. Doug rejoined the Pioneers back at Pavuvu, but I still have no idea what happened to Tennessee.[14]

The American assault on Peleliu had the highest casualty rate of any amphibious invasion in terms of men and materiel in the entire Pacific war. The Japanese suffered 10,695 killed and only 202 were captured while the American death loss was 2,336 men along with 8,450 wounded.[15]

Postlude

James Seidler survived both Peleliu and the future Battle of Okinawa. He claims to have had no other close calls during the rest of the war. He remained a buck private through the war years because he and his top sergeant simply did not get along very well.

James left the Corps in October 1949 and stated, "I got out with an ex–Navy Wave, a one-year old son and one hash mark." He and his wife, who passed away after nearly 40 years of marriage in 1987, had seven children and many grandchildren and great-grandkids.

He maintains a membership in the 1st Marine Division Association with the Tennessee Chapter. In 1994, he returned to Peleliu for the 50th anniversary of the battle, where he met a Marine who had carried Kenneth White to the aid station, his body white by the time he got there. The hole from the explosion underneath the bulldozer was still there and the dozer blade was still lying in the ocean just off the beach. Because most of his military friends are now dead, James no longer attends reunions.

In 1999, James married a lovely Colombian woman, 12 years his junior, whom he claims keeps him young. He states, "Every day, I thank God for this day!"[16]

I received a letter and pictures from James Seidler, dated 9 May 2006, in response to the ad that I placed in the *Old Breed News*. His accounts of his close calls were very good. A second letter, dated 23 May 2006, arrived with some personal background information that I had requested from him.

8

USN Hospital Corpsman First Class Beryl Bonacker

> Luck is when opportunity knocks and you answer it.
> — Author unknown

Prelude

Beryl Bonacker was born on 6 September 1922 in Titonka, Iowa. He was one of four brothers and one sister of a dairy farm family. Two of his brothers would also serve during the Second World War. After his senior year in high school, Beryl moved to Woodlawn, Oregon, where he joined the Navy. "The Navy had always intrigued me. Going to sea on a battleship was something I had in mind, but the Navy had other plans for me." He entered Navy boot camp training on 20 April 1943 at Farragut Naval Training Base in Idaho. Since Navy corpsmen were in great demand, he was "volunteered" and entered Hospital Corps school at the Farragut Base after boot camp graduation. The school was followed up with a two-month assignment at the base hospital. "One day my name appeared up on the bulletin board to go to Camp Elliot, north of San Diego, California, for further training with the Marines. I was now a Hospital Corpsman 1st Class."[1]

A History of Navy Corpsmen

Although corpsmen go back to the very beginning of the Navy, the Hospital Corps was officially established in June 1898. In 1814, Navy Regulations mention a "loblolly boy" who was to serve the surgeon and surgeon's mate. The loblolly boy prepared for battle by filling containers with water to hold amputated limbs. His duties also consisted of maintaining the braziers of charcoal to heat tar, which was used to stop the hemorrhaging from the amputations. During battle, he was also tasked to keep the deck safe for the surgeon around the operating area by placing sand on the blood-coated, slippery surfaces.

The "surgeon's steward" eventually replaced the loblolly boy. Surgeons recognized a need for additional trained help so they selected promising young men for training in elementary medicine. More than a cleanup person, this specialist was probably the true forerunner of today's corpsman.

When Congress established the Hospital Corps, the Secretary of the Navy appointed 25 senior "apothecaries" as pharmacists. These 25 are the charter members of the Hospital Corps. Today's Hospital Corpsmen provide medical services for the Navy and Marine Corps throughout the world. Lieutenant General Lewis "Chesty" Puller was quoted as saying, "You guys are the Marines' doctors. There's none better in the business than a Navy corpsman."

Prior to World War I, four Medals of Honor were awarded to Hospital Corpsmen. During the war, there were 16,000 enlisted men in the Hospital Corps. Seventeen were killed and another 146 were wounded or gassed. Two Medals of Honor, 55 Navy Crosses, 33 Distinguished Service Medals and 27 Letters of Commendation were awarded to these heroes.

During the Second World War, approximately 200,000 men and women served in the Corps. The corpsmen suffered 889 killed and 1,724 total casualties. Seven earned the Medal of Honor, while there were 61 Navy Crosses, 465 Silver Stars and 982 Bronze Stars awarded to Corpsmen. One of the men raising the famous flag on Iwo Jima was Corpsman John Brady.

During the Korean conflict, corpsmen once again performed admirably, earning an additional five Medals of Honor. In the Vietnam War, the corpsman ranks suffered 620 killed and another 3,353 were wounded in action. They were awarded the following medals: 3 Medals of Honor, 29 Navy Crosses, 127 Silver Stars, 2 Legions of Merit and 290 Bronze Stars.[2]

The Hospital Corpsman's Pledge: "I solemnly pledge myself before God and these witnesses to practice faithfully all of my duties as a member of the Hospital Corps. I hold the care of the sick and injured to be a privilege and a sacred trust and will assist the Medical Officer with loyalty and honesty. I will not knowingly permit harm to come to any patient. I will not partake of, nor administer any unauthorized medication. I will hold all personal matters pertaining to the private lives of patients in strict confidence. I dedicate my heart, mind and strength to the work before me. I shall do all within my power to show in myself an example of all that is honorable and good throughout my naval career."[3]

1944
Cape Gloucester, New Britain

I went overseas with 78 other corpsmen in the 40th Replacement Battalion. We joined the 1st Marine Division at the end of the Cape

Gloucester Campaign in New Britain, where I was assigned to Company E, 2nd Battalion, 5th Marines [2/5]. After the fighting was over, we went the island of Pavuvu to prepare for our next battle at Peleliu. By now, I had earned the nickname of "Bonny" given to me by my senior corpsman.[4]

15 September 1944
Peleliu, Palau Islands

We had come to Peleliu on an LCI [Landing Craft, Infantry]. We prepared to disembark, loaded down with our gear and supplies around our waists and over our shoulders. Believe me, we were not going for a hike. We had to go over the side of the ship onto a smaller boat called an LCVP [Landing Craft Vehicle, Personnel] that would take us ashore and then return for more men. We crouched down in the craft, each person trying not to tangle the gear on his back with the guy next to him. The boat was crowded, elbow-to-elbow. When an LCVP was full, the person in charge pulled away from the ship and got in line with other small craft as they circled the ship. There were hundreds of circling LCVPs as they massed for the assault, going ashore in waves.

It was a very bright, hot day with no cloud cover or wind. The sea was calm, except where the LCVPs were stuck in the chop created from the ship's wake and the crosscurrents from the circling boats. As a corpsman, I was very concerned about the possibility of heat stroke. The outside temperature was already hovering around 95 degrees and it was not yet 0900. From time to time the LCVPs would stop. The exhaust from all of the ships and boats created a blue haze, which settled around us each time we stopped. There was no way to avoid the nauseous clouds of exhaust and carbon monoxide. By this time, it had risen to 100 degrees.

We were all woozy from the fumes and, in addition to being half-sick, the extreme heat was difficult to deal with. We were also very scared of what was about to happen, because for many men, including myself, this was the first time we would see action. It seemed like our LCVP circled for hours. The Navy had laid down a lot of firepower zeroed in on the beach prior to us disembarking. For that reason, we weren't drawing any fire from the beach. We were still a quarter of a mile out and hadn't yet received word to head for the beach, but we knew it was just a matter of time. We had been told to keep low in the craft to avoid being hit, and it was tough not to be able to stand or sit upright. To be honest, we were a mess and we hadn't started for the beach yet.

Finally, the word came and the LCVP made a beeline for the beach. Our unit was in the eleventh wave and landed on Orange Beach. It was now over 110 degrees and water was already at a premium. It seemed only minutes had passed before the craft made a sudden stop, striking a coral head. We went out the front, stepping into about three feet of water and still several yards from the beach. Marines and corpsmen alike were tripping over each other as they struggled over the bumpy coral. Once on the beach, we lay all bunched together until, with a few choice words from the lieutenant in charge, we spread out while trying to take as much cover as possible.

The beach itself was very shallow and rose only about four feet from the sandy margin to the top of the airport runway. There were no trees, rocks or anything to provide protection. It was all open ground. We would have to face all that exposure when we crossed the airfield. The enemy was starting to lob in shells, which were hitting some of the LCIs just off-shore and the LCVPs. We were also starting to get mortar shelling and small arms firing from inland. It was time to get off the beach!

Finally, we got word to move out across the airport runway. As we ran across the tarmac, the temperature was unbearable. The heat radiated off the cement runway, which made it feel even hotter. At this point, we were not getting any casualties, with the exception of a few scraped knees and elbows. We could see buildings in the distance that would afford some protection against small arms fire. Reaching the buildings, we could see they had been bombed extensively and still smelled of sulfur. We felt good to know that we had a little protection from the enemy. There was no evidence of any life in the area, just a lot of destruction. The Japanese remained underground in their coral caves and bunkers. We thought we had gone far enough for one day, but the higher-ups thought differently. We were told to move out again, this time going through a swampy area with the constant sounds of rifle fire all around us. We finally set up for the evening but it was obvious that lack of water was taking its toll and we would not receive water until the next afternoon. As our first day ended, we were hungry, thirsty and scared of what lay ahead for us.[5]

19 September 1944
Peleliu

Four days later, I was assigned to a patrol that was going to dynamite Japanese cave entrances. Four demolition Marines would drop dynamite by placing it on the end of a line, which would then be dropped or swung into the cave entrances. Marines with M-1s and carbines would lay down cover fire to protect this tricky operation. Another corpsman, Kenneth Blewitt, who was right next to me, took a bullet in the flesh just above his right shoulder blade. As I was attending his wound, a Japanese mortar round landed within a few yards of us and miraculously, neither of us received any shrapnel. We did get hit with hot pieces of coral that left burn marks on my right arm. We were both extremely lucky; however, Kenneth would later be hit by shrapnel again in the stomach. Unfortunately, he would not survive his gaping hole. He had been part of the same 40th Replacement Battalion when we had earlier joined the 1st Marine Division. There were so many caves on Peleliu. One particular cave was a medical cave and we found medical supplies of all sorts once we secured it. This was just one of many close calls that I experienced during the war.[6]

Postlude

Following Beryl's service time, he went to dental tech school in Seattle on the G.I. Bill. However, since dental technicians did not receive a very good salary at the time, he went to work for Boeing Aircraft and continued there for eleven years. He married and had three children in the Seattle area. They would later move back to Oregon. He went to work for United Bakery, where he retired in 1984. He has been married for 58 years!

For years since retirement, I've maintained both a flower and vegetable garden. I have been a lifetime member of the First Marine Division Association since 1978. For many years, I attended reunions all over the United States. I am a current member and former board member of the Camp White Museum in southern Oregon. The Museum displays war artifacts, most of which are from the Second World War.

My combat experiences, and there have been many, bothered me to the point that it was hard to sleep at times! I, along with many veterans who saw just enough death and destruction, found it difficult to talk about our experiences when asked to tell about where we had been and what we had done. The first time I did talk about my duties as a corpsman was when I went to my first, 1st Marine Division Reunion. Sixty-two years have passed and I very seldom think and talk about our war. I was a Christian when I went into the service and I still am! I'm certain that it was the love of God and family that got me through it all.[7]

Postscript

Beryl Bonacker had many close calls during his time as a Navy corpsman, but he was not the only family member to survive near-death experiences during the war. His younger brother, Marlyn, was an Army Air Force tail gunner on a B-17 bomber. On his second bombing mission on 6 April 1945 over Germany, another American bomber crashed into his plane. He was the only survivor out of his eight-man crew, parachuting into Germany, where he was quickly captured. After moving to several different POW camps, he and a few others managed to escape during an American attack on the city. They were eventually picked up by friendly forces and returned to England.[8]

On 10 July 2006, I received an e-mail from Beryl Bonacker, who had read my ad in *Military Magazine*. He said he had a couple stories for me that might interest my readers. We continued a series of e-mails on 11 July, 6, 14, and 17 August 2006. I received a letter package from Beryl dated 21 August 2006 which included his story, pictures and a copy of the January 2006 *Military Magazine* which had a story on both Beryl and his brother Marlyn. On 24 October 2007, I received permission from the editor of *Military Magazine* to use anything in this article.

In a note from Beryl's wife, dated 3 September 2007, I learned that he had suffered a stroke on 24 February 2007 on his left side, which has caused him extra problems since he is left-handed.

9

USMC Sergeant George Peto

I find that the harder I work the more luck I have.
— Thomas Jefferson

Prelude

George Peto was born on 18 September 1922 in Akron, Ohio. His early years were spent on a farm in the Portage Lakes area, south of Akron. His family grew most of their own food. As a youngster, he fished, hunted and ran a trap line for muskrat. Prior to the Second World War, the family never had an indoor bathroom.

> We did have a two-hole outhouse, which was considered a luxury in those days. I still recall those trips at night to the outhouse in a foot of snow. It was a very primitive life. Growing up in those conditions helped me survive the war. My hunting and use of guns at an early age also proved useful.

George joined the Civilian Conservation Corps (CCC) when he was 15 and spent his 16th birthday on a desert in Utah. Since there was a two-year maximum limit on service in the CCC, he and a friend went to Cleveland to take the physical exam for the Marine Corps. George passed, but his friend was rejected for being colorblind. He put off joining for a year but finally enlisted on 25 August 1941. At that time, prior to the war, there were only about 18,000 Marines in the entire Corps. After Pearl Harbor, that number would greatly increase.

> I enlisted in the Marines for "travel and adventure," and besides, finding a job in 1941 was no easy task! I served in four Pacific campaigns during the war including eastern New Guinea, Cape Gloucester, Peleliu, and Okinawa. During my entire time overseas, I was assigned to the 3rd Battalion, 1st Marines (3/1), 1st Marine Division.[1]

A Brief History of the 3rd Battalion, 1st Marines

The "Thundering Third" 3/1 was first activated on 1 March 1941 and was assigned to the 1st Marine Division. The Battalion deployed to New Zealand in June 1942 and participated in the Pacific campaigns for Guadalcanal, New Britain, eastern New Guinea, Peleliu and Okinawa during World War II. After the war, 3/1 helped in the occupation of northern China.

During the Korean War, it first deployed to Kobe, Japan, and then made the amphibious landing at Inchon, Korea. They continued in operations near Seoul, the Chosin Reservoir and along the Western Front. After the armistice, the Battalion remained in Korea and helped to protect the Korean Demilitarized Zone (DMZ). The Battalion relocated to Camp Pendleton, California, in 1955 and was part of the contingency force during the Cuban Missile Crisis in 1962.

During the Vietnam conflict, 3/1 fought from January 1966 to May 1971, operating from Chu Lai, Da Nang, Hoa Vang, Ca Lu Combat Base, Cua Viet, Go Noi and the DMZ between North and South Vietnam.

The Battalion took part in Desert Shield and Desert Storm, going ashore by helicopter and landing craft at Ra Al Mishab, Kuwait, in support of the 2nd Marine Division in 1990–91. 3/1 is currently taking an active role in the War in Iraq.[2]

September 1944
1st Marine Division
Peleliu, Palau Island

I was assigned to K Company, 3/1, when we landed on Peleliu. That very first night, the Japanese surrounded 235 of us and we held on by our fingertips, totally cut off from our battalion. I was a machine gunner that night and we held our position, but only 18 Marines were still standing by the next morning! I often still think back to that night and, by comparison, most problems in civilian life have been just a small bump in the road.

Religion had never played a big part in my life until several days later on Peleliu. I was on my way back to K Company from the beach; my canteen was empty, it was 130 degrees in the shade and mortars and machine gun fire were raking us from all over. I was in deep despair and thought, "This would be a good time to ask the Lord for help," which I proceeded to do. The Jap guns, however, continued relentlessly. Consequently, it was in a shell crater on Peleliu, I am sorry to say, that I lost what little religion I had. Today, as I reflect back on those days, I must have had a guardian angel on each shoulder or I would have never survived. As I was thinking about that day sixty years later, I recalled that right after I had asked for help from above, I had jumped into another shell crater and, as I looked over the rim of the crater through that smoke and hell, an old man appeared carrying an M-1 rifle. Except for his age, he looked like any other Marine. That old Marine was none other than the legendary Lewis Burwell Puller, known throughout the Corps as "Chesty," our regimental commander. As we parted, he said, "How are you doing?" I managed a grin and said, "Hanging in," and we proceeded on our separate ways. Had the Lord himself spoken to me, I would not have been more motivated. Who knows, maybe he did.[3]

1 April 1945
Okinawa, Japan, Ryukyu Island Group

Okinawa was the first battle held on the Japanese home territory. It was located south of the four larger islands of Japan. The land battle began on 1 April 1945 with the largest amphibious assault during the Pacific campaign of World War II. It would also be the largest sea-air-land battle in history. Army General Simon Bolivar Buckner commanded the American forces of 548,000 Marines and soldiers. At his disposal was the III Corps, consisting of the 1st and 6th Marine Divisions along with the 2nd Marine Division, which was used as an afloat reserve, and the XXIV Corps, which included the 7th, 27th, 77th and 96th Army Infantry Divisions. The Japanese defenses were under General Mitsuru Ushijima in the south, and the lesser known General Takehido Udo in the northern part of the island. They commanded the 32nd Army, which consisted of the 9th, 24th and 62nd Divisions along with the 44th Independent Brigade. Their total force numbered 107,000 soldiers and 24,000 civilian troops. What was very different from previous island battles was that there were also several hundred thousand civilians living on Okinawa at the time.[4]

By the time we landed on Okinawa, I had over two years overseas and three campaigns to my credit. I would definitely say I was a seasoned veteran. I had already been through so much combat and seen thousands of dead bodies, that I had become used to all the mayhem. I had two Marines shot on either side of me and I don't think my blood pressure changed at all. Either you adapted to your environment or you were led to the rear by a corpsman and the war is over for you and you then had to live with it for the rest of your life.[5]

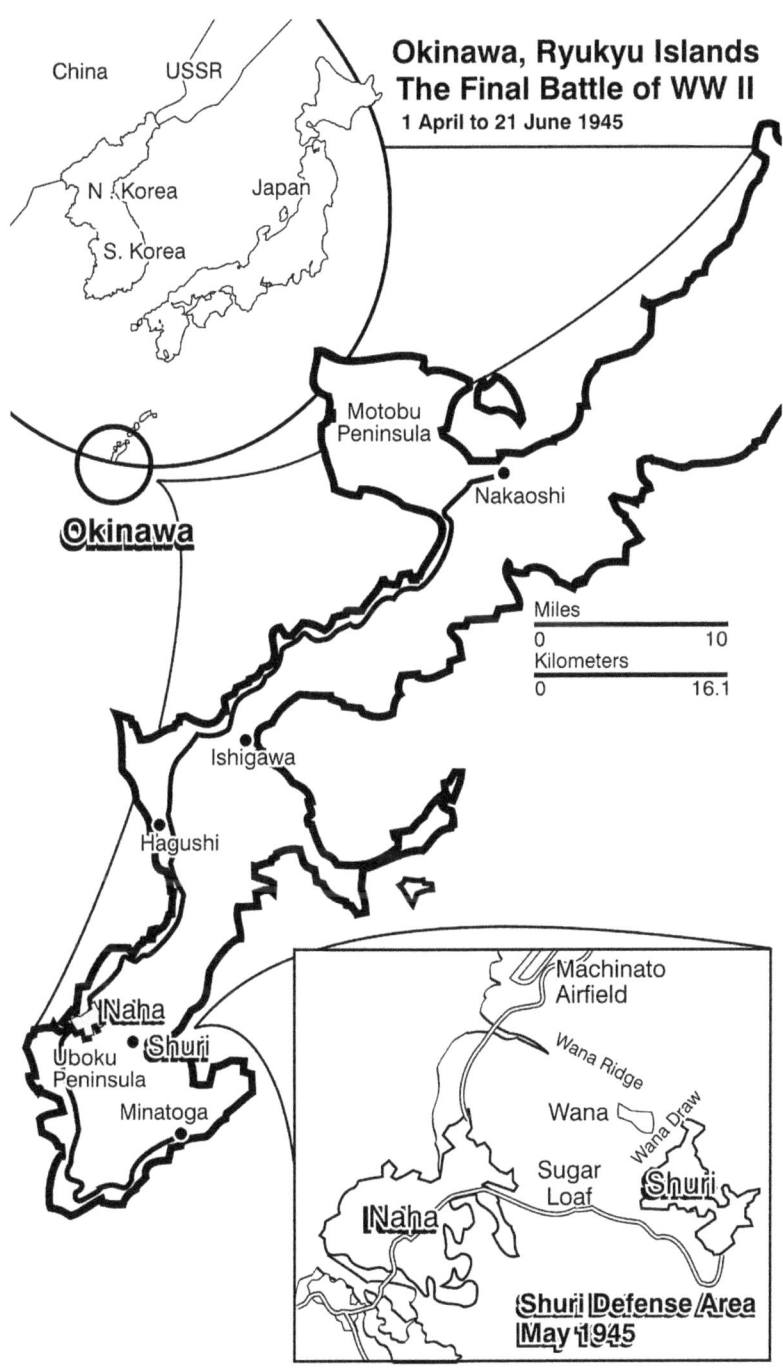

General Ushijima realized he could not defend the entire island, so he centered his defenses and troops in the southern part of the island around the historical capital, Shuri Castle. This provided a heavy defense line that could only be flanked from the sea. For the first time in the Pacific War, the Japanese not only had time to dig in fortifications but they also had large numbers of tanks and artillery pieces. With relative ease by World War II standards, the entire north end of the island fell a few weeks later on 20 April. The southern phase of the battle, however, would be different and much bloodier. Before the Americans could take Shuri Castle, they had to conquer several strategic areas, including Sugar Loaf Hill, Dakeshi Ridge and both the Wana Draw and Ridge.[6]

14 May 1945
1st Marine Division
Wana Draw, Okinawa

The 6th Marine Division's celebrated assault on Sugar Loaf Hill occurred at the same time that the 1st Marine Division entered against the Japanese Wana defenses. For this reason, historians paid little attention to the Wana battles, but they were no less important and the fighting was just as ferocious. The complex was first attacked on 12 May; the fight for the Ridge began on 13 May and for the Draw on 14 May. All three regiments of the 1st Marine Division would participate in the heavy fighting.[7]

Beyond the village of Wana lay Wana Draw, a broad, shallow basin, entirely bare, which dropped down from the coral heights of northern Shuri to the Asa River and the coastal plain north of the city of Naha. On the south side of Wana Draw, a high coral ridge, similar to Wana Ridge on the north, climbed steeply to the Shuri Heights at the southwestern corner of Shuri. Wana Draw was completely exposed to enemy fire from high ground on three sides.[8]

According to Marine General Oliver P. Smith, "Wana Draw proved to be the toughest assignment the 1st Division was to encounter." The Draw was defended by the remnants of the Japanese 62nd Infantry Division to their near extinction. They were dug deeply into caves, linked together by underground passages.

On 20 May, Lieutenant Colonel Stephen V. Sabol's 3/1 improvised a unique method for eliminating Japanese defenders from their reverse slope positions in the Draw. In five hours of muddy, backbreaking work, Marines carried several drums of napalm up the north side of the ridge. There, they split the barrels open, tumbled them down the gorge, and set them ablaze by dropping white phosphorus grenades in their wake, which played havoc on the Japanese troops.

For the first several days of the fight, the weather had been dry and the ground solid, enabling coordinated ground and air attacks against the enemy. However, by 22 May, heavy rains began which flooded the Wana Draw with mud and water until it resembled a lake. Life and fighting became nearly impossible. Living conditions for the front-line troops were indescribably bad. Gains were measured by yards won, lost and won again.[9]

At the time of my close call story, I was a sergeant assigned as the 3/1 Battalion forward observer [FO] for the 81mm mortars. The incident took place one day in late May 1945. My job kept me with the advancing companies. When one would be relieved, I would join up with the next leading element. The other observer, a very close friend, was killed on 4 May. His assistant died on 11 May and my platoon commander was wounded on the 9th. This left me as the only 81mm mortar observer for the next 52 days of intense combat with the Battalion.

We were moving into Wana Draw with our right flank heavily wooded with lots of small brush. The artillery had taken care of the big trees. I saw a small black object moving up and down and thought at first it was an animal. As I continued to watch it proceed towards me, I realized it was on an enemy soldier's belt. So, I placed my rifle over a fallen log and patiently waited. Three feet in front of me lay another log, and when the Jap got there, his head came up and he stared right into the muzzle of my rifle. His startled look lasted about one tenth of a second, then my bullet hit his brain and his head dropped. I am sure he died instantly. Before I could check him out, I heard the call to move out so up the draw we went.

We paused briefly before starting up, at some tombs directly above. The observer for the 60mm mortars gave an order to his guns to cover the area ahead but his calculations were off and they dropped right on top of us. There were cries for "corpsmen up!" I glanced over at the observer and he knew it was his rounds killing fellow Marines. He totally lost it and began sobbing uncontrollably. It is every observer's nightmare to drop short rounds and I believed the war ended for him that day. We advanced to the Okinawan tombs and around the burial place was a two-foot-high concrete wall, which was a perfect place to take cover and fire over. We were under heavy machine gun and rifle fire and knee mortar rounds were falling like rain. While returning fire, I felt a tap on my shoulder and thought it was the Marine next to me. I glanced over at him, but he was firing over the wall. I then looked over my shoulder and saw an enemy mortar round that must have just grazed me, lying on the ground. Had I chose to throw myself on it, I would have been killed and probably put in for a Medal of Honor. However, our training was to grab it and pitch it away. As I picked up the mortar round, the Marines in close proximity realized what was happening as it left my hand. There was a resounding explosion and I came within a millisecond of losing my hand and possibly my head. The incoming fire from the other side was so intense that we had no time to think about our narrow escape.

The Division received the Presidential Unit Citation for its performance at the battle of Wana Draw. For the Marines, it was just another day at the office. We were on our way to the next objective, which was the medieval Castle of Shuri.[10]

By the end of May, General Ushijima began pulling troops out of Wana Draw and the Shuri Line, which finally allowed Marines to pour into Shuri. One grizzled veteran recalled that Wana Draw "was the most awful place conceivable for a man to be hurt or to die." For every 100 yards of advance through the Wana complex, the 1st Marine Division lost 200 Marines![11]

Okinawa finally fell on 21 June 1945. The American commander, General Buckner, was killed just 5 days before the end of the battle, while visiting the front lines, by ricocheting shell fragments. His counterpart, General Ushijima, committed suicide (seppuku). The losses on both sides were staggering. The Japanese had 110,000 men killed, 7,455 captured (which was an unusually large number compared to other Pacific island battles) and lost 16 ships and 7,800 aircraft (many from kamikaze attacks). Over 150,000 civilians also died in the intense fighting and shelling, referred to as the "Typhoon of Steel." Many civilians, believing in the propaganda that Americans were barbarians who committed horrible atrocities, killed their entire families to avoid capture. Several simply jumped off the steep southern cliffs, hundreds of feet above the ocean, to their deaths.

The American losses were also dramatic. Over 12,500 men were either killed or listed as missing. Thirty-eight thousand were combat wounded, along with another 33,096 who were listed as non-combat wounded, most of whom were rendered as combat ineffective due to battle fatigue. The United States suffered its highest-ever casualty rate for combat stress reaction during this battle.

Neither side realized that the Battle of Okinawa would be the last battle of the war. Plans were already in the making for the invasion of the main Japanese islands, which would never happen due to the surrender of Japan after the two atomic bombs were used against Hiroshima and Nagasaki in August 1945.[12]

Postlude

After 4½ years, I was discharged at Great Lakes in Chicago, Illinois, on 25 November 1945. I was given a handshake and told, "There would always be a job for you in the Corps." I went down to the Sherman Hotel in Chicago and proceeded to wash away all those bad years with good whiskey, until I found myself a week later in Cicero with a bad hangover and no money. I figured it was now time to go home! I considered myself fortunate that I did not see a psychiatrist or I would still be under his/her care. I went home, got a job and went to college. In June 1948, I married and had two children. It took me about five years to get the war out of my dreams and thoughts and I truly believe the experience helped me through life. I am still married today to the same woman after 58 years! I was a merchant in Columbus, Ohio, for 36 years.[13]

George is a member of the 1st Marine Division Association and recently was the Grand Marshall at the 30 May 2006 Memorial Day Parade in Worthington, the largest parade in Ohio. He is also the webmaster and historian for 81mm Mortars for the 3rd Battalion, 1st Marines: 1941 through 1947.[14]

George Peto e-mailed me on 25 April 2006, in response to my 1st Marine Division ad in the *Old Breed News*, telling me he would like to participate in my book. He wrote his story and included his personal information in a letter dated 3 June 2006.

10

USMC Corporal Jim Anderson

> Life and death are balanced on the edge of a razor.
> — Homer, *The Iliad*

Prelude

Jim Anderson was born in the rural town of Dallas, Wisconsin, in 1925. Assured that if he left early he would still get his high school diploma, at the age of seventeen he joined the Marine Corps on 9 March 1943. His basic training was in San Diego, followed immediately by infantry training at the nearby Camp Elliot. Several months later, he found himself aboard the troop transport ship *Rochambeau*, headed for New Caledonia in the South Pacific. After a short stay in New Caledonia, his next trip took him to New Guinea, where his outfit, Company K, 3rd Battalion, 5th Marines, 1st Marine Division, landed after the main action was over. "I never fired a shot. We went looking up in the hills for the Japanese, but we never found any."

Cape Gloucester, New Britain
December 1943

After a month on New Guinea, the next stop was at Cape Gloucester, where they arrived a few days after D-Day, just after Christmas of 1943. "It was a very heavily dense jungle and it rained every afternoon." On the second day, as Company K headed inland, they began taking some sporadic fire from unseen enemy positions. As they approached "Suicide Creek," Jim was second in the column, acting as a second scout. "The first scout was out in front of me and all of a sudden there was a burst of machine gun fire and down he went. I crawled up to him but could see he was obviously dead. I immediately took a bullet in my left side, knocking me over. I managed to drag myself out of there and made it back a ways. I nearly passed out when the Japs threw a mortar near my position which filled my left leg with shrapnel." Some Marines came to his aid and brought him back to the battalion aid station where his wounds were stabilized. He had just survived his first close call with death. He was eventually transported to an Army hospital back on New Guinea. The larger pieces of shrapnel were removed, as was the bullet that was lodged in his stomach. After a short recuperation, he went back and joined his company on New Britain. From there, the 1st Marine Division was sent to Pavuvu, a rest camp near Guadalcanal.

September 1944
Peleliu

In August 1944, they climbed aboard an LST and were told they were headed for Peleliu, an island about 600 miles east of the Philippines. The trip took five weeks. When it came time to hit the beaches at Peleliu, the Marines were told that they expected the island to be taken in just 72 hours. "We jump over the side of amtracs and were immediately hit by machine gun fire. My first thought, on the island, was that I would not make it. I didn't see how anyone could live through what was happening on that beach. It was indescribable. To this day, I can't find words to describe it."

K Company was one of the first units ashore in what was estimated to be 115-degree heat. "They told us on the ship that the beach was a good place to get killed, so we headed inland right away." Jim's most memorable moment on Peleliu came in the early fighting. "We had just run up against a pillbox with a machine gun and the commander told me to go back and get a couple of tanks to come up. I was going down a path and as I turned a corner, there was a Jap soldier! I had my rifle in my hand and pulled up and fired without getting it to my shoulder. The shot went wild and the enemy soldier did bring his rifle to his shoulder and fired. I can still see the flame coming out of the gun barrel. The shock of me shooting first must have unnerved him because he missed. He had a bolt action and I had a semi-automatic. He was working the bolt when I got my rifle up to my shoulder and fired. That was the closest call I ever had."

Shortly thereafter, K Company worked its way down the western part of the island and then jumped on some tanks that took them to the northern tip of the island. From there they boarded some amtracs and were taken to the nearby Ngesebus Island. They spent a few days clearing out some pockets of Japanese and then returned to Peleliu. The outer portions of the island had been taken but the Japanese were now holed up in caves and fortifications in the central highlands with places that the Marines would call Bloody Nose ridge, the Five Brothers and the Five Sisters. "At night we would stay in our positions. You knew if you moved, you'd probably get shot at by our own troops. The Japanese would move at night as they brought in more replacements."

By now the Marines, who had been constantly fighting, were tired from their heavy combat loads and lack of sleep. "We were extremely tired. I was as low as I could get. I could hardly put one foot in front of the other. The place was full of dead Japanese and the smell was awful."

At the end of October, K Company was transported back to Pavuvu, after having lost nearly two-thirds killed or wounded. They slowly recuperated and began getting replacements. It was evident that another island and another battle were on the horizon. In February 1945 they once more boarded an LST and, once at sea, were told they were headed for Okinawa.

Okinawa
April 1945

The Marines landed without a shot being fired. It was Jim's fourth landing. Okinawa was an agricultural island and the men were able to live off the land, digging up sweet potatoes and onions as they advanced. After the 1st Marine Division had cleared the northern part of the island, they headed south and were placed in the center of the island. Soon the fighting became very intense. "We'd be on one ridge at 0600. We'd then call in artillery on the next ridge and after two hours of shelling, we'd move on to take that ridge. Sometimes we couldn't and we'd have to try again.

"At one point, our artillery was coming awfully close to our position one night. We couldn't move back because you just didn't move at night. You'd get shot. The commander came to me and said, 'Andy, do you think you could get back to that artillery and have them stop?' I said, 'I'll give it a whirl, sir.'

"I had a very rough time getting to the rear, getting shot at by our own men and everything else. I finally found the officer in charge of the artillery and told him the situation. He told me I was full of baloney. I had to use strong language. I told him if he kept shooting, somebody was going to get killed. It's not easy for a corporal to talk that way to a lieutenant, but I really laced it to him." The officer finally decided to halt the bombardment. For this effort and for other incidents of bravery, Anderson was awarded the Bronze Star.

The fighting continued from April to August. The rains came and made life miserable and difficult to wage a war. The Marines finally reached the south side of the island, just one week before the atomic bomb was dropped on Hiroshima. The Marines were ecstatic. Okinawa had been tough on K/3/5. Their 220-man Marine company had been reduced to just 110 men. Many of the survivors had enough points to rotate back to the United States. Corporal Anderson, who now was just one of 19 survivors of the company that had landed much earlier on back at New Guinea, did not.

Postlude

After a brief rest, Jim's company was again placed on LSTs and this time headed off to China, where their duty was to disarm the Japanese soldiers and send them back to their homeland. It was relatively pleasant duty for the Marines, especially after the past years of heavy fighting. By January 1946, Jim qualified to return to America.

He was discharged at Great Lakes, near Chicago. Within two years, he married Beverly and they had three children. Anderson worked as a mechanic for 20 years and then became postmaster at Colfax, Wisconsin, for the next 21 years. He currently lives on the outskirts of Cameron and volunteers during the summer months at the nearby Barron County history complex.

Postscript

During the 1990s, Jim became curious about a Japanese battle flag he had taken off a dead enemy soldier on Okinawa. He located a translator and discovered the name of the soldier who had died. Through the Japanese welfare agency, he was able to track down the soldier's son, Isao Kito, who lived in Tokyo. Jim wrote Mr. Kito a letter about the flag, and soon after, a reply came indicating that he had been conceived while his father was on leave and he had never known him. He also wrote, "I most humbly request that you return my father's flag." Jim couldn't think of any reason to keep it, so he mailed it to the son. Kito later wrote that he "broke down and cried because I knew my father had touched that flag." To this day, the Andersons and the Kitos still exchange greetings every year.[1]

On 24 October 2007, I came across the online story of Jim Anderson from a newsletter link on the Minnesota American Legion website. I was able to locate the story's editor, Al Zdon, who writes "War Stories" for the website. He also produced a book, titled *War Stories: Accounts of Minnesotans Who Defended Their Nation*. On 14 November 2007, Mr. Zdon e-mailed me and granted me permission to use portions of Jim's and three other stories from the website and book.

11

USN Hospital Corpsman Second Class Benton Corry

> Diligence is the mother of good luck.
> — Benjamin Franklin

Prelude

Born on 19 September 1925, Frank Corry was raised in Oakman, Alabama. In 1940, when he was just under 15, his Boy Scout troop was assigned to assist the National Guard at the local railroad yard in preparation for a visit by President Franklin D. Roosevelt, who was helping to escort the body of the late Speaker of the House, Will Bankhead, to his funeral in Jasper, Alabama.

> Early in the afternoon, a large impressive automobile drove up by the tracks. The driver parked the car and walked away from it. My cousin Corry and I gave the automobile the once-over, inside and out. Corry was in the driver's seat and I was in the back seat when a very agitated colonel came running towards us. He ordered us to get our asses out of the car and impressed on us that not only the limousine but also all around it was a forbidden area. The train pulled in and Roosevelt came out. Using the handrails, he hand-walked down the ramp and entered the back seat of the car where I had been sitting. That impressed on us the gravity of his polio.
> It was a different time in those days; a time when two young Boy Scouts could come face to face with the President of the United States and cavort in his car. A time when, after the Japanese bombed Pearl Harbor and the United States entered World War II, every boy and every man, regardless of age or physical condition, was ready to sign up and go to war for his country. I graduated from Oakman High School in December 1942, a semester earlier than I would have graduated, had it not been for the war. I had tried to enlist in the military the prior summer but had been turned down and told to first finish high school.

On 11 February 1943, I enlisted in the Navy. I had no inkling of what commitment I had just made to myself. The Navy literature stated that there were fifty-two trades from which to choose. That statement was correct, but what the literature failed to say was that they let you make your choice and then they place you in whatever trade they damn well pleased! In my case, I listed airplane mechanic as my first choice and gunner as my second choice but I was placed into the Hospital Corps!

I entered boot camp in San Diego, California. The first few days, I thought Navy boot camp was rough. Then, I got a look at the Marine boot camp through the chain link fence separating our two facilities. Our training was like child's play, compared to what the Marine boots were going through. Ignorance is bliss! At that time, I had no idea that the Marine Corps drew their medical personnel from the Navy, nor of the high casualty rate of the corpsmen attached to the Corps.

Following boot camp, Frank went to the Hospital Corps school at Balboa Park in San Diego. After graduating, he was assigned to a guard company at the San Diego Navy Hospital, which he considered as excellent duty. All good things eventually end and, after several months, Frank reported to field medical school at Camp Elliott in San Diego. The three months of training with Marines was very rigorous. Frank's first impression of working with Marines was not positive. There was quite a bit of animosity between the corpsmen and Marines. "We were treated like the lowest of the low!"

Frank's group finally left the States for New Caledonia and then on to Pavuvu Island, where they joined up with the 1st Marine Division. He and several of his corpsmen friends were attached to Company G, 2nd Battalion, 5th Marines (2/5).

Pavuvu, in the Russell Islands, was called a rest camp, but it was far from that, with rains, mud, falling coconuts, mosquitoes, malaria, huge rats racing around the top of tents after dark, jungle rot [severe fungus seeping infections] and men becoming "Asiatic" [not crazy but doing strange things].

The animosity between Marines and the corpsmen was totally forgotten on Pavuvu. The battle-hardened Marines accepted and respected the corpsmen. No longer were we given the dirty details. I remember our battalion commander stating that the corpsmen would take care of the casualties and it was the duty of the Marines to protect them at all costs. And that was the way it was. A strong bond that has lasted a lifetime was formed between us.

The Division finally left Pavuvu for their first combat campaign. Frank remembers along the way, that they picked up a Tokyo Rose broadcast, where she basically stated, "To the members of the 1st Marine Division, the butchers of Guadalcanal, I have a message for you boys. On or about 15 September, you will invade an island called Peleliu. Well, boys, we have a nice reception committee waiting for you. What's left of you can go down Broadway in two street cars!"[1]

15 September 1944
1st Marine Division
Peleliu, Palau Islands

I was transferred back to Headquarters Company to be a part of the Battalion Aid Station (BAS) shortly before we landed on Peleliu. In the first afternoon, when we started to move the BAS area, we went through a horrendous artillery bombardment. The concentrated fire was devastating. When it was over, the Battalion Sergeant Major and his clerk to my immediate right were dead. The Corpsman to my left was OK. The man next to him was dead. A Corpsman directly behind me had his legs blown off. One of my friends received shrapnel in his leg. There was a total of seventeen killed or wounded. From that time on, I had a horror of artillery and mortar fire. This was the first of many lucky close calls that I would experience during the War.

Another one of our problems was the lack of water and our reserve water had been contaminated. There were many casualties caused by dehydration, exhaustion and sunstroke. On 16 September (D-day + 1), by 1000, the temperature was 110 and climbing. We passed a large shell hole with water standing at the bottom. There was also a Jap body partially submerged in it. There was serious discussion of filling our canteens and using our water purifying tablets. This was only a fleeting thought, but it illustrates our dreadful plight.[2]

* * * *

On 17 September 1944, I was assigned to the 3rd platoon in Easy [E] Company for the balance of the campaign. That day, I learned what "friendly fire" was. First, our Navy planes strafed us, then we received an artillery barrage of airburst from a Marine unit and then it was topped off by friendly mortar fire. Most of the 34 casualties our battalion sustained that day were from three forms of friendly fire, the largest portion from shrapnel raining down from the airbursts, referred to by the Marines as "Hell Fire."[3]

* * * *

I celebrated my 19th birthday on D-day + 4. It had been a long, long year since my 18th birthday; the longest period being between D-day and this birthday. We moved into a new position after dark. The next morning three Japs, just a few feet from me, jumped up and started throwing grenades. We had no casualties except a man who had a seizure when the action started. The platoon moved out, leaving the patient and myself behind until stretcher-bearers could come and evacuate him. Fright is putting it lightly, being alone in the area where I knew there could be more Japs and armed with only a .45.[4]

* * * *

My platoon made a sweep down the beach and then started toward the Japanese-controlled hills. Taking a break and sitting on the edge of a large shell crater, I saw something that was unbelievable. A large shell was skimming the ground, coming directly at me! I fell over backwards, there was a loud "whish" and the shell exploded behind me. When a shell is fired pointblank and is coming at you eye level, you can see it in flight.[5]

* * * *

At dusk, we moved up a high coral ridge without opposition and formed a line along the top. We spotted three Japanese, opened fire and only one escaped. Later that night, "Punchy" told our sergeant that he heard Nips below us but was quietly told that he was just imagining things and to try to get some sleep. Then we heard an unmistakable loud click of a gun bolt being pulled back. All weapons on our line opened up. At daybreak, we could see a heavy machine gun pointed up the hill with several dead Japanese soldiers around it. We would have been slaughtered if the Japanese had gotten the gun into operation. We had very little cover. You can't dig foxholes in coral.[6]

* * * *

After we had a brief relief from the front lines, we started up the East Road, which was on the opposite side of the island from where we had been fighting. A flat piece of shrapnel came from afar. I didn't even hear the explosion of the shell or bomb. It hit nearby, striking another Marine with a glancing blow to his forehead, knocking him unconscious. The huge chunk of iron lay on the side of the road, smoking. I bandaged his wound and had him evacuated. He rejoined us a few days later.[7]

November 1944
Pavuvu Island

By November 1944, the 1st Marine Division had defeated the Japanese on Peleliu and returned to Pavuvu Island to rest, regroup and refit to begin planning for their next campaign at Okinawa. Frank Corry found himself transferred back to G Company, 2/5.

Back on Pavuvu, it was not uncommon to hear a shot at night. Some poor soul had committed suicide. What the men had been though, living conditions, anticipation, not knowing what was going to happen, weighed heavy on our minds. Immediately, the training for the Okinawa campaign began. We were told that the landing would be heavily defended. Later, because Pavuvu was not suitable for full-scale maneuvers, we were first transported to Guadalcanal to practice landings. We finally boarded LSTs for the journey back into combat. On Easter Sunday, April Fools Day, 1 April 1945, we loaded onto amphibious tractors and started the long journey to the beach.[8]

1 April 1945
Okinawa, Japan

The picture given to us of the landing was incorrect. Remembering the slaughter during the invasion of Peleliu and the briefings we had received on what could be expected on the Okinawa landing made us expect annihilation. We expected to be blown out of the water at any time. Upon stopping on the beach, the ramp of the amtrac dropped and we charged out. Surprise! No enemy fire or steep cliffs that we had been warned about faced us. It was unbelievable. Our battalion had only one casualty the entire day. We moved inland and when we stopped for the night, we had a panoramic view down to the beach and beyond. From our vantage point, we could see the battle between our Navy and the Japanese kamikazes. We could see that the Navy was catching hell. Kamikazes were coming in one after another. What fireworks! One couldn't see how a plane could get through the concentration of fire.

While the U.S. Army turned south and engaged the enemy, we spent the entire month of April in the hills of the north, searching for Japanese. I personally did not see any action during this time. On 1 May 1945, we loaded onto trucks and headed south, unloading in the rear area before going to the front line. As we neared the front line, we started up a long hill. There was one ambulance after another coming down the hill. It seemed that all the patients had head wounds. Having the memories of Peleliu and the slaughter there, I got sick at my stomach and threw up.

On 10 May, 2/5 attacked the Awacha Draw, known to Marines as "Death Valley" for obvious reasons. I was in the company command post when the fighting began, but not for long. There was a continuous stream of casualties. At the mouth of the Awacha Draw, there were two ridges running perpendicular to the Draw, one behind the other with the back ridge being higher than the front one. Machine gun fire was raking the front ridge. A Marine climbed the ridge, almost to the top, when he was then hit. He tumbled down the incline and there was a call, "Corpsman." I knew there should be a medic in the vicinity but the call kept up. Looking at the front ridge being sprayed by the rapid-firing Nambu machine guns, I made up my mind not to go. But, after the call kept up, I charged over the hill. The man was lucky because it was only a flesh wound. I was lucky because I wasn't hit going to the man or returning to my outfit. It was much harder to get up the nerve to cross the ridge again and I hesitated awhile before I charged out again.[9]

* * * *

A tank was called up for support at Awacha Draw. It went by a ditch where I was lying. I looked over and saw that the tank treads had dug up a huge mine just a few feet away from me. Needless to say, it did not explode or I wouldn't be writing this.[10]

* * * *

I replaced a wounded corpsman in a platoon that had pulled back to a better position. We started to advance again, crawling up the Draw. There was a muffled explosion and the platoon leader beside me slumped down. I rolled him over and observed that his hand was blown off and he was riddled with shrapnel. We surmised that he had set off an antipersonnel mine. Another Marine screamed hysterically that he was bleeding to death. He was running across the mouth of the Draw when a bullet pierced his canteen. His buttock and leg were wet with warm water. I laughed when I saw that he was unharmed, but he could not see the humor in the incident.[11]

* * * *

Torrential rains were the norm for most of May. It created a supply problem. There were times when airdrops were required to supply us. Most of the drops came down in our area but there were times when they landed in enemy territory. We were forced out of our foxhole by a downpour that filled our hole one night. Lightning struck a burial vault a very short distance from us. There was a blinding flash and a thunderous crash. It left us unable to see for quite awhile. The charge followed our telephone line and gave the Marine on watch, holding the phone to his ear, a severe shock. He refused to stand watch again![12]

* * * *

Next up was the Wana Draw. Just before dawn, on 16 May, a Marine brought his wounded platoon leader up to the company CP. After daylight, we radioed for an ambulance jeep, which had to stop several hundred yards away from us because the soft ground was saturated with water. A buddy and I evacuated him under direct antitank fire. The Japs fired round after round, zeroed in on us, and reloaded rapidly as we ran across a long open space. The lieutenant took a beating because we hit the deck every time the Japs fired. He must have weighed 245 pounds at the time, but with our adrenal glands pumping, we had no problem running with him. The three of us were lucky to reach the jeep with rounds hitting so close. His danger didn't end with being loaded on the ambulance jeep. The Japs were determined to destroy the jeep. The rapid fire continued until the vehicle was out of sight. As each shell exploded, I thought the next one would be a direct hit. There must have been a Higher Power looking after him.[13]

* * * *

We dug in late one afternoon behind a railroad embankment. There was a swish of a mortar falling and a thump. It hit between my foxhole and the foxhole of a Marine called Butch. There was no explosion! We saw a round hole in the wet, soft ground. My foxhole mate and I immediately dug another hole, but Butch and his buddy were not going to move. Eventually, they decided later it would be wise to relocate and they, too, dug another hole.[14]

* * * *

We received word that the Japs had pulled out of the Shuri line. They were moving to set up a new defense line. After Shuri fell, we advanced rapidly, meeting very little resistance from the Japanese. Our main obstacle was the deep mud. A good friend and I walked in front of a cave and sat down beside the mouth. The whole hill suddenly shook and debris shot out of the cave, showering us as we sat. The cry "Corpsman" came from the other side of the hill and I ran over the ridge. Before getting to the wounded, there was another terrific explosion and a long sheet of fire shot across my path. I found three E Company Marines killed and fifteen wounded![15]

* * * *

We moved to a position near the coast. I slept next to a building. During the night, I woke up, hearing someone running fast. It was a Japanese sailor, who ran right over me. He didn't get far before he was killed.[16]

* * * *

We were now at the Kunishi Ridge. I thought the Jap artillery barrages were bad until the Army shelled us. How long we were under fire, I don't know, but it seemed all night. There would be intense shelling, a lull and then intense shelling again. Every gun would open up at the same time. I don't know of anything that is more terrifying than a concentrated artillery barrage except lightning striking near you. To make matters worse, shells were hitting into the bank we were up against, causing many casualties. We would have been safer if we were on open ground. Dirt was thrown all over me several times with shells hitting on the crest of the bank. I received a concussion when one shell exploded beside me. The cry "Corpsman" was a terrible thing to hear, knowing that someone was wounded and we would be completely exposed. We treated several casualties that night.[17]

* * * *

Later, we found ourselves preparing for an attack against the last organized fight of World War II, Hill 81. Late one night, a Japanese soldier crawled across the road and into our hole. It was mass confusion, all a blur! All I know is that we survived and the Japanese was killed. On 21 June, we took this last hill in the war.[18]

Postlude

Frank Corry had survived Okinawa and the war. On Okinawa alone, he was the sole corpsman not wounded out of the eight in his G Company. Out of the 232 original G Company members making the invasion, 131 were wounded and 31 killed (70 percent total casualties). When taking into account their 129 replacements during the battle, the company suffered a grand overall total of 234 casualties. "In the cartoon book, *Up Front*, Willie tells Joe, 'I am beginning to feel like a fugitive from the law of averages.' That was exactly the way I felt. At the end of the Okinawa campaign, I was the only G Company corpsman out of eight that was not a casualty."[19]

Following the end of hostilities, G Company, 2/5 moved and set up camp in northern Okinawa, where they later heard about the two atomic bombs on the Japanese homeland and the ultimate surrender, ending the War in the Pacific. "The news of Japan's surrender was welcome news. Our entire group was battle veterans and we knew that the invasion of Japan would be much fiercer than any we had experienced in the past."[20]

The 2/5 was sent to China for duty as a show of force and to calm things down between the Communist and Nationalist Chinese. Overall, the Marines considered this excellent duty and the liberty was great. Eventually the Marines were sent home based on their time spent overseas. Frank arrived by ship in San Diego. "As we disembarked, the Salvation Army greeted and handed us each a quart of fresh milk, the first we had in approximately two years. That gesture meant a lot. I have a high respect for that organization. I finally arrived at home after a three-year absence."[21]

Frank attended college and joined the Navy Reserves to supplement his G.I. Bill funds. Three months after getting his pharmacy degree, he received orders to report to active duty in the Korean War. He was able to stay out of the war and was assigned at the Naval Air Station in Jacksonville, Florida, as a pharmacist. Once he was discharged, he did not reenlist. Frank eventually married and had a family. He worked for years as a pharmacist with the Veterans Administration.[22]

He has spent many years successfully searching and helping old 2/5 friends with whom he shared the horrors of war. He belongs to the First Marine Division Association and has remained especially close with his World War II G Company, 2/5 comrades.

> In 1993, I attended my first annual reunion of G Company, 2nd Battalion, 5th Marine Regiment personnel who served in World War II. It was in Orlando, Florida. My plan was to visit for a day or two and move on to Disney World and Sarasota. Five days later when the reunion ended, I was still there, and it seemed like it was just starting. That reunion turned out to be the highlight of my year. Meeting with old friends was exciting. Memories came back, memories of heroic actions, memories of Marines protecting their corpsmen and memories of the good times as well as the bad.
>
> In our reminiscing, I would bring up an event that I considered unforgettable. Other members that were with me at the time and place would have no memory of it. By the same token, I had no memory of some of the events others would bring up. I believe that forgetting is necessary for keeping one's sanity while in the horrors of war and in the

ensuing decades. What we can never forget is the bond that was forged between young men, boys actually, half a world away. Deprived of all the comforts of home, not sure they would ever return home. Many did not. And, of those who did, not many remain. And so, I offer some of my memories of that war, to those who remain and to those who come after us.[23]

I first received a phone call from Frank Corry on 8 August 2006 and then a series of follow-up e-mails on 14 and 17 August. He also sent me his 63-page war memoirs with permission to use it all. He did request that I also get permission from Tom Evans, author of *Hold Your Head High, Marines*, a 2006 self-published book which included most of the same memoirs. Mr. Evans e-mailed his approval on 16 August 2006. Frank also promised that he would send me answers to a personal questionnaire that I had sent him, but he was about to receive a pacemaker and to date, I still have not heard back from him.

12

USMC Private First Class Charles Nichols

> Better an ounce of luck than a pound of gold.
> — Old proverb

Prelude

Charles "Nick" Nichols was born on 20 March 1926 in Norwood, Massachusetts. He grew up on a farm with four brothers in the area of Washington, Maine. All of his brothers would eventually serve their country in various military branches. After attending one year, Nick quit high school to work as a ship-fitter helper on destroyers along with his mother, who was a welder at the same Bath Iron Works Yard in Bath, Maine. Shortly after turning 17, he joined the Marine Corps. He entered boot camp at Parris Island in June 1943.

> I was assigned to the 1st Marine Division and met up with them at Henderson Field on Guadalcanal. They had just returned from Cape Gloucester, New Britain. I was placed in the Headquarters and Service Battery of the 3rd Battalion, 11th Marines (3/11). We were then relocated to Pavuvu in the Solomon Islands to regroup for the Peleliu battle."

September–October 1944
Peleliu, Palau Islands

> I was walking alongside a tank on 3 October 1944 on the west road of Bloody Nose Ridge when we were hit by mortar and machine gun fire from higher up on the ridge. I took a piece in my right shoulder, about the size of a shotgun shell. Initially, I felt nothing and then my shoulder got extremely hot. The tank also took a direct hit. My sergeant, Carl Mazur, moved me to cover behind a rock formation, and gave me a car-

bine and took my BAR. It was a lot lighter, and he asked me if I could make it back to get help from a corpsman. Jap snipers kept me pinned down a few times but I managed to get back and patched up. The corpsman asked me if I wanted the chunk of metal and I said, "Hell no, send it back to the States and tell them to melt it down and send it back to these bastards with my compliments."

* * * *

One day on Peleliu, I was on a detail lugging ammo and water up to our guys on Bloody Nose Ridge. I had a five-gallon can of water on my shoulder, and heard a ping and then felt water running down my back. A sniper put a hole through the can. At first, I figured it was blood and not water. I thought the war was over for me. After realizing what had happened, I got mad as hell and hollered, "You son of a bitch." I had to go back down again for another water can.

* * * *

Another time I was walking down a narrow road and a tank was coming from one direction and a jeep from the other. I took off for a ditch in heavy underbrush and lay down. The tank took off to the ditch I was in to let the jeep pass. Sure enough, the tank straddled me as it ran over me. A Marine came over to me and said, "Jesus Christ, you were run over by a tank!" I looked down and saw two arms, two legs and no visible signs of blood. He said, "Do you feel run down?" I replied, "No, I feel run down and very lucky." Then we started laughing, rolling on the ground and laughing our asses off. I guess when you get tired and hungry and not giving a damn, you get giddy and foolish; besides, the temperature was over a hundred degrees.

When we returned to the Solomons after Peleliu, the guys kidded me about my experience. They'd say, "There goes Nichols, who was both shot in the head and run over by a tank." Earlier, I had also taken a Jap sniper round that had glanced off my helmet.

1945
Okinawa

On Okinawa, to the best I can remember is that one morning at daybreak, Sergeant Mazur told us to, "Saddle up. We're moving out." We were set up at Shuri Castle and I was a machine-gun crewman and a BAR man (Goddamned heavy weapon). My buddy, Wilbur, carried a .30 caliber machine gun. I thought we were headed to Naha but found out later we were going to Kunishi. This is really all I remember. One minute I was walking beside a 105mm gun, pulled by a 6-by-6 and the next minute a nurse in a tent at Yontan, Okinawa, woke me up and said the war was over, we dropped a bomb on Hiroshima. She brought me a shot of whiskey (the God's truth). I was bandaged up, from my head, neck and chest. She asked me if I was ever on a plane. I said no and she replied, "Well, you will be tomorrow." I flew to Guam the next day and then went by hospital ship to Pearl Harbor. Then I traveled through a series of hospitals from San Francisco, California; Klamath Falls, Oregon, to a rehab center; Seattle, Washington; Boston Chelsea Hospital and finally ended up at the Philadelphia Naval Hospital. More than likely, I should have been killed that day on Okinawa, but lady luck was still with me. Sadly, I would later learn that Sergeant Mazur was killed in December 1945.

Postlude

Charlie got out of the Marines in March 1946 but reenlisted for two more years before ending his Marine career in 1948. "I drove trucks for my entire life. I had bad legs that were operated on at Quantico, Virginia, in 1947 while I was attached to the 22nd Marines. Driving was the only thing I could do."

Charlie is now a widower, living alone. His wife died in 2005 and two of his six children are also deceased.

I am very active in the Marine Corps League # 394, Portsmouth, New Hampshire. I attend all military funerals, blood drives, reunions and greet troops coming back and leaving for Iraq and Afghanistan from the Pease Air Force Base in the Newington-Portsmouth area. We Marines are there whether it is 0300 or 1500, 24 hours a day. They stop to refuel and change flight crews. We have coffee and donuts, cold drinks, toilet articles, books, magazines, pizza, cookies, candy, etc. We get to "shoot the breeze" with them and cheer them up. It means a lot to them and to us Marines as well.

It gives me a great feeling of doing something for our troops, as well as it does to all of my Marine brothers. "Once a Marine, always a Marine." When it is Marines leaving for Iraq, I tell them I wish I could be going with them, but they don't take 80 year olds. Once I did sneak aboard a plane and the young Marines hid me until I got caught.

I could tell a lot more about my war experiences, but it would be too long of a story and until just recently, I never talked about the war.

I used to have bad nightmares about the War, but they've eased up over the years. My children tell me my war story would make a great movie![1]

I received a referral from Diane Kuebler, a daughter of a World War II Seabee, regarding Charles. I sent him a letter and he responded with a letter dated 27 November 2006 answering all of my questions along with his close call descriptions.

13

USMC Private First Class Kenneth Stevens

> Luck is the residue of design.
> — Branch Rickey

Prelude

Kenneth Stevens was born in Long Prairie, Minnesota, on 23 July 1924. He left school after the 8th grade and began an early, hard life of farming and ranching. When he was 19½ years old, he joined the Marine Corps on 29 February 1944. "I enlisted in the Marines because I had two older brothers who did not pass the physical to join the service and two younger brothers, so I thought I had better get in where I could do some good."[1]

I went to boot camp in San Diego. I got through boot camp with no problems. I didn't mind it because I had bounced around the country since I was fourteen. I had worked on threshing crews, farms and ranches, so they weren't getting a kid fresh off his mama's knee. In boot camp, they gave us a choice of the branch we wanted to get in. I told them I wanted to get into the Fleet Marine Force. That's the outfit that does the beach landings. The sergeant in charge told me, "In six months you're going to be dead." I told him, "I don't want to come back and have to ask somebody how you fight a war."

When I finished boot camp, they sent me to Camp Elliot, California, for combat training. Then I went to BAR [Browning automatic rifle] school, and then scout and sniper school. The instructor told me, "Overseas, there are only two kinds of BAR men, the quick and the dead." So, I really practiced with the BAR every chance I got. I tried to compare myself with the gunfighters of the "old west" because that's how they stayed alive. We then left Camp Elliot and went to Camp Pendleton for about two weeks. I was assigned to Company E, 2nd Battalion, 21st

82

Marines (2/21), 3rd Marine Division. We did some amphibious training at Oceanside before we went overseas.

We eventually left for Hawaii, where we stayed for seven days at the Marine Transit Center. From Hawaii, we left for the Marshall Islands and stayed aboard ship a week, waiting for the 3rd Marine Division to land on Guam. We joined the 3rd Marine Division on Guam. After we finished off the main Jap resistance, they sent my battalion to the north end of the island. We set up a perimeter camp and we patrolled every day, hunting for stray Japs. We had to stand guard around a perimeter fence. One day, I was walking guard duty when a stray Jap took two shots right at me and missed. Most of the Japs on Guam couldn't shoot very well.[2]

* * * *

Once on patrol I was in the lead in very thick jungle. We came around a corner on the trail when we ran smack into four Japs with rifles. I dropped three of them right on the spot. The first one's brains were splattered right onto my face. The fourth one ran back down the trail and we went looking for him, because I knew I had hit him. A Marine named Carlos was in front of me when I saw the guy lying in the brush besides the trail. He was trying to get a grenade out of his jacket and I hollered to Carlos to look out. He spun around and split the guy's head from the top of his head to his chin with his M-1 rifle. We did these patrols until November 1944, when they finally declared the island secure.[3]

* * * *

The Army sent a bunch of guys, all from New York City, to operate a radar station that they had set up on the north end of the island. Our guys were mostly from the central states, including Montana, Texas, Tennessee, Oklahoma and Iowa. One day we were coming back from a patrol and we met some New York guys and they had about an eight-hundred-pound heifer on a rope and we asked them what they were going to do with her. They told us they wanted to keep her for a pet, but their CO wouldn't let them keep her. So, I told them we would take her over to our camp and they could come and see her. That was about 1600 and by 1700, we were eating steak! We all knew what steak looked like on a hoof, as we hadn't had meat to eat in months.[4]

* * * *

Private First Class Stevens survived his close calls on Guam and his unit then began training and preparing for their next island campaign. They eventually loaded on the USS *President Jackson* and headed for their Iwo Jima destination.

I had two close calls on the ship while en route to Iwo Jima. One time, I went to the head [toilet], which was one deck above the sleeping compartment. When I came out the doorway, I saw sparks fly. It was pitch black in there. When I went down into our compartment, it was full of smoke. I asked the guys what happened and they told me that Leach had shot himself in his hand with a BAR. I looked up and saw three holes in the deck right where I stepped out of the head. They couldn't have missed my feet but by a couple of inches. I never saw Leach again.

* * * *

The day before we landed on Iwo Jima, I was going up the stairs to the top deck when I heard a tremendous blast just outside. A bunch of guys came flying down the stairs. The Japs had just dropped a shell right on the deck from an on-shore battery. A few minutes latter and I would have been on the deck, totally exposed.[5]

February 1945
Iwo Jima

Iwo Jima is one of the Volcano Islands in the Ogasawara Island group about 670 miles south of Tokyo and 700 miles north of Guam. It is part of the Tokyo Prefecture and thus constituted the first part of Japan's home territories to fall to the Allies during World War II. After the fall of the Marianas during the summer of 1944, the Japanese were fully aware that Iwo Jima would be one of the next major campaigns for the Americans. The strategic importance of this Island was based on three major factors: the vast distances involved for B-29 bombers from the Marianas to Japan; the Japanese radar on Iwo Jima that gave early warnings; and thirdly, the Japanese fighters on the Island that were capable of shooting down American B-29s.

By February 1945, the Japanese had over 21,000 soldiers under the able leadership of General Tadamichi Kuribayashi, a direct descendant of samurai warriors. He had lived in the United States for three years and believed that Japan could never win against a country that possessed such great resources. Nevertheless, he accepted the challenge to defend Japanese soil and die for his country. He had built an underground fortress of tunnels, bunkers and reinforced caves with the help of mining engineers. He also tried to have a food reserve to last for two and a half months since he knew, once the Americans had circled the island, there would be no more resupply of men, equipment and food.

Kuribayashi's defense plan was a radical departure from previous island battles. He did not return fire with Japanese artillery during the pre-landing

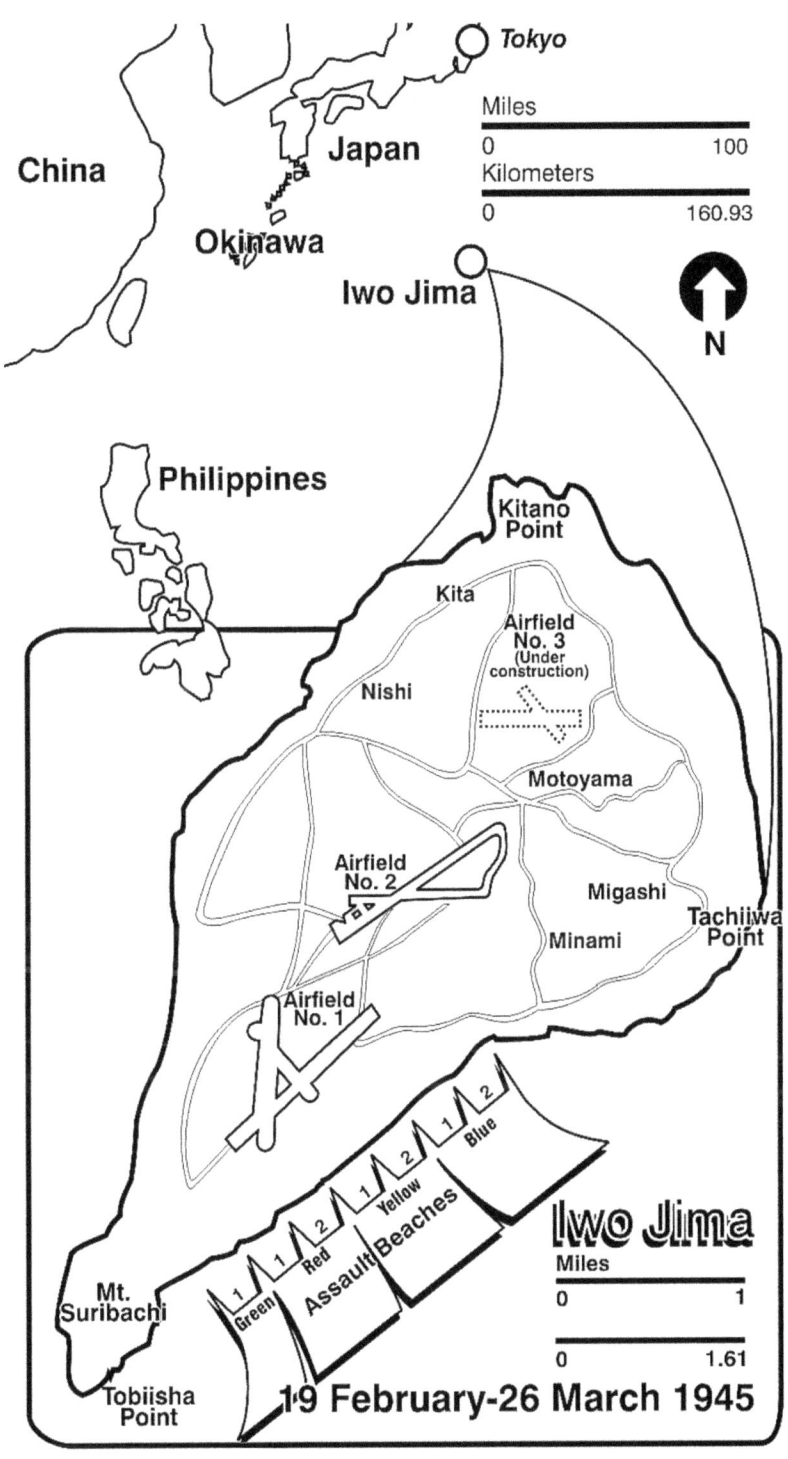

bombardment so as not to give away his positions. He did not oppose the initial landings on the beaches and did not start to direct fire until the Marines had advanced 500 meters inland. The Japanese knew they could not win the battle and so their main intention was to provide the Japanese homeland more time to prepare for the eventual attack on Japan. Kuribayashi planned to fight a defensive battle and did not want any major counterattacks, withdrawals or banzai attacks, which, in his mind, were a waste of soldiers' lives. He asked his men to kill ten Americans for every one of their own lives, and at first, they would successfully fulfill this order.

Marine General Holland Smith, who had the 3rd, 4th and 5th Marine Divisions under his command, led the American ground forces. The total American forces numbered close to 100,000 men. The operation was designated as Operation Detachment. On 16 February 1945, a massive three-day air and naval bombardment began.[6]

19 February 1945 (D-Day) Eastern Beaches on Iwo Jima

At 0200 on 19 February, battleship guns signaled the beginning of D-Day. Soon 100 planes attacked the island, followed by another volley from naval guns. At 0830, the first of an eventual 30,000 Marines of the 3rd, 4th and 5th Marine Divisions landed on Iwo Jima and the battle commenced. Another 40,000 Marines would land in the following days.[7]

> We were supposed to be in floating reserves, but they lost so many people in the morning landings that they started unloading us in the first afternoon. The beach was so crowded that they couldn't get most of us ashore; however, my Higgins boat made it to the beach. I started up the beach in the sand and just took a few steps when the Japs hit a big ammo dump on the water's edge and blew it up. It sent mud and sand all over the guys right behind me. I could have walked all the way up the beach on dead bodies. I dug a foxhole next to the 5th Division and spent the night. The next morning, the rest of my 21st Marines came ashore.
>
> The second day we started moving up to the second airfield and we ran into a Jap pillbox. Two Marines in my fire-team were wounded in the action, but we killed the four Japs in the pillbox. On D-Day + 4 we watched them put the flag up on Mount Suribachi. It gave us a good feeling to see the flag go up.[8]

* * * *

General Holland M. Smith said we had to take that second airfield at all costs. We tried to take it from the end of the runway. Almost every time we tried to get on the airfield, we got heavy small arms fire from across the runway. Our bazooka man's name was Stag. He put one bazooka shell right in one pillbox but it didn't go off because of the loose sand. I reloaded for him and as he rose up to fire again, the Japs hit him and split his scalp just as if you would with a knife. I grabbed the bazooka so it wouldn't go off and he rolled over and sat up. He told me he just had a headache. He had a perfect part in his wavy blonde hair and it was cut dead center. I then saw one Jap who was about seven or eight hundred yards across the runway and it looked like he was carrying ammunition boxes between two pillboxes. I lined him up with my BAR, but the first round hit the ground. I could see the dirt fly up in the air. Some of the guys said, "You'll never hit him that far away." I said, "You just watch me!" I kept raising the BAR up, firing four rounds. On the fourth round, he threw the ammo box and fell to the ground where I could see him. That was a long shot. I think on his last trip, he was doing a little dance, taunting me and thinking I could not hit him. His dance was now over forever. The Japs on Iwo Jima, unlike those on Guam, were excellent shooters.

They sent the 5th Division up the west side of the airfield and the 4th Division along the east side. Our 3rd Division followed behind the 4th Division to where the runways crossed. Then, we all crossed the airfield with bullets buzzing by like a swarm of bees. I was in the lead fire-team. We were on the left side of the company so my fire-team jumped down off the runway and into a big shell hole. We ended up right in front of a big heavy machine gun bunker. Rounds were firing all around us. The fire-team leader told us to take off for a ditch alongside of the airfield. Pfc [Private First Class] Bumps took off first and was hit and killed at about the halfway mark by the machine gun. Next, Corporal Rearden took off and he was also killed. It was now my turn so I grabbed my BAR by the sling and went out there, like a bat out of hell. I did a somersault into the ditch as bullets kicked up right underneath me. Following me was Pfc Grobe but he hesitated just before jumping into the ditch and was struck seven times in the chest. I reached up, caught him by the jacket and placed him in the ditch. He was from Iowa and just seventeen years old.

I got myself into a small ditch where I could see the enemy machine gun position. The Japs couldn't get the gun low enough to hit me, but I could shoot into the gun and soon put it out of action. I then crawled along the ditch until I could see the entrance to the bunker. The Japs kept coming out of the entrance trying to get at the rear of my company. I put the BAR on single shot and kept picking them off all afternoon long. After dark, I got out of there and looked for E Company, but when I found them, we only had 22 Marines left!

Lieutenant McCann came along and told me he had seen what I had done earlier and told me he was going to see that I got a Medal of Honor. He then told me to cover him as he went to check on the rest of the men. Minutes later, he was shot through the head, so there went my Medal.

The 22 guys left dug in on a little rise at the edge of the airfield. We were alone and cut off from any other outfit. I only had one magazine of ammunition left. I laid my fighting knife in front of me and said a prayer. I knew that every Marine in our group was ready to fight to the death. We could hear Japs all around us that night, but they didn't attack because they didn't know how few of us were alive. The next morning they sent a bunch of tanks right up behind us and there was a big tank and artillery battle right above our heads. The Japs had a 37mm antitank gun. The battle sounds were nearly loud enough to split your eardrums. They blew the turret off a tank right behind me and killed four men. Finally, we were taken back to friendly lines and had our first chow in several days. There were some guys in the 5th Division who told me that I had earlier killed 74 Japs in front of that bunker.[9]

* * * *

We thought we were all done fighting. I was wandering around the area in a daze and didn't know where I was. A corpsman got a hold of me and gave me a couple of pills that snapped me right out of it. He told me I had a blast concussion. They put us in different outfits because there weren't enough of us guys left to make a company. I spent another 30 days on the front lines serving in all three divisions.

We next moved on to airfield #3 and then on to the sulfur flats. You could dig a hole six inches deep and put a can of C-rations in it. It would then get so hot you couldn't eat it. One morning I was sitting alone out on those stinking sulfur flats and as far as I could see were Jap and Marine bodies. As I looked at this terrible sight and wondered how I could still be alive, I saw the most beautiful sunrise that I had ever seen. At that moment, I felt God's hand on my shoulder. I have never forgotten that feeling.

We crossed the sulfur flats to the rocks and caves near the north side of the island. One night, I was kneeling on the edge of my foxhole when something hit me on the back, knocking me face down into the dirt. Everything felt numb in my back. Sully was in the hole next to me and I asked him to check my back for blood. He responded that, "There's no blood but it sure raised hell with your jacket." A four-by-twelve inch shell fragment had hit me flat. If it had come in sideways, it would have cut me in half. Those narrow escapes happened all throughout the campaign.[10]

* * * *

One day we were pinned down on a ridge and totally out of water. They pulled a water tank with a jeep to about 400 yards behind us. I volunteered to go after some water and I took a 5-gallon expedition can and an M-1 rifle with me. About halfway to the water, a Jap shot the stalk right off the rifle I had in my hand. I still managed to get the water and return safely. That same afternoon, I was showing the squad leader some Japs on a hill behind us. They were digging out a gun in a cave about 500 yards away. We were standing with our arms touching and he was shot right through the forearm.[11]

* * * *

One night the guy in the hole next to me was bayoneted by a Jap who came in behind us and then ran right past my hole. I pulled the trigger of my BAR once and hit him three times in the neck, side and thigh. He fell just five feet in front of my hole. Later that same night, another Jap came at me from the front. I let him get about 25 yards from me and then let him have a round in the belly. He was carrying a Molotov cocktail that was about a quart bottle filled with aviator gas with a fuse in it. They'd throw them at us and burn everything, but fortunately, he never got a chance to throw it. He lay out there and burnt all night.[12]

* * * *

One night, Sully and I were in a foxhole together right next to a steep bank and I was sitting with my BAR across my knees when I looked around over my left shoulder and saw a Jap kneeling on the edge of the bank. He had a bayonet about a foot from my face. I jerked the trigger and fired three rounds with my BAR. He disappeared and I couldn't see him in the dark. Sully threw two grenades, but they went off too far away. I said, "He's gone now." The next morning when it got daylight, he asked me, "Is that the Nip you were talking about last night?" He was face down on the edge of our foxhole. I lifted up his helmet and saw that he had three holes over his left eye that you could have covered with a half dollar. He had a cavalry carbine with a fold-over bayonet. The next day I was standing up on a ridge and there were some tanks down below. They were shooting at some caves while I was picking Japs off when they came out of the caves. Our battalion major came up and asked me what I was doing up there by myself. I just told him to watch. About that time, some Japs came out of the cave and I let go with my BAR. He shook his head and said, "You've got to be the coolest son of a bitch I've ever seen."[13]

* * * *

During the next few days, we headed north. General Smith put out the word that he would give two cans of beer to every man in the unit who first reached the north end of the island. So, myself and eleven or twelve other guys went on patrol out to Kitano Point. I sat with my shoes off and my feet in the ocean water. It was the first time I had taken my shoes off since the landing. Someone said, "How are they going to know that we made it to the ocean?" I took off my canteen and filled it with saltwater and taped a message on it saying "for inspection, not consumption." We then sent a runner to the division command post with the canteen. That night we had our two cans of beer and it tasted pretty damn good! It was the first beer we had since we left Guam.

Later, they took us back to the rear areas where they had showers set up by the Seabees. It felt great since we hadn't bathed since the landing. They also sent in a bunch of replacements and we were able to reform the 21st Regiment.[14]

Postlude

The battle for Iwo Jima ended on 26 March 1945. As was the case with most island battles, the Japanese fought to the death. Nearly 21,000 were killed and just 216 captured. Many bodies were buried forever in their underground cave and tunnel systems.[15] Japanese accounts indicate that General Kuribayashi committed hari-kari, the Japanese ritual of suicide, in his cave near Kitano Point on 23 March 1945, the 33rd day of the battle. His body was never discovered. "Of all of our adversaries in the Pacific," said General Holland Smith, "Kuribayashi was the most redoubtable." Said another Marine, "Let's hope the Japs don't have any more like him."[16]

American casualties were also extremely high with 6,821 killed and 20,000 wounded. One-third of all Marines who died in World War II were killed during the Iwo Jima battle. Twenty-seven Medals of Honor were awarded to Marines and corpsmen during the battle. This was over one-quarter of all such medals awarded during the entire war to Marines. It also represented the most Medals of Honor ever awarded in a single battle to date.[17]

We left Iwo Jima on Easter Sunday 1945 and relocated back on Guam to prepare for the invasion of Japan. I believe we were about two weeks away from the invasion when we heard the war had ended. I left Guam on 1 December 1945 and was discharged on 2 January 1946.[18]

Ken went on with his life, drove trucks, and ranched for a living. He still has livestock today and enjoys roping steers at rodeos. He married Phyllis and raised five boys and four girls. His wife passed away in 1995 and two years later he married Audrey. She had two boys and six girls, so combined, they have one very large family.

Ken is a lifetime member of the 3rd Marine Division Association, Iwo Jima Veterans, Veterans of Foreign Wars and the American Legion.[19]

I received a phone call from Ken in July 2006, in response to my ad in the 3rd Marine Division's *Caltrap* newsletter. He sounded a little frail but he promised me he would send me a copy of his World War II stories that he had typed up several years ago. I received his five-page, single-spaced, typed memoirs on 17 August 2006. The pages were full of great close call stories on Guam and Iwo Jima. I followed this up with a questionnaire for personal information, which I received back on 5 September 2006.

14

USMC Warrant Officer-1 George Green

Actions are the seeds of fate and deeds grow into destiny.
— Harry S. Truman

Prelude

George Green was born on 20 February 1922 in Chicago, Illinois. His father was a disabled World War I veteran who had served with the Army's 58th Infantry Regiment and was gassed while fighting in Europe. George was the oldest of six children and the Depression greatly affected their lives. George and the two oldest children had to be placed in a Catholic orphanage and were later sent to foster homes where good families took them in. During the summer of 1930, their father picked them up in an old Model A Ford truck with a mattress in the back and took them to Philadelphia. Along the way, the truck broke down and a farmer allowed them to camp out in his front yard. His dad eventually was able to trade his truck for Greyhound Bus tickets to Philadelphia.

In Philadelphia, the family lived in several different houses. His father, however, was unemployed and the family soon found themselves eight months behind in rent and evicted from one of their homes by a landlord who also desperately needed money. His father found an old circus wagon once used for animals and, with some help from a friend, he purchased the wagon for $9. He then rented a place for the wagon for just $3 a year. The family made their new one-room home as comfortable as possible. Eventually, the State Housing Commission forced them to move out due to the unhealthy conditions that existed for a family of eight living in just one room. His father finally received a small veteran's disability check. The World War I gassing he had earlier endured had weakened his lungs and he was unable to work. Things got a little better with the help of welfare benefits and the disability checks.

Despite the Depression, the family had fond memories of Philadelphia. George and his oldest brother both became First Class Boy Scouts and, as they grew up, did all the normal kid things. In 1937, the family paid a neighbor $25 plus gas to take them back to Chicago, where George went to high school. He remembers walking 26 blocks to school every day. During the summer, George worked in a small store helping to deliver groceries to the well-to-do Chicago suburbs for a $1 a day.[1]

In the spring of 1939, my sophomore year at Harrison Technical High School, our ROTC instructor advised us cadets about an Army training program called the "Citizens Military Training Camp." Several of us applied and we were all accepted for the 30-day summer training camp at Fort Sheridan, Illinois. If, after successfully completing four years of training during the summer months, we would be selected as 2nd Lieutenants in the Army Reserves. We had classroom training, close-order drill, field exercises, daily inspection and rifle marksmanship. We were given a certificate indicating we had successfully completed the basic course and were qualified to return next year for the red course.

In the fall of 1939, while looking in the *Chicago Tribune* want ads for a part-time job, one ad struck me as interesting. It offered a full day's pay for one night's work a month. I went to the designated room in the old impressive courthouse. I entered and inquired about the ad and a Marine dressed in greens told me that they were accepting men for the United States Marine Corps Reserve. After explaining the program, I agreed to sign up. I was soon assigned to Company B of the 9th Marine Corps Reserve Battalion. After learning that anyone who recruited two more men for the Marines would get a set of dress blues, I quickly went out and found two willing friends. We drilled one night a month and that was considered a day's pay. At that time, a private's pay was $21 a month, so we got $1/30$ of $21 for each drill period. This was enough money to get my white shirts done by the Chinese laundry for my ROTC Friday inspections.

I was promoted to Pfc and spent two weeks of active duty summer training from 7 to 21 July 1940. We spent most of the time on the firing range and I was able to qualify as a sharpshooter. On 1 September 1939, Hitler invaded Poland and started World War II, so whenever we got together for drills afterwards, there was always talk of whether we would be involved in the war. The consensus was that somewhere along the line, we would be involved and it would be important for us to train as hard as possible, which we did.

While I was a senior in high school, my unit was called to active duty due to the impending possibility of war. We left for the Marine Corps Base in San Diego, California, on 7 November 1940. We arrived four days later and I was assigned to H Battery, 2nd Defense Battalion in the .50 Caliber Anti-Aircraft Section. In May 1941, I was promoted to corporal and transferred once again, to E Battery, 2nd Battalion, 10th Marines, 1st Marine Brigade. At the end of the month, we boarded ships, went through the Panama Canal, and eventually ended up in Iceland on 7 July 1941, where I was placed in charge of one of the antiaircraft gun sections. Although the United States was still not committed to the war, our orders were to fire on any German aircraft that appeared to threaten us. We learned about the 7 December 1941 Pearl Harbor attack while still in Iceland and began preparing for the Army to take over our position. We all knew that we would soon be headed for the Pacific. In March 1942, we arrived back in the United States. After a leave, we reported in to Camp Elliot, San Diego, California, where I was promoted to sergeant.

After a few more transfers to different units, I was sent to Camp Lejeune, North Carolina, where I was assigned to F Battery, 2nd Battalion, 12 Marines, 3rd Marine Division on 25 July 1942. Training began immediately and we were issued new 75mm howitzers.

On 15 August 1942, I married my sweetheart, Betty, from Philadelphia. Initially we were told we were too young as she was just 16½ and I was 20½. We then lied about our ages and managed to pull it off. I spent every spare minute with her whenever I could get away from the base.

On 17 November, we entrained for the west coast and ended up at Camp Dunlap in Niland, California, where our training continued. Betty joined me on the west coast and we soon learned that she had become pregnant. After getting our orders for overseas, Betty returned to Chicago to live with her family. We boarded the USS *Lurline* in San Diego for the South Pacific on 14 February 1943. We arrived in New Zealand at the beginning of March and began serious training in all facets of combat activities. We left New Zealand in July and sailed first to New Caledonia and then on to Guadalcanal. We later embarked aboard the USS LST 341 [sic] on 13 November and headed for Bougainville in the British Solomon Islands.[2]

November 1943
Bougainville, Solomon Islands

Bougainville is the largest of the Solomon Islands with a length of 120 miles and a width at its widest point of 40 miles. The mountain chain that forms its backbone rises to 9,000 feet at Mount Balbi, an active volcano in the northwest end of the island. Rabaul, on the island of New Britain, was considered a Japanese stronghold and military leaders deemed it very important to encircle it with Allied forces. Bougainville was determined to be the next step in the process to cut off Rabaul and provide an airfield for land base fighters. The Japanese forces were concentrated at the northern and southern ends of the island where they heavily defended important airfields. It was therefore decided to land at Empress Augusta Bay on the west side and middle of the island. This area was lightly defended, but the terrain was terrible. The Marines were used to establish a strong beachhead and, after a few months of heavy fighting against Japanese forces, were able to move inland and provide a good perimeter. By 15 December, the Army had relieved most of the Marine positions. By December of the following year, Australian troops took over the fight and still faced nearly 40,000 Japanese soldiers.[3]

During the Bougainville campaign, I received a battlefield promotion to platoon sergeant. We provided artillery support for the infantry troops and were quite often bombed by both Japanese planes and artillery. One bomb landed within 15 feet of about 20 of us. None of us was hit, but one Marine got a piece of shrapnel in the heel of his boondockers! Everything above the ground was a shambles as the shrapnel tore into our hammocks and everything that was hanging in the trees.[4]

In writing the story of the Bougainville campaign, the main emphasis has usually been placed on the front-line action. Unfortunately, the fate of artillerymen, the engineers, pioneers, Seabees and service troops remains in the background. Yet it is they who carry out the extremely difficult and sometimes thankless tasks that are always necessary in every military campaign.

Out of the hundreds of Japanese killed in the Empress Augusta Bay area, it is estimated that half died as a direct result of artillery shelling. The preparation that was fired before the Piva Forks battle constituted a new high in artillery bombardment in the South Pacific theater of war. The miles of torn jungle and pockmarked ground bear testimony to the devastating fire of the 12th Marines. A total of 72,643 rounds were fired during the campaign. General Allen Hal Turnage said of the artillery fire at the completion of the action, "Probably the most accurate I have ever known."[5]

George and his 12th Marines left Bougainville on 15 January 1944 and arrived back on Guadalcanal three days later. He shortly received a promotion to gunnery sergeant. On 21 July 1944, his unit returned to war, landing in the 5th wave on Guam in the Mariana Islands.[6]

July 1944
Guam, Mariana Islands

We landed at Red Beach 2 in the Assan Beach area. This area had 100 yards of coral reefs and our LCVP came up to the reef and dropped its ramp. There had not been enough LVTs to bring us all the way up to the beach. All hands pitched in to unload the guns, ammunition and equipment and then dumped it into the water on the reef. While we were unloading, the Japs were dropping mortar shells on the beach and reef. Fortunately, when they hit the water most of the explosion was upward and had little effect on our personnel.

No sooner than we unloaded the last equipment and our LCVP brought up the ramp and backed off the reef, a mortar shell landed alongside. The craft sunk but all three sailors survived and managed to get aboard another LCVP. With mortars continuing to fall on the beach and reef, we had to carry our guns and equipment to shore. Somehow, we all managed to make it to shore with no casualties and we were ready to fire missions that same afternoon. Luck was still with me.

While on Guam, George was promoted to the warrant officer ranks at the end of September. Following the fighting came the inevitable reforming and training for the biggest battle of his life: the Iwo Jima campaign. George was put in charge of a forward artillery observation team (Fox FO-2) consisting of eight Marines. He embarked on the USS *Bolivar* (APA-34) on 11 February 1945 and sailed for Iwo Jima.[7]

19 February 1945 (D-Day)
F Battery, 2nd Battalion, 12th Marines
Fox FO-2 Team
Iwo Jima

We were told we would be in Corps Reserve on D-Day. We got up early, had a good breakfast and packed up just in case we had to go in. The weather was clear, a little on the cool side and we could see Mount Suribachi being struck by naval gunfire. We went down to the wardroom to have coffee and to listen to radio reports from the first waves. These waves hit the beaches with little opposition. I spent the rest of the day observing and listening to reports. The fighting was getting tougher, but the 5th Division had made it across the island and Airfield #1 was in our hands. The rumor was that we were going in the next day. The Japs were now hitting the beach with everything they had.

We got into the LCVPs early the next morning. We spent the entire day going around in circles and getting sick from the diesel fumes. We were finally recalled back to the transport in the early evening. I was sure glad to get out of the landing craft. We had a good meal and another opportunity to sleep on a bunk. We were told that we were wanted on shore but it was too congested with men and wreckage spread out all over. It was a nice day to spend my 23rd birthday, 20 February 1945.

Finally, on D-Day + 2, we were able to land and set up in a large shell hole about twelve feet deep. Japanese heavy mortars and artillery were constantly coming down around us. We were told that we were now attached to the 4th Division and would soon be moving out to continue the attack. We were assigned to K Company, 3rd Battalion, 21st Marines (a 3rd Marine Division unit, also temporarily assigned to the 4th Division).[8]

* * * *

On D-Day + 5, we moved up to Airfield #2. I spread my team out as we hit the runway. There was enemy high-velocity gunfire, at about head level going right over us, but we couldn't determine its origin so that we could call in an artillery mission. Captain Heinze, the CO [Commanding Officer] of K Company was sitting on the edge of the runway about ten feet away from my position when he suddenly yelled at me to look out. I turned around in my two-foot-deep shell hole and saw a sputtering Nip grenade about three feet in front of me. I was staring at it as it exploded and instinctively ducked my head. I brought up my carbine in the direction that the grenade had come from and, as I aimed, another grenade flew out of some bushes. It landed in almost the same spot as the other and exploded, wounding me slightly for the second time in the last few seconds. I felt my face expecting a handful of blood, but only got a little. I had several fine grenade particles in my face, but fortunately, none hit my eyes. Captain Heinze came sliding down into my hole, holding his leg. He had taken a large chunk from the grenade on the inside of his right thigh. I tried to get a BAR man to spray the bushes where the grenade had come out, but as he walked up towards them he toppled over, shot in the stomach. I could now see the Nip in a foxhole with a top that he moved up and down, which we called a spider trap. We got a fireteam directed at him and they finished him off with grenades. The next time I looked at him, he was plastered to one side of the hole and quite a mess.[9]

* * * *

Right after this incident, I looked to the rear and saw 4.5 rockets coming down at us. They were easy to see, as there were so many of them and they were making such a loud racket. From a good, deep shell hole, we sat helpless watching those rockets creeping up on us and exploding on our rear troops, mostly on our machine gun positions. Finally, they stopped after the last one exploded about ten feet behind us. I heard later that this barrage was from our own rocket trucks and they had just about wiped out the Company's machine gun section. Lieutenant Archambault came up to replace the wounded Captain Heinze as the Company CO.[10]

* * * *

Since K Company had been reduced from 220 Marines to just 90, on D-Day + 7, we were attached to L Company, under the command of Captain Stephenson. We attacked behind artillery falling about 200 yards to our front. We just ran on a compass heading and didn't stop until we were out of breath. As we approached a cliff, we stopped to determine where we were and to get a rest. Right in the middle of us, out pops six Japs from nowhere! Where they thought they were going, I didn't know, but I'm sure they were as surprised to see us as we were to see them. I raised my carbine to my shoulder and pulled the trigger, aiming at the first one. I heard a bang and pulled the trigger again. No bang! I grabbed the bolt to put another round in the chamber and pulled the trigger once more. No luck, it still didn't go off. By this time, all of the Nips were dead so I checked my carbine to see what was wrong. It dawned on me that I had never unlocked the safety catch. The first bang I heard when I pulled the trigger was the Marine's rifle next to me. I took the safety off and never put it on again until we returned to our rear gun positions.[11]

* * * *

We moved out again and, by this time, most of the fire we were receiving was from small arms, whereas before, it was mainly from mortars and artillery. We soon came to a rise or hill in which it was necessary to go over the top. I could tell that the Japs had the crest zeroed in by the sounds of the bullets and they had already wounded several of our men. I passed the word to dive over the top and not to stop. Over we went, one at a time. No sooner did we get over the hill than we came face to face with two Jap tanks, only 50 feet to our front. They were dug into the ground with only their turrets exposed. One of the tanks had been hit by our artillery and was burning, but the other suddenly pulled up out of its position. We did not have any antitank weapons, not even a bazooka. All we had were hand grenades and rifles. With everyone shooting at it, it noisily clanked out of its hole, turned to our right and then went down behind some rocks to safety. We were all in the open, but it never even tried to fire on us. Once more, I had escaped sure death.[12]

* * * *

Later, taking off after another barrage, we went through the village of Motoyama and the sulfur refinery and into a maze of jagged rocks along the footpaths. We had to keep jumping over dead Japs lying in our paths and there were two Nip tanks burning with their ammo inside exploding like popcorn in a kettle. We spent the night dug in amongst the rocks. We had a rather active night from the Nips. We could hear them running their tanks and on several occasions, they appeared headed towards our position. I fired many barrages before dawn. Just as the darkness of night was changing to the soft gray of dawn, I got out of my hole and was talking to Captain Stephenson when we heard several hand grenades go off. Right behind us, four Japs came running out, one behind the other, about two paces apart. I reached for the first weapon I could find and picked up a Thompson submachine gun, but by the time I got it in position to fire, there were no more live Japs.[13]

* * * *

On D-Day + 8, 27 February 1945, we began moving along a path between jagged rocks about five paces apart when all of a sudden a white phosphorus shell exploded, spreading its phosphorus all over the place. Luckily it missed me and my FO team, but it did get several men from L Company. I'm sure this was one of our shells because as we proceeded to advance on the double, I happen to glance to my right rear and my eyes caught sight of an artillery shell arching down from the sky. I watched it sail down to about fifteen feet from where I was in a crouched position. I was so amazed to see this projectile that I watched it explode. The air sung with fragments flying, but there was not a mark on me or any of the other men close by. The going got tougher, from both the Japs and the lay of the land. We finally held up to get organized. I now believed we had gone too far to our right and the 4th Division was behind and attacking us.[14]

* * * *

After another move we were stopped and pinned from small arms fire and mortars, probably mixed in with some of our own artillery. I found a nice spot behind some rocks at the bottom of a hill and put my radioman there with the radio. He had radio contact with the battalion and they advised me we were to attack again at 1600 and wanted me to fire the pre-attack barrage. I found an observation spot on top of a hill in front of the radio position and started to register in for the barrage. This required me to spot the round, run down to the radio, give the correction and run back up the hill to see where the shells landed. I could tell that some Nip was shooting at me whenever I appeared at the top, as the bullets were zipping past me. After observing one round, I started down the hill on the double and about halfway down, something hit my left arm just below the shoulder and spun me around, knocking me over. When I got to the radio position, I saw what had happened. A bullet had pierced my utility and field jackets, going in one side and coming out the other, but just touching and only giving me a red spot on my arm. I had four bullet holes in the two jackets.

I went back to my V in the rocks to see if I could observe any shells hitting at the start of our barrage when I was told that Captain Stephenson wanted to see me. I turned and took five steps when someone said, "Your sergeant is hit." I turned around and saw that it wasn't my sergeant, but rather the company's mortar observer, who had just taken my spot at the V. He had been shot in the forehead and died instantly. I don't think he ever knew what had hit him. I was told that no sooner than I had left the position, that this Marine had stuck his head through the V and was shot immediately. Unfortunately, Captain Stephenson was also killed several days later.[15]

* * * *

On D-Day + 9, we were relieved and by noon that day, we were on our way back to our battery positions. I was able to take a bath using buckets, shaving out of the canteen cup, and then crawled into a niche in the fire battery-direction center and slept until noon the next day. For the balance of the battle, I acted as battery executive officer but we did not do too much firing as the infantry was now clearing out bypassed pockets and caves.[16]

George left Iwo Jima on 17 March 1945 from the west beaches, and went aboard the cargo ship *Santa Isabel* (C-2) and arrived back on Guam on the 21st. He had survived numerous close calls and had earned a Bronze Star with Combat "V" and two Purple Hearts.[16]

Postlude

On 3 April 1945, George and several of his compatriots, boarded the LST-27 and sailed for San Francisco three days later in a convoy of 15 other LSTs. "The Pacific was smooth as glass most of the time and we enjoyed a pleasant cruise with good food, fresh water, showers and bunks with sheets. We briefly stopped at Pearl Harbor before arriving in San Francisco on 6 May. From there, I boarded a train for a furlough before reporting for assignment at the tent camp, New River, North Carolina, to help train new Marines for overseas duty. I remained at the tent camp until the end of the war when I was transferred to Camp Lejeune, Hadnot Point, as assistant camp fire marshall."[17]

George was discharged in April 1948 and then joined the Marine Corps Reserves. He regained his warrant officer status in June 1949. He went to college on the G.I. Bill and graduated with a B.S. in architectural engineering. He and Betty had six children but, unfortunately, she passed away in 1965, the same year that he retired as a chief warrant officer-4 from the Marine Reserves. George married a second time in 1971 but in February 2006, his second wife also passed away.[18]

Over the years, George worked as an architect and in the field of sales promotion with both U.S. Gypsum and a large drywall, painting and partition contractor. In 1967, he moved to St. Louis and continued in sales promotions. He started his own company in 1980, which his son now runs.

Although physical conditions are now limiting him, he still occasionally enjoys golf and fishing. He belongs to both the 2nd and 3rd Marine Division Associations, and in 1995, he and his second wife, Yvonne, traveled to Iwo Jima with several other Marine and Japanese veterans to attend the 50th anniversary memorial.[19]

Postscript

In George's last letter to me, he mentioned that he was attending a preview that night of Clint Eastwood's recent Iwo Jima movie, *Flags of our Fathers*. I could easily tell that the Marine Corps and the battle of Iwo Jima were still strongly embedded in his everyday thoughts.[20]

Later I received an e-mail from George that included an article written by Bob Dart of the Cox News Service. The 85-year-old George was mentioned as an attendee at the opening ceremonies of the Marine Corps' new museum in Quantico, Virginia, which opened on 10 November 2006, the Marines' 231st birthday. He was quoted as saying, "The Marines were the most exciting part of my life."[21]

I received an e-mail from George Green on 17 August 2006 briefly telling me that he had several close calls during World War II. He asked me if I would like to receive a copy of his war memoirs. Besides immediately saying yes, I also sent him an e-mail questionnaire on 21 August to gather additional personal background information. I also followed up the e-mail with a hardcopy reminder, sent by USPS in early September, since I had not received anything back. In a letter dated 11 September 2006, he told me he had sent his memoirs and was still working on the questionnaire. On 18 September 2006, I received his memoirs and was very excited. The package was over an inch thick and included his memoirs, pictures and other pertinent information about his war experiences. In a letter, dated 11 October 2006, I received the answers to my questionnaire. George sent me another e-mail on 21 November 2006 containing a Cox News Service article describing the opening of the new USMC Museum in Quantico, Virginia. George has lived a very interesting life and I feel privileged that he has shared everything with me through his writings.

15

USMC Private George Smyth

> It takes a better man to survive good luck than bad.
> — Duc de La Tochefoucauld

Prelude

George Joseph Smyth was born on 22 May 1926 in Brooklyn, New York. He was the second oldest of five siblings, three sisters and one brother. His father died when he was just ten years old. With the loss of his father and living during the Depression era, George felt a tremendous responsibility to his family, so he began working at an early age to help out with expenses. He worked as a soda jerk making egg creams in Long Island and was also a delivery boy for the local newspaper, the *Brooklyn Eagle*.

Like many patriotic Americans during the Second World War era, George Smyth enlisted in the United States Marine Corps prior to graduating from high school at the age of 17. He was filled with anger towards the Japanese for the bombing of Pearl Harbor and wanted to do his duty for his country. The young man stood 5 feet, 8 inches tall (he grew 2 more inches while in the service), had blue eyes and brown hair and was ready to face the enemy at any cost.[1]

Although 28 March 1944 was his official enlistment date, Private Smyth actually began his active duty on 27 April 1944 when he entered boot camp at Parris Island, South Carolina. He qualified as a rifle marksman and, after he graduated, was assigned to Camp Lejeune, North Carolina, where he continued his combat training and waited for his overseas orders. He became very proficient with the bazooka and would soon be officially designated as a bazooka operator.[2]

A Brief History of the Bazooka

The bazooka was the world's first antitank rocket. It utilized a shaped-charge rocket and became an important weapon that helped Marines and soldiers to destroy enemy armor and field fortifications during World War II. In 1942, the Army was the first to adopt the M1 Antitank Rocket Launcher built by General Electric. The soldiers soon nicknamed it the "bazooka" after a musical instrument developed by entertainer Bob Burns.

The Marine Corps started testing the weapon in June 1943, and it was first utilized by them in combat during the Bougainville operation in October of that same year with limited success. After several modifications, the next model was developed and named the M1A1 Bazooka. This was the weapon that the Marines used successfully during the Marianas and Peleliu Campaigns. By mid–1944, this bazooka was assigned to the general service within the Fleet Marine Force. The table of organization for each Marine division by May 1944 was authorized 172 bazookas, including 43 for every regiment, of which 16 were assigned to the weapons company and 9 for each infantry battalion. Each rifle company was allotted 3 to be utilized at the company commander's discretion.

In October 1943, the Army's Ordnance Department developed an even better bazooka, the M9/M9A1 model. There were many improvements over the earlier models, including a trigger-operated magneto, a safety switch, a tube that could be broken down for easier carrying and an improved rocket (M6A2 high explosive rocket). Its basic operational and maintenance simplicity, especially under rugged combat situations, made it an ideal weapon for Marines fighting in the Pacific theater of operations. It wouldn't be until the battles for Iwo Jima and Okinawa in 1945 that the Marines were able to use this newer and much better version.[3]

Private George Smyth finally received his orders for overseas. After traveling to California, he boarded a ship on 14 August 1944 and headed for Guam in the Mariana Islands and to his assignment with the 3rd Marine Division. The battle for Guam had begun earlier on 21 July 1944 and the island was officially declared secure on 10 August 1944. George arrived after the main battle was over, but until the Division departed for the Iwo Jima campaign, the Marines continued to take part in mopping-up operations and training. Private Smyth was assigned to K Company, Third Battalion, 21st Marine Regiment in the 3rd Marine Division.[4]

Iwo Jima
February 1945

After finally arriving at the Iwo Jima staging area, Private Smyth and the rest of the 3rd Marine Division, now commanded by Major General Graves B. Erskine, remained afloat as reserve forces on the first day of the battle. Hearing the battle take place, with explosions everywhere and naval gunfire all around them, the waiting Marines had many thoughts going through their minds: excitement, anticipation, and fear of the "great unknown" which lay ahead of them. It was soon determined that reinforcements were needed right away.

The 21st Marines, commanded by Lieutenant Colonel Wendell H. Duplantis, was the first regiment from the 3rd Marine Division to receive orders to join in on the battle. By 21 February (D-Day + 2) all units in the 21st Marines including the three rifle companies (I, K and L) had made it ashore. It would not be until 24 February that the entire 3rd Marine Division would be committed to the action. During its initial days on the island, the 21st Marines was attached to the 4th Marine Division.[5]

The 21st Marines quickly filled in gaps along the beachhead and dug foxholes for protection. The chaos of the battle was unyielding as mortars, rockets, artillery and automatic rifle fire were continuous. "It made us feel good that we were finally going to see action, but we soon changed our minds after a day or two. That first night none of us were able to sleep in our sandy foxholes."[6] On 22 February (D-Day +3) the 21st Marines became an organized and cohesive unit and moved towards the front lines by passing through the 4th Division's 23rd Marines.

The next day, 23 February (D-Day + 4), as they were crossing the captured Motoyama Airfield No. 1, they noticed the American flag flying atop Mount Suribachi. "The cheer that arose drowned out the sound of the Jap shells. Many a Marine had tears in his eyes."[7]

When they finally hit the front lines, the Japanese unleashed everything they had in their arsenal against the newly arrived Marines. One of George's buddies, a Brooklyn kid, was badly wounded charging a machine gun position pillbox. "He saved many lives by doing it."[8]

Most of the remainder of the 3rd Marine Division had landed by 24 February (D-Day +5) and the 21st Marines returned to their parent unit. The Division continued the attack against the Motoyama Airfield No. 2 at 0915. They were placed between the 4th and 5th Marine Divisions and spearheaded the drive from the middle island position.

The ground around this airfield was very treacherous because the Japanese had sighted their guns down the runways and the surrounding areas. They had artillery and mortars preregistered for the anticipated Marine assault and had dozens of machine gun nests and riflemen hidden in strategic and well-fortified positions. The heights to the north of the airfield made the entire sector a "no man's land" that was defended by the best troops in the Japanese Army. Minefields covered both flanks and each new attack brought heavy casualties on both sides.[9]

> For hours, with mud and sand up to my waist, mortar and artillery fire falling around, I lay in a hole, but those hours were not wasted. I

prayed nearly every minute of the time. I was then told to take out a Japanese light tank to our front.

When I finally decided to get out of the hole, I made ready for a long dash. I was a bazooka man and had three rocket shells strapped to my pack. As soon as I started to rise, the rockets were the first thing to appear above my hole. A second later I felt the thud of bullets as they hit my pack. I was more afraid that the rockets would explode than I was of anything else. I got back down in the hole and removed my pack. The bazooka shells were stitched with bullet holes. Thank goodness none of them had hit a detonator.[10]

By now, the Japanese had zeroed in on Private Smyth's bazooka team's location and bullets from machine gun pillboxes and hidden snipers flooded the air above their heads with lead. The enemy tank that had been their objective was to their front and the Japanese knew that there was a definite threat from this Marine's bazooka position. Rockets, mortars and artillery shells began landing close to their protected shell hole. The next few minutes of Private Smyth's life are hazy as he has little or no memory of the events that took place. He was later told that he had knocked out the enemy tank, killing several Japanese soldiers. As the team rose to once more move forward, George was shot by a sniper's bullet through the right temple and out the left. At the same time, an enemy rocket landed right next to their position. "It seemed as if 10,000 baseball bats hit the back of my head at one time. From that time on everything was a blank."[11]

The other team members were also injured. Smyth had lost consciousness and was bleeding about the head. Later another buddy from Brooklyn, whom he met in the hospital, told him what had happened to him. This Marine saw the bazooka team go down after the explosion and he immediately sent for stretcher bearers to bring the wounded back to the beachhead. Although it took awhile, several brave men came out under heavy sniper fire and, regardless of the fact that another rocket barrage might begin at any time, picked up all of the injured Marines. By the time they made it back to the staging area on the beach, Smyth appeared quite dead and, therefore, was placed in a long line of dead bodies waiting for eventual burial. He was tagged as dead and his mother, Gertrude, would later receive a telegram notification that he had been killed.

After George had lain unconscious for over 24 hours, a burial party began checking the pockets of the dead to obtain any personal belongings. When they reached Smyth, they soon found out that his body was not cold and stiff like the others and realized that he was still alive. One of the men radioed for instructions on how to bring him out of shock. A Navy corpsman soon arrived, treated his wounds, and was able to revive him. He bandaged his bleeding head and realized that Private Smyth needed a blood transfusion as quickly as possible. The corpsman helped him up and managed to get him to stagger along the beachhead towards a field medical station near the evacuation point.[12]

As they struggled through the sand they came upon a shell hole lined in ammunition boxes and up popped out a Marine combat correspondent, Eugene S. Jones, with his camera. Jones took what would soon become a legendary World War II and Iwo Jima picture. The touching and memorable photo, showing the young Private Smyth's swollen and bloody face with his fists clenched in pain, was nearly as well known as Joe Rosenthal's famous flag-raising picture on Mount Suribachi. It appeared in wartime magazines and newspapers throughout the country.[13]

Upon reaching the temporary medical aid station, George received two pints of blood plasma. He would eventually need a total of 13 pints of blood over the next year in order to save his life. George's casualty tag was changed to "wounded in action" and dated 26 February 1945. Although wounded on the 24th, this date remained on his Marine Corps records as the official date of his Purple Heart.[14]

On 26 February (D-Day + 7), the USS *Lowndes* (APA-154), a troop and cargo carrier, delivered needed supplies to the beachhead with its smaller boats between the hours of 0800 and 1200. They then returned later in the day to the No. 2 hatch on the starboard side of the ship to deliver casualties from the island, including George and 56 other injured Marines and sailors, by 1600. Sometime around 1830 the ship headed off for its normal night deployment, continuing a zigzag pattern throughout the evening.

There was an ever-present possibility that Japanese aircraft would bomb any ships left moored around the island and the threat of submarine attacks was also a fearful consideration. This became the ship's normal routine: delivering supplies and receiving casualties during the next several days and then heading out to sea in the early or sometimes late evenings. Occasionally some of the wounded men were transferred to other ships or returned back to their units to continue in the fighting. With a severe concussion and head wounds, George probably remained in and out of consciousness during most of this time. His obvious head wounds were tended to on a daily basis with cleaning and fresh bandages. Finally, during the very early morning hours of 2 March (D-Day + 11), the USS *Lowndes* steamed away from Iwo Jima and headed off in a small convoy for the Mariana Islands.

The USS *Lowndes* arrived in Guam in the early hours of 5 March and moored in Berth No. 6, Apra Harbor, Guam, in the Mariana Islands. At 2200 hours, George and approximately 335 other wounded passengers were transferred to the United States Fleet Hospital #111 where they were to receive much better care than was available aboard the ship.[15]

Besides his apparent head wounds, George was diagnosed as having a severe concussion and head trauma resulting from the bullet wound and explosion. He developed chronic, traumatic, subdural hematoma.[16] Basically, this is an accumulation of blood and blood breakdown products between the surface of the brain and its outermost covering, called the dura. The chronic phase of a subdural hematoma begins several weeks after the initial bleeding. Tiny veins called bridging veins run between the dura and the surface of the brain. The subdural hematoma develops when these veins tear and leak blood, usually as the result of a head injury. A collection of blood then forms over the surface of the brain. Surgery is often required. This may include drilling small holes in the skull to relieve pressure and allow blood to be drained. Large hematomas or solid blood clots may need to be removed through a larger opening in the skull.[17]

George continued to have his blood drained and, at the same time, received more blood transfusions as they were required. As luck would have it, he had no permanent brain damage, but he did lose hearing in his left ear.

> I know how concerned I was at that time over the adequacy of the blood supply at the hospital, and how deeply grateful I was to the people at home when I found that a sufficient amount was available to restore me to health. I knew at the time that it was impossible for myself and the other boys who lay beside me in the hospital to make a direct appeal for the blood that would save our lives but I made up my mind that if I should be fortunate enough to return home that I would not only give back the 13 pints I had received but would try through relating my own combat experiences to impress upon all Americans the important part that blood plays in our keeping up the morale of our fighting men and in winning wars.[18]

After about a month in the hospital in Guam, George was reading a copy of *Time* magazine and saw the photograph taken of him and the unknown corpsman by Eugene Jones on the beach, back on Iwo Jima. Later it was also reproduced in *Life* magazine. He clipped out the pictures and sent them home, but subsequently forgot all about it until years later.

Also during his time in the Guam hospital, George was able to communicate with his family to let them know that he was alive and not dead as had been previously reported. He also wrote about his combat experiences for the *Brooklyn Eagle*, where he had worked before joining the Marines. The *Eagle* printed his story under the title, "Carrier Boy Is Iwo Hero."

On 9 May 1945 George left the United States Fleet Hospital #111 on Guam and flew to Oahu in the Territory of Hawaii, where he was assigned to the United States Naval Hospital #10.

George would stay in Hawaii until 23 May when he was again reassigned to a Naval hospital in San Francisco. He had finally made it home to the United States mainland. Several weeks later, on 15 June 1945, he was relocated for the last time, to the United States Naval Hospital at Camp Lejeune, North Carolina.

George stayed in four separate hospitals for over a year, as blood clots continued to form on his brain. He was promoted to private first class on 6 March 1946. He was finally able to leave the hospital and was considered physically fit despite the fact that he had metal plates in both temples and had hearing loss in his left ear. He received an honorable discharge on 23 March 1946. The Marine Corps gave him a grand total of $148.87, which included travel pay home at 5 cents per mile and other miscellaneous monies due him on his discharge date, and he headed home to Brooklyn to begin his new life.[19]

Postlude

Following the Marines, George went to work for the U.S. Rubber Company in Manhattan. He finished high school and earned a degree in business administration from Pace College by going to school at night. He met a pretty brunette named Loretta Smith, who also worked at U.S. Rubber, and they married in 1949. They settled in Levittown, Long Island, and later adopted two children, Chris and Jeanne. Loretta had developed heart disease related to childhood rheumatic fever which had prevented her from having her own children. In the early 1950s George changed jobs and went to work with Western Union where, as an up-and-coming executive, he was promoted quickly to a supervisory level position.[20]

On 25 June 1950, the Korean War began, and once more the Marines were called to duty in another far-off land to fight for their country.

George had already begun to fulfill his promise of donating his 13 pints of blood back to the American Marines and soldiers. George was quoted as follows in a 22 January 1952 news release put out by the Western Union: "Thirteen pints of blood saved my life. That represents the blood of 13 donors. The wounded men in Korea and the veterans in military hospitals are in critical need of blood. Military authorities say 2,800,000 pints of whole blood must be collected by July 1952. The goal is 300,000 pints a month. We can do it if we all work together. I urge everyone who can, to help, not once, but often."[21]

Besides donating blood, George continued to maintain his strong patriotism and Marine Corps roots by joining the Marine Corps League and the 3rd Marine Division Association. He served at one time as the commandant of his Marine Corps League's General Smedley D. Butler Detachment and attended nearly every Marine convention that he possible could. He also enjoyed reading books about the Marine Corps. George lived the motto, "Once a Marine, Always a Marine."[22]

In late 1951 and early 1952, the "famous" Iwo Jima picture of George appeared in Red Cross blood drive posters throughout the nation. After seven years, the wounded Marine in the picture still remained an unidentified mystery man. Then, an employee at Western Union recognized the picture as that of a fellow worker, George J. Smyth of Levittown, Long Island. Modestly, George acknowledged that indeed, he was the wounded Marine in the picture. Identification was confirmed when a meeting was held between the photographer, Eugene S. Jones, who by now was a cameraman-correspondent for NBC-TV News Department in New York, and George Smyth at the 21 Club in New York City. Mr. Jones had recently spent some time in Korea as a combat photojournalist. In the meeting, Eugene asked George to describe what kind of day it was, what the area looked like around him and other details. After George answered all of his questions, especially when he recalled that Jones snapped his picture on the beachhead from a shell hole lined with ammunition boxes, there was no longer any doubt that the man in the photograph was indeed George Smyth.[23]

George soon became somewhat of a celebrity, especially on the East Coast, as his story and pictures appeared in numerous newspapers and Red Cross blood drive posters and advertisements, primarily in the New York and New Jersey areas. He also appeared on TV, including *The Ed Sullivan Show*, to promote blood donations. He had used his temporary notoriety to further the cause to encourage all Americans to donate as much blood as possible to the Red Cross. On 26 February 1952 (the anniversary of the day that he received his Purple Heart), George stood at the head of a line of 235 people at the Western Union offices in New York, to donate his seventh pint of blood to the Red Cross.

> Somewhere there's a man in a field hospital whose chance of coming home may depend on me. I don't know him and he doesn't know me, just as I never knew whose blood was saving my life. I still owe six pints to somebody and it doesn't matter who.[24]

By September 1955 George had donated his fifteenth pint of blood and would continue to give blood, far exceeding the original 13 pints of blood that he had promised while recuperating in military hospitals. He had also helped lead several Red Cross blood campaigns in the New York area.[25]

George's life would take several twists and turns, some good and some bad. His wife, Loretta, died at the early age of 40 due to heart complications. He was later introduced to another wonderful woman, Teresa, who herself had lived through a traumatic experience when her husband was killed in an unfortunate accident when she was seven months pregnant. The newborn son was named Harry after her late husband. The two fell in love and married in 1966 when George was 40 years old and they started off with a combined family of three children. They would later have three children of their own, Carol, Michael and Eileen.

As a younger father, George was fairly regimented, probably due to his Marine Corps training and the fact that he had to help his mother raise his fatherless family as a child. He was devoted to his job and well liked at his Western Union position. He thoroughly enjoyed reading and could often be found reading a good book by the pool and drinking his favorite drink of blended ice and orange juice.

George loved to travel and always tried to take his family on a big trip every year. A favorite spot was Hawaii, where he could lie on the beach and read to his heart's content. As he grew older, he loosened up and became more affectionate and began to laugh more. His war demons were finally leaving his soul. He seemed to have kept a lot inside of himself for years. He never really talked about the war unless he was asked and he never felt heroic about his notoriety.

He was a devout Catholic and made sure that his family went to church every week. It was probably his faith that got him through the war, his long recovery in the military hospitals and the death of his first wife. He made sure that all of his children received what they needed and provided them with an upper-middle-class upbringing in the suburbs with excellent schools.

George suffered heart attacks in 1970 and 1972 and had open-heart surgery in 1974. After living for a few years in Texas, the family returned to the East and settled in Ridgewood, New Jersey. George continued working for Western Union until the early 1980s. Upon his retirement he took up cooking and baking, and he and his wife enjoyed hosting small dinner parties for friends. Although George could no longer give blood due to his heart condition, his family continued the tradition of donating blood as often as possible to honor their father.

He died from his final heart attack at his home on 26 February 1986, just short of 60 years old. Ironically, once again, this was the same day 41 years previously that he had received his Purple Heart. He had been a wonderful husband, father and friend. George's six children all went on to raise their own families.

George would be known as an honorable, honest and moral man. He was highly regarded by many people. His wake was several days long because of the number of people who came to show their final respects. His youngest daughter, Eileen, says, "I hope he is now relaxing in heaven, with a good book and listening to big band and Frank Sinatra music, because God knows his life on earth wasn't always an easy one!"[26]

George Smyth was a true American hero, not just on the sands of Iwo Jima or by his determined efforts to survive his serious wounds, but more importantly, as a former Marine who returned the life-giving gift of blood to so many other military men and women in need. Another famous Marine Corps motto is "Semper Fidelis" (Always Faithful). George once said, "Semper Fidelis represents the real moments of my life."[27] George Joseph Smyth was always faithful to his God, his family, his country and to the Marine Corps.

    In April 2007, I received an e-mail from Eileen Judd, daughter of George Smyth, asking if I was still looking for close call stories. She had seen an old ad on the 3rd Marine Division website. At the time, I had completed my first manuscript draft, and told her no. She did briefly tell me his story, which was quite amazing, and later, in June 2007, I decided to write her father's story for her family and possibly as a potential magazine article. The completed family project ended up at 50 pages long. In August 2007, while rewriting my manuscript, I decided to include a shorter version of the story and inserted it with the Iwo Jima chapters.

16

USMC Private First Class William Byrd

> Impossible situations can become possible miracles.
> — Robert Schuller

Prelude

Born in 1925, William "Billy" Byrd grew up during the Depression years. His father, who had served his country during World War I and was gassed in the trenches in France, was a sharecropper in the cotton fields of Mississippi. The family, with six boys and one girl, constantly moved from one farm to another. Even though the years brought on hard times, Billy had many happy childhood memories of growing up including fishing, hunting, playing games and climbing trees. However, one unfortunate day, his family was torn apart. Both of his parents had tuberculosis and were sent to a sanatorium, and all of the children were dispersed amongst friends and relatives throughout several southern states. Quite often homeless, Billy would hitchhike from place to place to find work and shelter amongst his relatives. He eventually found a job in the kitchen department of a hotel and lived at the YMCA for just three dollars a week. One day his draft notice arrived in the mail and he was ordered to the nearby Camp Shelby. It was then that he decided to join the Marine Corps.

He arrived at the Marines' San Diego boot camp by train and bus. In six short weeks, Billy learned the basics of becoming a Marine, and upon graduation, he was promoted to private first class. He was next assigned to the Marine Raider battalion that was located a few miles further north. He enjoyed this duty, even though the training was very tough and included nearly daily 20-mile-long hikes. A few months later, the battalion was disbanded and he was then placed with the 2nd Battalion, 28th Marines (2/28), 5th Marine Division at Camp Pendleton, California. Training continued as this new unit was brought up to strength and they were then relocated to Camp Tarawa in the Territory of Hawaii.[1]

A Brief History of the 5th Marine Division

The 5th Marine Division was created during World War II for the Battle of Iwo Jima and the planned invasion of the Japanese homeland. The Division was activated on paper on Armistice Day, 11 November 1943, and officially began operating at Camp Pendleton on 1 December, at which time men and equipment began streaming into the base. The official activation date was 21 January 1944. Its infantry regiments consisted of the 26th, 27th and 28th Marines.[2] The new division was never a truly "green" outfit, even from the very start. Thousands of combat veterans joined fresh new Marines, barely out of boot camp. Included in these experienced Marines were former members of the First Marine Parachute Regiment, the Raider Training Battalion, the Parachute Training School and the Parachute Replacement Company. Most of these Marines had already served in combat and gave the Division an edge in training and battle. Additionally, seasoned Marines who had not yet fought were located and transferred in from all over the United States to provide more stability to the new outfit. The nickname for the Division was "The Spearhead."

After months of training, the Division relocated to Camp Tarawa, near Hilo, Hawaii, between August and November 1944. The Fifth continued to hone its combat skills and, after receiving its first combat assignment of Iwo Jima, began intensified training on terrain that was similar to their invasion objective. In December 1944, transports began arriving at Hilo and loading commenced on 16 December. The last units of the Division pulled out of Camp Tarawa on 4 January 1945.[3]

> We left Hawaii and boarded a large troop ship, heading off for an unknown destination. I watched as the sun set on the vast Pacific Ocean and can still remember how beautiful it was. On the second day out our D Company was called below to a conference room. We huddled around a big conference table and I got a close look at a lifelike model of an island. I remember thinking that it looked like a pork chop. You could see and feel the rough terrain and at the bottom, there was a mountain.[4]

18 February 1945
Iwo Jima

> We were all put onto a smaller ship called an LST or Landing Ship Tank and were then sprayed with disinfectants even though we had already gotten a series of seven shots. At some point during the night, we climbed into amtracs, amphibious crafts that used treads to move through the water and onto the land. I don't remember anyone sleeping

that night. In the early hours of 19 February, I looked west into the darkness, and in the distance about ten miles out, I could see flashes of light. This was my first sight of war.[5]

* * * *

At about 1030 on the first morning, after most of the first waves of Marines made it ashore, all hell broke loose. Shells from the enemy's big guns began screaming down on us. Mortar shells were exploding everywhere. The machine gun fire was deadly across the area. Rifle fire found easy targets. The sound was deafening with 500-pound shells exploding overhead. Land mines were sown together like wheat in a field and they would explode every time a Marine stepped on them. Every square inch was under attack and we had no defense whatsoever.[6]

* * * *

In battle against a dug-in enemy, nothing was funny about our situation, but I laughed briefly when our company bugler, William Buise, dove into a foxhole at the same time one of our mortars was fired by one of our guys. The mortar shell flew right between his legs.[7]

* * * *

During one trip to bring back ammo, bullets started popping all around me so I dove into the nearest foxhole. I waited a few minutes and started running again. It was on this run that a mortar exploded nearby and almost blinded me with sand and ash. I held onto the ammunition and somehow made it back safely. Getting back to our lines without being hit was somewhat of an accomplishment. A little prayer here and there helped too.[8]

* * * *

During the second night, the Japanese attacked our lines. They came from everywhere, yelling and swinging swords. Many had bayoneted rifles. With the help of flares, we cut them down like bowling pins. Just when I thought things were letting down, a lone Jap crawled into our three-man foxhole with a bayonet on his rifle. One of the guys shot him in the leg and another grabbed his rifle while I hit him in the face with the butt of my carbine. One Marine then put him into a chokehold and I yelled one of the only Japanese words I knew, "Surrender!"[9]

* * * *

On the third day, the clouds were very low and the ground still wet. The smoke haze was so heavy I couldn't see the top of the mountain.

Small arms fire started up again with bullets popping around us. They were firing mortar shells at us again with their sickening thuds. I heard screaming of the wounded and the moans of the dying. A mortar hit and exploded about 30 yards away. A large fragment hit my helmet and almost broke my neck. A Marine near me was hit just under the helmet and he was blinded by blood for a while. I was going to pour some water on his face but found my canteen was hanging by just one hook. It was empty because of a three-inch hole near the bottom.[10]

* * * *

I'll never forget what happened to the third platoon, led by Lieutenant Herbert Worry. One day during the confused fighting, they found themselves surrounded by the Japanese. They were in a deadly trap. I was on the east side of the ravine along with Sergeant Mulligan. We decided that I should go for help, running across some open ground. I ran for dear life! I found a tank and the crew followed me back, but we didn't make it back in time. Lieutenant Worry and his men were wiped out, including Sergeant Mulligan.[11]

* * * *

One night after a flare went out and just before daylight, I heard a dragging sound. Then, all of a sudden, two enemy soldiers jumped us from behind. One had a gun and the other, a bayoneted rifle. It seemed like the struggle lasted forever. I had one in a vise-like grip around the neck. I remembered how he smelled. My buddy, Pfc Orville Carriveau, was cut on his hand and arm but he was still fighting. I was hit with a rifle butt under my left eye. It was the hardest blow I had ever received and I still have a scar from the incident.

I vaguely remember another Marine coming to help. One of the Japanese was stabbed to death while the other was shot. I remember blood running into my mouth. I was so weak, almost lifeless. I was carried to a medical tent where they put in stitches. I soon felt guilty laying there so, after about twenty minutes, I slipped out and returned to my company. Orville must have done the same thing after me because I heard he was later killed in action.[12]

Postlude

Somehow, luck stayed with Billy throughout the deadly battle. He survived the war and would eventually be promoted to corporal before getting out of the Marines. He married, had a family and worked in the music radio business. In 2005, he wrote and self-published his short war memoirs, titled *By the Dawn's Early Light*.

The 5th Marine Division received a Presidential Unit Citation for their actions on Iwo Jima. They suffered 2,416 deaths and 6,860 wounded.[13] On 27 March, the last Marines of the Division left Iwo Jima and again returned to Camp Tarawa. After the war ended with the dropping of the atomic bombs on Japan, the Division was sent overseas for occupation duty, mainly on the island of Kyushu. Beginning on 23 November 1945, the Fifth began their long-awaited return to the United States and home. On 5 February 1946, the 5th Marine Division was deactivated and its colors encased. It would be 20 years later, in 1966, that the Division was once again activated due to the War in Vietnam. Both the 26th and 27th Regiments were sent to fight in Vietnam and would continue to uphold the Spearhead's highest traditions.[14]

Postscript

The author was part of the reformed 5th Marine Division and fought in Vietnam with the 27th Marines from February though September 1968. His story may be found in Chapter 34.

Diane Kuebler, a daughter of a World War II Seabee, gave me another lead that led to Marvin Veronee, a Navy ensign who served at Iwo Jima as a naval shore gun fire-team leader. Marvin told me about Billy Byrd and sent me a copy of Billy's war memoirs, which he edited and helped to self-publish. I received e-mail confirmation on 2 December 2006 that allowed me to include some of Billy's close call stories from this book.

17

USMC Private First Class Lee Bergee (Part 1 of 2)

> The best luck of all is the luck you make for yourself.
> — Douglas MacArthur

Prelude

Lee Bergee was born on 13 January 1927 in the city of Fort Madison, Iowa. From the early age of just 12, Lee already knew that he wanted to be a Marine. He had learned everything he could about the Marine Corps, from their history to close-order drilling. He takes pride that in 1940, while in high school, he was a member of the marching band that took the first place award in the National Marching Band Contest in Topeka, Kansas.

As soon as he graduated from high school, Lee joined the Marines in July 1944 and attended boot camp at Parris Island, South Carolina. After short stays at Camp Lejeune, North Carolina, and Camp Pendleton, California, Lee found himself headed for the Philippines in the latter part of the Second World War. Although there was a significant Marine attachment (4th Marines) in the Philippines during the 1941 Japanese conquest, only Marine air squadrons and a few Marine ground forces were involved in the retaking of the islands by the United States Army's 1944–45 campaign.[1]

1941
The Philippines

The 7,000 islands of the Philippines are located in the northeastern part of the Malayan Archipelago. At the outbreak of the Second World War, the Philippines were a commonwealth of the United States with a population of about 19,000,000 people. General Douglas MacArthur had been sent to the islands in 1935 to help organize the Philippines' defenses. He retired from the

Army in 1937 but stayed on in the Philippines as the military advisor until June 1941, when President Roosevelt recalled him to active duty because of the potential Japanese threat.

On 8 December 1941, the Japanese began bombing the Philippines and soon followed with a ground assault, quickly capturing the capital city of Manila. MacArthur then ordered a general retreat to the Bataan peninsula on Luzon and the small adjacent island of Corregidor. On 22 February 1942, MacArthur was ordered to leave Bataan and go to Australia to take over as the Supreme Allied Commander Southwest Pacific Area. It was in Australia that MacArthur made his famous "I shall return" speech on 20 March 1942. The Philippines, now under the command of Major General Jonathan Wainwright IV, held out against the Japanese until early May before surrendering.

October 1944
Leyte

It was not until 1944 that MacArthur received permission to begin the campaign to recapture the Philippines. His first objective was the invasion of Leyte, an island located between Luzon and Mindanao, on 22 October 1944. By December, the U.S. Sixth Army had defeated the Japanese on Leyte.[2]

January 1945
Luzon

The invasion of Luzon, the largest island in the Philippines, began on 9 January 1945. It was on Luzon that Private First Class Bergee had his first close call experience.

> On 11 January, while [I was] walking point down a jungle path, a Japanese soldier suddenly jumped out from behind a tree and pointed his rifle at my head. Before I could react, he pulled the trigger but nothing happened. I killed him, walked up to where he was lying and took his rifle to look into the chamber. The bullet had been struck by the firing pin, but had not fired! I kept that bullet for years, but finally lost it. God was certainly with me that day.[3]

Manila was recaptured on 4 March and the remaining Japanese continued fighting from isolated mountain positions. While the battle continued on Luzon, the U.S. Eighth Army landed on Mindanao on 10 March and began advancing through the southern Philippines, including the islands of Panay, Cebu, Negros and Bohol.

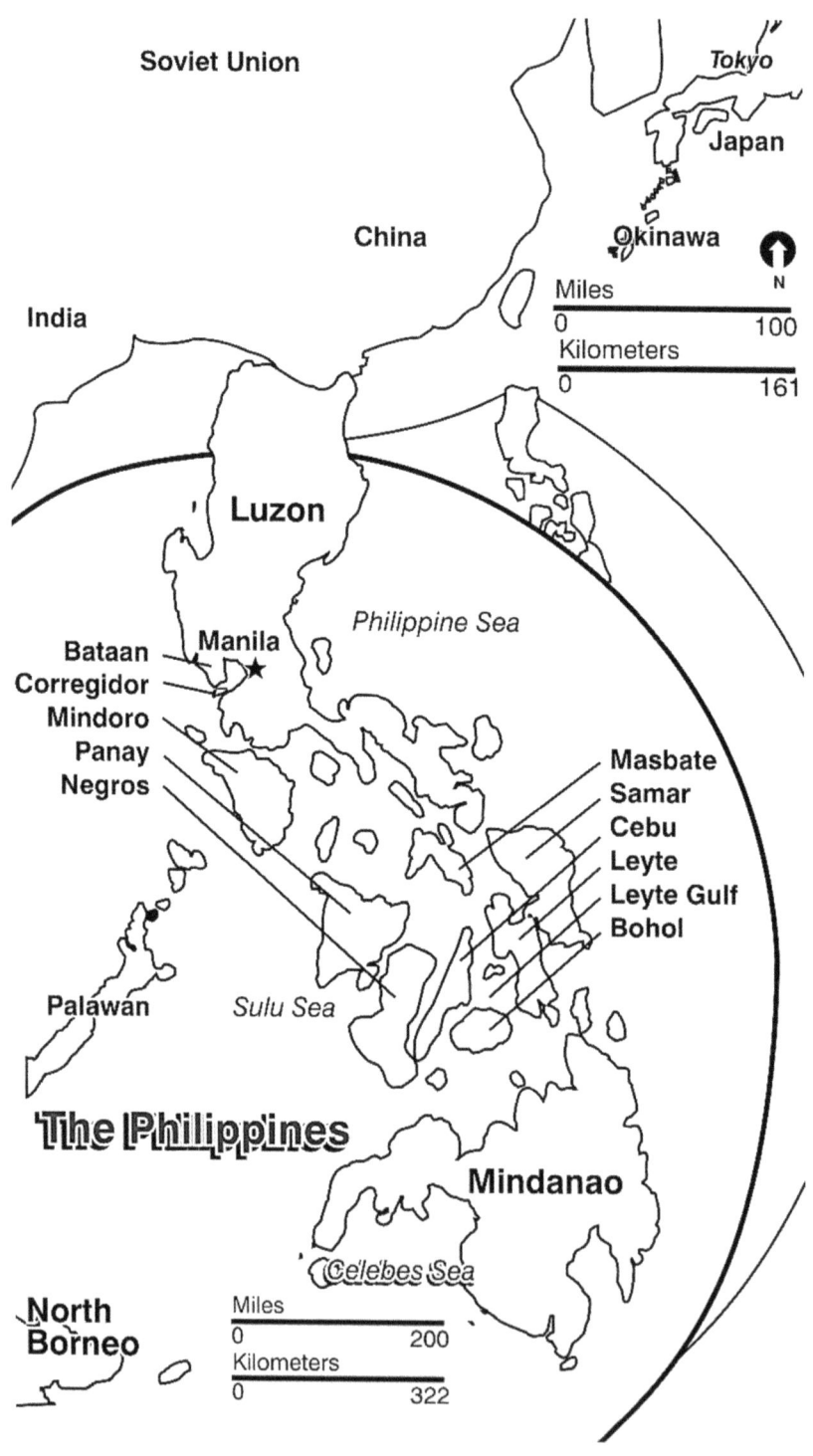

After hearing that their Emperor had announced that Japan had surrendered, the final 50,000 Japanese troops stopped fighting on 2 September 1945.[4]

Postlude

Lee was eventually wounded in the Philippines by a grenade blast and was finally returned to the United States on 13 December 1945. He reached his home in Iowa on Christmas Eve, with the temperature hovering at 34 degrees below zero, quite a difference from the steaming hot jungles of the Philippines. Little did he realize that five years later he would be fighting again, shivering in the subzero cold of North Korea.[5]

Postscript

To read the rest of the story about Lee Berger and several more of his close call incidents during the Korean War, please go to Chapter 20.

Lee Bergee first contacted me by e-mail on 14 August 2006 and we continued communicating with e-mails on 15, 16 and 18 August. Lee later sent me a copy of an interview that was done for *Military History* magazine in the December 1995 issue. Permission was granted from the editor of *Military History* for the use of the interview on 7 November 2007.

Part Two: Korea

>Fates, we will know your pleasures.
>That we shall die, we know; 'tis but the time,
>And drawing days out, that men stand upon.
>— William Shakespeare

18

USMC Private First Class Herbert Luster

> In life, the only certainty is uncertainty.
> — Robert Levine

Prelude

Herbert Luster was born on 21 June 1931 in the Robertson County city of Hearne, Texas. As a youngster, he loved to play marbles and at just six years old, he received his first BB gun. When he was ten, he got a worn-out .22 Winchester pump rifle, which he carried for miles in the rural McGregor, Texas, area where his family had moved when he was in the 3rd grade after his father had died and his mother remarried. He was now the eldest of six children, including three from his stepdad. He played all sports in season at both junior and senior high school. During World War II, children were asked to donate toys, so he donated over 800 marbles. Years later, he saw Korean children playing marbles and wondered if they were part of his old collection.

At the age of sixteen, he joined the Air National Guard as a medic and drove a field ambulance. He also gave shots to the other Guard members. When he was seventeen and still in the 11th grade, his stepdad urged him to leave home. On 19 August 1948, he joined the Marine Corps in Little Rock, Arkansas. He figured that he was a replacement for his favorite cousin, Dick Stewart. Dick was a Marine who had fought in the Pacific and used a bulldozer to help seal up Japanese soldiers in caves during the Second World War. Although Dick had survived the war, he later died in a barracks fire in Northern China in December 1945.

Herbert attended boot camp in San Diego, California, with Platoon #83. He is still proud to this date that his platoon bested their rival and more senior platoons, #81 and #82, at the rifle range. After boot camp, he was posted to guard duty for a month before being assigned to Midway Island with a guard company of 50 men and officers. The Midway duty was intended to be a one-year tour. However, when Colonel Chesty Puller took over the

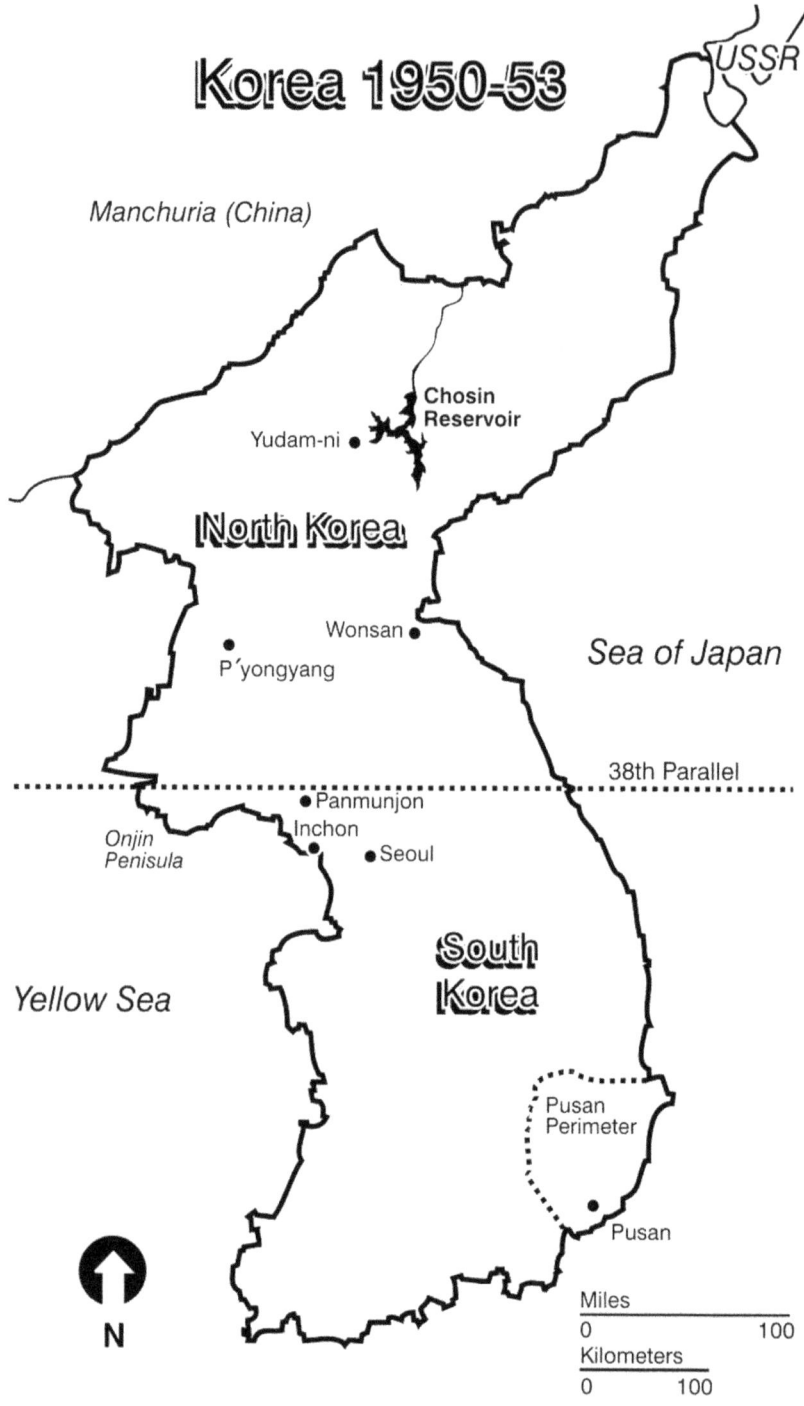

Marine Barracks at Pearl Harbor, he reduced the 50-man contingent to just six and Herbert, along with 43 others, was deployed back to Hawaii. At the Marine Barracks in Pearl Harbor, Luster made Chesty's rifle team and was honored that he got to shake hands with the legendary Marine.[1]

25 June 1950
South Korea

The North Korean People's Army (NKPA) invaded South Korea on 25 June 1950, ending a five-year-old peace. American President Harry Truman quickly responded by deploying United States air and naval assets, followed by a ground commitment on 30 June. The newly formed United Nations (UN) joined in with a 22-nation force, all under the command of General Douglas MacArthur.

When the war broke out, the Marine Corps, like most United States services, was under strength and still equipped with older and sometimes outdated World War II equipment. As the Marines called up reserves and transferred men and equipment to form an entire Marine division (1st Marine Division), it initially put together a provisional brigade designated as the 1st Provisional Marine Brigade. The Brigade was formed from assets of the 1st Marine Division and 1st Marine Aircraft Wing at Camp Pendleton, California. Nearly 7,000 Marines were transferred from the 2nd Marine Division at Camp Lejeune, North Carolina, for both the Brigade and to begin the rebuilding of the 1st Marine Division. The Brigade was activated on 7 July 1950 and built around the 5th Marine Regiment and Marine Aircraft Group 33 (MAG-33). The Brigade was commanded by Brigadier General Edward Craig, who at the time was the 1st Marine Division's assistant commander, while the 5th Marines was led by Lieutenant Colonel Raymond Murray.

At the time, the 5th Marines' three battalions had only two rifle companies each, and every one of these six companies was short about 50 men. The three artillery batteries were short two 105mm howitzers each and the antitank company had no tank platoon. Regardless, the Brigade left from San Diego by ship between 12 and 14 July 1950 and headed initially for Japan. On 25 July, however, it was redirected to South Korea because conditions were deteriorating as the North Koreans were sweeping down the South Korean Peninsula and overwhelming the South Korean Army (ROK) and the American Eighth Army units.[2]

By 2 August 1950, the Eighth Army had crossed the Naktong River and, along with the ROKs, began forming a small toehold defensive perimeter on the southeastern portion of South Korea around the major port city of Pusan, called the Pusan Perimeter. By 4 August, they finally had one continuous line, anchored on the sea at both ends: the Sea of Japan and the Korean Straits. The perimeter was roughly 50 by 90 miles. The defenses also had natural mountain and river barriers, which helped in positioning the Allied forces.

2 August 1950
1st Provisional Marine Brigade
Pusan Perimeter, South Korea

With great timing, the 1st Provisional Marine Brigade landed at Pusan on 2 August, arriving in time to help blunt a North Korean offensive along and west of the Naktong River. Private First Class Luster found himself assigned with Company A, 1st Battalion, 5th Marines (1/5) on those early hot August days in the southwestern part of the Pusan Perimeter. "My fire teammates were Ellis, Koehler and Burton,"[3] Herbert recalls.

On 3 August, the 1st Battalion departed Pusan by motor truck and arrived in Ch'angwon at 1000 hours. All Regimental units joined the 1st Battalion by 1500 that day.

> The road was crowded with people who were loaded down with children and personal belongings. Fear and uncertainty were on their faces. Where were they coming from? Where were they going? They all looked very tired, as they must have walked a long way. Most of the people were going the opposite direction that the Marines were traveling. The road wasn't wide enough for two-way traffic, so the whole scene was a dusty mess.[4]

Routine security patrols continued around Ch'angwon and then at 2130, 5 August, the 5th Marines were told to prepare to move to the vicinity of Chindong-ni, further west, for possible offensive operations against the North Koreans.

> Corporal Evans brought me my mail. I had a letter from Peggy! It didn't take but a few moments to read, "Dear Herbert, I have a boyfriend now and feel I must ask you not to write me again. You will probably be pleased to know that he is a Marine too." It was the old "Dear John" letter so often talked about by sad Marines too far away to compete. I had named my BAR (Browning Automatic Rifle) "Peggy" and decided not to change it. I still liked her anyway.[5]

Now the Marines moved north through the city of Masan and then headed west with an overall objective of Sach'on. By 12 August, the Brigade had advanced as far as Ch'angch'on, where the 1st Battalion, 5th Marines had fought off several NKPA attacks. The Brigade was only four miles away from the objective at Sach'on. The Eighth Army's General Walker now told the Marine brigade to pull out because a large enemy offensive by the NKPA's 4th Division was underway further north near Obong-ni, which was centered in the middle of a looping bulge formed by the Naktong River. The enemy's 4th Division had crossed the Naktong River and was threatening a major breakthrough.

Normally, the Korean summers were drenched with monsoon rains, but in 1950, there was a drought and temperatures soared above 100 degrees. With some difficulty, the Marines were able to pull out and headed towards the Obong-ni area by trucks. Arriving on 16 August, the Marines found the 24th Army Division on their right flank. The battle had been going on in the area for ten days and the Marines were given three ridgeline objectives, each heavily defended by the enemy. The plan was for the Marines to attack the next day at 0800. The coming three-day battle was to be called the First Battle of the Naktong Bulge. The 2nd Battalion, ordered to take the first ridgeline objective at Obong-ni, arrived at their assembly area at 0130. Just one air strike and no artillery, prior to their 0800 attack, hit the ridge. The action was ferocious; the Obong-ni Ridge was taken and lost three times by 2/5, due to intensive enemy automatic fire and the heavy use of grenades.[6]

17 August 1950
Company A, 1/5, 1st Marine Provisional Brigade
Obong-ni Ridge, South Korea

While 2/5 held ground about halfway up the objective, 1/5 was ordered to move forward and pass through 2/5 to continue the assault.

Up ahead was an enemy T-34 tank that had been burned by napalm. To the right was a small hill and the left side dropped off into a swampy flat. The column stayed to the right, against the hill. We could hear a battle raging beyond the hill. Off the road to the high ground, Company A was ordered to wait. I pulled out my food and decided to eat a can of peaches but my stomach protested and I gave the can to my new assistant BAR man, Pfc Baxter.

The company hit the road again. The T-34 sat where the road turned to the right and the column halted once more. Baxter and I took positions up the hill from the tank beside a bean patch. The pole beans offered some shade from the high sun. I placed my rifle near Baxter, laid on my back, and through the leaves of the bean plants looked up at the blue sky. I had just begun to feel better when I started to notice something hit the top of the vines. I couldn't see a bird or grasshopper. It happened again

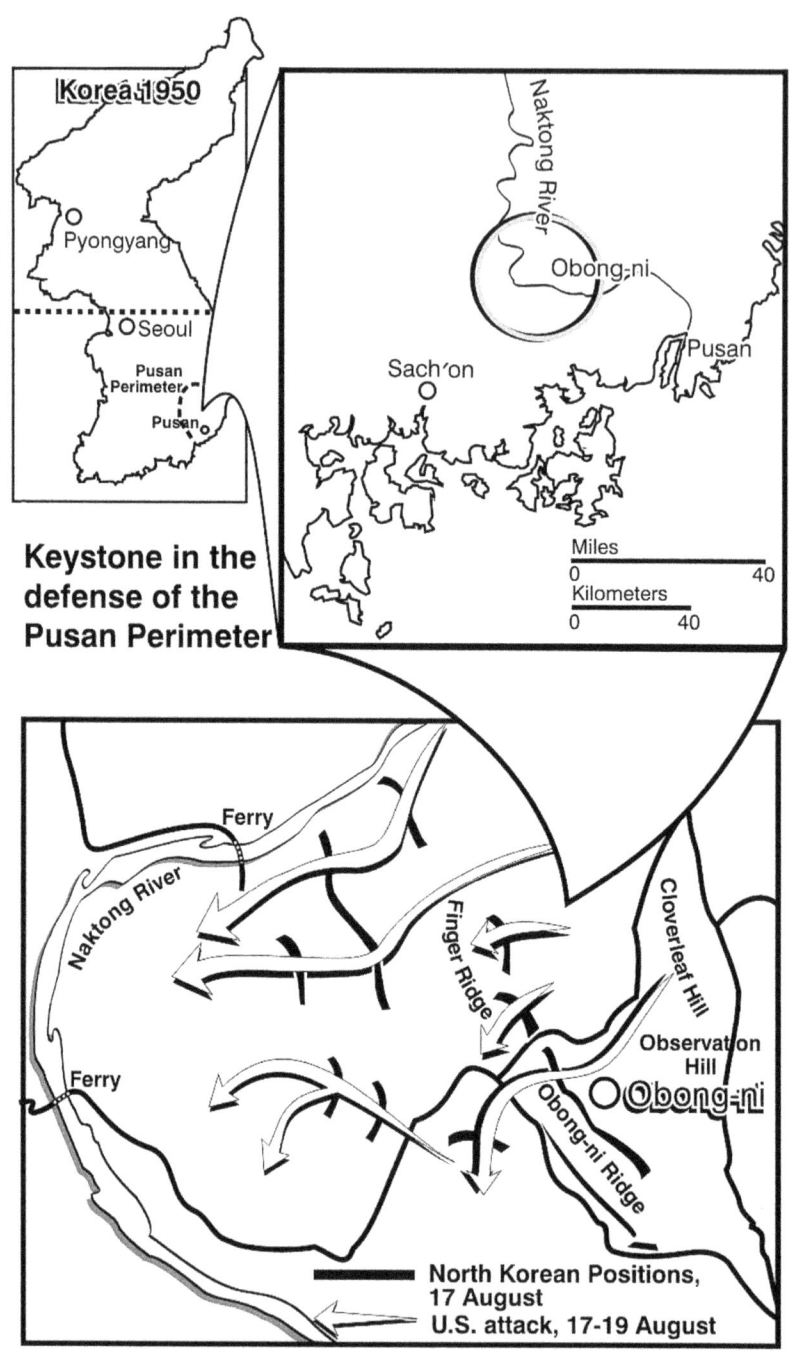

First Battle of The Naktong Bulge

and this time it was no mistake. Someone was shooting at our hill and hitting the beans above me. The order came to "saddle up."

Waiting on the side of the dusty road, I began looking above a little village situated up on the hill. I saw a soldier get shot as he tried crossing an open space near a clump of pines. I then watched him work his way down to the road. By the time my fire-team reached the cut in the road, I had seen many wounded men carried out of the valley. A Pershing M-26 tank sat just past the cut where the road turned to the right around the hill. It served as a shield. Nearby, a dead soldier lay face up on a slab of rock. As we took a path leaving the main road, we walked past a grass hut with three dead soldiers lying beside it. One had his eyes open; they were blue and seemed to say, "It's not my time to get up for guard duty."

The valley of rice paddies was divided by a small creek lined with cool, shady willow trees. Beyond the creek stood a large beautiful tree, with enough shade for all of A Company. From where I stood, it looked like a big Arkansas oak. For a second, I wondered if I'd see Arkansas again. We stopped at the creek for final orders. The gunny gave it to us straight. He wanted my fire-team to flank a saddle about 400 yards away. He pointed out a machine gun position and said they would provide fire support if needed. I asked about the high ground to our backs. I didn't want to be shot in the back like some men had experienced earlier on the Kosong and Sach'on roads. "Don't worry about that hill," the sergeant reassured. "Good luck, men."[7]

By 1300, the 1st Battalion had passed through the depleted remnants of the 2nd Battalion. The 2/5 had suffered 23 dead and 119 wounded since their morning attack.

Off we went, passing the .30 caliber air-cooled Browning machine gun. As we started up through the dry fields above the valley floor, the gunner wished us well. The men spread out five yards apart to present a poor target. The scrubby pines were thick and a whole platoon of enemy could be concealed there. As the hill got steeper, I slipped the rifle sling over my head so both hands would be free to climb. It was so hot and humid that our sweat never dried. We were constantly soaked. My BAR hung in front of me so I could fire quickly if needed. Suddenly, a recoilless 75mm rifle opened up on our objective. The whole team stopped. "Move out," came a shout from the valley! I moved ahead faster.[8]

It was useless to be cautious. Because the young pines were thick, I couldn't see ten feet ahead of myself. Suddenly, I broke through on the top of the ridge. Although I couldn't see the other side, I could see everything on this side. There was the saddle. Gunny didn't say what to do when we got to the top. Everything was quiet except my heart. Had the enemy gone from the hill while I was climbing? No, men began to crawl quickly from the crest to the saddle and uncovered their guns. By now, it was around 1600 in the late afternoon.

"Evans, do we have anyone in that direction?" I quickly asked. "No," was his reply. "Send some machine gun fire up that draw," I ordered. I could see a fire team of four men in A Company walking right towards the enemy position I had spotted. Someone asked, "Do you still see them?" It was evident that no one saw the enemy but me. I started to throw a grenade, but remembered the sarge said to save them for use at night. I pulled back the bolt to cock the action of the BAR, pushed off the safety, settled back on my right foot and opened fire. The flying dirt and tracers told me where my rounds were going. I emptied the rifle. I pulled the sling back over my head, pushed the magazine release, but it didn't fall out. I pushed the release with my right thumb and pulled the empty magazine out. I stuck it in my pocket, reloaded and raised the BAR to my shoulder. Before I got it all the way up, red dirt kicked up in my face. A big jerk at my right arm told me I'd been hit. I looked down and saw blood squirting onto the broken BAR stock.

I had taken a four-round automatic burst from a Russian burp gun. One round had exploded my rifle stock, exposing my cleaning gear that I stored in the base of the stock. I was truly lucky that only one of the four rounds had hit me. I should have died right then and there. Remembering my first aid, I lay back in the shallow ditch and tried to relax my body. "I'm hit, pretty bad," I called to my team. "Where?" came the reply. "In the arm," I returned. Then the whole ridge exploded. My teammates were all wounded and Koehler was killed.

A Corsair aircraft swooped down to fire on the saddle area. I put my left arm over my face to protect it from the falling empty machine gun shells. Soon Corporal Evans appeared and tore open my right shirtsleeve. He then disappeared as fast as he had come. "Corpsman! Corpsman up!" Then there was silence. Evans had spoken to me and I was sure he was the one who had called for the corpsman. I got in position to roll to the brink of the ridge. My right arm flopped loosely. I began to scoot down the hill until my wounded arm was caught on a scrub pine. I was stuck!

All I could do was wait. Because of the loss of blood, my eyesight was failing. However, I could still identify the valley below and the place where I had earlier seen the dead soldiers.[9] As my blood gushed out of my arm, I asked God to "Please give me one more shot at life on this earth."[10]

Two corpsmen, Green and Babbick, finally found me and we continued on the journey towards the aid station. They eventually retrieved a litter and, after great difficulty, were able to get me on it. "Don't worry, Marine," they assured me. "We can get you back now." I could see my beautiful tree again and knew that I was only 300 yards away from the road. We made it to the road and a tall black man lifted me off the stretcher and onto a small ambulance jeep. "You're going to be all right, Marine," someone calmly said. The next thing I knew, I was inside a large tent. After checking my blood type and trying to find a vein that hadn't collapsed, the doctors finally were able to perform a blood plasma transfusion. Soon I felt a cooling in my arm, chest, legs and feet. I would later learn that of the corpsmen that had initially helped me, Babbick was killed and Green lost a finger.

With some of the other wounded men, I was quickly loaded into a field ambulance. The driver and guard continually talked as they drove down the rough road. Each time the ambulance hit a bump, all of the men in the back groaned. By the number of the voices, I guessed about six or eight men were taking the ride. Someone shouted, "Slow down, you're killing these guys." "I can't," the driver returned, "or we won't make it."

One time, the ambulance was fired on and the guard returned the fire with his dinky little carbine. It was a long ride before we jerked to a stop. Relaxed and confident voices appeared at the back door and strong limbs picked us up. Soon we were boarded onto a train, nicknamed the "Purple Heart Express." I now had lost all track of time, but I did recognize the dimly lighted rail yard at Miryang, a friendly town with lots of water, cool and peaceful.[11]

While Private First Class Luster and other wounded Marines were making the painful journey back to a naval hospital, the Brigade was preparing for its first night on the Bulge battlefield. The 1st Battalion's two rifle companies had not been able to dislodge the North Koreans from the hills that dominated the Obong-ni Ridge. They dug in for the night as the sun went down. The night brought counterattacks with tanks, automatic weapons and extensive use of enemy grenades that came raining down upon the Company A Marines, eventually diminishing at daylight. In the morning of 18 August, 1/5 brought the attack against the NKPA and finally retook the Obong-ni Ridge. The 3/5 now moved through 1/5 and carried the fight to the second objective at Hill 207. By the next day, things had stabilized with the enemy in full retreat.[12]

On the way to Pusan, I was restless and could not move. My right hand burned and there was no relief. How long could I last? I asked myself how much I could endure. My limit was fast approaching. The train finally stopped and the side doors slid open. "Over here," someone called hurriedly. "This guy is in bad shape." Two Americans quickly moved me to the door of the railcar. I was placed on the dock and a line was lowered from the boom of the ship. The handles of my litter were fastened to the cable and up I went, suspended in midair above the Pusan pier. [Luster had been loaded onto the hospital ship, the USS *Consolation* (AH-15).] Before I knew it, someone had placed a mask over my face. "Breathe deeply, please," came the matter-of-fact command. Time was gone and I dreamed.

I awoke, moaning and groaning. I slowly moved my body to stretch, all except my right arm. It seemed to be anchored to the bed. I strained to look at it to see what was wrong. All I could see were clean white sheets. My right shoulder was anchored to the hospital bed. A pulley with about five pounds of weight was where my arm used to be. I was alive, but part of me was gone![13]

Postlude

Except for mopping-up operations, the First Battle of the Naktong Bulge was over. The fight had cost the Marines 66 dead and 278 wounded. The NKPA had lost all of its heavy equipment and weapons and had been virtually destroyed. Only 300–400 men were left in the 4th NKPA Division. With the Naktong Bulge safe, at least for the moment, the 1st Marine Brigade was released and went into the Eighth Army reserves. On 20 August, the 5th Marines moved down into the vicinity of Masan. By 1 September, the North Koreans launched another offensive along the Naktong Bulge and, once again, the Brigade was ordered back to counterattack. After four days of severe fighting, the Marines were again pulled off on the night of 5 September. In the 65 days in the Pusan Perimeter, they had suffered 148 men killed and 730 wounded. It was estimated that the enemy had over 9,900 killed and wounded. General MacArthur had now conceived a new and bold plan where he would soon utilize the services of the Brigade. The 1st Marine Provisional Brigade was deactivated and again became part of the 1st Marine Division on 13 September 1950.[14]

After leaving Pusan on the hospital ship, Luster was first taken to a remote island with what he describes as lots of tree and birds. The ship's next stop was Japan and then on to Wake Island. From Wake Island, he boarded a plane to Hawaii, where he soon left for the Travis Air Force Base in California. He finally ended up at the Naval Hospital at Oakland, California. Luster spent a total of 7½ months in hospitals, including a month's leave from California to Arkansas. In Los Angeles, he got on a quiz show and won four new $10 bills. "I was rich!"

He was medically retired from the Marine Corps at Treasure Island, California. "I was the first amputee to be released from the Korean War. I received my Purple Heart in a hospital gown at the Oakland Navy Hospital. I was now known by my new nickname, 'Lefty,' and attended colleges in Hawaii and in Arkadelphia, Arkansas. On 24 December 1951, I convinced Romaine Hall to marry me."

After a full life of working, he retired in November 1996 due to heart problems. He and his wife had five sons and two daughters. They now have 16 grandsons, two granddaughters, two great-grandsons, one great-granddaughter and "two more on the way!" He also teaches a men's Bible class in Big Spring, Texas.

Lefty is still a gunman. He hikes every day and shoots regularly at a target in his backyard with his small-bore rifle. In the 1980s, Lefty took his wife, Romaine, to tour Korea. "We stayed on to teach English conversation at Masan and other places, but eventually had difficulty with our visas because the Korean government was paranoid." They both walked the same roads that Lefty and his 1/5 unit had taken in 1950.

I have been a member of the Veterans of Foreign Wars, the Disabled American Veterans, and am still active in the local Marine Corps League. I never miss a Marine Corps Birthday (10 November). I attended many reunions until my health prohibited it, including the 1st Marine Division, A-1/5 and B-1/5. I am now the sole survivor of my Korean Fire Team. I still constantly think of my wartime experiences. I never miss a day with my empty sleeve as a reminder. I had asked God for another chance at life and it was granted. Amen![15]

In April 2006, I received a postcard from Lefty briefly telling me about losing his arm in Korea. He told me that everything about the incident was already reported in a book by Don Knox, titled *The Korean War: Pusan to Chosin, An Oral History*. Curious, I purchased a used copy from Amazon.com. At first, I was not sure if I wanted to use the story, so I filed the card away. On 30 June, he sent me an additional postcard because he had read another ad that I had placed in *Military* magazine. I revisited his story and realized that I wanted a chapter centered on the early Pusan Perimeter Battle to round out my Part II on the Korean War.

I sent Lefty a questionnaire to retrieve additional information and he quickly responded on 26 July 2006. Sadly, in a note dated 9 September 2007, I learned from Lefty's wife of 55 years that he is now suffering from Lewy Body Dementia.

On 30 October 2007, I receive non-exclusive permission to reprint portions of Don Knox's book from Harcourt, Inc.

19

USMC Sergeant Kermit Wilhelm

> Go and wake up your luck.
> — Persian saying

Prelude

Kermit "Kurt" Wilhelm was born and raised in south Minneapolis, Minnesota, and upon graduating from Roosevelt High School in 1948, he found himself without a full-time job like many other young men. They were competing with thousands of servicemen who had recently returned from World War II overseas duty. He and three friends decided to join the military together and flipped a coin to pick the branch of service. The coin toss was for the Navy and the young men went down to the recruiter the next day. The Navy representative told them that there were no openings right then, but there would be in a week and they would all be called back in. A couple of days went by and while Kurt was working a part-time job, he missed the phone call from the recruiter. By the time he showed up at the Navy office, his friends were gone. A little upset that he could not join in with his buddies, he crossed the hallway and joined the Marines! After boot camp in San Diego, California, he ended up in Guam for the next two years. "We trained, and we trained and we trained. We chased each other around the jungle. It was a real challenge to try to outdo each other. It never got boring, as there was always something to do. I think we were the best-trained Marines ever. Nobody ever had that much training."

In early 1950, the Marines in Wilhelm's unit returned to Camp Pendleton, California, because their Guam base had been devastated by a tremendous typhoon. The Marines began a rotating 30-day leave, one-third of the group at a time. When North Korea attacked South Korea and the American troops stationed there in June 1950, Wilhelm's unit was sent overseas again, this time with the newly formed 1st Provisional Marine Brigade.

August 1950
Pusan Perimeter
1st Provisional Marine Brigade

We were supposed to go to Korea and form a division, but we were told that Korea was going to go down the toilet if we didn't get there fast. Our transport went directly to Pusan. The perimeter around the town at that point in early August had shrunk to about 50 to 75 miles. It was the Allies' last foothold in the country. We were a pretty "gung ho" group of guys. We could hardly wait until we got into battle. That lasted until the first firefight. I was a machine gunner in charge of one assistant gunner and six ammo carriers. The machine gun weighed 30 pounds and the men would take turns carrying it on a long march. After a while, your arm and fingers became numb. Someone would have to take the gun from you because you couldn't put it down.

The 1st Marine Brigade's job was to take the hills around the perimeter and begin to push the North Koreans back. Looking back at the situation, I saw that the Army personnel were in a difficult situation, lacking proper wartime training and having been sent there as peacetime occupational troops. At the time, though, there was some animosity between the Marines and the Army. Sometimes we'd take a hill, turn it over to them and then a few days later we'd have to go back and take it again.

The going was very tough at first. The men only carried ammunition and C-rations and there was little transportation. I think we only had hot food once or twice in the first 30 days. We got pretty beat up and we lost several people. When they finally pulled us back, we set up in a soybean field. Our clothes were just rags by then. It was 95 or 100 degrees every day with humidity about the same, and the clothes just rotted off our backs. We just threw them into a pile and burned them.

I only carried one canteen at first, but soon acquired another. Guys were getting dizzy and passing out from the heat. You didn't dare drink out of the rice paddies because they were fertilized with human excrement. If you did drink the local water, you immediately went to sickbay to get some paregoric to plug up your butt.

The basic operation was for the Marines to head down a road until they encountered enemy fire from a surrounding hill. Then they would go and take the hill. Sergeant Wilhelm usually set up his .30 caliber Model 1918-A1 (BAR) machine gun in a position where he could cover the attack, often firing directly over the charging Marines' heads. The gun could fire 250 rounds per minute, with every fifth round a tracer so the gunner could adjust his aim.

I loved being a machine gunner. We had practiced so much. It was great when you set up, and gauged the distance and fired off a burst and you saw the hat flying off the enemy. You knew you'd done it just right. I had become so familiar with the weapon during the training on Guam and probably cleaned it a thousand times, that I think I could still take it apart with my eyes closed.

The success of the Marines in pushing back the North Koreans was due in part because most of our NCOs and officers were World War II veterans with lots of combat experience. One of them was our gunnery sergeant. He had eyes like an eagle and he saved my life more than once. We probably took 15 or 20 hills in 30 days and each one was a challenge. Guys would get to the top of the hill when it was over and they'd just start babbling. The adrenalin was going so fast. It just took a while to slow down and to realize that we're on top of the hill and alive.

September 1950
Inchon and Seoul, Korea
1st Marine Division

With the perimeter secure around Pusan, the Brigade pulled out on ships and once again became part of the 1st Marine Division. Wilhelm's parent unit was now Company G, 3rd Battalion, 5th Marines (3/5), 1st Marine Division. General MacArthur planned the landing at Inchon, on the west side of the peninsula, for 15 September 1950. Wilhelm's unit was assigned the task of taking Wolmi-do, an island that strategically controlled the port of Inchon. The island had been hit by shelling for several days before the landing. Most of the North Koreans who had survived the shelling were in bunkers and caves, and had to be coaxed out or killed.

We took the island in two or three hours and then we were done. There was kind of a dome shape to the island and we sat on top watching the landing at Inchon. It was like watching a movie. We were too far away to fire so we just sat there and watched. It was a great show.

The fighting moved through Inchon and up into Seoul. At one point, they dumped us off in a field and the North Koreans were all around us, running in all directions. We felt like Custer at his last stand. It was a hell of a wild fight that lasted maybe three or four minutes. That was one of the luckiest and wildest times that I remember in Korea.

In Seoul, Wilhelm's unit happened to be the one that captured the National Capitol Building and the men were able to raise the American flag

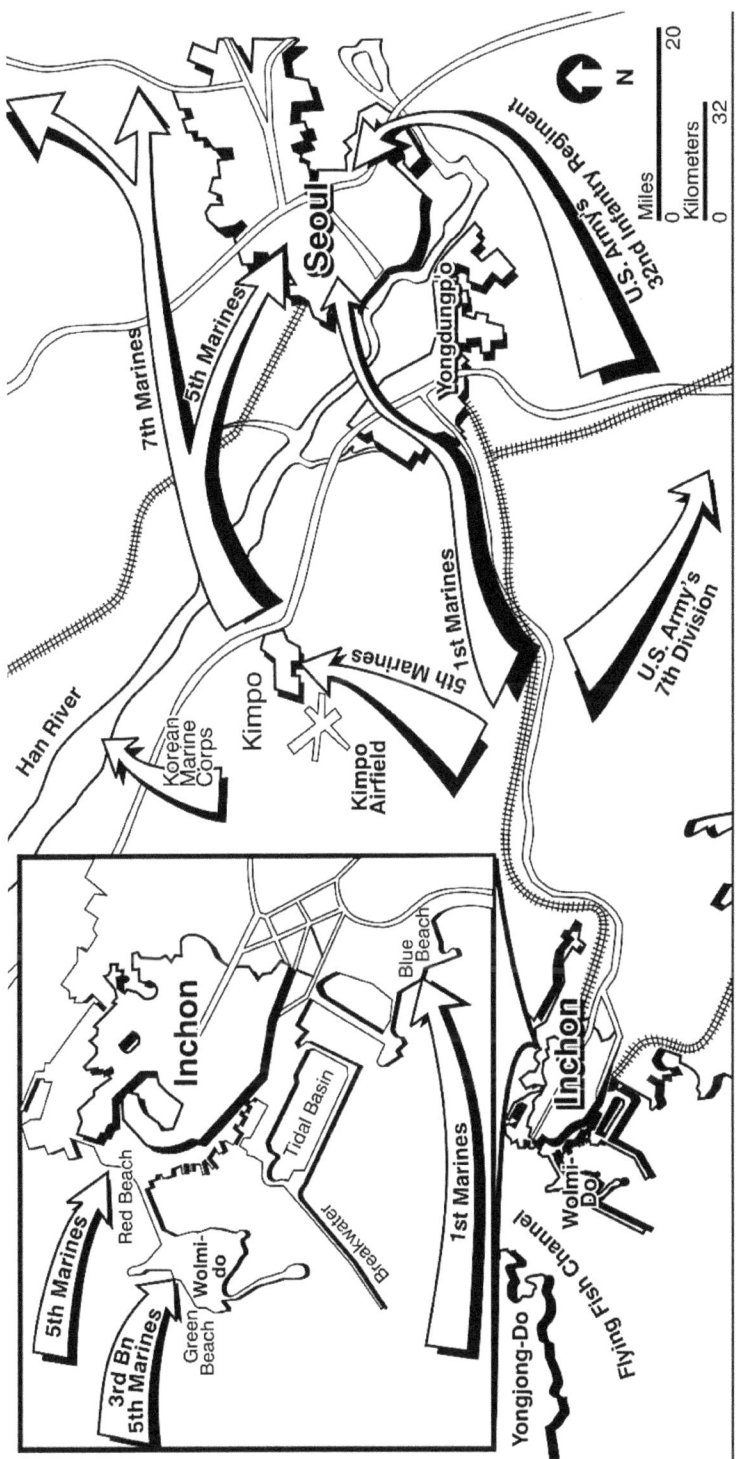

Inchon To Seoul, 15 to 29 September, 1950

atop the building. The area was soon host to Allied dignitaries. "I saw MacArthur and all the other officers with their chrome helmets. 'Dugout Doug' [MacArthur] had an ego as big as a truck. He had an opportunity there to back off, but he didn't. Once the Chinese intervened, it was another three more years of war." Not long after, Wilhelm and the 3/5 were brought back to Inchon where they were loaded on transports again and brought up to the east coast of Korea.

November 1950
3rd Battalion, 5th Marines
Chosin Reservoir Area

The 3/5 headed up to Hagaru-ri on the southern edge of the Chosin Reservoir and then took a position on the east side of the Reservoir for a couple days before being relieved by an Army unit. Wilhelm and his comrades then marched up the west side of the Reservoir to a spot near Yudam-ni, about 14 miles northwest of Hagaru-ri. It was about 15 degrees below zero at night. The 3/5 was the northernmost force on 27 November 1950.

It got kind of wild and wooly. I was sleeping on a frozen rice paddy and I just had time to get my boots on when a bunch of Chinamen came around a hillside. We were lined up along a road and the Chinese were on the other side of the road.

The Marines beat off the attack and recaptured the hill that overlooked the valley where they had been.

As the fighting continued, Wilhelm was at his machine gun and the bullets were whizzing by. "The assistant gunner was bringing up more ammo but he got wounded. I got up to get the ammo. I had just picked up the other can and was asking him how he was when the lights went out. The next thing I knew I was on my hands and knees and there was a singing in my ears. It was like a siren going off and there was blood everywhere." One bullet had passed through Wilhelm's parka and cut a pack of cigarettes in half. Another severed the chinstrap of his helmet. A third hit him in the cheek, slicing through the bottom of his nose. A fourth bullet glanced off the middle of his forehead. "It just sort of bounced off this thick head of mine. I'll never know for sure what hit me, but I am almost positive it was a Russian-made burp gun." At the time, Kurt did not know just how lucky he had been.

"We called for a corpsman, and I was helping my assistant when he looked at me and said, 'Christ, Kurt, they shot your nose off!' I wanted to put my hand there and touch it to see how bad it was, but I couldn't. I didn't have the courage to touch my own face." The corpsman gave Wilhelm a shot of morphine and wrapped bandages all around his head, leaving only a narrow slit to see through. He and three other wounded men walked down the hill as darkness was settling in. "The walking didn't bother me but I had a really bad headache.

"The aid station was in a farmhouse and the doctor re-bandaged me with some smaller stuff. I wanted a cigarette and that's when I saw my pack had been shot in half. A corpsman took me over to a corner and gave me a little pill and one of his cigarettes. I took three or four drags and that was the last thing I remember until the next morning."

Wilhelm was strapped to the hood of a jeep in a sleeping bag as the Marines began their slow withdrawal from the Yudam-ni area. "The heat from the engine kept me warm, but after a couple of days, I noticed a guy who was shot up really bad. I told them I could walk and this other guy could take my place on the jeep. I walked and I rode on a trailer full of dead and wounded for a while. It took us four days to go 16 miles. We weren't moving too damn fast."

As the column neared Hagaru-ri, an officer began gathering up all of the walking wounded into a temporary unit. "He got us organized and we marched into Hagaru. I heard someone say as we marched by, "Look at those magnificent bastards." The temperature was still sub-zero and Wilhelm was taken into a hospital tent with a heater. "I hadn't eaten in three or four days and I was just so damned tired. In the tent, there was a big bowl of Tootsie Rolls there and we helped ourselves. Within minutes, the whole group of us was asleep. Half of the guys fell asleep with the Tootsie Rolls in their mouths."

Postlude

From Hagaru-ri, Kurt was flown by a C-47 to the Korean coast and then on to Japan, where he stayed at an Army hospital for two months. "It was so nice to be warm again." All good things must come to an end, so in late February, he rejoined his old unit that was now fighting in central Korea around the line that was later drawn to divide North and South Korea. After just three weeks back on the front lines, he received his orders to return home due to a rotation schedule that gave extra credit for being wounded.

On my last day in Korea, we were involved in a firefight. We had been sent out to rescue a patrol. As it turned out, the enemy was on one side of the hill and we were on the other side. We were lobbing hand grenades back and forth at each other. All of a sudden, a runner came up and said the gunny and I were to report to headquarters to be sent home. I took my last grenade and threw it over the hill and then I walked down. That was the end of my career at war.

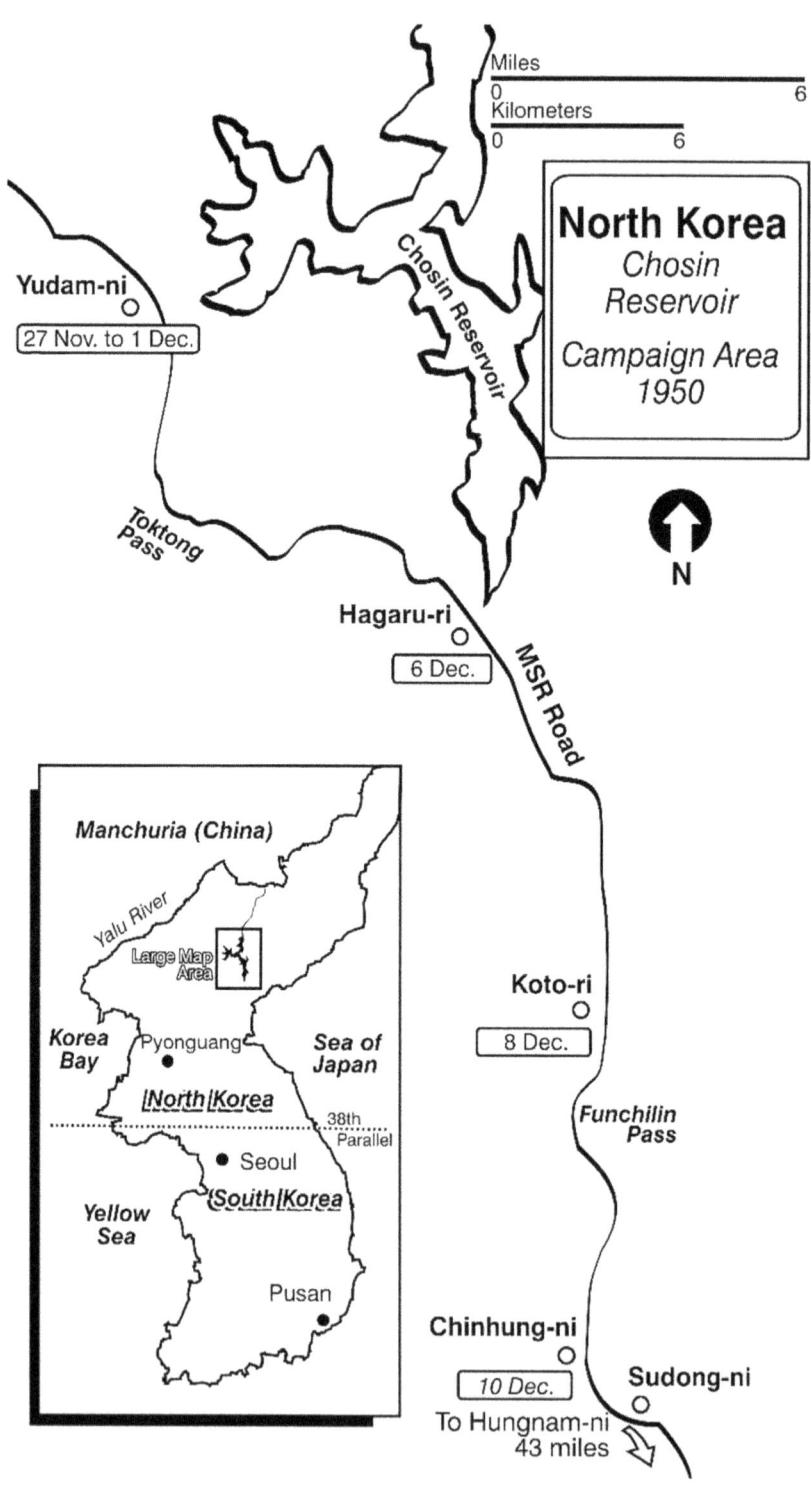

Kurt finished his enlistment at the Naval Air Station in Memphis, Tennessee, and was honorably discharged from the Marines in August 1952. He had signed up for three years, but ended up serving for four. He became a surveyor in civilian life and became the chief surveyor in a nine-state region for the United States Department of Fish and Wildlife. He retired in 1986 and now resides in Burnside, Minnesota. He and his wife, Fern, had two daughters. It has taken over four operations over the years to allow Wilhelm to breathe through his nose correctly.[1]

On 26 July 2006, I came across the online story of Kurt Wilhelm from a newsletter link on the Minnesota American Legion website. After several attempts to locate Mr. Wilhelm and the Minnesota American Legion, I finally located the editor, Al Zdon, who writes the "War Stories" for the website. He also produced a book, titled *War Stories: Accounts of Minnesotans Who Defended Their Nation*. On 14 November 2007, Mr. Zdon e-mailed me and granted me permission to use Kurt's and three other stories from the website and book.

20

USMC Staff Sergeant Lee Bergee (Part 2 of 2)

> If fate means you to lose, give him a good fight anyhow.
> — William McFee

Prelude

After World War II, Lee decided to remain in the Marines and spent the next few years on bases at Camp Pendleton, California; Camp Lejeune, North Carolina; and Little Creek, Virginia.

At the outbreak of the Korean War in June 1950, Lee Bergee was a staff sergeant assigned to a scout-sniper platoon attached to the newly formed 1st Provisional Marine Brigade. Lee was about to live a charmed life with a series of no less than four very close calls, prior to his luck finally running out during the Chosin Campaign.[1]

August 1950
South Korea

Lee arrived in Korea on 4 August 1950 and assisted in the defense of the Pusan Perimeter. While fighting in the Naktong River area he had his first of several near misses. "I felt my left shoepac [World War II winter-issued boots] suddenly become untied. A bullet had severed the shoelace!"[2]

* * * *

After the Pusan Perimeter fighting, Lee and the 1st Marine Brigade joined the 1st Marine Division on ships and landed at Inchon. Lee was now assigned as a platoon sergeant with E Company, 2nd Battalion, 1st Marines (2/1).[3] About two miles east of Ascome City, which was on the outskirts of Inchon, Lee's unit hit their first enemy resistance.

It was 17 September and our company outflanked a North Korean roadblock and came across an enemy force. We killed about twenty of them who were entrenched on Hill 208. I remember throwing a grenade at their position and in turn, they would throw three right back at me. Later I located a hidden T-34 enemy tank in a hut. I found one of our tanks and instructed them where the tank was hiding. It fired and both the hut and tank blew up before the enemy crew could shoot at us. The next day we took the city of Sosa. It was during this battle that I had my canteen shot off my cartridge belt. Later that night, when I grabbed for my entrenching tool to dig my evening foxhole, I found that the handle had also been shot off.[4]

He was with the Division as it retook Inchon and Seoul, the capital city of South Korea. After the fighting stabilized and now favored the United Nations' forces, the Marines once again loaded onto ships and went around the southern peninsula and northwards to the North Korean port city of Wonsan. From Wonsan, the Marines continued heading north in vehicles and on foot along the eastern side the country towards the Chosin Reservoir. The 1st Marines, under Colonel Chesty Puller, was responsible for maintaining the main supply route from Koto-ri to the Chosin Reservoir area.[5]

I will never forget the temperature in December 1950, which averaged around 40 degrees below zero. The water in our canteens froze. We had to work the operating handles on the breechblocks of our M-1 rifles every now and then so they wouldn't freeze shut. Standing watch, you stomped your feet constantly and wiggled your toes inside your shoepacs to keep the circulation going. The cold seeped through your clothing and you were always miserable. The wind hit your face until it was raw and the blinding snow whipped into your eyes and half-blinded you as you searched for enemy activity. You dreamed of being close to a roaring fire. I remember at Koto-ri when several of us set a railroad boxcar on fire and climbed inside until the flames drove us out. One morning at Regimental Headquarters, the thermometer registered minus 54 degrees!

I first realized that we had been surrounded when our battalion mail jeep came back full of holes after running into an enemy roadblock. We had been told that there were six Chinese divisions around us, but it didn't sink in until that jeep came back.

I just got out of my sleeping bag one dark night, took two steps, and a burp gun cut loose and sent about 20 rounds into my bag. The down feathers really flew.[6]

* * * *

"Compared to the Japanese, the Chinese were not very good fighters. They would try to overwhelm you with sheer manpower. They were, however, extremely disciplined and tough. We killed so many Chinese who attacked us that they were finished as a fighting unit. That unit never entered into combat again during the Korean War. There were individual acts of heroism by Chinese soldiers, but generally, they depended on their strength in numbers. I shall never forget the many nights of massed attacks by the enemy. The damn bugles blaring in the cold night air, the yelling of the Chinese as they swarmed toward our positions wave upon wave. Those sights and sounds will always remain in my memory. Everywhere you looked, there were charging Chinese. It reminded me of knocking over an anthill and watching the ants scamper to and fro.[7]

* * * *

On 7 December, I had a Chinese grenade land on the top of my pack. I could hear it sizzling but I just couldn't shake it off and it remained stuck. It never did explode![8] I vividly remember another time when a Chinese soldier hit me with his fist right on my frozen nose. Well, that made me mad and I grabbed him and bit off his ear. Yep, I really did. I bit his ear off and then killed him.[9]

* * * *

The corpsmen and doctors were superb, as always. Those Navy people had to administer first aid and operate under severe conditions and always with a good possibility of being killed. Several times, Chinese infiltrators would tear a long slit in the medical tents and try to get inside, shooting anyone who got in their way. One ambulance, on the road between Koto-ri and Hagaru-ri, was machine-gunned viciously and the chaplain of one of our regiments was killed, along with his assistant and the wounded on board. Yes, the medical personnel were heroes in the truest sense of the word. They were under constant fire and there was no such thing as a hospital. The corpsmen had to keep the hypodermic syringes taped in their armpits to keep the liquid in the syringes from freezing solid. They also stuffed morphine ampules inside their mouths to keep the doses from freezing. One corpsman told me, "By the time you would cut through the different layers of clothing to reach the wounds, your hands would be numb from the cold." One thing I might mention is that it was so cold that when one was wounded, the blood didn't run as it did in the tropics. The blood coagulated, which saved many a Marine's life.[10]

* * * *

On 9 December, on the road just outside the Koti-ri, an enemy 122mm mortar shell ended my good luck. It hit six of us, killing five and sending shrapnel into my legs, left arm, chest and my back. I was evacuated via air from the Koti-ri airstrip.[11] I barely remember the field hospital down in the valley at Hamhung. In the hospital tent I overheard a doctor telling a corpsman, "Put that one over there. He won't make it." How I prayed it wasn't me he was talking about.[12]

Postlude

Lee was initially flown to the bottom of the mountain and then on to the Naval Hospital at Yokosuka, Japan. On his birthday, 13 January 1951, he landed at the Naval Hospital at Oak Knoll, California. He was eventually transferred to the Philadelphia Naval Hospital to be closer to home. After recuperating, Lee remained in the Marine Corps and served as a recruiter, senior drill instructor, staff NCO Leadership School instructor and a special ceremony drill sergeant.[13]

I was finally medically retired on 11 May 1956, after a 12-year shortened career. In 1956, I visited Lieutenant General Lewis B. "Chesty" Puller at his home in Virginia and the first thing he said to me as we shook hands was, "Have you thawed out yet, Sarge?" After 15 years, the first thing he mentioned was the cold. Yes, we all have our memories of buddies killed, of the hordes of Chinese assaulting our frozen lines and the long, dangerous walk out, but I truly believe the uppermost thought in our minds, when we think of that campaign, is the cold! [The first thing] I said to myself, when I awoke at a naval hospital in Japan after being evacuated from Koto-ri, was, "I pray that I NEVER am this cold ever again."[14]

We Marines always knew that in the morning light we would find our buddies still next to us, dead or alive. The Corps' justifiable pride in itself is not built on braggadocio but on actual accomplishment. Writers who were not there have written many articles about the Chosin fight. We were a band of brothers and we were coming out of that trap like Marines, or we weren't coming out at all.[15]

Lee eventually married and had four wonderful children: Cheryl, Lynda, Eric and Michael. He attended 3½ years at State University of Iowa, majoring in creative writing. Lee has written two books. His first book, *Rendezvous with Hell*, published in 1963, is about the Korean War. His 1987 book *Guests of the Emperor* is the story of a former Japanese prisoner of war, Corporal Frank O. Promnitz. This latter book was selected for the Bataan Memorial Museum library in Santa Fe, New Mexico. He has held numerous jobs including newspaper managing editor, freelance writer and photographer. He has participated in Civil War reenactments, given speeches to high schools about his combat experiences, coached Little League, served as a Scoutmaster, and run a self-storage facility during his long life. He currently is retired and enjoys writing and reading.

Lee belongs to the Military Order of the Purple Heart, the Marine Corps Association and the "Chosin Few."[16]

> I believe that God walked with me through the valley of the shadow of death, believe me.[17] As they say, one sign of age is a tendency to live in the past. I now understand why. It is only after a life filled with living and sharing love with someone you cherish and adore that you can savor the meaning and importance of an experience such as the "Chosin Few" shared. The bad memories I can live with and the good memories I treasure. I have come to believe that I have an obligation to the future, to give young people the chance to have a meaningful understanding of the past and the glory that was, though only in retrospect. It is important, not to me, but to the future."[18]

This second chapter on Lee continues his Marine Corps Career after World War II and into the Korean War. The editor of *Military History* magazine authorized permission to use a December 1995 interview article about Lee on 7 November 2007.

21

USMC Sergeant Joe Ohman

> Whatever the universal nature assigns to any man at
> any time is for the good of that man at that time.
> — Marcus Aurelius

Prelude

Joe Ohman grew up on the north side of Minneapolis, Minnesota, where he graduated from high school in 1947. He was one of five brothers and the oldest suggested that he join the Marine Corps, which he did. He enlisted in the Marine Corps Reserves with the 4th Infantry Battalion. For the next four years he continued his part-time Marine career by attending two-week training at various east coast bases during the summers and weekly evening drills at the local Naval Air Station in Minneapolis.

In 1950, the 20-year-old Joe was working as a store manager at the Minneapolis Honeywell Company. At the time, the fighting in Korea had begun and the Marines of the 4th Battalion knew there was a possibility that they would be called up to active duty.

"We knew there was a chance we'd get called up, but we really didn't believe it. This was during the time when they pushed those guys off the beach. We were pretty concerned, but it was all scuttlebutt."

At one of their weekly drill meetings, the rumors finally came to an end. The reserve Marines were called to active duty on 1 August 1950 and departed two days later by train to the west coast, destined for Camp Pendleton, California. Once at the base, the Marines trained intensively and began preparations for war. "It seemed like we went 24 hours a day there. We were getting all of our gear and we were firing all of our weapons." The 4th Battalion was broken up and filled gaps in the 1st and 2nd Battalion, 7th Marines, 1st Marine Division. Joe, by now a sergeant, was assigned to Fox Company in the 2nd Battalion as a squad leader in charge of rocket launchers designed to be used against the Russian T-34 medium tanks that were being used by the North Koreans.

With just two weeks of training, the Marines boarded ships and headed out to sea and towards an unknown destination. "We thought we might be going to Hawaii. The scuttlebutt was flying around the ship, but as usual, it was all wrong. We got to Hawaii and went right by it." The ships landed later in Kobe, Japan, and the men were allowed a few hours of liberty. "There was just enough time for a few beers and then back on board."[1]

Inchon, South Korea
September 1950

The ships landed four days after the initial attack at Inchon while some fighting was still going on within this port city on the mid-western part of the Korean peninsula. The Marines went ashore at Wolmi-do Island and moved across the causeway and onto the Korean mainland. "It was our job to punch through and go north of Seoul into the mountains. We would cut off the retreat of the North Koreans as they headed north." By now, Ohman's nine-man squad had uncrated, and were carrying, their new rocket launchers. They were a larger version of launchers that had been used earlier, but unsuccessfully, against the T-34s.

The Marines loaded onto trucks in the dark and headed north. They were told not to fire back if they were fired upon. "I suppose they didn't want the North Koreans to know we were sending troops north." The truck convoy didn't get far before the men could hear the heavy fighting going on in the distance. Artillery shells started whistling overhead but fortunately Fox Company made it to their mountain destination without any problems.

A few days later, Fox Company was ordered to relieve another company that had been under fire on a hill. When Ohman arrived he found a nice white wool blanket that had been previously left by a Korean soldier. He told his foxhole partner that they would be warm that night. Unfortunately, the white blanket also served as a zeroing in point for the North Koreans to fire on from their nearby position on a hill. "Pretty soon there were these beautiful, blue-white tracers going right over our heads. For awhile we wondered what they were doing, but then we realized they were marking our position for a mortar attack." For the next two hours mortars exploded all around their foxhole, some coming as close as ten feet away. "There were all sorts of stuff flying over our heads. It all went back to that dumb white wool blanket."[2]

* * * *

On 14 October 1950, Sergeant Ohman was with a group of Marines on a hill who were firing down the hillside at a retreating enemy force. As he watched the action for awhile, he noticed a mortar round hit at the base of their hill, soon followed up by a second round that landed about halfway up the hill. This was a situation that many men did not notice, or if they did, they did not put two and two together. This is always the difference with men of action and how the results could either be a close call or death. It is just that simple.

"In a split second, I realized they were walking that mortar up the hill and that the third round would be right on top of us. In fact I could hear it coming. Those big mortars sound like ripping paper and it gets louder as it gets nearer." Ohman shouted to a Marine next to him and the two took off running as fast as they could. "We had about three seconds I suppose and we dove off the embankment." The round landed right on top of the other Marines and the explosion dazed Ohman. "My rifle had been destroyed. My pack looked like it had been hit by a shotgun blast. I had a nick on my leg, but mostly I had a hell of a concussion. I had a hard time hearing and I was in a fog."

Up on the hill at the other Marines' position, the scene was devastating. "Seven of those guys were killed and eight had been wounded. A few seconds earlier, I had been standing right with them." Ohman was taken to a MASH first aid station and was soon evacuated to a hospital in Yokosuka, Japan.[3]

Postlude

Several days later in Japan, Joe had sufficiently recuperated and was scheduled to return to his unit, but his luck was still with him. "I was supposed to return to Korea but the confusion in Yokosuka was unreal. I got on a plane and I thought they were taking me back to Korea, but instead, I was transferred to Hawaii." In Hawaii he spent some time at the Trippler General Hospital and was then shipped back to the United States, where he completed his active duty time.

"I considered myself a really fortunate person, especially when you see what happened to my company." Yes, luck had continued to stick with Joe. Fox Company, 2/7 ended up south of the Chosin Reservoir during the end of November 1950. They were holding a hill overlooking and protecting the MSR road. Five days later only 50 to 60 of the Marines were left out of the 300-man Fox Company. Five Medals of Honor, seven Navy Crosses and 16 Silver Stars were awarded to the Marines in the company. "All I could think about was that I'm one lucky guy to have missed it."[4]

Postscript

In 1990, Joe Ohman was convinced by family and friends that he had to go down to Fort Snelling to fill out some paperwork relating to his service time. What he was not aware of was that his four brothers had arranged for him to receive the Purple Heart that he never received for his wounds in Korea. In front of friends, family and a military entourage, he received his well-deserved medal. Ohman's brothers, following in their father's footsteps, had all seen military action. Their father served in World War I; three brothers, Joe, John and Jim, fought in Korea; and Bob was a Vietnam veteran.

For Joe, the Korean War will never be a "forgotten war." He believes that even at the time of the war, Americans really never understood what was happening in those Korean mountains. "Most people weren't aware of even where Korea was. They didn't seem very concerned about it. You've got to remember that this was in the shadow of World War II. Sometimes it seems like the only guys who remember it were the guys who were there."[5]

On 24 October 2007, I came across some online close call stories from a newsletter link on the Minnesota American Legion website. I was able to locate the editor, Al Zdon, who writes "War Stories" for the website and also produced a book, titled *War Stories: Accounts of Minnesotans Who Defended Their Nation*. I sent Mr. Zdon a letter at Moonlit Eagle Productions requesting permission to use parts of his stories for my book, and he e-mailed me back on 14 November 2007, granting me permission to use portions of two stories from the website and two from his book, including this one about Joe Ohman.

22

USMC Corporal Renald Valkenburg

> It is in your moments of decision that your destiny is shaped.
> — Anthony Robbins

Prelude

Renald "Bud" Valkenburg was born 6 January 1929 in Paterson, New Jersey. He attended school in both Paterson and Clifton, N.J. His parents divorced when he was twelve years old and at the age of just thirteen, he got his first job as a dishwasher in a restaurant.

> This may not sound good, since I was so young, but it was one of the best things that could have happened to me. I worked from 5 to 9 every night except the weekends. I got out of school at 3 P.M.; however, the people who owned the restaurant made me come in at 3:30 to do my homework, which they reviewed. If they thought I did not do it correctly, I had to do it over. I was paid ten dollars a week, which I gave to my mother who worked in a sweatshop to support us. She gave me back a dollar. That way, I could go to the movies on Saturday and have enough left over to buy candy for the rest of the week. This was good for me. It kept me off the streets and out of trouble and gave me a head start on a work ethic.

Bud's mother eventually remarried and his family moved to Phoenix, Arizona. On his seventeenth birthday, 6 January 1946, he told his parents that he was going to the recruiting office to join the Navy.

> The men in my family had been in either the Navy or the Merchant Marines. However, the Marine recruiting office was one block before the Navy's. For no known reason, I went into the Marine recruiting office. The sergeant gave me a test, which I passed. I don't remember the contents of the test. Perhaps he just wanted to see if I could make an "X." This was soon after World War II so they weren't too fussy who they sent

to boot camp. He gave me papers for my mother to sign. She cried and said she didn't want me to join the Marine Corps, but my stepfather, a great guy, told her that the war was over and it would do the kid good. Although I wanted to join the Navy, I never regretted enlisting in the Marine Corps.

On 9 January 1946, I arrived at the U.S. Marine Corps Recruiting Depot in San Diego, California, to begin a two-year enlistment. I said I never regretted joining the Corps. Actually, it was that first night in boot camp that I had lots of regrets. At the time, I probably regretted ever being born!

After boot camp, I went to Sea School and then served with the Marine detachment on the battleship USS *Iowa* for about a year. This helped to satisfy my sailor inclinations. I like to tell people that I spent almost a year in the brig on that ship. I was a brig guard. In 1947, I was transferred off the ship to the Marine detachment on Ford Island in Pearl Harbor. It was great duty.

In November 1948, Valkenburg was discharged after spending 22 months in the Corps; however, he and the Marines were not quite done with each other. Just 3 months later, he re-enlisted in February 1949. He was initially stationed with the Marine detachment at the U.S. Naval Ordnance Test Station in Ridgecrest, California. Due to the outbreak of the Korean War on 25 June 1950, Corporal Valkenburg was transferred to Camp Pendleton, California, on 15 July, where he was assigned to Company I, 3rd Battalion, 1st Marines (3/1) and placed with the 3rd section, light machine gun platoon.[1]

About the middle of August, we departed San Diego for Japan on the troopship USS *Buckner*. Arriving about nine days later at Kobe, Japan, we then traveled by train to Camp Otsu, a former Japanese Army camp. After three weeks of training, we returned to Kobe, boarded LSTs [Landing Ship Tank] and headed for Inchon, Korea.

September/October 1950
3rd Battalion, 1st Marines
Western South Korea

Around 1700 on 15 September, we departed our LST in an amtrac [amphibious tractor] and went for the beach at the port city of Inchon, South Korea. Actually, it wasn't a beach, but a wall. When our amtrac butted against the wall, we used ladders to climb to the top and over. Our objective was a hill south of Inchon. It looked as if the city was completely destroyed by offshore bombardment from our ships. Strolling along as if I was going to the company picnic, I heard these zzzz sounds going by my head. Hey, it finally occurred to me that somebody was shooting at me! Instead of zigzagging, I kept strolling along. I must have been a great target. He kept shooting and I kept strolling. He must have run out of ammo or quit in frustration for the zzzzs stopped. If this had been a Marine shooting, he would've got me on the first shot. Yeah, I know that was stupid on my part but I've never had anybody shoot at me before. This was my first combat experience. Without realizing it, this was my first of ten close calls that I would have in the next 6 months in Korea.

* * * *

About three days later, our objective was Hill 123. Hills and mountains were named for their height in meters. Therefore, Hill 123 was nearly 400 feet high. That doesn't sound like much; but when you're humping it, carrying your pack, carbine, machine gun ammo and spare parts to the gun, that hill was a mile high.

Setting up our positions on the forward slope of the hill, we were hit by mortars. One landed close and I was hit. That is, I got hit on the nose by a small stone. Putting my hand to my nose, I noticed there was some blood. My foxhole mate, George, tried to pull my hands away from my nose but I wouldn't let him. I just knew my nose was gone! Finally, getting to see my wound, he turned away with an apparent "no big deal" attitude. I felt my injured nose. Whew! It was still there. It had a tiny scratch on it. Heck, no Purple Heart medal for this one. That was my second close call.

* * * *

The next day we headed for Yong Dong Po, a city on the south side of the Han River. By this time my poor wounded nose with the tiny scratch, was almost healed.

Following a dry flood-control ditch, we made an abrupt right flank and ran into a whole bunch of North Korean soldiers dug in facing to our right. We were crossing the "T." This was a "turkey shoot." Bullets were flying all over the place. A sergeant immediately to my left grabbed his chest, spun around and fell to the ground. Though shot in the chest, I later learned he survived. Two steps to the left and that could have been me. That was my third close call.

* * * *

The following day we went to a hill overlooking the Han River. From my position, I could see the city of Seoul. It looked like we were in for an awesome fight. That night, at about 2200, we crossed the river. Soon after the crossing, I went on a patrol to recover the body of one of our Marines who had been killed. Anticipating house-to-house fighting made it a sleepless night.

Early in the next morning, we entered Seoul. Civilians lined both sides of the roads shouting "Mansai." In Korean, this meant something like "Victory." They cheered us on. Our objective was a hill in the center of the city with a schoolhouse on it. Going along the main street, we found the road partially blocked by sandbags about 14 feet high and 4 feet thick. The center part was open through which machine guns were pouring lead. While we were unscathed staying on the sidewalks, many civilians were shot trying to cross the street.

Behind these barriers were Russian T-34 tanks manned by North Koreans. The route to our objective was on the other side of these tanks. However, thankfully, we found the tanks had been knocked out. Starting to go up the hill, a loose telephone wire somehow wrapped around my pack, holding me so I couldn't move. I immediately became a target. I could hear bullets hitting the wall behind me. A Pfc, another one of my foxhole mates, freed me in quick time. I was sure glad those North Koreans were poor shots. I had survived my fourth close call.

November/December 1950
3rd Battalion, 1st Marines
Northeastern North Korea

After Seoul, it looked like the war was over. General MacArthur gave orders for us to cross over to North Korea and destroy the North Korean Army. So, we boarded LSTs and traveled around the Korean Peninsula to Wonson in North Korea. On Thanksgiving Day, we moved north to a place called Hagaru-ri located at the southern edge of the Chosin Reservoir. We relieved the 7th Marines, which with the 5th Marines headed west to the Chinese border at the Yalu River. The weather was getting cold!

The next morning our platoon patrolled to a village about a mile and a half southwest of town. On the way, a civilian came by and told us that there were thousands of Chinese soldiers in the houses. Without verification, we continued on. I guess we were to be the verifiers. About a hundreds yards in front of the line, machine-gun fire from a low ridge caught us in an open field. We immediately hit the deck! Bullets kicked up dirt all around me. Then our company mortars, bless their souls, opened up on the ridge. This quieted the machine gun fire and we were able to get back to our company line. It was a miracle. They had caught us out in the open with no possible cover, spraying us like a hose and only one man was wounded. Close call number five.

* * * *

Because the temperature had dropped to minus 30 degrees, our foxhole had to be blasted open by shaped charges. The frozen ground was harder than cement. There was no way we could dig them by hand. One evening, about 2130, George and I were told to go to the warm-up tent for 30 minutes. I don't think we were there for 5 minutes when we heard, "Here they come!" Even today, when I hear those words in normal conversations, I remember that night and get a little tense.

We rushed back to our positions. Bullets were flying all over the place. It was dark and I couldn't see anything but I began shooting into the dark ahead of me. George asked, "What are you shooting at?" Right then a grenade exploded on the edge of the hole. He grabbed his forehead and cried out, "I'm hit!" I tried to see if he had a hole but he wouldn't pull his hand away. When he did lower his hands, he only had a bump. A chunk of frozen dirt, blasted by the grenade, probably caused this. Remembering my nose incident in September, we began to laugh. We both began to shoot and throw grenades into the darkness that night. Number six close call.

Being in the battle of the Chosin Reservoir was like having a hundred close calls. I often think of that time. We were Marines, we were well trained and we were brave, but only God Almighty brought us out of that fight. Even though we had 12,000 casualties, we came out fighting, bringing our wounded, some of our dead and most of our equipment. We came out intact as an organized fighting unit. It was neither a rout nor a retreat. It was a 71-mile fight to the sea.

After fighting our way to the sea and transported by ship to South Korea, we rested for a couple of weeks in a place called Masan. Boy oh boy, did we eat well during those days. However, these good days were about to end.

January through March 1950
3rd Battalion, 1st Marines
South Korea

On 6 January 1951, my birthday, we headed north to a place called Andong. There was no combat in the area; however, there was a problem of friendly, faulty artillery rounds. One day, while [I was] sitting on a "fourseater" head [toilet], a short round hit about 25 feet in front of me. Instead of exploding on impact, it arched up high in the air and blew up. If that round had exploded on contact, the head, I and other disgusting things would have been flying through the air. I called this close call number seven.

* * * *

On 14 March 1951, we arrived at our objective early in the day. I spotted what I thought was a Chinese soldier looking at us. I asked our company commander if any of our men were in that direction. His reply to me was, "Shoot him!" By the time I looked up, he was gone. We received orders to patrol the surrounding area. We left our packs and went out to see what we could see. We weren't out of there 5 minutes when Chinese mortars blanketed the area we had just left. Evidently, that soldier I had seen was a Chinese mortar spotter. Close call number eight.

* * * *

The next day, 15 March, we awoke to the sun and a treat for breakfast. We got a slice of bread and a hardboiled egg. I just knew it was going to be a great day! It did turn out to be an exciting day. After our "gourmet" breakfast, we moved along the ridgeline of a heavily forested area, then down a draw and started up another hill to our right. Leading my squad around the slope of a hill, I heard a bullet hit right behind me and then another in front of me. I stopped and sure enough, the next bullet hit where I would have been. I ran back several feet next to a tree. I tried it again; but sure enough, the same pattern occurred. This time while jumping back, I felt a tug on my trousers. I didn't get shot, my pant legs did! Suddenly, a tracer bullet whizzed by my face. That round intended for me, hit another Marine. I still feel bad about that. It was my bullet and someone else got it. Yes, close call number nine!

* * * *

On 23 March 1951, it appeared that we were once again fighting North Koreans instead of Chinese. Our platoon was in the rear while the others pushed forward to attack. Our First Lieutenant called us up to tie in with How (H) Company to make a flanking attack. How Company got delayed, so our Item (I) Company started without them. My gunner cried out, "I'm hit!" Looking at him, I saw that a bullet had gone through his ankle. Next, a recent replacement hollered, "I'm hit, I'm hit bad!" He died right there! CRAACK! It sounded like a bullet went off inside my head. This was my number ten and last close call![2]

Postlude

Corporal Valkenburg had been shot through the neck, shoulder and chest. After nine months in the hospital, he was medically discharged from the Marine Corps in early 1952. After leaving the Marines, he went to college and held numerous and diverse jobs. His last "real" job was as a marketing director for a company. For the last 6 years, he has written a weekly article for the local *Depoe Bay Beacon* newspaper. He and his wife, Peggy, live in Depoe Bay, Oregon. "I am married to a great woman who puts up with me. We have three daughters, six grandchildren and three great grandchildren."[3]

These many years later, I'm still a Marine. You see, when a "boot" graduates from boot camp, he has earned the right to use the title Marine for life. I still get goose bumps whenever I hear the Marine Corps Hymn being played.

I think anyone going through the things we did back then were affected by the war. For me, survivor's guilt was a problem. I still feel bad about those around me who were killed. Of the seven men in my original squad, six of us were casualties. I think of these young men like and many more who would never marry, never have children or grandchildren. They would never have a full life or grow old like me. In a nutshell, war is terrible, it is insane, it is suffering and it is most of all without glory. The price paid for war is not money. It is paid with the lives of the flower of our youth. Today, my heart and prayers go out to those men and women of the military in Afghanistan and Iraq.[4]

I received a phone call from Bud Valkenburg, another Old Breed 1st Mar Div Marine, in late April 2006 in response to my ads. He told me that he wrote a weekly newspaper column for his local paper and that he was preparing a Memorial Day article that might have some information that I could use. I anxiously waited for the article and I have to admit that I was almost giving up when I received a letter, dated 14 June 2006. In it was his article, titled "Close Calls in Korea" (how perfect could that be?), along with his complete bio. He also gave me written permission to use any or all of his article. I received further permission to use the article from the *Depoe Bay Beacon* newspaper on 21 November 2007.

23

USMC Private First Class John Bastian

> Luck marches with those who give their very best.
> — H. Jackson Brown Jr.

Prelude

John "Jack" Bastian was born in Reed Springs, Missouri, on 28 August 1930. With the outbreak of the Korean War in June 1950, John entered the Marine Corps and after boot camp was assigned as a rifleman with Easy Company, 2nd Battalion 7th Marines (2/7), 1st Marine Division.[1]

A Brief History of the 2nd Battalion, 7th Marines

Initially activated in Cuba on 1 January 1941, the Battalion was assigned to the 1st Marine Division. Known as the "War Dogs," 2/7's motto is "Ready for all, yielding to none." During World War II, it battled on Guadalcanal, Eastern New Guinea, New Britain, Peleliu and Okinawa. 2/7 relocated back to Camp Pendleton, California, in 1947 where it was deactivated until the Korean War in 1950.

During the Korean War it fought at Inchon, Seoul, the Chosin Reservoir, and both the East Central and Western Fronts. It also manned the defense of the DMZ following the war until 1955, when it was relocated back to Camp Pendleton. During the Vietnam War, from 1965 to 1970, 2/7 operated from Qu Nhon, Chu Lai, Da Nang, Dai Loc and An Hoa.

Once again returning to Camp Pendleton after the Vietnam conflict, it relocated to its present base at Twenty-nine Palms, California. 2/7 was deployed for Operations Desert Shield and Desert Storm in the early 1990s in Southwest Asia. They are currently involved in the war in Iraq.[2]

25 June 1950
South Korea

At the beginning of the Korean War, NKPA (North Korean People's Army) units moved southward through the Korean Peninsula with relative ease. MacArthur countered by dramatically using the 1st Marine Division, under General O.P. Smith, to land behind enemy lines at Inchon on 15 September, which opened the door for an apparent Allied victory. Then, along with the Army's 7th Infantry Division, the combined force retook the South Korean capital city of Seoul. Continuing to push north, the Americans and their allies forced the NKPA back across the border at the 38th parallel. The fighting then continued all the way to the Yalu River at the North Korean border with China. The 1st Marine Division had relocated and moved north along the eastern side of the country intending to attack from the Changjin (Chosin) Reservoir area. By now, the different Army and Marine Corps Units had been separated by MacArthur, which most commanders felt was a major mistake.

On 19 October 1950, Communist China entered the war and sent huge numbers of their soldiers across the border into Korea. The UN command proved to be hesitant in their appreciation of the facts that the war had now taken a major change. With the Eighth Army in the west, the Marines' 1st Division, elements of the Army's 7th Infantry Division and the 41st Independent Commando Royal Marines, combined as the X Corps, were separated by a mountain range in the east and had little communication with each other. MacArthur still failed to comprehend the extent of the Chinese involvement and discounted reports that nearly 300,000 Communist troops were massing at the Yalu River. The early battles with the Chinese were intense, but they slowly backed up northward again, luring the Americans deeper into enemy territory.

Time was on China's side as a pleasant October autumn was rapidly turning into an early, bitter winter.

2 November 1950
7th Marines, 1st Marine Division
Sudong Valley, North Korea

2 November was a clear, crisp day as all three battalions of the 7th Marines were spread out in the hills around the Sudong Valley in the northeastern Korean Peninsula. Dog (D) Company, 2/7 moved out on foot and entered the valley, located about 16 miles south of Koti-ri and just one mile south of the town of Sudong-ni. The Marines came across several Republic

of South Korean Soldiers (ROKs), who were running south and shouting that the Chinese were attacking. D Company was ordered to seize the steep-sided Hill 698, which was high ground west of the MSR road. They immediately came under heavy automatic weapons fire. The attack continued throughout the day and into the early evening, with D Company sustaining heavy casualties. The steepness of the hill made the attack very difficult. Upon darkness, the crest still had not been achieved. Lacking ammo and with mounting casualties, Easy (E) Company entered the foray and relieved the faltering D Company positions. There was no doubt in anyone's mind now that the facing enemy was not North Koreans but the Chinese Army, specifically the 371st Regiment of the 124th Division.[3]

3 November 1950
Easy (E) Company, 2nd Battalion, 7th Marines
Hill 698, North Korea

On the morning of 3 November, E Company ate their C-rations and continued the attack up the steep slopes of Hill 698. They started their assault with a force of about 190 men. The Chinese Communist Forces (CCF) fought intensely by raking the Marines with heavy rifle fire from their bunkered positions on top of the hill.

With a determined enemy shooting at you and rolling grenades down on you as you climbed to dig him out, it began to feel like we were ascending Mt. Everest in our bare feet. Something I have often wondered about was on that 3 November date, we knew we were fighting Chinese but the generals in Japan still said there were no Chinese in Korea. Perhaps if the generals had left their safe haven and visited the front lines, they would not have been surprised by what was about to take place 3 weeks later during the Chosin Reservoir onslaught.

We finally reached the summit of Hill 698 and established an Easy Company perimeter of defense. Most of us simply moved into foxholes that had been dug by the Chinese. We counted 40 dead enemy and our losses were five Marines killed and 90 wounded. We were a seriously depleted company!

By the time I got to the hilltop perimeter, most of the available holes were already taken by Easy Company Marines except for one that had an apparently dead Chinese leaning against a tree next to it. Lying next to his body was an enemy potato masher grenade. The soldier had a large wound in his chest, most likely from a .50 caliber bullet from a strafing American plane. His foot stretched out over my newfound foxhole. Exhausted, I kicked his leg aside and crawled into his vacant hole.[4]

Easy Company Marines prepared their positions for the evening with the knowledge that they would not only be facing a possible Communist counterattack, but also another extremely dark and cold night, probably in the minus 30 degree range.

I was thankful that I had not drawn guard duty for the night, so I placed my rifle on the ground and climbed into my sleeping bag, hoping for a good night's rest. As the frigid evening wore on, I put my head inside the bag to stay warm and to protect my ears from freezing. After dozing off, I awoke to sounds and the feelings of debris coming down on top of me. Terrified, I popped my head out of the bag and saw a man moving above me. I then attempted to unzip my zipper but found it had apparently frozen from my breathing on it from inside my bag! I found myself trapped and completely helpless. I did manage to wiggle myself into a standing position but still could not force the zipper open.

Standing, I saw my "dead" Chinese, barely moving due to his injuries, but still attempting to detonate the grenade that I had left lying outside the hole. I started yelling and cussing because I knew that if I couldn't get out of my bag, I would be one dead Marine!

Suddenly, I saw a white flash and heard a loud blast! I thought for a second that I was surely dying. I do not recall the name of the Marine next to me who had heard my cries and shot the enemy soldier dead. His bullet passed within just a few inches from my head. Needless to say, I didn't sleep the rest of the night. I knew that I had been very lucky and had narrowly escaped almost certain death."[5]

Postlude

On 4 November, the Chinese once again attacked the 7th Marines' positions. During the fighting on the 3rd and 4th of November, the 7th Regiment and Marine air wings killed 696 Chinese and inflicted nearing 3,000 casualties on the 124th Division. The Sudong-ni area battles ended on 7 November and the 7th Marines then continued northward, still unaware that they were being sucked in by the communist forces and a major attack.[6]

John Bastian's Korean service ended a few weeks later on 17 November 1950. He earned a Purple Heart, a Navy Presidential Unit Citation, the Korean

Service Medal with two stars, the United Nations Service Medal and the National Defense Service Medal.[7]

On 14 June 2006, while searching websites on the Korean War so that I could leave requests for information, I came across two perfect stories for my book project. John's brief personal vignette, titled "Frozen Zipper," was both somewhat funny and unique.

My publisher later discovered that that these two stories actually came from a book, titled *Korean Vignettes: Faces of War,* edited by Arthur Wilson and Norman Strickbine.

My first attempt to locate Arthur Wilson and Artworks Publications came back undeliverable from the post office. I then did an online white pages search for Mr. Strickbine and came up with a few possibilities. I sent out the letter again and on my first attempt found the right person. Norm e-mailed me and reported that Mr. Wilson had passed away in April 2006 and that he now solely controlled the rights of the book. Not only was he enthusiastic that I wanted to use some of their stories to further promote the Korean War and the men who fought in it, but he also offered to let me use stories from their second book, *Red Dragon: Faces of War II.* He also reported that both books are nearly out of print and will never be reprinted due to old age and health reasons. I purchased *Red Dragon* from Norm and he sent me his written approval to use the stories on 26 October 2007.

Norm also reported that John Bastian unfortunately died several years ago.

24

Korea: "Hell Fire Valley"

> Luck never gives; it only lends.
> — Swedish proverb

Prelude

This chapter relates the stories of two lucky Marines who found themselves in the thick of a major battle on 29 November 1950 with the Chinese Army along the MSR road between Koti-ri and Hagaru-ri, below the Chosin Reservoir and on the northeastern side of North Korea. They were both part of "Task Force Drysdale" when it was attacked in an area that soon earned the nickname of "Hell Fire Valley."

"Task Force Drysdale"
29 November 1950

On the morning of 29 November 1950, Major General O.P. Smith, Commanding General of the 1st Marine Division, ordered Colonel "Chesty" Puller (commander of the 1st Marines) to put together a task force to open up the MSR road between Koti-ri and Hagaru-ri where the bulk of the division was currently located. Puller put together the only forces readily available to him, which ended up being a mixed bag of troops, under the command of Royal Marine Lieutenant Colonel Douglas Drysdale. The group consisted of Drysdale's 41st Royal Commando Battalion, Company G, 3rd Battalion, 1st Marines (G/3/1), B Company, 31st Army Infantry Regiment and various Headquarters and Services Marines that Puller could spare. The total force was about 900 men and 140 vehicles.

The task force left Koti-ri at 0930 but by 1630 they had only reached the halfway point to their objective due to heavy enemy resistance along the route. At this halfway point, the Chinese ambushed the force and cut it to pieces! The units bogged down and became separated with little radio contact amongst the split-up groups. This is the area that Drysdale would later name as "Hell Fire Valley." After being reinforced by tanks from D Company, 1st Tank Battalion, Drysdale was ordered to continue on at all costs by General Smith.

By the evening, most of the men from the 41st Commando, G/3/1 and the tanks had made it to Hagaru-ri, but in the confusion along the MSR, approximately 400 members were left stranded and out of radio contact. The stranded forces comprised about 60 Royal Marines, most of B Company, 31st Infantry Regiment and the Headquarters and Service Marines. They were strung out in roughly four pockets along a nearly mile-long stretch of road.[1]

Private First Class Charles Suplee
Company D, 1st Tank Battalion

Private First Class Charles "Chuck" Suplee was born in Salem, Oregon, on 8 April 1930. Shortly after joining the Marines, he found himself in Korea in September 1950 assigned to tanks with Company D, 1st Tank Battalion.

I remember that long trip north on November 29, 1950, from Koti-ri to Hagaru-ri through what became known as "Hell Fire Valley." I was the assistant driver/bow gunner in an M-26 Pershing tank at that time. We began drawing sporadic fire late in the afternoon from what we thought were North Koreans. Suddenly, we were met with a hailstorm of small arms fire. I could hear the crump of antitank weapons. The driver and I quickly buttoned up our hatches. The tank commander, in his haste to find targets for his 90mm main gun, failed to close the TC [tank commander] hatch on top of the turret. As we raked the area with our weapons, I was startled to hear a loud "clank" behind me. I turned to see what it was. The driver and assistant driver both sit in the lower, forward part of the tank. The turret deck is just even with their shoulders and slightly behind them. Some Chinese soldier had lobbed a grenade through the open hatch that the tank commander had failed to close.

The "clank" alerted the tank commander. He gingerly picked it up and threw it out of the open hatch. It was an older type Chinese hand grenade that failed to detonate. Needless to say, if it had detonated, I would not be here today to relate this story. He then closed the hatch to prevent a reoccurrence. To say I was scared is a classic understatement.

After the fire tapered off, we continued on our way to Hagaru-ri. A few minutes later I heard another "clank," but that one was outside the tank. I knew we had been hit with something that had a high velocity, which later proved to be a .51 caliber antitank rifle. As we continued up the MSR I heard a grinding noise which reminded me of the noise a bearing makes as it burns out. That is exactly what was happening. A .51 caliber AP [armored-piercing] round had hit the idler adjusting wheel. The shaft in turn failed and we lost our right track. Well, the best that a tank can do with but one track is turn in circles, so we knew we had a major problem. Although we were under fire, we hooked a cable to the tank ahead and towed into Hagaru-ri. From then on, we were used as an artillery piece and cannibalized for spare parts. It was a sad ending for a tank that had performed valiantly in its duties.

The following days at Hagaru-ri were mostly spent freezing our buns and swapping C-rations to obtain the higher valued "wieners and beaners," which traded 3 for 1 when it came to "spaghetti and meatballs" and 10 to 1 for "corned beef hash." Each tank was equipped with a small portable one-burner gas stove which we used to heat rations. Water was boiled in a helmet and then the unopened ration cans were immersed in the water until thawed and heated. The nights were spent repelling the constant human wave attacks of bugle-blowing Chinese attacking down the hills surrounding the town.

I recall one particular night when a group of us were in a warming tent gathered around a diesel-burning stove, soaking up the heat, a commodity in scarce supply at the time. I had just begun to feel warm for the first time in weeks when the Chinese picked that moment to launch an attack. I had just said I wasn't leaving this warmth no matter what, when a couple of rounds passed through the warming tent. Changing my mind, I grabbed my mummy bag and hauled ass towards my tank for cover. That was when I noticed the snow kicking up in little spurts behind me as I ran. You can't believe what it feels like when the enemy has you in his sights and is trying to nail you. You also can't believe how fast you can run under these circumstances!

Chuck made it though this Korean tour and returned for a second tour from June 1953 to April 1955. He remained in the Marine Corps and served later in Vietnam. He retired at Camp Pendleton, California as a Gunnery Sergeant in 1969.[2]

Staff Sergeant Charles Fieldson
11th Marines, Post Office Detachment

Staff Sergeant Charles "Chuck" Fieldson was born on 16 June 1930 in Pemberton, New Jersey. Upon arrival in Korea on 15 September 1950, he was assigned as a mail clerk with the 11th Marines (an artillery battalion) which one would normally expect to be a fairly safe position.

While serving with the 11th Marines, I worked as a mail clerk at the unit post office. We had a 6 × 6 truck two-thirds filled with mail for Yudam-ni. "Ski," our T/Sgt who was the honcho for our mail unit, had his men all picked for the mail run. I was not one of them. But I sure admired one of the guys who had been picked. Well, maybe not the man, but I did admire his new cold-weather parka and brand new snowpack boots. They were something! The cold weather had hit and my footgear didn't keep out the cold. My toes were about to drop off. Nobody knew where he had gotten these prizes and he wasn't talking. But he was talking about how he would just as soon not make the Yudam-ni run. So we made a deal. I would make the run. He, in trade, would give me his new snowpack boots and heavy parka. It was a fair trade. We both got what we wanted.

So in the early morn of 29 November 1950, we took off from base. There were four of us including the driver and three mail clerks. We barreled up the MSR, past Majon-dong, Sudong, Chinhung-ni and through the Funchilin Pass and into Koti-ri. Here, we joined a Hagaru-ri-bound relief convoy, "Task Force Drysdale." It was a mixed bag of Marines, Royal and USMC, Army and ROKs, spearheaded by tanks. Enemy was spotted in the hills to the east. We could hear firing ahead. It was stop and go. Half way to Hagaru-ri we were hit by a large enemy force.

The column was broken. The fore half with tanks went on in to Hagaru-ri. The rear half headed back to Koto-ri. In the middle, with no choice, we fought. The battle became know as "Hell Fire Valley." Halted, with Chinese closing in, we bailed out of the truck by slitting the side canvas. The back was open to enemy fire. I took position by the front wheel. About midnight, I was firing across the road, kneeling. I had emptied several clips from my M-1. A clip jammed due to the extreme cold. I had just gotten it out and a new one in when I spotted a grenade being lobbed at a 75mm recoilless firing some 10–15 feet away.

I just had enough time to turn my face away when it went off. I came to in a ditch across the road with my face a bloody mess. The parka and those boots went a long way in keeping me from freezing that night while being "out of it." It was almost daylight when I heard the voice of a gunnery sergeant talking to the Chinese. Then someone said, "Let's go, we're surrendering. The wounded are going back to Koto-ri." We never got there. The Chinese took us to a farm house. The yard was full of people. One of the Marines on the porch, [whom] I later knew as Lieutenant Colonel Chidester, pointed and said, "Take care of that man." My head and face were then quickly bandaged.

I was held captive for seven days. We were fed potatoes. The second day, Corsairs strafed all around the house. They must have figured out we were inside. When the Chinese headed north, they told us to come, lest we be killed by our planes. It was 30 below and I was weak, so I decided to stay. It was a very lucky move. Those who left were gone almost three years, the few that survived. The guard group that left was replaced by another group who were a lot meaner. One of them stripped me of my parka and my boots. I had a hell of a time with my right boot. My foot was swollen. He jerked it off, skin and meat along with it. On the seventh day we heard rumblings on the MSR. It was our guys coming back from Hagaru-ri. They put us on stretchers and gave us blankets. I was helped to the top of a tank and held on to a mounted machine gun until we got to Koti-ri. I arrived with no boots or parka but with my pride as a Marine fully intact.

By 9 December 1950, Chuck was evacuated out of Korea for the last time. He had earned a Purple Heart, a POW medal, and several other unit and Korean service awards.[3]

Postlude

Of the 900 original members of "Task Force Drysdale," about 300 made it to Hagaru-ri. Another 300 were killed or wounded and about 135 were taken prisoner by the Chinese. The remainder somehow made it back to Koti-ri. Over 75 vehicles were destroyed by the enemy. Although some believed the task force was ill conceived and doomed from the start, General Smith felt that it was a partial success as it delivered some 300 infantrymen along with a tank company that was desperately needed for the defenses at Hagaru-ri. Lieutenant Colonel Drysdale, although wounded, had made it to Hagaru-ri, while the captured Lieutenant Colonel Chidester was never seen again.[4]

"Task Force Drysdale" was the first time since the Boxer Rebellion in China in 1900 that Royal Marines and U.S. Marines had fought together. After the "Hell Fire Valley" battle, their respect for each other would continue to grow.

This is another story that Norm Strickbine allowed me to use from his book, Korean Vignettes-*Faces of War*.

25

USMC Sergeant Elbert Koonce

> There is no fate but your own fate.
> — Leslie Grimutter

Elbert "Gene" Koonce was born in Evansville, Indiana, on 6 April 1926. Gene joined the Marine Corps and by August 1950, he was transferred to the war zone in Korea, where he was assigned as the platoon guide with the 1st platoon, George (G) Company, 3rd Battalion, 5th Marines.

November 1950
Hill 1282 Adjacent to Yudam-ni

Funny things, odd things, crazy things, a million to one odds against things, happen in war. No rhyme, no reason, no known cause, just happenstance. It was 30 November 1950. My company, George 3/5 had just relieved Item (I) 3/5 on Hill 1282 overlooking Yudam-ni. It had been under constant Chinese attack since the night of 27 November when it was defended by Easy (E) 2/7. Very heavy casualties resulted in Easy 2/7 being reinforced by two platoons from Able (A) 1/5. Later in the morning of 28 November, two platoons from Charlie (C) 1/5 were sent up the hill to reinforce E/2/7 and A(-)1/5. Attacks were being hard pressed, the Chinese seemingly careless of losses. Our casualties were also high. The need to hold the high ground of Hill 1282, vital to the defense of Yudam-ni and the MSR, overrode all other considerations. Over 200 wounded were taken off that hill. E/2/7 had suffered the most.

Continuous enemy pressure and an increased tempo in the attack resulted in How (H) 3/5 being sent on 29 November to relieve units holding the hill. Still under unrelenting attack, Item (I) 3/5 climbed the hill to relieve H/3/5 and to give care to the many wounded men, still fighting, but unwilling to leave their battle positions. On 30 November, George 3/5 was ordered to Hill 1282 in relief of I/3/5. We were the sixth rifle company to occupy the hill in four days of continuous battle. It was like making sausage out of the Chinese, except that the Chinese being fed into the sausage grinder kept taking deadly whacks at the guys turning the crank. It is an axiom of warfare that the defense suffers about one-third the casualties of the attacker. The way they kept coming reminded me of that Ripley cartoon of 50 Chinese marching abreast and, due to birth rate, being able to go on forever. The 1st platoon, in which I was the platoon guide, relieved a platoon from I/3/5. The Chinese launched another heavy attack with their main effort at our 1st platoon. In the first few minutes, the platoon leader and the platoon sergeant were both killed. Two squad leaders were wounded, as was I. As the ranking NCO, I took command of the platoon. Due to all the wounded being cared for in Yudam-ni, our orders were to hold Hill 1282 at all costs. No withdrawals!

After repulsing the attack, I took a pair of binoculars off the body of an 81mm FO [forward observer] and tossed them down the slope to acting squad leader Jochum. I told him to try to locate the snipers, who, between attacks, were raising hell with us. The brushy area from which the Chinese were launching their attacks was about 40 yards below us. We called in an air strike, but only strafing runs were made because the enemy was too close to us for our Corsairs to bomb or napalm them. After the air strike, Jochum yelled for me to come down. I ran and jumped into his hole. It was a small, round Chinese-dug foxhole, a real tight fit for two Americans. He said he had not been able to locate any snipers.

We rose up slightly to better scan the terrain. I was looking over Jochum's left shoulder as he used the binoculars. Then the lights went out. When I came to, my head was ringing like a bell. Jochum was moaning, saying he had a head wound. I looked him over and felt around his head. He had no head wound but he had no left ear, either. No blood! The cold and the shock must have stopped any bleeding. My helmet had a crease in it; almost vertical. Apparently as I looked over his shoulder, a sniper had nailed us. In our cramped position, if his left ear had not deflected that bullet, just a tad, I would have had a third eye midway between the ones I was born with. His ear deflected it just enough to go over the brim of my helmet instead of under it. St. Peter and his whole choir of angels were with me that day. I have never doubted my luck since, but neither do I press it!

Gene was promoted to staff sergeant and his luck would continue until he rotated home in April 1951.[1]

This story from *Korean Vignettes: Faces of War*, jumped out at me when I first read it and I knew right away that it would be perfect for my book.

26

USMC Sergeant Forest Heistermann

> Control your destiny or someone else will.
> — Jack Welch

Prelude

Forest "Fritz" Heistermann was born 8 October 1926. His hometown of record upon entering the Marine Corps was Fountain Valley, California. By the breakout of the Korean War in June 1950, Fritz was already a seasoned combat veteran of World War II. He had fought on both Guam and Iwo Jima during the Pacific campaigns. He arrived in South Korea on 15 September 1950 and was initially assigned as an artillery forward observer (FO) with Fox Battery, 2nd Battalion, 11th Marines.[1]

Late October 1950
United Nation Forces
North Korea

By late October 1950, General Douglas MacArthur's United Nations (UN) force was well on its way to victory by taking the offensive and pushing past the border between South and North Korea at the 38th Parallel and had approached the Chinese border at the Yalu River. The Eighth U.S. Army moved northward on the west side of the Korean Peninsula, while units of the Army's 7th Infantry Division, the 1st Marine Division and the 41st Independent Commando Royal Marines, which combined were called the X Corps and placed under the command of Army Major General Ned Almond, marched along the eastern side. The Army units of the X Corps, however, were spread too thin and completely out of supporting distance from each other. Furthermore, the Eighth Army and the X Corps were separated by a mountain range and had little or no communication with each other. Meanwhile, MacArthur continued to ignore claims that Marines had been fighting Chinese forces as early as 19 October and that they were staging attack troops above the Yalu River. The basic plan in the east was for the Marines to attack from Yudam-ni at the Chosin Reservoir, moving north and west to ultimately meet up with the Eighth Army and cut off the North Korean People's Army (NKPA). In the Chosin area, the Marines in the west and the Army units in the east were separated by the reservoir. Most commanders in Korea were outraged that MacArthur had divided his forces, leaving them extremely vulnerable.[2]

Late November 1950
1st Marine Division
Northeastern Korean Peninsula

Unsure of the Chinese threat, Major General O.P. Smith's 1st Marine Division moved north carefully, keeping its units close together and stockpiling supplies and ammunition along the Division's main supply route (MSR). The 5th and 7th Regiments of the 1st Marine Division began their northward attack on 27 November from Yudam-ni, while the 1st Regiment, under legendary Colonel Chesty Puller, protected the MSR. Unknown to the X Corps, a massive force of 18 Chinese divisions had already attacked the Eighth Army in the west on 25 November and had nearly destroyed it.

The 5th and 7th Marine Regiments quickly ran into a heavy Chinese force of nearly 70,000 poorly equipped, but well-organized, enemy troops which attacked all over the northeastern peninsula. The MSR was cut off in several places. At the time of the attack, the 11th Marines (artillery) along with the 5th and 7th Regiments were at Yudam-ni at the Chosin Reservoir area. General Smith's Division Headquarters was further south at Hagaru-ri, Puller's 1st Marines was based at Koto-ri with its units spread along the MSR, and the Army units were still mainly east of the Reservoir. Nearly everyone was surrounded! By 29 November, MacArthur had received the negative reports and finally decided to withdraw the X Corps southward to the port city of Hungnam while ordering the Eighth Army to try to hold onto P'yongyang in North Korea. His delayed action would have serious consequences during the next few weeks. The X Corps would fight for their lives trying to break out of the Chinese trap. By now, there were 120,000 enemy troops battling against 40,000 UN forces in the northeast with orders to annihilate the Allies to the last man!

On 30 November, General Smith heard MacArthur's orders to withdraw and reportedly stated, "It took them two days to decide this!" He then ordered his surrounded Marines in the Chosin sector to somehow withdraw and pull back to Hagaru-ri. Although not verified, Smith was quoted by a reporter as saying, "Retreat hell, we're just attacking in the opposite direction." Not stopping there, reporters also sought out the always-colorful Colonel Chesty Puller and he provided them with this quotable statement: "We've been looking for the enemy for several days now. We finally found them. We're surrounded. That simplifies our problem of finding these people and killing them."

It took the Chosin area Marines and Army personnel over three days to reach Hagaru-ri, only 14 miles away, on 3 December. Once there, all the units regrouped. Through intelligence gathered from captured Chinese prisoners of war (POWs), the Marines learned that there were seven Chinese Communist Force (CCF) divisions around the city. On 6 December, the men at Hagaru-ri began a 9-mile, 38-hour fight to reach the next major town of Koto-ri. Despite communist control of the MSR and numerous roadblocks, nearly 10,000 men and 1,000 vehicles reached Koto-ri. Most of the 1st Marine Division (1st, 5th and 7th Marines) was again reunited. Wounded were evacuated from the airstrip and the X Corps now prepared for the last 43-mile trek southeast to the sea at Hungnam, where ships would take them out of harm's way.[3]

Having served as an FO at Hagaru-ri, on return to Koto-ri, I was once again assigned to the 1st Marines and placed with Baker (B) Company of the 1st Battalion, 1st Marines.[4]

8 December 1950
Company B, 1st Battalion, 1st Marines (1/1)
Chinhung-ni, North Korea

On 8 December, 1/1 was located in the hills around the city Chinhung-ni, which was 10 miles south of Koto-ri. Lieutenant Colonel Donald M. Schmuck's 1st Marines was rested and prepared for what would be the last major battle of the Chosin campaign. The night of 8 December would bring snow and temperatures reaching minus 40 degrees with a wind chill factor of minus 60 degrees.

A young lieutenant came up to me and said, "Fritz, I want you out on that OP [Observation Post]," pointing to a position roughly 200 yards in from of our MLR [Main Line of Resistance]. As I was taking off, our Captain said, "Be careful. We lost a man up there last night!" I really didn't need to hear that! Initially, two wiremen went out with me, to lay wire and hook up a crank phone, but they soon returned to the friendly lines and left me by myself. At around 1600 hours, it started snowing and getting dark. I was definitely not looking forward to this night. I settled in and checked out the phone hookup, which proved to be OK.

Sometime later that night, I heard muffled voices and equipment sounds. I realized there were Chinese up the ridge, separated from me by only a shallow draw. I cranked the phone and said, "They're coming and I'm heading in. Watch for me." Suddenly, a flare went off and I now realized that they were almost on top of me. I had to do something quick.

I emptied my 30-round clip in the direction of the enemy and ran for our lines. It soon became evident that I couldn't safely make it all the way back so I jumped into a shell hole. While [I was] trying to get another clip from my cartridge belt, a concussion grenade went off at the top of the hole. I landed on my back with the wind knocked out of me. I was having trouble breathing, when a young Chinese soldier looked over the rim of the hole and pointed his rifle with fixed bayonet at my face!

He pulled the trigger but the only sound that came out was just a "click," an apparent misfire! He then reversed his rifle and gave me a blow to the left side of my chest, breaking a few ribs. Next came a butt stroke to the chin and a slam to my face, which broke my jaw. I knew that I was close to dying when he tried to stick his bayonet in my face. Fortunately, I was able to turn my head just in time to avoid the thrust, which just missed my ear and stuck into the dirt. This gave me an opportunity, as he was now off balance, so I grabbed his quilted jacket and pulled. As I did, his rifle went off, causing some permanent damage to the hearing in my left ear.

I fumbled for my old World War I 32/20 revolver that my father had given to me prior to leaving the States for Korea. I was able to pull the weapon from my holster, put the barrel in his face and fire. He fell on top of me and I passed out. Later, when I came to, I heard Chinese talking and moving about. They must have believed that we were both dead. I stayed quiet and they soon moved away to another position. Once again, I passed out, only to awaken later to dead silence. It was freezing cold!

I remained the rest of the night with the dead Chinese on top of me, his body warming me in the 30 below zero temperature. Early next morning I again heard noises, only this time it was Fred, my buddy, who was looking for me. He had followed the commo line out hoping to locate me, or my body. Fred found me and helped me down to an aid station. From there, I walked across a blown bridge and down the mountain to Chinhung-ni. I then caught a ride to Hungnam and boarded a ship, which took me to the Bean Patch area at Mason and eventually to the Naval Hospital in Yokosuka, Japan. I will never forget looking at the barrel of that rifle and hearing the "click." I was one lucky Marine.[5]

The 1/1 had successfully held off the Chinese at the Funchilin Pass near Chinhung-ni on the snowy night of 8 December, thus ending the final major

CCF offensive in the northeast. They would continue to launch minor assaults, but they too were suffering from the weather conditions and lack of food. Their supply lines were seriously overextended.[6]

Postlude

General Smith's 1st Marine Division finally reached Hungnam on 11 December and, by the 15th, Navy ships transported them to safety where they would once again become combat operational within just one month and would continue in the fighting. General Smith and his experienced regimental commanders and other key personnel provided the necessary leadership that pulled the overmatched unit together and ensured a successful withdrawal.

During the Chosin Campaign, the Chinese endured 25,000 killed and 12,500 wounded, and lost another 30,000 men to frostbite. Seven of the ten CCF divisions never entered combat again during the Korean War. United Nation losses amounted to 2,500 dead, 192 missing in action, 5,000 wounded and 7,500 cold-related injuries. Of these friendly casualties, the 1st Marine Division suffered 604 KIA (killed in action), 114 DOW (died of wounds), 192 MIA (missing in action), 3,508 WIA (wounded in action) and 7,313 non-battle casualties, mainly frostbite.

Today, the Marines still consider the Battle of the Chosin Reservoir to be one of the proudest moments in their history. They call it the "Frozen Chosin" and the veterans are part of the "Chosin Few." Likewise, the Chinese Army considers the battle of the Chosin Reservoir an honor. This campaign along with its victory in the west against U.S. forces was the first time in a century that a Chinese Army was able to defeat a Western army in a major battle, despite their heavy losses.[7]

Fritz Heitermann's Korean service ended on 30 July 1951. During his service in both World War II and Korea, he earned the Bronze Star for valor, the Purple Heart and numerous unit, campaign and service medals.[8]

The second Korean vignette, titled "Click," that I located on my 14 June 2006 online search (see chapter 23 notes) told the story about one very fortunate Marine.

27

USMC Sergeant William Palizzolo

> There is much to be said for challenging
> fate instead of ducking behind it.
> — Diana Trilling

Prelude

I was born in South Boston [10 July 1931], which had the highest number of combat deaths of any neighborhood area in the country during the Vietnam War. This has nothing to do with the Korean War except both were ["Generaled"] by politicians. As youngsters, our major entertainment was tossing coins against the wall. The closest coin to the wall won all the coins. Starting at ten, with pennies, at 18 we were pitching quarters.

Little did Bill know at the time that, within a few years, a simple coin toss would determine his fate between life and death.

At 16 I joined the Marine Corps Reserve to have new clothes, shoes and underwear. I was 19 when the war began in Korea. On 6 November 1950, I was sent to Parris Island, SC, then on to Camp Pendleton, CA, and finally boarded a ship to Korea.[1]

14 April 1951
Korea

On my first day in Korea, seven of us were helicoptered to the front lines. I stayed there one full year as a rifleman and bazooka gunner leader with Bravo (B) Company, 1st Battalion, 7th Marines. Getting off the helicopter that first day, I noticed a canvas tent spread flat on the ground. Underneath it were seven bodies. The sergeant told us that we were replacements for these men. He also announced a typist was needed for

Headquarters Company. I was tempted to volunteer but did not want to repeat the drudgery of my last job as a typist for a trucking company. One of my buddies did volunteer. I was momentarily concerned I might have made a mistake. As it turned out, I did not. The six of us trudged to the top of the hill to join our units. I had no sooner reported in when, in an effort to evade incoming rounds, I hit the dirt. My canteen came loose, rolled over the cliff, never to be seen again. Our medic, a black man, saw what had happened and gave me one of his two canteens. That simple act of kindness has stayed with me over the years. I hope he reads this and contacts me. "Doc" received several awards for bravery, risking his own life on numerous occasions as he treated front-line casualties.

The Chinese would attack at night, bugles blowing and shouting, "Marine, you die." More Chinese died than did Marines. Photos taken at the time attest this truth in graphic detail. I never thought I would leave Korea alive, or at least without a crippling wound. As it turned out I took my only wound in a mortar attack where a hunk of shrapnel gashed my upper thigh. I was one lucky guy! On Hill 673 I went down with an attack of malaria with a fever of 105 degrees. The lieutenant saw the sweat on my face but could not evacuate me for two days due to the ferocity of the battle at that time. When it was over, I turned myself in to a MASH hospital. I suffered three more malaria attacks in Korea. Later, back in the States, the VA gave me a "sure cure." Thankfully, I haven't had another attack these past 50 years.

* * * *

I really was one lucky Marine. We changed positions to an area 15 miles away, moving out with full packs and weapons. It began to rain. It was September but it felt like January. Cold, very cold! We had ponchos yet were soaked to the skin. At 2300, after a hard hike, we arrived at the new position. Ordinarily we would have dug individual foxholes, but because it was so cold we decided to dig a bigger hole to sleep together and benefit from each other's warmth. We finished the hole and crawled into our sleeping bags. We had just begun to warm up when the company commander showed up with the other bazooka team leader. A Chinese tank had been spotted and one team had to move towards the road to guard it. Neither team wanted the duty. We flipped a coin and I lost. My team members screamed at me for losing. We moved a few hundred yards to a new position overlooking the road. Again we dug in, sleeping two at a time with one man on lookout. A mortar attack began that lasted hours. At daybreak, we rejoined the company. The rain had stopped but it was still cold, muddy and miserable. On our way back to join our platoon, we passed by our original large, 3-man foxhole. It had taken a direct hit from a mortar shell. Had we not been posted to tank guard overlooking the nearby road, we would have all been dead. With a direct hit, it would have been a tough call to link body parts with names. My comrades were now patting me on the back in congratulations for losing the coin toss! We were known as the "Lucky Bill's Bazooka Team" for the next few weeks. Fifty-one years ago, I remember it as if it were yesterday. Every time I go to Vegas I keep thinking I can't lose. I had won the most important coin toss of my life in Korea![2]

Fate plays such an important part in men's lives while engaged in combat. This is the first of two chapters that I used from Arthur Wilson and Norman Strickbine's second book, *Red Dragon: Faces of War II.*

28

USMC Private First Class Richard Aiple

> One meets his destiny often in
> the road he takes to avoid it.
> — French proverb

Springfield, Ohio, was the home town of Richard "Ricardo" Aiple, who was born on 6 March 1931. Twenty years later, on 4 August 1951, Ricardo arrived in Korea as a United States Marine assigned as a rifleman in Baker (B) Company, 1st Battalion, 5th Marines.

It was a warm day in early September 1951. My company, Baker, 1st Battalion, Fifth Marines, was positioned on Hill 1310. The hill across from us had been heavily shelled by U.S. Navy guns in an action some days earlier. One round had been a "short" and had hit about 100 yards down the mountain in front of our position. The hole filled up with spring water. We began to use this hole as a watering point, much to the relief of the struggling draftees of the Korean Labor Corps. These middle-aged and elderly men had been lugging heavy 5-gallon water cans on their A-frame packs up the mountain to us several times a day. In addition, they brought up rations and ammunition.

Men in various squads would take turns filling canteens. Two men from a squad would make up a watering team. One man would fill canteens while the other would provide cover for him. We would usually string the canteens onto a pole, threading them through the chains that held the cap to the canteens. Going down the hill, canteens swinging on a short pole sounded like jingle bells, so we generally used a long pole to space the canteens and minimize the clatter. Since most men carried two canteens, we could end up with 20 or so canteens on a pole, which made about a 50-pound load.

This time it was my turn to fill canteens. Private Hooper was my water guard. I was to fill while he stood watch. We took off down the hill, then over to the shell-hole spring. Hooper took up position atop a big rock above me. It was a warm day. Lying there, he could scan the surrounding area, thus covering me while I knelt in a bent-over position. It was a tedious job to fill a lot of canteens. Each must be held at just the right angle to the surface of the water to allow air to escape from the canteen while the water fills in. While it is possible to fill a canteen by submerging it, it is much quicker to allow water in and air out at the same time. One thinks of little things like this when in an exposed position as possible prey to any guerilla sniper who happens to spot you through his scope.

About half an hour passed and most of the canteens had been filled. I straightened up to rest my aching back. Still crouched, I looked straight across the pool from me and square into the eyes of three North Korean soldiers armed with burp guns. I stared at them thinking that this was my last day on earth. I knew I had had it! My next thought was where in the hell was Hooper, my guard, my man on watch who was supposedly covering me. I had no weapon, just my trusty K-Bar. I didn't know what to do so I did nothing, figuring I could only be dead once. Not a pleasant thought, but the only one I had.

Without a change of expression, they lifted their burp guns and dropped them to the ground! They piled their hands, one on top of the other, on their heads and surrendered. I was one very startled, no longer scared, but very puzzled Marine. I yelled at Hooper and he awoke with a grunt. He had dozed off lying in the sunshine on that warm rock. We escorted the three North Koreans back under arms to the company headquarters. I carried the three burp guns and the Koreans carried our filled canteens. Hooper acted as an escort guard for the North Koreans who were now POWs.

Pfc Aiple and Private Hooper had a long private conversation later about the duties of standing watch when detailed as water guard on canteen-filling detail. We remained good buddies in spite of it. Since that day, if I am startled, that scene comes to mind. But it isn't as bad. I don't have to reach up and cram my heart back in my mouth and swallow hard to put it back where a heart is supposed to be. That day, for sure, I thought I was one dead Marine. God was with me in that day of my youth.[1]

The circumstances surrounding Richard's story should have had a much different ending, but God was on his side that day. Another Marine on any other day, under similar conditions, would have had his body riddled with bullets.

29

USMC Private John Graham

> It is choice, not chance that determines your destiny.
> — Jean Nidetch

Prelude

John "Lucky" Graham was born in Wilson, New York, on 21 January 1930. After joining the Marines and just prior to the Korean War, he was stationed at Camp Pendleton, California, in Colonel "Chesty" Puller's battalion. One payday, and with a weekend pass in his pocket, he set off for Tijuana, Mexico.

> Several of us sat in a bar having a beer when a group of noisy tourists barged in. One of our guys went to the head, leaving an empty chair at our table. This big guy came over and took the chair. I got up, put my hand on the chair, and told him it was taken. He gave me a shove and I shoved back. That started it! The barkeep called the "Policia." When the dust settled we both had sore knuckles and I had a broken nose. The big guy turned out to be Robert Mitchum, not long out of the Army. The ruckus got me busted back to Pfc. I ended up a few weeks later as one of a sixteen-man guard detachment at our embassy in Seoul, Korea.[1]

John had arrived in Korea just before the war broke out and within five months he would be captured and would spend nearly 23 months as a Prisoner of War (POW).

A Short History of American POWs During the Korean War

A total of 7,245 (677 Marines) Americans were captured and documented as prisoners of war during the 3-year war. Of these, 2,806 (26 Marines) died while in captivity due to the dire conditions, extreme cold and lack of proper medical care. An additional 21 refused repatriation at the end of the war on 27 July 1953. It is also important to note that 4,759 Americans (385 Marines) died while missing in action (MIA). The total death toll of the war for United States forces stands at 33,686 (4,268 Marines) as of 1 June 2000.[2]

Prisoners were severely mistreated, probably on both sides. Many accounts report of beatings, forced labor, starvation and death marches imposed by the communist forces on United Nation prisoners. North Koreans have also been attributed with conducting several massacres of captured American troops, especially during the early mopping-up actions of the war.[3]

Korea 1950–1952

That's where I was on June 25, 1950, when the North Koreans crossed the parallel. The Embassy was closed and we went south where we were flown to Japan. A few weeks later, I was back in Pusan, South Korea, and assigned to the 1st Marine Provisional Brigade. I fought on the Pusan Perimeter as part of the "Fire Brigade," running around the southern end of the perimeter. It was then on to Wolmi-do and I was among the first ashore at Inchon. From there, it was Seoul and Uijongbu and finally back on transport ships to Wonson in north eastern North Korea, where we were greeted by Bob Hope. We headed north and on 7 November 1950 we ran into the Chinese in a night long battle that somebody termed as "Nightmare Alley." Thousands of screaming Chinese! I was in Weapons Company (4.2 mortar section), 2nd Battalion, 7th Marines when we pulled out and headed further north for Yudam-ni.

When we got the orders to pull back, the 7th was on the right flank, facing south, and the 5th Marines were on the left. My squad ran smack dab into some Chinese in white uniforms. In the snow, we didn't see them until we were on top of them. We all fired at once. I was hit in the jaw by a burp gun slug which knocked me out. When I came to, I was in a Korean hut with several of my buddies. There were six of us. Some of the prisoners were Army from the other side of the reservoir. Almost all of us were wounded. Oddly enough, my jaw was not broken. It must have been a ricochet, but the concussion was enough to put me under. It made my face a bloody frozen mess.

The Chinese turned us over to the North Koreans, who herded us along for several days at bayonet point. Those who could not keep up were bayoneted. After a few days we reached a little village. We were interrogated and separated. I wound up in a group going to a North

Korean prison camp. After a couple of weeks over goat trails, hiding by day and traveling at night, we ended up at Manpojin, on the North Korean–Manchuria Yalu River border. It was a hellhole prison camp, both for Marines and Army. We learned that the prisoners were considered "hard cases" and for that reason were left to the tender mercies of the North Koreans. One of our guys was not a hard case. He was a turncoat. I spent ten days in "The Hole" with no food and only water, by being disciplined for talking about escape from our captors. The turncoat was an informer named Dickenson from Tennessee.

Late one winter day after 23 months in that camp, a flight of Corsairs came over the hill in an attack on nearby Chinese positions, followed by a second. Three of us who had talked escape took off in the pandemonium of ack-ack, bombs, strafing and napalm that hit a nearby building. By daybreak, we had jogged many miles south. We hid in some brush. A pattern was set: travel at night, catch a chicken and wring its neck, eat and sleep. It was cold, but not as cold as Yudam-ni. In about two weeks we could hear guns and knew we were close. We hid in a ravine all night, and at dawn came out in the 1st Cav lines northwest of Seoul. We sure were glad to see those dogfaces!

John would be promoted to corporal and left Korea on 28 November 1952.[4]

Had John and his friends not escaped when they did, they would have faced another eight months of captivity before the war ended with their fate unknown. No wonder that John's nickname is "Lucky."

John's lucky story was an inspiration when I first read it in the book *Korean Vignettes: Faces of War*. Quite often, POWs are not given credit for their survival instincts and bravery. He truly made his own luck.

30

USMC Acting Sergeant James Larkin

> Men of action are favored by the Goddess of Luck.
> — George Clauson

Prelude

James Larkin came from a loving and hard-working mother and father living in the Bronx, New York. He was born on 24 August 1932 and was one of five children, with two brothers and two sisters. He looks back on his early family life as both healthy and happy. He played all sports and considered himself a very good athlete.

At the age of 17, James joined the Marines in June 1950, mainly because of a family Marine Corps tradition. He attended boot camp at Parris Island, South Carolina. After graduation, he was assigned to the communication section of Headquarters Battery, 1st Battalion, 10th Marines at Camp Lejeune, North Carolina.

James left for Korea in early October 1952 and was sent to the headquarters section in Able Battery, 1st Battalion, 11th Marines as a forward observer (FO). By November, his unit had moved up to the Main Line of Resistance (MLR) in the Nevada City Outposts area.[1]

1952–1953
Nevada City Outposts
Jamestown Line, Western Korean Front

Northeast of Panmunjom and above the 38th parallel lay a series of hilltop outposts in front of the MLR defended by the 1st Marine Division along an area called the Jamestown Line. The 5th Marines' area of responsibility included three prominent hills named after the Nevada gambling cities of Carson, Reno and Vegas because the Marines maintained it was a "wide-open gamble" to be there. These three hills commanded an ancient invasion route to Seoul which Genghis Khan's horde utilized when he conquered this area of Asia centuries ago. In 1950, the North Koreans had cut across this same route when they attacked the South and pushed away the Korean and American armies. Now, the 120th Chinese Communist Division were located to the north, on higher hills overlooking these outposts, and if nothing else, the Americans manning the positions were to provide advance warning of enemy attacks on the MLR.²

March 1953
Nevada City Combat Outposts

I was on an FO team attached to Baker Company, 1st Battalion, 5th Marines (1/5). My parent outfit was Able Battery, 1st Battalion 11th Marines (1/11). The 1st Marine Division was assigned to the central sector of the right side of a 32-mile front called the Jamestown Line. The 1/5 (Able, Baker and Charlie Companies) was given the task of holding the center of the line. Baker, 1/5, was in the middle, Able to the left and Charlie was positioned to the right. To the right of Charlie, was 3/5, while 2/5 was in reserve, as was the 7th Marines. The 1st Marines and the Korean Marines were situated to the left of Able Company. Just slightly east and directly in front of the 5th Marines' sector of the MLR were three hills called combat outposts [COPs], Carson, Reno and Vegas in that order from left to right. The Marines named the hills because it would be a gamble to hold and defend them. Carson was about 800 yards out from the MLR, Reno 2,000 yards, and Vegas, the highest hill, approximately 1,200 yards out. Each outpost was manned with 40 to 45 infantry Marines, two artillery FOs and one 4.2" mortar FO.

21 March 1953
COP Vegas

Charlie Company, 1/5, had one platoon each on Carson and Reno, while How Company, 3/5, had one platoon on Vegas. It was my day to relieve an FO on Vegas. The procedure was that FOs went up for five days at a time, while riflemen rotated every three days. When I left the MLR for Vegas, I carried a crystal radio set on a pack board, along with an extra battery. I also carried my weapon, cartridge belt, extra ammo and some personal items. It was going to be a tough go, crossing 1,200 yards of rice paddies from the MLR to a trench line at the foot of Vegas, totally exposed

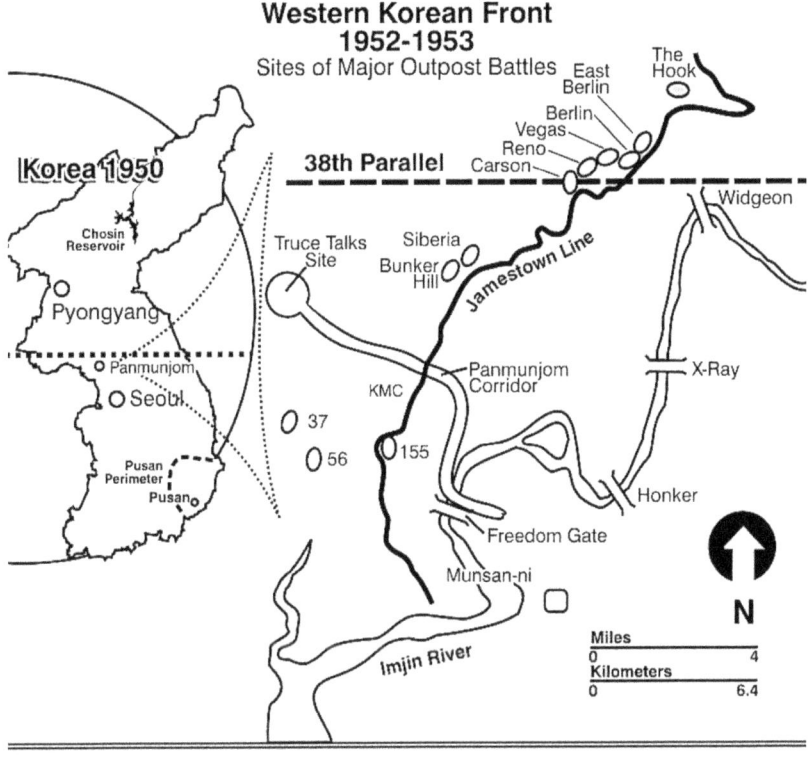
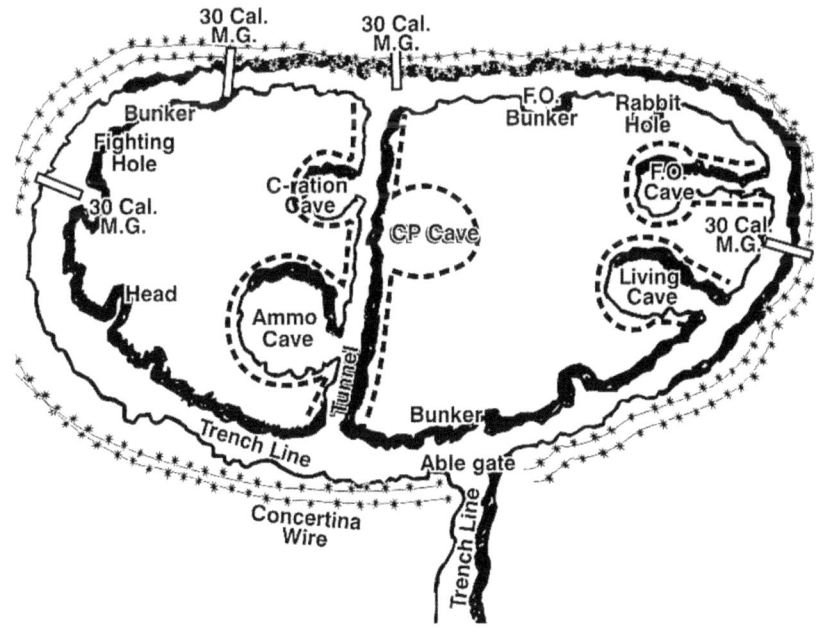

to Chinese observers. I made it after an hour without any problems and entered the south perimeter at the Able Gate. I joined the other FO, called "Jonesy," and stored my gear in a small cave dug into the topographical crest of the hill. I then took a break since I was pooped from my trip up the hill. We were both amazed that not one enemy round had been fired at me crossing no-man's land. Jonesy then took me through the base showing me the defensive positions in the trench line that encircled the outpost. The depth of the trench line varied from 4 to 12 feet deep.

One of the first things that I noticed was that the trench line had a mass of cut and broken communication wire from the enemy incoming. EE 8 phone lines and sound power lines from Vegas to our fire direction center [FDC] back at the MLR, in addition to our communication lines to the command post [CP] on Vegas, lay strewn throughout the trenches. When a line was knocked out, a new line was laid since it was nearly impossible to locate and repair a damaged line. On top of that, we had the weather problem. The ground was still frozen in some places and muddy in the heavily traveled areas.

Jonesy pointed out key terrain features, possible enemy positions, routes and most importantly, we talked about "box-me-ins," only to be used when under heavy enemy attack. Equally important was that I had good communications at all times with the MLR by 619 radios and EE 8 landlines. It seemed as though our defensive posture was well planned and laid out. The situation on 21 March was quiet with no Chinese activity or incoming. That's how it is before the shit hits the fan, which it would, much sooner than we would realize. It was a sure bet that the Chinese were getting ready for a big spring offensive.

We continued to work our way around the trench line and came to the FO observation bunker on the forward right slope of Vegas. In front of us were three prominent hills: 190, 150 and 153, all held by the Chinese. Throughout the perimeter were fighting holes, bunkers and caves carved into the walls of the trench lines. There were four .30 caliber machine guns positioned to the front and sides of the outpost. Down the center of the hill was another trench, with caves for the CP, ammunition, food, water and medical supplies. There were also three rows of concertina wire and mines surrounding the hill.

We met with the CO [commanding officer] on the hill, Lieutenant Kenneth E. Taft [great-grandson of former President William Howard Taft], who told me to come back when it got dark to see what the Chinese positions and surrounding terrain looked like at night. He reported that Chinese activity seemed to be increasing in the last few days.

22–24 March 1953
COP Vegas

The second day we started to receive our first incoming at about 0700. It was very sporadic at first, but as the day wore on, it increased in intensity and was more consistent. We had four WIAs and one KIA before the day ended, who were brought down by Korean laborers, whom we called chig-ee bearers, who also brought up supplies and replacements at dusk. I did not call in any fire missions to the FDC this day. On days three and four [23–24 March], we received massive amounts of mortar fire. Each day the intensity was greater than the day before. "Artie" came up that night to Vegas, and replaced Jonesy as my FO partner.

25 March 1953
COP Vegas

I asked Lieutenant Taft if he felt it advisable if Artie and I lay a secondary phone line to the FDC at the MLR as backup because of the recent increased incoming intensity. He agreed and said he would give us a fire team for protection and that we should plan to be back before 1900 so that we did not interfere with other night patrols. As Artie and I made it back to our cave, a heavy enemy machine gun opened up on us from Hill 190. We decided not to wear our bulky restricted winter clothing so as not to hinder our movement down and back up to Vegas. We hooked up our new phone line from the CP and then left out through the Able Gate, along with a rifleman and a BAR man, and headed off the hill. We decided that if we made contact, we would try to make it to a smaller hill between Reno and Vegas, called Reno Block, which was manned by a Marine squad during the night. The rifleman led the way, while I followed, laying the new communication line. Artie was next in line, carrying two payouts of wire, tied to a pack board. The BAR man brought up the rear. After what seemed like a long time, we made it to the MLR and after answering challenges from a listening post, we made our way into the friendly lines. We went to the communication bunker, which was on the reverse slope of the rolling hills that made up the Jamestown Line. Soon we had hooked up our new line to the switchboard. We did a quick line check to our CP on Vegas and then headed back up. This time we took a separate route from the one that we had taken down. We avoided obvious ambush locations, ridgelines and stopped every 100 yards or so to listen for any sounds at all. We finally made it back to Vegas at about 2000 and checked in at the CP to report to Lieutenant Taft. Artie then went back to our cave while I headed for the FO bunker. The 4.2 mortar FO, "Beck," was already there and he brought me up to date.

The enemy incoming had now increased, about one heavy mortar every five seconds or so. At about 2100, just after Beck left, I observed through the bunker aperture a brightness coming from behind Hill 190 and heard what I thought sounded like a convoy of trucks. After checking with Lieutenant Taft, I called in a fire mission on the enemy area with the FDC. They were not used to fire missions that late unless it was interdiction fire or "box-me-ins." The officer in charge of the FDC, a 1st lieutenant, questioned my mission, so Lieutenant Taft got on the line to confirm the truck noise and lights that we had observed. After a one-round adjustment, I called the battery for "Fire for effect." It seemed like the whole hill of 190 was blown apart from left to right for about 100 yards. You could only see flames and smoke and we heard many secondary explosions. We deemed the mission successful with a probable enemy ammo dump destroyed.

Artie and Beck came up to relieve me at around 2300 and I went back to our cave, being very careful when passing through the area that the Chinese machine gunner had zeroed in. When I got in the cave, I laid down on broken C-ration cartons, which insulated us from the damp and wet ground. I went out like a light and slept through the night. Artie and Beck let me sleep through the intensive Chinese incoming throughout the evening.

26 March 1953
COP Vegas

When I awoke, it was 0500 and my mouth was like sandpaper. I was cruddy and dirty, wearing the same utilities, socks and underwear for the last five days in the mud, snow and rice paddies. My body odor was so bad it would drive away even the rats. Today was my day to leave Vegas. In the past, the relief was normally made at about 1700 or later. This past week, however, the relief for a rifleman or FO would come at either daylight or at dusk. The exception was for casualties. They would try to get them off as soon as possible. I told Artie I was going to wait at the Able Gate and hope that my relief would come that morning. At the Gate, I was told that three wounded and one KIA were already taken off by a corpsman and stretcher-bearers. I waited until 0700 and knew my relief was not coming until that evening. I was pissed! All I could think about was getting off Vegas and getting a hot shower and clean clothes.

I went to the FO bunker to join Artie and Beck to keep myself and my thoughts occupied until that night. Although the incoming was not letting up, there were no targets of opportunity for us to call in a fire mission. After talking for a while, Artie and I went back to our cave and slept for a few hours. My gear and radio were ready to go. I decided to remove the battery from my 619 radio and leave it, along with the extra one that I had originally brought up. Artie woke up and we talked for a while. He asked me if I knew who my relief was going to be. I told him I had no idea and wished him well, as I headed out again for the Able Gate. When I arrived, a Marine joked about my relief, saying he had probably missed this second attempt. That was not what I wanted to hear. As we talked, a mortar round hit on the reverse slope in front of his position. He was lucky he was wearing his heavy parka over his flak jacket because a large piece of shrapnel had penetrated his jacket. The tempo of the incoming was now greatly increasing. There were several of us at the Able Gate. Two were wounded and three were waiting to be relieved. Finally, my relief entered our base. It was an old friend, "Drum." I was surprised because I knew he only had a month left before he rotated home. We moved down the trench line and I gave him a brief rundown of things on Vegas. I told him that Artie would fill him in completely.

We shook hands and I wished him the best. I waited no longer, as I was the last man to leave that night. I took my radio and my weapon and left Vegas through the trench. I made it to the foot of Vegas and kept as low as possible as I headed out. My thoughts were if I got to the halfway mark, I would be in good shape. I don't think I made 100 yards before they spotted me. The first rounds were over, the next couple a little short. They were bracketing me. To my left front, a couple hundred yards away, was a large dip in the ground. If I got to it, it would offer some concealment. They adjusted their range on me, one round hit close to my right. I took my radio off and got on the ground fast. The next round was so close I could feel the hot air from it and pieces of frozen ground hit all around me. The next round was even closer. I could not believe they were hitting that close and shrapnel was not hitting me. At that moment, if I were an atheist, I would surely have found God.

They ceased fire on me because I was sure they thought I was dead. My radio was damaged beyond repair. I lay there for a little longer and then grabbed my weapon, got up and ran all out for the dip that I had previously seen. I think I made it in record-breaking time. It took a few minutes to catch my breath and to settle down. It was starting to get dark as it was now close to 1800. I planned to wait until full darkness and then move out towards the MLR, hoping not to run into a Chinese patrol. While waiting for the darkness, I couldn't help thinking of Drum, Artie, Beck and Lieutenant Taft, along with all of the other men on Vegas. The Chinese were plastering the outpost as if to reduce it to an anthill. With the kind of barrage that the enemy was pounding on Vegas, Reno and Carson, it was now obvious that a major attack would soon follow.

It was much easier to move without my radio to hamper me if I had to move fast or run. I got up and moved out. The sounds of the incoming, exploding on all of the Nevada City outposts, was deafening. Cannon fire and white flashes were coming from our MLR. It was counterbattery fire from the 11th Marines' artillery. There was no doubt that the Chinese were going to jump off. My problem was walking into artillery rounds falling short of the MLR fired by the Chinese. I kept walking and hoped I was closer to the MLR than I thought I was. I finally came up to a small, vacated bunker used as a listening post and I knew that I was now close to the MLR. I approached the friendly lines and was challenged by the sergeant in charge. When I came up to him, he looked at me as if I had come from Mars, not because I was so filthy looking and had a beard, but because I had just come through all of that incoming hitting Vegas and Reno. He probably thought I was a ghost. I was taken to the CP and was asked about the situation on Vegas by the lieutenant in charge. He then had someone take me to the hygienic unit where I showered and changed my filthy clothes for clean ones. After the shower, I felt ten pounds lighter after washing all that filth and grime from my body and hair. When I was finished, I made it back to my Baker Company, 1/5. I soon learned that the situation on Vegas and Reno was in doubt but Carson appeared to be holding on. Later, I discovered that 36 Marines, including Lieutenant Taft, had been killed and my three FO buddies, Drum, Artie and Beck, were all captured along with five others. I was the last and only survivor to escape Vegas, and without receiving even one scratch![3]

Postlude

After several days of continuous enemy bombardment, in the early evening of 26 March 1953, the Chinese 358th Regiment stormed the three Nevada outposts. Carson held on but Reno was soon overrun in short order. Survivors retreated into caves; however, the Chinese quickly sealed the caves while the riflemen passed out from lack of oxygen. Elements from 1/5 went to their aid but they were ambushed near Reno Block and incurred numerous injuries.[4]

On Vegas, the situation was equally serious. Lieutenant Taft fearlessly exposed himself to the murderous enemy artillery and mortar fire and skillfully effected an urgently needed reorganization of his intrepid garrison of Marines in an effort to stem the onrushing hostile troops. When the enemy gained the friendly trench line and overran the position, forcing the platoon to withdraw to the command post bunker, Taft provided a stirring example of leadership and courage during those crucial moments. He opened fire with his pistol in a final courageous effort to stave off the attackers, personally killing several of the enemy, before a hostile satchel charge was hurled into the bunker. Lieutenant Taft (later Captain Taft) was posthumously awarded the Navy Cross.[5]

Colonel Lewis Walt, CO of the 5th Marines, quickly organized a counterattack with the help of 2/7. At dawn on 27 March, air strikes, artillery and mortars opened up on the now enemy-controlled Vegas hilltop in preparation for an infantry assault. As three Marine companies launched their attack, they came under hundreds of enemy artillery rounds in an effort to stop the Marine advance. The battles continued back and forth and finally, by 30 March, all of the Nevada outposts were back in Marine control. Total friendly losses were 156 KIA, 801 WIA and 19 captured, while the 358th Chinese Communist Regiment suffered 1,200 killed, sealing their fate for the remainder of the war.[6]

The outpost battles continued until the end of the Korean War in June 1953, during which time the truce talks were underway at the nearby city of Panmunjon. In the entire Korean War, from 1950 to 1953, 4,262 Marines were killed. In the campaign of the outpost wars, 1952–1953, 1,689 Marines were killed or 43 percent of all Marine KIA casualties.[7]

I stayed in the same area, even after the 23rd Army Division and a Turkish brigade replaced the 1st Marine Division. Our 11th Marine artillery stayed in support, mainly for the Turks. I joined a new FO team and was assigned to a battalion with the Turkish brigade. We stayed with them until the 1st Marine Division came back on line. I think this was sometime in late May 1953. I then joined another new FO team and we were assigned to 1/1 that was protecting the MLR overlooking the Panmunjon Corridor.

I returned to the States in November 1953 by ship aboard the USS *John Pope*, a troop carrier. We landed at Treasure Island in San Francisco, California. After a few days of processing, we were given a 30-day leave. I later reported in to my new assignment with the 1st Battalion, 10th Marines at Camp Lejeune and I was discharged in July 1954.

When I left the Marine Corps, I worked for the First National City

Bank of New York for one year, but realized banking was not for me. I then went to college (New York City College and NYU), while working for Parents Magazine. After college, I was employed in the hotel business in public relations, which I retired from years later. I now enjoy reading, cooking, putting together photo albums and politics.

Never married, James stays in contact with his Marine friends. He belongs to the 1st Marine Division Association, the Marine Corps Heritage Foundation, the Marine Memorial Association and the Marine Corps Association. He attends reunions and visits his old buddies as often as possible.[8]

I received a phone call from James Larkin in April 2006 in response to my article in the *Old Breed News*. He was very excited to tell me his story, but said it would take a long time to write since the battle descriptions were very dramatic and he wanted to get the story accurately reported. I almost gave up on him and wrote him a note of encouragement. We exchanged several other phone calls over the months and finally, I received a 21-page handwritten letter, detailing his exploits on Outpost Vegas on 22 September 2006. He also included maps and some pictures. On 1 October 2006, I received my answers from a questionnaire that I had previously sent him.

31

Korea: "Calls of Nature"

> Luck does not favor hesitation.
> — Roman words of wisdom

Prelude

An interesting dilemma that most people never even consider, unless they have been in a bogged-down fixed-position war like World War I or the last years of the Korean War, is how to go to the bathroom without getting killed! This chapter tells two stories, one of a Marine and the other a Navy corpsman, who both had "calls of nature" that very easily could have had disastrous results.

USMC Private First Class Melvin Boland

"Mel" Boland was born on 25 April 1930 and grew up in St. Louis, Missouri. Twenty-one years later, to the month, Mel found himself assigned to Baker Company, 1st Battalion, 1st Marines (1/1) in the hills of Korea as a Marine rifleman.

It was in late June or early July 1951. I'm not sure; dates are a bit hazy in my mind after 50 years. I and my foxhole buddy, Dale, were dug in near the crest of a large hill east of Chunchon, Korea, near the 38th parallel. It was about five miles across the valley to the next range of hills where the Chinese positions were located. Shortly after daylight, the Chinese began sniping at us with what sounded like a 76mm recoilless rifle. For sure, it was a flat trajectory "whiz-bang!" When the round went by, we knew it was a high velocity weapon. You could tell by the whistle. The rounds either hit the side of the hill where we were dug in, or kept on going to give some of those in the rear areas a taste of what it was like on the line. Everything was quiet the second morning we were on the hill and I told Dale I felt like a cup of cocoa. I mashed the round block of cocoa from my breakfast C-ration, poured it into my canteen cup, filled it with water and began to warm it over a small can of "liquid heat." It was soon hot, almost too hot to drink. I lifted it gingerly to my lips. As I did so, the first 76mm round of the day came in, right at us. In a mad dash, I scrambled back into our foxhole, spilling cocoa all over Dale.

When the Chinese gunner finally decided to halt his daily pot shots, we had a chance to dig our shoulders out of our helmets. Dale looked over at me and said very seriously, "Boland, they saw the steam from your cocoa." I spent the rest of the day trying to convince him that it was impossible for the gunner or anyone for that matter who was five miles away, even with binoculars, to see the small amount of steam from my cup of cocoa. Even though I did not fully convince him, he put up no argument the next morning when I tried again to start my foxhole day with a bracing cup of hot cocoa. You guessed it. I don't have to tell you what happened! My cup of hot cocoa gave Dale another hot bath of sticky cocoa. After that, all the talking in the world could not have convinced him, even if our division commander, Major General Thomas, had passed the word! He was firmly convinced that the Chinese had spotted the steam from a distance of five miles away. I tried to tell him it was me, out in the open warming my cocoa, not the steam from the cocoa that the gunner had spotted. It was useless. Dale and I were foxhole buddies for many months after that. He carried the conviction that steam from cocoa was a dead giveaway. Anytime I fired up a cup of cocoa, Dale left our foxhole to go elsewhere.

While in that same position, the Chinese gunner persisted. He seemed to take a vindictive delight in taking shots in our vicinity. After I had spilled the second cup of hot cocoa over Dale, I stayed in our foxhole during daylight hours. That gunner was too damn good. I didn't care to risk my hide further to his accuracy and unlimited supply of ammo. We had now been in the same position for three days. As with most of humanity, my body had long ago reached a state of regularity with the elimination function common to all mammals. Every morning my "urge" was as regular as clockwork. My problem in taking care of the "urge" over the past three days was an alert Chinese gunner. He was active from daylight to dusk. I had gained great respect for his abilities. I no longer challenged him by leaving our foxhole. The third morning at my usual time, I reached a point of desperation. I told Dale, "I gotta go! I'll have to stay in our foxhole while I attend to the call of nature." Dale said to me in all seriousness, "Boland, you'll just have to get yourself killed. You are not going to use this hole to relieve yourself." He damn well meant it too. I began timing the interval between rounds.

There seemed to be eight seconds between each round. I had a huge wad of paper in my hand. I knew I would have little time for delicacy of manners. I worked my fatigues down around my ankles, ready to spring out of our foxhole. When I heard the next round, I was out of that hole with the speed of a cheetah and the leap of a gazelle. I moved about five feet away from our foxhole, stuck my behind down hill and let it fly. It sounded like a small explosion. I used one hand to pull my fatigues part way up my legs. The other hand with the wad of paper was busy doing what I told it to do. Finished with my wad of paper, I tossed it downhill. I used that hand, now free of encumbrance, to pull the other leg of my fatigues around my waist while simultaneously emulating a base runner sliding home, just in time to escape the gunner's next round. I sang the Hallelujah Chorus with deep feeling! Handel would have been proud.

Dale was laughing. I had to join him. Even then it was funny, but also damn serious. Literally, my butt was on the line! We talked about entering "Bolands's Eight-Second Bowel Movement" into the *Guinness Book of World Records* but decided there was no apt category.[1]

USN Hospital Corpsman Third Class Robert Wickman

Robert Wickman or "Doc" and "Wick," as he became referred to, was born on 25 March 1931 in Keizer, Oregon.

I enlisted 28 September 1950. I specifically joined the U.S. Navy to "see the world," have a clean bunk and eat hot chow. It looked as if it would all work out until I took the placement test at NTC [Naval Training Center] Boot Camp. Because my vision was not the best (I had memorized the eye chart to enlist), I wasn't qualified for Naval Air. My second choice was hospital corpsman since I had a desire to pursue a career in medicine. The interviewer, who knew a lot more about the services than I did, said, "Are you sure?" I told him I was sure. I went to hospital corps school at the Navy Hospital in San Diego. A little more than two years later, I received orders to the fleet medical service school at Camp Del Mar in Camp Pendleton, California.

I shipped to Korea aboard the transport ship *Meigs* in June of 1953, arriving in Korea about three weeks later. The medical corpsmen, a part of the 33rd Replacement Draft, were assigned where needed. I went to Item (I) Company, 3rd Battalion, 7th Marines. When I joined the 7th Marines as a corpsman, the 1st Marine Division was in Corps reserve. On the 4th of July, after a huge Independence Day celebration, we moved to the "Boulder City" area, where the 25th Army Division was waiting to be relieved.[2]

The "Boulder City" area was located along the Jamestown Line east of Outpost Vegas and roughly between and south of outposts Berlin and East Berlin.[3]

For some unknown reason, I was sent to make a sanitation inspection of the area the army was leaving. During the process I spied a brand-new, latest-style flak jacket lying on a bunk in a vacant tent. There was no doubt the jacket needed a more careful owner. I left the war-torn and tattered flak jacket issued to me on the bunk. I tried the new jacket for fit. It could have been larger, but it covered me in the vital spots. A few steps away from the tent, an Army lieutenant stopped me and inquired about my new flak jacket. I knew I had been had. At this most appropriate moment in an awkward situation, the chaplain's driver drove up to tell me a corpsman was needed to go to East Berlin. I had been assigned that duty. The lieutenant wished me "good luck" as he held my old flak jacket in his left hand and waved goodbye with his right. The driver took off for the Item Company CP as soon as I could climb in the jeep.

The first relief patrol took a wrong path ending in a heavily mined saddle between Berlin and East Berlin. A mine detonated! A lieutenant was killed and several others were wounded. The wounded were treated and sent to the rear. We went to East Berlin. An almost constant H & I [harassment and interdiction] fire battered us. Days were hot and bodies were bloating. The stench was terrible. In front of our "crab hole" was a mound. It didn't take long to find out what it covered. Shrapnel gouged the mound. The bloated body in the mound was in full decay. The blow flies came. My "crab hole" was on the forward slope, towards "goony land." Nature called! I asked a seasoned Marine, "Where do I go to relieve myself?" All he said was, "Stand up, Doc." The trench parapet was only three feet high and there wasn't much cover. I had just begun a good stream when I noticed puffs of dirt "walking" toward me. I had been zeroed in by a gook machine gun. Immediate problem solved. The gooks were experts with mortars. They would "walk" our trench line at their leisure. I lost my hearing for about eight hours. An area where I was treating a wounded Marine was too close to their incoming fire. My ears have rung incessantly ever since.

A four-holer [field toilet] was in an area targeted by their mortars. One Marine had just positioned himself on the "throne." I have never seen anyone run so fast with his pants hanging below his knees. He dove into the trench just as a direct hit landed on the four-holer, and scattered its contents over a wide area.

Several days before the cease-fire, fighting intensified. The "goony" attacks penetrated our trench lines. Our casualties were heavy. At times my hands were so slick with blood I could barely start an IV. I have since learned from our Company XO that the final battle for "Boulder City" was one of the most severe of the entire war. I feel privileged to have survived the last battles of the Korean War and to have been on the hill the night the cease-fire flares were fired at 2200 hours on 27 July 1953. I feel proud to have served my country as a Navy corpsman with the United States Marines. At reunions, I come in contact with several Marines who say I treated their wounds. They are very emotional moments.[4]

Postlude

The Korean War, known by its veterans as the "Forgotten War," took a terrible toll of casualties in just three years. The military casualties for the NATO forces totaled over 474,000 dead, wounded and missing. The armies of South Korea and the United States had the highest casualties. The United States alone suffered 36,516 killed, 92,134 wounded, 8,176 missing and 7,245 prisoners of war. The communists (North Korea, China and the Soviet Union) lost somewhere between 1.2 and 1.5 million soldiers to casualties. The total Korean civilians killed and wounded on both sides are estimated to be in the millions![5] Within ten years another Asian war would erupt, this time in Vietnam, and once again the Americans would be heavily involved. The South Koreans would, in turn, commit troops to aid the American cause.

Postscript

Another factor in dealing with "calls of nature" during the Korean War was the extreme cold that the Marines endured during the winter months. Lee Bergee (see chapter 20) states, "We would wait until the heat of the day, which was normally around 1500, and then do our best to get the job done. It wasn't easy, and hundreds of men were constipated throughout the campaign."[6]

These stories, from *Red Dragon: Faces of War II*, jumped out at me for both their unique and humorous content.

Part Three: Vietnam

All of us have bad luck. The man who persists
through the bad luck — who keeps right on going — is the man
who is there when good luck comes — and is ready to receive it.
— Robert Collier

32

USMC Private First Class Bruce Horton

> Luck is a dividend of sweat. The more
> you sweat, the luckier you get.
> — Ray Kroc

Prelude

Bruce Horton was born on 7 September 1948 in Burke, South Dakota, but was raised in the town of Gregory within the same state. His family was poor and he had two brothers and two sisters. As a child, he and his best friend would catch tadpoles, frogs and turtles and go camping during the summer. In the winter, it was sledding, building snow forts and shoveling driveways for extra money. When he was five, his Uncle Vern showed up at his house, decked out in his new dress blues Marine uniform. Bruce knew right then that he wanted to be a Marine too. In his teenage years, Bruce started to get into trouble. He soon felt it was time to change his environment and joined the Marines in August 1966.

He entered boot camp at MCRD in San Diego, California. After boot camp, he headed off to Camp Pendleton, where he went through both the Infantry Training Regiment (ITR) and Advanced Infantry Training (AIT) schools. It was during AIT that Horton received the nickname, "Charlie." This name stuck with him throughout his Marine Corps enlistment. Whenever they went out on practice patrols during war games, he always brought up the rear, which was called "Tail End Charlie." Without getting a regular stateside assignment after his infantry training, he was immediately shipped off to Vietnam in March 1967. Upon arrival in Vietnam, he joined up with the 1st Battalion, 9th Marines (1/9), where he was assigned to Company C.[1]

A Brief History of the 1st Battalion, 9th Marines

The 1st Battalion, 9th Marines was activated on 9 September 1942 and became part of the 3rd Marine Division. Its role is to "locate, close with and

South Vietnam and the I Corps

destroy the enemy with fire and maneuver." During the Second World War, the unit heroically participated in the battles of Bougainville, Guam and Iwo Jima.

During the Vietnam War, 1/9 was given the unique nickname of "The Walking Dead." The Battalion had the highest killed in action rate in Marine Corps history. It was engaged in combat in Vietnam for 47 months and 7 days, during which time 749 of its Marines and corpsmen were killed.

In the late 1980s, 1/9 was deactivated to make room for one of the three light armor reconnaissance (LAR) battalions. In late 2005, the Battalion was once again activated for service in the Global War on Terrorism.[2]

1967
1st Battalion, 9th Marines
Quang Tri Province, Vietnam

The 1st Battalion operated in the northern I Corps region in Quang Tri Province. It was headquartered on the high ground at Dong Ha, which was visible to the critical area around Con Thien. In spring of 1967, the North Vietnamese Army (NVA) decided to concentrate on the Marine strong point at Con Thien, located 14 miles inland and 2 miles south of the Demilitarized Zone (DMZ). This outpost was crucial to Marine efforts in the area. Con Thien overlooked one of the principal enemy routes into South Vietnam. Capture of this outpost would open the way for a major invasion of the Quang Tri Province by the 35,000 enemy troops massed above the DMZ. The initial 1967 offensive aimed at Con Thien occurred in July 1967, and for the first time, the NVA would employ extensive artillery to support its infantry.

2 July 1967
1st Battalion, 9th Marines
Con Thien Area
Operation Buffalo

Operation Buffalo began on 2 July 1967 utilizing Lieutenant Colonel Richard J. Schening's 1st Battalion, 9th Marines in and around Con Thien. A and B Companies operated northeast of the strong point near a former marketplace on Route 51, while D and H&S Companies, along with the command group, remained within the outpost perimeter on Con Thien. C Company was at Dong Ha at the 9th Marines command post.

By 0900, both A and B Companies became engaged with the enemy,

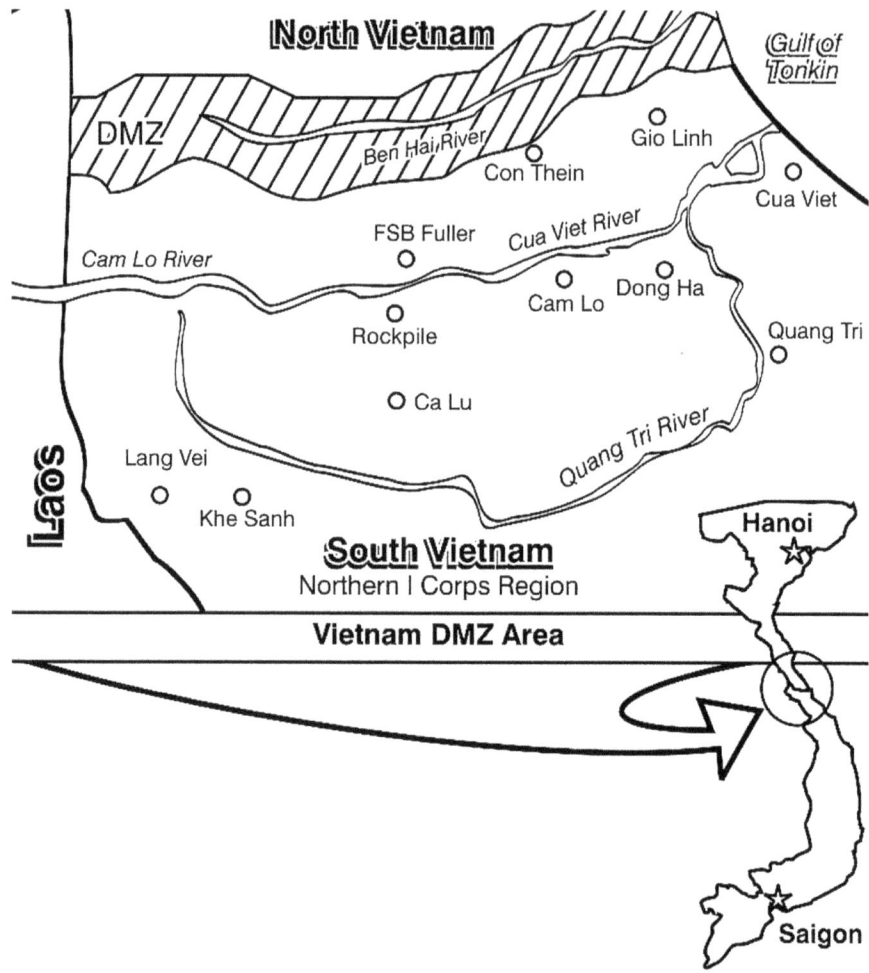

which was later estimated to be an NVA multi-battalion force. Besides heavy automatic fire, the North Vietnamese utilized artillery, mortars and flamethrowers against the outmanned Marine forces. The 1/9 battalion commander immediately ordered Company C to helicopter in from Dong Ha to link up with Company B and also sent in a platoon and 4 tanks from his Con Thien base to make a link-up and help with removal of the casualties. As C Company arrived, the advanced units were met by a heavy artillery barrage, which wounded eleven Marines. By this time, most of the officers in Company B had been killed, including the commanding officer, Captain Sterling Coates.

By 1500, Lieutenant Colonel Schening notified the 9th Marines' regimental commander, Colonel George Jerue, that he needed outside assistance as all of his units were heavily engaged and that he had no more Marines to commit to the critical fight. Jerue responded by sending in 3/9, which took control of Companies A and C while the rest of the 1st Battalion units returned to Con Thien. This increased pressure caused the NVA to temporarily break contact. 1/9 had lost 84 killed in action (KIA), 190 wounded in action (WIA), and 9 missing in action (MIA), with enemy losses unknown. Included in the wounded was the C Company commander, Captain Hutchenson. Due to the heavy losses, Companies A and C were combined with approximately 80 men under the command of Captain Al Slater.

During the next few days, BLTs (Battalion Landing Teams) 1/3 and 2/3 joined the 9th Marines, as they attacked northwards in search of missing Marines and kept applying pressure against the NVA. The fighting continued under intermittent NVA artillery and mortar fire, with skirmishes occurring every day. Both sides incurred losses with the advantage now favoring the Marines, as they were able to use their own artillery in close support. On the afternoon of 5 July, an air observer spotted a large concentration of NVA 3,000 meters northeast of Con Thien. He called in artillery and air strikes and later reported observing 200 dead enemy soldiers.[3]

6 July 1967
Combined Companies A and C, 1/9 attached to 3/9 Operation Buffalo

On 6 July, the combined A and C Company, along with a detachment from the 3rd Reconnaissance Battalion, were moved 1,500 meters to the north-northeast to cover the main Marine forces' left flank. This maneuver was unseen by the enemy and they were able to dig in and establish a strong fighting position. At 1600, the main Marine units came under heavy artillery fire, estimated at nearly 1,500 rounds. During this barrage, 400 NVA crossed the Ben Hai River and approached in marching formation, still unaware that they would be crossing the unseen A and C Company position. When the enemy was within 150 meters, Captain Slater's small group opened up and totally confused the NVA, who never knew the true size of the opposing force. They continued probing the perimeter, but with the aid of accurate friendly artillery, sometimes as close as 75 meters from their lines, the Marines held their ground.[4]

In the early evening, our 3-man fire team was assigned to our nighttime position by our platoon sergeant and squad leader. My two teammates were Lance Corporals Baker and Rogers, who had both just joined the Battalion about 10 days prior to 6 July. We were positioned in an area that had tree saplings or bushes about eight feet high all around us except for the direct front. It was like a horseshoe design with bushes to our back and along both sides for about 40 feet. We started to dig our foxhole, but quickly discovered that the ground was as hard as cement. While the other two continued digging, I located an empty hole that had been previously dug by the NVA. After checking it for booby traps, I notified my teammates and we moved in. The new hole was in a much better position as we were now at the top of the horseshoe. We had a better field of fire and could see Marines to our right, about 100–150 feet away by a big tree.

The three of us had discussed our strategy in case we had enemy contact that night. It was concluded that Lance Corporal Baker and I would provide cover fire so that Lance Corporal Rogers could throw the grenades. We each had two grenades and gave them all to him. He was the biggest of us and would be able to throw them further. I took the first watch while the other two sat in the hole, eating. It was just starting to get near dusk when I heard several gooks talking. Almost instantly, about 30–40 NVA came running out of the bushes and trees at about our 10 o'clock. It took me a couple of seconds to realize they were the enemy since the first two had on Marine helmets and flak jackets and were carrying M-16s.

I opened up with two magazines on full automatic and hit between six and eight of them before I went to semi-automatic and continued to fire. I heard Rogers say, "I got one." I could see some of them crawling in the grass due to the green leaves and branches that they tried to use as camouflage. It wasn't too hard to see them against the brown ground. I continued to fire and stopped eight or nine of them. Then, there was an explosion and I felt pain in my left leg and said, "I'm hit!" I looked down at my leg and in doing so, saw that Baker had been seriously wounded in the hand by a chi-com [Chinese Communist] grenade. Rogers appeared to be in shock and was just sitting in the bottom of the hole. I yelled to the Marines in the next hole and asked for assistance. They replied that they had their hands full and could not offer any help.

For some reason, and I don't have an answer to this day, I suddenly turned to my left at about 8 o'clock and saw a gook with his hand and arm in the air. I fired five or six times and hit him with three or four bullets. His body jerked and fell to the ground. When I hit him, his eyes got the size of silver dollars. Almost immediately, I heard a thud, knew it was another grenade and covered my face with my left arm. The chi-com blew and shrapnel tore into my arm, shoulder and left side of my head. My rifle and helmet landed outside of the foxhole. I turned to my companions but they were both combat ineffective at this time.

I jumped out of the hole, grabbed my rifle, yelled to where I thought another Marine foxhole might be and once again asked for help. I took a step back to get into my hole when I felt a new pain in my right ankle. It was as if someone hit my shin with a baseball bat.

I must have passed out because the next thing I knew was that it was pitch black and I was about four to five feet away from my foxhole. I couldn't see anything and called out for my fire team several times but heard no response. Finally, a flare went off and I saw that no one was in, or around, the hole. I also realized that my rifle, flak jacket and all of my gear was missing. While I was passed out, the NVA had come in and stripped my gear off thinking that I was dead! I had no idea where my team was.

I started to crawl through the bushes to the foxhole on my right and felt stinging in my wounded left leg. There were several pieces of wooden splinters sticking out of my leg. I pulled them out and continued along until another flare went off and I saw my squad leader in a small hole. I called out and made it over to his position. I told him that I needed a weapon so I could find my missing teammates. He replied that all he had was a .45 pistol and that the two of us were going to stay put until morning. I must have passed out from time to time because he kept telling me to be quiet. I remember feeling as if ants were biting or eating at my wounds.

In the morning of 7 July, we moved back to a road to link up with some of the other Marines. Once on the road, two men sat me on their rifles in a carry position and another gave me a flak jacket, which was way too large for me. They carried me to a landing zone [LZ] and sat me on a tree stump. As I was sitting, every time I moved, the oversized flak jacket rubbed against my shoulders and arm. It hurt like hell and I tried to take it off but the platoon sergeant insisted that I leave it on. A corpsman walked by and I asked him to remove more of the bamboo sticking out of my head. He told me it would be better to leave them in until I got to the hospital because if they were taken out I might go into shock. I replied that I had already taken some out of my leg and he retorted back sternly, "Leave them alone!"

Finally, a medevac chopper landed nearby and I lumbered in. It was already full of dead and wounded Marines, including Baker and Rogers sitting in the front. I nodded at them and passed out. We all ended up on the USS *Sanctuary* hospital ship.[5]

During the previous evening, heavy enemy probes, mortar fire and small arms fire had continued to maintain pressure on the Marines until 2200. Throughout the rest of the night, small arms and mortar fire harassed the combined Company, but most of the NVA had begun withdrawing. In the morning, 154 enemy bodies were found strewn around the Marines' position. There were only 12 friendly casualties! The Company was ordered to return to the Battalion's perimeter. Just after leaving, a 30-minute NVA artillery barrage landed within their old lines.[6]

Postlude

Operation Buffalo continued through 14 July 1967. There were a few more significant battles, but those on the 2nd and 6th were by far the largest. NVA bodies were located everywhere and it was difficult to get an accurate count since so many had perished due to heavy artillery supporting fires. The Marines even resorted to counting enemy canteens because the bodies were horribly torn apart. It was also not possible to cross the Ben Hai River to search further because it was still too dangerous. The Marines reported 1,290 dead NVA and two captured while their losses totaled 159 killed and 345 wounded. Of the known enemy killed, more than 500 came from air, artillery and naval gunfire. In addition, supporting arms destroyed 164 bunkers and 15 artillery and rocket positions. To accomplish this, Marine aviation used 1,066 tons of ordnance, Marine and Army artillery consumed more than 40,000 rounds and Navy ships fired 1,500 rounds of 5" and 8" naval guns. On the other hand, enemy artillery accounted for half of the Marine casualties during the operation and posed a constant threat to logistical support installations.[7]

In mid July, my former fire-team members came into my ward on board the hospital ship, but frankly, I was not very happy to see them. I felt as if they had let me down. They both returned to the States and I went back to Charlie Company, 1/9 at the end of September 1967.[8]

In April 1968, Horton completed his tour and returned to Camp Pendleton, California. After just two days of stateside duty, however, he again volunteered to go back to Vietnam. He completed a second tour, assigned to both 3/27 and 3/5, and eventually left the Corps. He attended college briefly and held a variety of jobs including working for the Postal Service. He reentered the Marines in 1975 but was discharged two years later due to military-related disabilities. He married and had one son, Craig, but would later divorce in 1999.

Today, Bruce enjoys fishing and taking care of his large landscape. He belongs to the Marine Corps Association, Disabled American Veterans and the Vietnam Vets of America. He receives treatment for his medical needs through the Veterans Administration. He has attended one 1/9 reunion that was held in Las Vegas in 2002.

The Marine Corps gave me a sense of belonging to something special. They taught me what loyalty and honor were. I made more friends, and I mean ones that I could trust, than I ever knew possible.[9]

I received a phone call from Bruce Horton in early January 2006, in response to a request for info that I had placed in the January issue of *Leatherneck* magazine. He briefly told me about his close call experience and I requested that he write his story down and send it to me. Within a short time period, I received an 8-page letter, dated 9 January 2006, and his first words were, "Welcome Home." This is a common greeting amongst Vietnam veterans, who never did receive their welcome home from the American public. A second letter arrived on 2 June 2006, with his personal information that I had requested earlier.

33

USMC Captain John McLaughlin

> A pound of pluck is worth a ton of luck.
> — James A. Garfield

Prelude

John Larry McLaughlin was an only child who was born in Atoka, Tennessee, on 19 November 1938. He lived in the rural South and, as a youngster, helped out with the family farm. He loved sports and lettered in football, baseball and basketball at his high schools. He attended both the University of Tennessee and Bethel College in McKenzie, Tennessee, where he also lettered in football and basketball. In June of 1959, he married and started a family, which would eventually include three sons. John graduated from Bethel College in 1960 with a B.S. degree with three majors: social studies, education and health, and physical education. His intentions were to become a high school coach and teacher.[1]

> During the summer of 1960, I saw a Marine, in full uniform, in the student center at Bethel College. I sat down with him and inquired who he was and what he was doing at Bethel. I then went home and told my wife that I had joined the Marine Corps. It is a good thing that tongue-lashings don't leave welts or I'd be horribly disfigured. Later, we went back together and with her full approval, I signed up. I had my teaching credentials, but the best job offer I had to teach and coach only paid $3,000 per year. I would later learn that my 2nd lieutenant's pay would be just $222 per month. Do the math![2]

John entered the Officer Candidate Course (OCC) at the Marine Corps Development and Educational Command (MCDEC) located in Quantico, Virginia, in 1960. He graduated as a Platoon Honor Man in a class that commissioned only 370 out of 1000 candidates. He then attended The Basic School (TBS), also at Quantico, where he ranked 17th out of 375 and was once again his Platoon's Honor Man.[3]

I never had any intention in making the Marine Corps a career! I was asked in passing, in the corridor of the TBS bachelor officer quarters, whether I wanted a regular commission. I asked, "What's that?" The staff platoon commander replied, "You have to do 4 years instead of 3." I said, "OK," and never gave it a second thought.[4]

John's early Marine career included various assignments with the Fleet Marine Force based at Camp Lejeune, North Carolina, including training Cubans prior to the failed Bay of Pigs invasion, serving on ships during both the Cuban blockade and the Santo Domingo crisis. He later served aboard the USS *Springfield* (CLG-7), which was the flagship for the Sixth Fleet. In 1964, he found himself back again at TBS at Quantico.[5]

When my four years were nearly up, I had reported to TBS as a Tactics Instructor where I had to do a year on station before submitting my resignation papers. When I heard that the Marines had landed in Vietnam in 1965, I immediately sent in a transfer request to join them, with no better reason than to determine whether I was a man or not. Time passed and I called the TBS' monitor and asked where my request was. He replied, "It was here in my file drawer with 2,000 others just like it!"[6]

McLaughlin extended his service time, but it would not be until 1967 that he finally received his orders for Vietnam. En route overseas, he first graduated as the top Marine in his Military Assistance Training Advisor class at Fort Bragg, North Carolina. His initial assignment in Vietnam was as a combat operations center, intelligence watch officer and briefer at the 3rd Marine Amphibious Force (MAF) Headquarters. Eventually, Captain McLaughlin was reassigned and became the company commander of Lima Company, 3rd Battalion, 4th Marine (3/4), 3rd Marine Division.[7]

May 1968
Company L, 3rd Battalion, 4th Marines
Hill 689 in the Khe Sahn Area, RVN

The basic strategy of 3/4 during the month of May 1968 was to base two companies on and around Hill 689 (L & K) and the other two at Hill 552 (I & M), which were both located northwest of the Khe Sahn Combat Base. Lima controlled the northern half of Hill 689, while Kilo was positioned on the south side. The surrounding rolling hills had dense undergrowth and were generally flat with sparse vegetation on the crests and tall elephant grass on the slopes. Occasional streams provided a good source of water for both the Marines and NVA. The May temperatures were in the mid–70s to upper 90s with a humidity of 85 percent. The NVA were hunkered down throughout the hills in well-constructed bunkers, with thick overheads of logs, bamboo, dirt and sandbags. Only a direct hit could eliminate one of these refuges. The Company L command post on Hill 689 was called CP Alpha and general artillery support came from the 1st Battalion, 11th Marines and the 3rd Battalion, 12th Marines. Platoon size patrols left the hill nearly every day searching for newly built-up NVA areas.

On 4 May, a Lima platoon discovered a 35 NVA bunker complex. The bunkers were destroyed and the area was planned for a later high explosive (HE) bombardment. The next day, Hill 689 received 10 incoming enemy mortar rounds and countered with their own 81mm mortars, causing an immediate cease-fire by the NVA. On 7 May, another 15 incoming mortars hit the hill. During the day, a platoon found four more bunkers, which were destroyed on sight. On 9 May, another platoon found two antipersonnel (AP) mines and eleven 82mm mortar rounds, which they returned to the S-2 section (intelligence) on Hill 689. Two days later on 11 May, the hill received 120mm incoming mortars and artillery was called in to halt the barrage. Once again, a Lima patrol found more bunkers in the surrounding hills, which were immediately destroyed. On 12 May, a Lima observation post observed seven 122mm rockets being fired, which resulted in a call for Marine artillery. Eighteen secondary explosions were seen in the NVA rocket-launching area. Word came down on 13 May that the Army unit on LZ Peanuts had vacated their position, so a Lima platoon was sent to check out the area. They found a large amount of 782 gear (miscellaneous packs, cartridge belts, canteens, etc.), weapons and ammunition left behind. All important items were returned to the hill. Once again, Hill 689 received enemy mortar rounds and responded by calling in artillery. It was quite evident from all of the recent activity that the enemy was very interested in Hill 689 and the surrounding area.[8]

0745 on 15 May 1968
Company L, 3rd Battalion, 4th Marines
Hill 758 North-West of Hill 689

At 0745, Lima Company's 2nd Platoon left Hill 689 and headed off northwest along a ridgeline to their first checkpoint, 200 meters away, on a high knoll designated as Hill 758. There was a narrow trail along the spine between the two hills with the sides dropping off steeply down into the valley below. Most of Hill 758 was covered with elephant grass, greatly reducing visibility, along with just a few trees on the crest. It was a common patrol area, one that was done quite often during the daylight hours. At night, ambushes would be situated in and around the hill. As the patrol approached the crest, the dead silence was broken at 0805 by shots from the elephant grass, instantly killing the point man, Private First Class Steven Amesca. At first, the fire stopped as quickly as it started and then the Marines began firing and tossing grenades at unknown targets to see if the enemy was still there. The NVA immediately responded with heavy automatic fire and chi-com (Chinese Communist) grenades, which overwhelmed the Marines. The platoon commander ordered a partial withdrawal. At 0850, additional elements of Lima Company, including Captain McLaughlin, joined the 2nd Platoon.[9]

I had been in combat for 5 months and felt that I knew as much or more than any other 03 [Captain] in Vietnam. I was one of those few rare individuals who had conquered fear! My radio call sign was Darting Star Lima 6 Actual. After the 2nd Platoon pulled back, I brought out the 3rd Platoon and my weapons platoon, with the intent of seizing Hill 758 and conducting a company combat patrol, minus the 1st Platoon to see what the NVA were screening by this unprecedented action. I left the 1st Platoon to man the perimeter back on Hill 689. First, I prepped the hill with arty (105s and 155s), air (Snake and Napalm), Naval Gun Fire (5" and 8"), mortars (81s and 60s) and sniper fire with absolutely no effect![10]

According to one squad leader from the 2nd Platoon, "Captain McLaughlin ordered all of Lima's leaders together during the bombardment. He looked tough as iron as he gave the attack order."[11]

I then ordered 2nd Platoon to again attack the crest of the hill. I was maybe 5 meters behind the assault line and heard no AK-47 fire and no enemy grenades, but the attack stalled once again. I issued a frag order [fragmentary order/change in mission] to the retreating lieutenant to withdraw to the attack position, reorganize and to be prepared to continue the attack on order. I then ordered the 3rd Platoon to pass through the retreating Marines and resume the attack. That platoon swept through in good order and assaulted up the steep narrow hill. At exactly the same point where the 2nd Platoon had faltered, so did they! But this time, the 3rd Platoon commander stepped out in front of his men silhouetted against a blue sky, turned his back on the enemy and, with his .45 pistol in his right hand, shouted something I could not hear. He then changed his .45 to his left hand because he had been shot in the right elbow. Next, he swept his good arm over his head as he pivoted and literally led the charge up and over! Damnedest thing I ever saw. He would later receive the Silver Star for this action.

During the mop-up and consolidation phase at 1154, we received incoming mortar fire. It was at this time that my close call experience happened. I looked down the slope of the hill and spied a small "rabbit hole." Stupid, but not too foolish, I took my .45 out of its plastic for the first time since it was issued. With some difficulty, because of the encrusted rust, I jacked a round into the chamber. I walked over, squatted down at the hole, and found myself looking right into the muzzle of an NVA, RPD light machine gun, the equivalent of our BAR [Browning Automatic Weapon]. I squeezed off rounds as fast as I could while executing a perfect backwards roll down the steep slope, as an enemy burst was fired between my legs where my head had been a nanosec before. A couple of somersaults and I sprang to my feet. I was pissed! I went back up and fired my pistol into the hole until I ran out of ammo. I looked up to see my gunnery sergeant and the CP group grinning at me from the top of the hill. Regaining my dignity, I ordered, "Gunny, reduce this bunker!" Holding back the laughter, he gestured with his M-16 and, with another man, leaped onto the concealed top and tore it away. As they did, the NVA soldier stuck his hand out holding a chi-com grenade by the handle. We scattered and he held it until it went off. The Marines went back to work and had his body out in seconds and on the ground by the hole.

I ordered a mop-up of the objective that disclosed other concealed bunkers. I believe to this day that we prevented a major attack against our sector because we forced out an NVA unit that was screening attack preparations further north.[12]

As Lima Company began withdrawing from Hill 758 shortly after 1200 hours, they were hit with 120mm mortar rounds, which wounded several more Marines. By 1420, all Marines had returned to the Battalion position on Hill 689. They had lost 4 KIAs and 38 WIAs. They had confirmed six enemy killed and captured quite a few weapons and gear. The next day, Kilo Company went right back into the same area and lost another 14 men including one KIA. May 1968 would be a bloody month for 3/4 as the NVA continued to apply pressure against the hills around Khe Sahn. Their losses for the month included 71 killed and 250 wounded.[13]

Postlude

Returning to the United States, John continued what would be a 20-year career in the Marines. He held dozens of positions and was assigned to duties at Forest Park, Illinois; Camp Pendleton, California; Quantico, Virginia; Okinawa, Japan; and finished up at Camp Lejeune, North Carolina. He also continued his college studies both during and after his time in the Marine Corps, earning master's degrees in education administration and in human resources management. He ended up teaching and coaching high school in Tennessee for nearly 22 years. He kids by saying, "What do you think my most dangerous job has been: 20 years in the Marine Corps including leading an infantry company in combat, or 22 years as a teacher in the outskirts of Memphis, Tennessee? Most people answer it right."

Retired and now married for 48 years, John enjoys reading, ballet, Broadway theatre, opera, symphony, "yardening" (his word) and travel.[14]

On 1 June 2006, I received a telephone call from Mr. McLaughlin in response to a request for information that I had placed on the 3/4 message board. After a great talk, he agreed to send me his close call story, which he did by e-mail later that same day, including a 6-page resume about his professional and private life. He also referred me to the 3/4 website where information about the battle had been posted in May 2006 by a fellow Marine.

34

USMC Corporal Robert Simonsen

> Amor fati — love your fate, which is in fact your life.
> — Friedrich Nietzsche

Prelude

Robert "Bob" Simonsen was born on 15 October 1947 in Hollywood, California. His family, including an older sister, later moved to Santa Monica, California, where he went to school from grades 1 through 12 and his first year of college. He loved sports and going to the beach. He played both Little League and Pony League baseball and lettered in varsity basketball at Santa Monica High School, graduating in 1965. As a teenager, he held a variety of odd jobs including parking lot attendant at a beach club, dishwasher at a hospital, and summer camp worker in the High Sierras. He always loved war movies and knew that someday he would join the military service. After one year at a local junior college, majoring in engineering, and seeing the war in Vietnam erupting on the TV every night, he knew it was time to enlist. He was a slender 6'2", quiet, shy and unassuming. He had never been in trouble nor had he ever fired a gun in his life. He did not quite fit the typical stereotype image of a tough United States Marine.

Bob joined the Marine Corps because he believed it was his best and fastest chance to get to the war in Vietnam. In October 1966, he headed off to boot camp at the Marine Corps Recruiting Depot (MCRD) in San Diego, California. Following boot camp, he went to Camp Pendleton, California, for the infantry training that all Marines receive, regardless of what their military occupation specialty (MOS) may end up being. For Bob, that initial specialty was to be a construction surveyor and he received his training at the Army's Engineering School at Fort Belvoire, Virginia. After graduating as the top Marine and second overall in his class, he was assigned once again to Camp Pendleton, with the 13th Engineering Battalion, 5th Marine Division.

Approximately 1700 on 14 February 1968
Headquarters and Services (H&S) Company,
13th Engineers
Camp Pendleton, California

For several days, rumors and scuttlebutt were circulating throughout Camp Pendleton about a manpower buildup in Vietnam. The Tet offensive had forced the generals and President Johnson to request additional forces for immediate deployment to the war zone. We had all wondered if we would be included in this emergency group. As I entered my old World War II wooden barracks from the mess hall that February 14th evening, all hell was breaking out. We quickly learned that the Marine Corps had been ordered to send an additional infantry regiment, the 27th Marines, to Vietnam. This regiment was vastly undermanned and had been mainly used as a training and replacement unit for overseas assignments. There were simply not enough riflemen stationed at Camp Pendleton to fill the empty ranks. We were all asked to volunteer and leave our engineering positions for combat duty in Nam. Many of us, myself included, did indeed volunteer, but regardless, nearly everyone was eventually assigned to one of the three battalions of the regiment.

The 3rd Battalion, being the last in the regiment to form up to full strength, was left with whatever was left over. The majority of our ranks were filled with non-infantry Marines, like me. Engineers, truck drivers, cooks, mechanics and you name it, were put together with just a few seasoned infantrymen to form the 3rd Battalion, 27th Marines (3/27). We would further prove the old Marine adage that every Marine is first and foremost, a basic rifleman. So, on that February 14 evening, I went from being a construction surveyor to a combat warrior! I was proud and very excited to be going to Nam after having tried to get there for the past 16 months.[1]

A Brief History of the 27th Marines

The 27th Marine Regiment was born out of World War II on 10 January 1944. It was formed at Camp Pendleton, California, as part of the 5th Marine Division. In August of that year, the Regiment relocated to Camp Tarawa in the territory of Hawaii.

In January 1945, the 27th Marines received its first combat assignment: the invasion of Iwo Jima. The Regiment landed on Iwo Jima on 19 February 1945 and repeatedly met the Japanese in hard, close combat. On 16 March, the island was declared secured. The severity of the fighting left 566 dead and 1,703 wounded within the Regiment alone. Four of its members were awarded the Medal of Honor. After returning to Hawaii, the 27th Marines was deployed to Japan for occupation duty from September to December 1945. On 10 January 1946, the unit was deactivated at Camp Pendleton.

Due to the intensification of the American effort in Vietnam, the 27th Marines was reactivated on 1 January 1966 and began intensive training for possible deployment to the Vietnam War zone.[2]

18 February 1968
Company I, 3rd Battalion, 27th Marines
(attached to the 1st Marine Division)
Cau Ha (3/27 Base Headquarters), Vietnam

Four days later, we arrived in Vietnam and were quickly assigned to the "rocket belt" area, to the south of Da Nang. I was placed in the first platoon of India (I) Company as a fire-team leader. We constantly patrolled looking for the elusive Viet Cong in an effort to prevent them from attacking this important port city with its strategic air base. The first three months in country could be easily summed up as a blur of booby traps, sniping attacks, ambushes, patrolling, sweeping, very little sleep, intense heat and way too many casualties. However, we did slowly hone our war skills and began to evolve into a good, cohesive combat unit.[3]

4 May 1968
7th Marines
Go Noi Island, Quang Nam Province
Operation Allen Brook

Go Noi Island was located 15 miles south of Da Nang, 5 miles east of An Hoa and just north of the Que Son Mountains, which the NVA used as an infiltration route from Laos. Although not truly an island, it was surrounded by rivers, streams and roads. Traditionally, the Go Noi sector was used as a staging place for NVA units building up for attacks against the Da Nang area. In May 1968, the 36th Regiment of the 308th NVA Division and elements of three VC battalions had found their way onto the island. Marine reconnaissance units had observed the enemy and it was decided to send in elements of the 7th Marines to make contact and stir up the action.

Operation Allen Brook began on 4 May 1968 with the 2nd Battalion,

7th Marines (2/7) who made their first large contact on 7 May and killed 42 NVA. On 9 May, another fight resulted in 80 more KIA enemy soldiers. By now, the 27th Marines had been notified that they would be joining the fight on Go Noi Island and would eventually take over total responsibility. It was first decided to send in India Company, 3/27 as the initial linkup to the 7th Marines while more preparations were being finalized.[4]

0600 on 13 May 1968
Company I, 3/27 attached to the 7th Marines
Hill 148, Que Son Mountains
Operation Allen Brook

We landed by helicopters on Hill 148 in the Que Son Mountains overlooking Go Noi Island to our north. We spent the entire day and evening on the hill, where we lost two Marines KIA and several others WIA due to booby traps. It was on this hill that my luck began and would continue through the end of my tour in Nam. In the late afternoon, we were ordered to pick up some supplies at the crest of the hill. My squad leader, Corporal Stephen Zucroff, led the way with Watson and myself following close behind. Just prior to reaching the top, Watson and I stopped for a breather. Seconds later, we were blown to the ground by a tremendous blast, covered with dust, blood and bone fragments. Zucroff, unfortunately, took most of the blast. His body was carried in the air right over us, killing him instantly. Watson suffered a broken eardrum but I was totally unscathed. Had we not stopped, our fate would have been much worse, if not fatal.

For the next few days, we linked up with the 7th Marines on Go Noi Island and had very little contact with the enemy. On 15 May, we left the island at Liberty Bridge and tried to give the impression to the NVA that we were leaving for good. We slipped back, however, at midnight under the cover of darkness and prepared for an attack against a large suspected enemy position.[5]

0900 on 16 May 1968
Go Noi Island
Operation Allen Brook

At about 0900, an explosion of war sounds suddenly interrupted the early morning calmness. The crescendo, somewhat hesitant at first, quickly increased into the chaos of an all-out battle of major proportions. NVA fire erupted from a tree line to my immediate front. Their AK-47 rifles and RPK machine guns [Soviet light machine gun that replaced the RPD in the 1960s] barked out a relentless barrage of fire with bullets whispering and cracking closely overhead. We returned the favor with the sting from our M-16s and M-60 machine guns. An occasional familiar "bloop" of an M-79 [U.S. grenade launcher] round being fired from behind me with its resultant explosion, was encouraging, but not very comforting. Fate had begun the battle, leaving me with no immediate, personal protective cover, so I simply dropped to my knees in a small opening and began shooting my rifle.

To my right, two Marines had found temporary shelter behind a small brick wall and were returning fire as fast as they could. Beyond them, "Speedy" Gonzales launched a one-man assault on an enemy bunker. On my left, Pfc Jack Henderson, Pfc Robert Burke (who the next day would earn the Medal of Honor, posthumously) and "Ski" all opened up upon the enemy. Henderson took an early NVA round in the stomach, which soon proved to be fatal. Somewhere behind me were "Tex" Massey, my new squad leader; Mitch, our platoon radio and M-79 man; and both our platoon commander and sergeant, who were all engaged heavily into the fight.

"Doc" Glick, our Navy corpsman, attended to our wounded as best he could under the dangerous conditions that existed. The rest of India Company was spread out along the left flank of the battle, somewhat disorganized due to the terrain and scope of the NVA positions. On the extreme right, companies of the 7th Marines were also engaged against what was later deemed to be the main body of the enemy. They would suffer large casualties during the day's fighting.

Marines shouted out all over, "I got one" or "I'm hit," followed by the phase we all hated to hear, "Corpsman up!" At the same time, because of the close proximity of the enemy, I heard the chatter of the hidden Vietnamese probably echoing out similar statements to their comrades. A chi-com grenade tumbled out of the tree line in my direction, followed closely by a second one. I hit the ground and covered up as best as I could, and fortunately, they both exploded short and caused little damage except for a bad cut across my nose which I neither felt nor knew about until much later. I heard the sounds of approaching jets and knew that soon their high explosive bombs and napalm would rain death upon the NVA. I also heard the rotor blades of medevac helicopters above the intense roar of the battle, which left little doubt that friendly casualties were quickly mounting. Pfc Vincent Coles was suddenly shot in the head and died instantly. "Speedy" was shot in the leg and then twice more as two NVA tried to finish him off, as he lay wounded behind a bunker.

Suddenly, a dead quiet and blackness overtook me as if someone had placed the final nail into my coffin![6]

Approximately 1000 on 16 May 1968
Near the Village of Phu Dong (2), Go Noi Island
Operation Allen Brook

When I regained consciousness, I found Doc, Tex and Mitch by my side. My head hurt and I was very groggy as they helped move me back to a relatively safe location next to the badly wounded Speedy. Mitch told me he had seen a three-round automatic burst hit right in front of me, which was followed by a fourth round that went through my helmet. Shrapnel from my helmet or bullet fragments had peppered the left side of my skull and knocked me out for several seconds and to this day, I still do not know how long it was. While Speedy and I lay side by side waiting for a medevac, shrapnel from a stray bomb hit all over our position, once again wounding my companion, but left me without any new injuries. Lady Luck was still with me. As the battle died down, a Marine came by with my helmet, showed me the small entry and large exit holes, and stated, "You're the luckiest guy I ever knew."[7]

Approximately 1800 on 16 May 1968
1st Medical Battalion Hospital — Da Nang, RVN

We arrived by helicopters at 1st Med with 10 wounded and 10 killed. Since I was the least seriously wounded Marine, I waited several hours before they were able to shave my head and dig out most of the shrapnel, although for years small pieces of metal would fester and I would simply remove them with my fingernails. I spent the next 4 days at the hospital, but while I was there, I continuously saw more 3/27 Marines come through wounded and heard their horrific stories of ferocious combat that I had fortunately missed. My India Company was practically wiped out on the day after I was wounded and evacuated. Nearly 30 were killed and scores wounded. If I had not been wounded on the 16th, I would have surely been killed or seriously injured along with my fellow Marines back on the island. I did return to the operation on 25 May for a week before 1/27 took over for my battalion. We later returned to Go Noi Island again from 13 to 31 July 1968.[8]

Operation Allen Brook lasted from 4 May through 24 August 1968. The operation, which mainly involved the 27th and 7th Marines, was considered a search-and-clear mission to neutralize enemy forces and installations, which affected the defense of Da Nang. The enemy was totally crushed on Go Noi Island, losing 1,017 known killed. Marine casualties were also high, with 172 dead and another 1,124 wounded.[9]

Postlude

Following Operation Allen Brook, I continued to serve with the 1st Platoon of India Company, 3/27 until September 1968 when the 27th Marines was ordered to return to the United States. Although we began with nearly 50 Marines, I was the lone original member left in my platoon.

After 3/27 returned home, Bob was assigned to the 7th Engineers stationed in Da Nang, where he completed his 13-month tour in Vietnam in March 1969. Returning to the United States, he was placed once more with the 13th Engineers in the same barracks that he had left prior to going to Vietnam. He got out of the Marine Corps as a sergeant in September 1969 and resumed his college education on the G.I. Bill at Santa Monica College, where he met and married his wife, Nan, in 1970. They are still married after 37 years and have one 30-year-old son, Erik. Bob completed a B.S. degree in civil engineering at Cal State University in Los Angeles by attending school at night while working for the City of Los Angeles in the Public Works Department. After nearly 20 years of city civil service work, he and his wife started a successful private business in 1985 and retired in 2006. There is hardly a day that Bob does not think about 16 May 1968 and his other Vietnam experiences. He helps maintain a 3/27 website (http://three27.com) and has written a book about his beloved Battalion, titled *Every Marine*. He is actively engaged in communications with other Marine friends and attends most of the 3/27 reunions. He currently enjoys walking, reading, gardening and writing. He deals with life on a day-by-day basis and constantly thinks about, not only his Vietnam comrades, but also the American fighting men and women currently in Iraq and Afghanistan.

One evening in June 1968, when I was acting as the Sergeant of the Guard while attending NCO School in Da Nang, I wrote a short story, titled "An Unforgettable

Experience," describing my time on Operation Allen Brook. The events were still fresh in my mind and the words flowed easily even though I was still thinking of all of my friends who had been killed and seriously wounded the month before. A few years after I got out of the Marines, I wrote another short story, titled "Insights of a Vietnam Bound Marine." The writing of both of these stories helped me through some tough emotional times. I used these stories as the basis for this chapter and they were the inspiration for seeking out other individuals who had close calls during their military service. Portions of these stories were also included in my first book, titled *Every Marine,* which was published in 2005, but everything was rewritten as original material for this chapter.

35

USMC Lance Corporal Arthur Riordan

> Good luck needs no explanation.
> — Shirley Temple Black

Prelude

Arthur "Art" Riordan was born in April 1945 at Wantagh on the south shore of Long Island, New York. He was about five minutes from the ocean and thirty minutes from Manhattan. He was the middle of five brothers (no sisters) of an Irish-American family. He learned early, practically from birth, how to receive and issue lumps. His father was an aeronautical engineer who worked in research development for Republic Aviation. "He was a good provider and friend." Art describes his mother as an "incredible housewife, cook, healer of hurts and wounds and someone who would help push a car when the battery was dead. They were great role models and I am sure they are now both saints in Heaven."

In school, Art wrestled, boxed and played baseball. Following high school, he attended two colleges but quickly became bored. The Vietnam War had just started and after receiving conflicting reports from professors and military friends, he decided it was time to find out for himself.

> I joined the Navy and soon became bored again so I transferred into the Marine Corps against Lieutenant Commander Lebonte's wishes. She did not understand this young man and his need for action. I attended Marine boot camp at Parris Island and ITR training at Camp Geiger, a satellite base on Camp Lejeune. I was then sent to Camp Pendleton, California. There were some boring times in the Marine Corps but usually they were short-lived. They kept us busy with constant training. We had physical training, wet net training, weapons, heavy equipment, helicopter deployment, cold weather, NBC [nuclear, biological and chemical warfare], desert and unit deployment training. I also received some of the best training in the bars of Southern California!

I was enjoying life but regretting the main reason I had in joining the Corps, which was for action. This came to a fast halt when the 1968 Tet offensive started in Vietnam and President Johnson ordered an additional combat regiment (27th Marines) to be deployed in short order. I was notified of my transfer at midnight and brought to the staging area where I was assigned to Lima Company in the Third Battalion (3/27). The following day we were placed on a C-141 [cargo and troop carrier jet] to deploy to Vietnam. At the time, I only had six months remaining on my enlistment.[1]

February 1968
Da Nang, South Vietnam

Upon arriving, we were trucked to Cau Ha, south of Da Nang, and began running patrols almost immediately. Four days earlier, I was on a beach in California and now I was on a beach in South Vietnam, carrying an M-14 rifle. This was typical of the 3/27 Marines. You could be sitting on your ass for hours but once you got moving, it was 0–150 MPH in a split second with no letup even if you ran out of gas. I arrived in Vietnam at 185 pounds and after two months of C-rations and tainted rice paddy water, I was down to 155 pounds.[2]

17 May 1968
Go Noi Island

On 17 May, India Company got into the hardest fighting of Operation Allen Brook. The company was decimated and was not being reinforced by other units in the area. The 3/27 Battalion commanding officer, Lieutenant Colonel Tullis Woodham, mobilized Kilo, Lima and Mike Companies, who were in other parts of our battalion's normal area of operations. I was with Lima Company and we were brought in from the bush, geared up and waited for the choppers to assist and relieve India Company. The first and last time I flew in a CH-53 helicopter was going into Go Noi Island. We were supposed to link up at the three o'clock position with the team that landed ahead of us.

We flew in and landed in a hot LZ, immediately taking casualties. The helicopter that I was on didn't stay on the ground long because of the small arms fire and incoming enemy mortars. I was on the ground as the chopper lifted off and out of the corner of my eye, I saw a body falling from approximately 25 feet in the air. I rolled to get out of his way and as he landed next to me with a sickening thud, his entrenching tool hit me in the helmet. I thought this Marine was crazy for jumping out at that height. It wasn't until 37 years later that I met that Marine, who was on a machine gun crew and he had the ammo for the gun. He damn near killed himself so as not to let his gun team down. To this day, I am amazed at the camaraderie in the Marine Corps. This became the start of a living hell. Most of us did not realize the island held a regiment of NVA and three VC battalions, which adds up to a lot of bad guys. During the initial confusion, we linked up with anyone we could find at the time.

I grew up five minutes from Jones Beach on Long Island, New York. I was a sun worshipper. Summers, from sunrise to sunset, were spent either on the beach or in a boat. I have experienced sun and heat. I have never been introduced to a heat so unbearable that you couldn't move ten feet without extreme effort. Between the heat and the humidity, it took an effort to breathe and then it was with short breaths, so as not to burn your lungs. We were all in terrific condition but with the helmet, flak jacket, extra ammo, full canteens, grenades and ammunition for crew-served weapons, the 120-degree temperature felt as if it would melt the soles off my boots. Little did we know when we entered that island we were going to be above ground while the enemy was below. They lived in the cool of the earth. Every time I see an ant farm, I am reminded of Go Noi Island. The first night on the island was relatively quiet.

18 May 1968
Go Noi Island

I, along with many of the men that returned from Vietnam, had numerous close calls without becoming a casualty. The one close call that still haunts me today occurred on 18 May 1968 on Go Noi Island. Lima Company moved out early the next morning to link up with India Company and the rest of the battalion. After taking a break for chow, my squad (1st squad, 1st platoon) was told to take point and approach a tree line. Private First Class George Botes was point man, while I was the fourth or fifth Marine in the column. Normally, we would have prepped or saturated the tree line with mortars or artillery but we were within rock-throwing distance where we had our chow break and no one expected the enemy to be so close. Surprise! The enemy was entrenched in spider holes beneath the ground, snipers in the trees and our butts were in the open. George Botes was approximately 50 feet from the trees when the enemy opened up with a barrage of small arms and automatic weapons fire. They hit Botes first and then worked their way down through the squad. The corpsman standing right next to me took a round through his helmet and two rounds in his cartridge belt. I thought he was dead.

I hit the ground fast and starting rolling to my right. There was a small tree line parallel to our march. Every time I rolled, a bullet hit where I had just been. Shit! This happened about four or five times. I rolled onto my stomach and just aimed in the direction of the tree line and emptied a magazine of my M-16 ammo. Aiming at nothing in particular, I was just trying to slow their deadly accurate fire. I raised my rifle and as I was exchanging a new magazine, my helmet slid down over my eyes. This generally happens when we were on the run and it used to piss me off. This time it didn't.

A round hit my rifle barrel, shattering my handgrip, and sprayed the front of my helmet with shrapnel. I caught a piece through my lip, hand and arm. Holy shit! Later on, I saw that the front of my helmet was peppered with shrapnel, which would have taken out my eyes with it. If my rifle wasn't raised slightly, that bullet was no doubt aimed at my head. I firmly believe my weapon saved me. That was enough for me. At this time, our men in the rear were firing back. Machine gun fire, small arms fire, grenade launchers and hand grenades were now buzzing in both directions, with me in the middle. I started rolling to my right again in an attempt to reach the parallel tree line and possible concealment. Rounds were still hitting where I had been. Some SOB still had me in his sights. Since I had finally reached some small undergrowth, and was not visible to the naked eye, I now realized I had a sniper trying to tag me. I reached the trees and was now doing a fast low crawl on my elbows and knees.

I was beginning to feel fairly safe and out of the line of fire when I came across a Marine sitting up against a tree while talking on a field phone. He was facing the enemy tree line of fire with his head above the brush. Since he was wearing camouflage, he was either a Recon Marine or a forward observer calling in air or an artillery strike. He was not from our company. I looked up and told him to get down because there were snipers out there. I remember him looking at me and then he took a round in his head. I couldn't believe I could move that fast on my elbows and knees but I was deep into the tree line in a flash. I firmly believe that the sniper thought that Marine was me. For years, I tried to interpret the look that Marine gave me as arrogant. "Hey asshole, can't you see I'm on the phone?" When you survive near death, you think at first you are lucky as hell. Then you puff up your chest and think, "I'm just damn good." Then reality sets in and you thank God and family for praying for your safety. I realize now that every time I moved I was out of the sniper's sight picture in his scope. When he reacquired me, I had to move again. If it weren't for that Marine by the tree who was killed, the sniper would probably have kept looking for me. You can't thank someone for taking your bullet. You can only pray for his soul.

On his way back to relative safety, Art came across a wounded Marine, threw him over his shoulder and brought him to a triage area. Returning once more to the front, he found a second wounded man and with the assistance of another, helped carry this Marine back on a poncho liner. By this time, the heat finally took its toll on Art.

My skin stopped perspiring and I was getting dizzy. I remember lying down in a puddle of water to cool off. I must have rolled face first because someone pulled me up and placed me on a helicopter. As soon as we got in the air, the cooler temperature revived me and by the time we reached the aid station in Da Nang, I was feeling fine. When we landed, I was met by two very large corpsmen. They asked where I was hit and I told them that I wasn't wounded and wanted to go back to my unit on the island. They grabbed me by the elbows and raced me into a room where my "good luck" clothes and boots were cut off and I had needles shoved into both arms, which were attached to bottles with some kind of solution.

The next day I made it back to our Cau Ha CP base and found another pair of semi–"good luck" clothes. I then went to the armory to have my M-16 repaired. I was told my barrel was too badly dinged and they would have to give me a new M-16. When I told them I just wanted a new front grip, they refused and replaced my "good luck," de-blued, three-prong flash suppressor M-16 with a new untested rifle. In combat, if you survive, luck plays a major roll. My old rifle wasn't just my best friend; it was part of me. My new weapon was green and hadn't been tested by the rigors of combat. It didn't even have a name yet. I now felt totally luckless as I returned to Go Noi Island.[4]

Postlude

Art's luck did continue and he completed his remaining months in the Marines in August 1968. He was discharged at El Toro, California, where he stayed for awhile to sort things out. After a week or so, he returned to New York and hit the bar scene and, in his own words, "became a partying drunk."

After a few months, his money ran out and he finally went back to work. He also tried to re-enter college but soon realized he no longer fit in. "In a little over three years, I had aged considerably. I met a wonderful woman and married. We divorced 15 years later after producing a beautiful daughter, Deirdre. I now have two granddaughters and a great son-in-law."

Art retired from American Airlines after 33 years. He currently splits his time between Massachusetts and Florida. "My hobbies were and still are girl watching, fast cars and fast boats." He belongs to the Marine Corps League and has attended many of the 3/27 reunions. "I still lift a drink to us combat Marines. Never to be forgotten!"

Combat, unlike other jobs when you leave, stays with you forever. It follows you day and night with its own unique form of excitement. I have always felt fortunate to be a part of the finest group of men this country has ever produced.[5]

I met Art years ago at one of 3/27's reunions. We have communicated over the years from time to time by e-mails. He also provided information for my previous book, *Every Marine*. Art saw my ad for close call stories that I had placed on the 3/27 web site's guest book and then asked me a few questions to find out what I was looking for. He then sent me a two page typed letter, dated 5 December 2006, describing his incident. I then sent him a questionnaire for some personal information and he responded with another letter dated 14 December 2006.

36

USMC Corporal John Wear II

> There is no armor against fate.
> — Shirley James

Prelude

John Wear II was born in Frankfurt, Germany, on 2 December 1946 to a United States Air Force career officer. His father retired as a full colonel after 30 years. John and his family, which included two sisters and a brother, moved around quite a bit and attended several schools throughout the United States and Japan on military bases. He was both a Cub and Boy Scout and was on his school's intramural soccer, track, swimming, touch football and softball teams. He also was involved in judo and varsity wrestling.

At the end of his college freshman year, he became dissatisfied with his life and went down to check out his options with the military recruiters. Since he had taken 3 years of Junior ROTC in military prep school, he leaned towards the Army. When he got to the recruiting station, the Army recruiter office was closed, the Air Force recruiter was out of town, and according to John, "the Navy recruiter had long hair over his shirt collar." It just happened that the Marine gunnery sergeant with his chest full of ribbons said the right thing to him: "Son, do you think you have what it takes to be a Marine?" and he replied, "Sign me up, Gunny!"

John entered boot camp at San Diego, California, in August 1966. In jest he said, "When I piled off the bus and stood on the yellow footprints, they issued me sunglasses, suntan lotion and surfboard wax." Upon graduation, he attended infantry training regiment (ITR), tank crewman school, nuclear, biological and chemical (NBC) school, embarkation school and non-commissioned officer (NCO) school, all at Camp Pendleton, California. He was assigned to the 5th Tank Battalion at Las Flores for about a year and picked up the rank of corporal.[1]

January 1968
1st Platoon, Alfa Company, 3rd Tank Battalion
Northern I Corps, Vietnam

I arrived "in-country" in the middle of January 1968 and was involved in the liberation of Hue City during the Tet [Vietnamese lunar new year] offensive of 1968, which was the most famous battle that I was involved in while in Vietnam. I was then assigned to the 1st Platoon, Alpha Company, 3rd Tank Battalion. We were mostly attached to the 2nd Battalion, 9th Marines (2/9) and utilized as infantry support.[2]

A Brief History of the 3rd Tank Battalion

The 3rd Tank Battalion was activated at Camp Elliot, San Diego, on 16 September 1942. Following training in at Camp Pendleton, the unit left for New Zealand in early 1943. The next stop was Guadalcanal, where it underwent final training for its 1 November 1943 landing at Empress Augusta Bay, Bougainville. Following this battle, the Battalion landed in Guam and went into action against the Japanese forces. The Battalion's last Pacific operation was on Iwo Jima in February 1945. Returning to the United States, the unit was deactivated in January 1946 at Camp Pendleton. Activated for the Korean War, the Third Tank Battalion relocated to both Japan and Okinawa, but never participated in the fighting in Korea.

The Battalion was called to war again for Vietnam, arriving in 1965. It had units in Da Nang, Khe Sanh and Con Thien, before leaving for Okinawa once more in 1969. In 1976, the Battalion detached from the 3rd Marine Division and moved to Twenty-nine Palms, California.

The 3rd Tank Battalion deployed to Saudi Arabia in 1990 in the wake of the Iraqi seizure of Kuwait in August 1990. It fought the four-day campaign of 24–28 February 1991 and returned to the United States in April. In June 1992, it was disbanded as part of force reduction programs.[3]

July 1968
Alpha Company, 3rd Tank Battalion
Dong Ha, Vietnam

During the month of July 1968, Alpha Company was headquartered at Dong Ha under the command of Captain E.V. Sullivan. The company participated in Operations Napoleon/Saline, Kentucky and Thor. During July

1968, they would lose 1 KIA and 14 WIAs as well as several tanks, damaged by mortars and mines.[4]

1 July 1968
Eastern Demilitarized Zone (DMZ)
Operation Thor

Operation Thor was a seven-day joint operation conducted by the United States Army, Navy, Air Force and Marines against the North Vietnamese enemy artillery, rocket and air defensive positions in the eastern end of the DMZ. In the summer of 1968, the NVA dominated the DMZ with their long-range, flat-trajectory 122mm, 130mm guns, and 152mm gun howitzers. The NVA had more than 100 artillery pieces that could outrange all U.S. artillery except for a select few Marine (8") and Army (175mm) gun batteries. The NVA could control the Marine logistical base at Dong Ha and the supply routes along the Cua Viet River and Route 9.

The first three days of Operation Thor were dominated by 210 B-52 arc-light strikes, followed by Marine and Army artillery, Naval gunfire and 350 fighter-bomber sorties.[5]

7 July 1968
Alpha Company, 3rd Tank Battalion attached to
Company F, 2nd Battalion, 9th Marines
North of Con Thien, Vietnam
Operation Thor/Kentucky

From 7 to 15 July 1968, Alpha Company, minus the 2nd Platoon, but reinforced with a flame section, operated with the 9th Marines around Con Thien. Their operations were probably a combination of the end of Operation Thor and the beginning of Operation Kentucky. They would provide direct fire and counter mortar fire support in sweeping with the infantry. Alpha was credited with killing 14 NVA during this one-week period.[6]

By now, I was a tank commander and flame-thrower tank section leader, working with Foxtrot Company, 2/9. We were involved in a search-and-destroy operation, sweeping in a huge arc around Con Thien. Later, I also learned the "brass hats" wanted us to observe the devastation that the B-52 arc-light bombing raids had made on the countryside.

July 7 was very hot and muggy with some saying it even reached 114 degrees that day. As we headed out in the morning with grunts alongside our tanks, we hit a massive amount of "shit" about 2,000 meters in front of our nighttime position. There were NVA .51 caliber heavy machine guns, RPG [rocket-propelled grenade] teams and so many AK-47s [Russian assault rifles] on full automatic that we could not count them all. There were also enemy 60mm mortars exploding everywhere. Due to the loud tank noises, communication radios blaring and the sounds of firing on both sides, I found it very hard to focus. At first, I didn't really see anything specific that was going on. I did observe some grunts standing up, firing from the hip like John Wayne. Some Marines were lying down and keeping out of the firefight, while others were just running all over the place not knowing what to do. The platoon sergeants and lieutenants tried their best to assume command but the huge amount of enemy fire made it very difficult.

I called over the tank intercom to my driver, "Steffo," to pull up past the grunts in front of our tank so that we could take the gooks under fire. As the tank lurched forward, I peered out of the tank commander's cupola when all of the sudden, a hot rush of air passed over me and I felt as if my face was burnt. I didn't have time to think about what had just occurred since there were lots of wounded Marines all over the place. Most of these men had been hit in the legs, arms and neck by shrapnel from mortar rounds.

The standard MO [modus operandi] of the NVA who were about to be overrun was to shoot like crazy and then fall back firing off their 60mm mortar rounds, which was exactly what they did. I looked in front of our position and saw Sergeant Towers standing inside of his cupola, frantically pointing to his left. There was a tree line and it appeared as if there were NVA firing between two large trees. I told Steffo to head over towards the tree line and said, "Charge the bottle, 'Flash,' we are going to burn some gooks!"

As we pulled up to the trees we started to get intense incoming arty from 152mm cannons that the enemy was firing at us from the mountains to the north. I mean, big impact blasts were now happening. Just as we were passing, Sergeant Towers caught a mortar blast off the side of his tank. We got maybe another 50 meters closer to the tree line when two grunts held up their hands to stop us. I yelled at the top of my lungs, "Get the f*** out of my way, you stupid assholes, we got to kill us some bad guys!"

All of a sudden, the tree line in front of us exploded, with hundreds of NVA shooting at us. Wounded grunts fell all around us. The two gun tanks on either side of me were firing their main guns while Flash was making our .30 caliber machine gun sing like an opera star. Sergeant Towers came over the radio and said, "Foxtrot three-one, I just got hit. I'm going to be medevaced but I want you to come over to my left and hose down the tree line from that pos [position]. Over." I replied, "Roger, Alpha one-two."

"OK, Steffo, kick it in the ass. Flash, get ready to work the main gun and keep hosing the tree line with the .30." We pulled right next to Sergeant Tower's tank and he called over the radio, "Foxtrot three-one, there are RPG teams all in the tree line. Hose them as I cover you with my 90mm cannon." Again, I replied, "Roger, Alpha one-two."

"OK, Steffo, kick it in the ass but be ready to stop for Flash to work his magic." We approached the tree line as the two gun tanks pumped round after round from their main guns into the enemy lines. By now, the grunts are also pouring it on. I saw tremendous explosions everywhere. "OK, Flash, let her rip!" The liquid napalm shot out of our gun tube from left to right and then all of a sudden, Flash hit the igniters and … BOOM, the whole tree line ignited in flames. The NVA then started to isolate their fire on my tank. "Steffo, back out of here on the double! Flash, keep up the firing into the tree line!" The grunts were now up charging, as were the two gun tanks. "Get some!" It was over before it began. The gooks took off and left only a few charred bodies behind. We continued to move throughout the day.

Later that evening, the grunt platoon sergeant asked me, "Did you see that RPG that almost took off your head?" I blurted, "Huh?" He then proceeded to tell me that the "warm air" that I felt on my face earlier had been a gook B-40 rocket that almost parted my hair. Holy Mother of God! I had almost "bought the farm" right then and there! They had been either trying to take me or my tank out, or both of us. Whew! If we had stayed still and not moved up, I would have had my head taken off by the most powerful antitank rocket in the NVA's arsenal.[7]

Operation Thor resulted in three friendly KIAs and 25 WIAs. The joint attack destroyed 93 enemy field, coastal and air defense artillery weapons and neutralized the North Vietnamese offensive potential in the DMZ area for the next three years. NVA manpower losses were unknown.[8]

Postlude

John completed his "12 months and 29 day tour," in what he calls the "Land of Oz," in February 1969. He then returned to the 5th Tank Battalion back at Camp Pendleton, where he was promoted to Sergeant E-5 and was later discharged from the Marines in July 1969.

He graduated with a B.S. degree in marketing from the University of Denver in 1971 and has held a variety of positions including department store buyer, merchandise manager, sales manager and independent manufacture's sales representative for several different companies.

He and his second ("and last") wife, Jeanne, currently live in New Hope, Pennsylvania, on a beautiful country lane. He has a son, John III, who is a 14-year Army Ranger, and three lovely daughters: Meghan, Brooke and Caitlin, who all have had children of their own.

Suffering from PTSD (post-traumatic stress disorder), John started to get involved again with his old and new Marine friends around 1999. He is a charter member and current president of the USMC Vietnam Tanker's Association. He also belongs to the 3rd Marine Division Association, the Marine Corps Tanker's Association, the Vietnam Veterans of America and the Veterans of the Vietnam War, although not as a very active member. He communicates regularly with several of his old Vietnam Marine comrades.

John currently enjoys scuba diving, running, gardening, wheel pottery and dog agility (he has three dogs and three cats). He and Jeanne are looking forward to retiring in a few years and moving to their 140 acres in New Mexico, where he plans to open up a pottery school.[9]

In response to a request for information that I had placed on Sgt. Grit's bulletin board (http://www.grunt.com), John e-mailed me on 14 April 2006 saying, "I normally don't give out my stories for free, but I feel good about your efforts. If you publish this, I would like an autograph copy of the book, OK?" He provided a very good action account of USMC tanks in battle. In a follow-up E-mail, dated 28 April 2006, John provided some background personal information that I had requested.

37

USMC Corporal Jay Vincens

Tempted fate will leave the loftiest star.
— Lord Byron

Prelude

Jay Vincens was born into a military family growing up on Army military bases around the United States and the world. He spent several years in the Canal Zone in Central America. He learned to speak both Spanish and French. While in Panama as a young man, Jay got his first taste of "guerilla warfare" by playing in the jungles and sneaking up on American forces without being seen. If he had been caught, all hell would have broken out, especially from his Army officer father. He adapted well to the jungle environment and learned on his own: camouflage, concealment and most importantly stealth. He felt natural in the jungle bush environment.

The 6' 3" tall, 165-pound, wiry Vincens graduated from college and was just beginning law school in Connecticut when he received his "notice from Uncle Sam." Jay elected to join the Marines to put his natural-born bush skills to practice in the Vietnam War. By 1968, he found himself assigned to the 1st Platoon of Hotel Company, 2nd Battalion, 1st Marines (2/1). With an expert mentor in his platoon staff sergeant ("The Boss"), Jay soon became a war expert in the "real bush," and would soon earn the nickname of the "Bushmaster." He quickly absorbed knowledge in map-reading skills, always knew where he was and had all the important radio frequencies memorized to assist in any combat situation that arose. He took pride in teaching these skills, and insisted that all of the Marines under him, in his fire-teams and squads, learned them. His basic weapons were the M-79 grenade launcher (blooper) and a .45 pistol.

Being several years older than the average Marine enlisted grunt and with a confident air about him, he was able to "acquire" specialized equipment for his Marines that was not normally issued. He usually got everything that he needed from the Army or other sources without being questioned or challenged. Because he rarely wore his rank on his collar, many believed he was an officer based on his age and bearing. He once even got into an "officers only dance" in Da Nang with Navy nurses.[1]

* * * *

Sometime near the middle of 1968, Hotel, 2/1 was positioned at the Khe Sahn combat base, where I had my first of many close call incidents. Because of the filth and mud in the trenches, I decided that a pile of wooden pallets on the outbound junk pile would be the perfect place to sleep. Besides, Charles (one of many nicknames for the enemy) had no doubt zeroed in on every square inch of the place, so why would they waste a round on a junk pile? I had kept a thin haversack on my back for warmth and tried to sleep face down while also wearing my helmet. Sure enough, the next night Charles had a "shitbird" fire a round that hit the junk pile and lit up something flammable. I woke up ten feet away with a helmet full of mud, my ears bleeding, my sleeves on fire and the old World War II–Korea style haversack smoldering, which saved me from getting my back burned. I had no idea who or where I was for hours. Someone walked me over to the battalion aid station, which looked like a scene from some outtakes for *The Texas Chainsaw Massacre* and nothing like the MASH unit on TV at all. I stood by, while the more seriously hurt and dying were treated. They patched me, up with some yellow goo, which burnt the hell out of me and then sent me back to the lines."[2]

* * * *

After Khe Sahn, I was assigned to serve temporarily as the English speaking RTO [radio tactical operator] to a combo ROK–RVN [Republic of Korea–Republic of Vietnam] outfit's skipper. One night we got a frantic call and went out to rescue some of their men who were trying to link up with a 1st Recon Battalion team. We had to get those folks out in the dark and one of them decided to light up one of those new nifty flashing sticks while we were bringing in the choppers. Training had taught us to bring in helicopters at night not by light, but rather by noise and voice directions. At that moment, the hills surrounding us on three sides lit up as Charles taunted us and it looked like one of those "Currier & Ives" postcards from Christmas in New England. Then they rushed us. A bad scene with fighting up close and personal but we were able to push them back. We got out with a third of the force wounded or killed. As I was pulling in one of the wounded onto the chopper evacuation site, the guy in front of me was cut in half, and two of us were slightly burnt when a flare in his pocket lit up. I also took what I later found out was a split round that went through his body and then through my left knee, leaving a strawberry-looking scar ever since. As three of us ran across the field firing, a rocket came in and turned the third guy on the right into steamy shreds with nothing to take back but a leg and a boot. Later, I was told at NSA [Naval Support Activity Hospital] in Da Nang that a guy on my left and I were peppered with his teeth and bone shards, making my face, neck and chest look like raw hamburger. However, back then I felt all of it was an endorsement of my being bulletproof.

Once again, my guardian angel came through for me. We landed at NSA around 0400, with most of the injured on my chopper not making it. After triage showed we could be helpful, we unloaded corpses and body parts until our time came to be examined. Six of us Marines received ROK and RVN medals for valor and Purple Hearts; however, none of that information made it into our 2/1 records back at company headquarters.[3]

* * * *

My third hit again turned out to be my angel's work in action.[4]

[According to Bobby Hingston, one of his teammates:] We were walking along a river, the countryside was beautiful, and the river seemed to have a lazy flow in it as it wound its way to the ocean. The water looked so good and cool I wanted to dive in. We'd been on patrol about an hour or so. To our left were trees and jungle. High grass lined the edges of the river, green as it could be. The air, unfortunately, hung thick and stale, as the mugginess could literally be cut with a knife. My shoulders were killing me as we moved along at a slow methodical pace. One thing about Vietnam, you never went running around as you saw John Wayne do in the movie, *The Green Berets*. You'd be dead in a heartbeat, most likely from a booby trap, or you would run smack into an ambush.[5]

[Jay continues:] On a patrol by a river, we came under fire. Rounds zoomed and cracked by my face. Thank heavens he was a shitty shooter or I would not be here today. As I hit the dirt, I saw flashes across the river in a tree and prepared to "bloop" the SOB. At that moment, I was punched on the left eye by something and my eye went red. I fired the M-79 anyhow and hit the bastard. The shooting stopped.[6]

[From Hingston's account:] There was a crack, crack crack! In a heartbeat everyone was down and scanning through the tree line to see who was sniping at us. You could hear people yell out to their squads asking if anyone was hit. Everything is OK here in Alpha Squad, Jay yelled up. Crack, crack as bullets again skimmed the earth near our heads. This guy's sights must be off, as you don't get any closer without scoring a hit. I want that man, The Boss yells out, now! Jay lifted up with his blooper and crack, crack again as Jay ducks down as the rounds all but burn his skin as they pass by his head. I see where he is firing from, Jay yells out. Well then, Vincens, kill him now! Injured in his eye, Jay yells out again, I don't want to lose this guy. Jay pops up quickly and bloop, smack! He quickly reloads another, and lifts up and fires again. That's two directly where I saw him, Jay yells out.[7]

[Jay continues:] I was sent to the rear, where they patched up my eye, and kept me for five days. The side of my head was the size of a melon in a variety of purple and black hues. Turns out, his round hit a concrete road marker, split, and just a sliver of a bullet went through my eyelid, grazing my eyeball, leaving a scar, but my head was still there. As they interviewed me to send me to the rear, I said no. I wanted to go back to my unit because we had many replacements and it was my job to help train them. I was a bit nuts back then, but weren't we all?[8]

* * * *

[Hingston concludes:] In early August 1968, a new Captain ("Skipper") took over Hotel, 2/1 and, like the platoon sergeant, he was a natural born leader. He was a former enlisted man with a previous Vietnam tour under his belt. These Marines, along with the help of Jay Vincens, started planning to put together and conduct five-man killer teams that would operate independently and bring the war to the enemy on their own turf. As August turned into September, 2/1 was relocated from the northern Cua Viet, Con Thien and Khe Sahn areas to replace a departing 3/27 in their area just south of Da Nang. This VC–controlled area was perfect for the killer team strategy. The Skipper selected members of the 1st Platoon to be the first killer team operators and Jay was placed in charge of the Alpha Team. Jay, who was scheduled to be transferred to a Recon unit, agreed to stay on for a while until the teams started operating on a smooth basis. Typically, the teams would go out on patrol with another full platoon and then peel off undetected and hide from the villagers and kids who were constantly seen around the battalion's new TAOR. Quite often, a two-man sniper team accompanied the killer teams on their operations.[9]

* * * *

[Jay continues:] One afternoon, we lost our new two-man sniper team while cleaning out some booby traps. One of the guys poked his head out and was hit by some shrapnel when we blew up one of the booby traps. Both snipers were evacuated but I still decided to continue, since there was another team out that night and we needed to support each other in case one of us got into trouble. There was a lot of activity that evening. We were ambushed and as I circled around to get the shooter, my foot went into a hole up to my crotch. My foot was wedged on a stick and I heard a loud boom! My right knee felt as if I had been shattered. Something against my upper leg in the hole started clicking loudly and something told me I had triggered a fuse and there was a countdown to getting myself blown away.

I threw away my gear to avoid wiping out the rest of the team, as I was carrying a bag full of blooper rounds, two sticks of C-4, two claymores, det-cord and about six grenades. While waiting to blow up, I decided to fire at the enemy shooter who had pinned me down but could not seem to hit me directly. When he saw me aiming in his direction, he took off running. I gave him six feet of lead and then fired, hitting the top of his head and killing him instantly. I now threw away my blooper and lit a cigarette while waiting to die. Something told me to try to and pull out my leg as just something to do while waiting. To my surprise, after four or five tries, my leg started moving. The clicking slowed down. My leg came out with my right knee on fire. I dragged and rolled myself away until I found an indent in the ground and stretched out and finished my cigarette. The hole had both a "bouncing Betty" and a booby-trapped 155mm round in it. We blew it up. I refused evacuation until both of our teams had finished their patrols and we were safely back in our CP. For weeks after this close call incident, I was called "the ghost who walks."[10]

* * * *

On another night to the southeast of the CP, in the Cam Sa area, two killer teams were operating a few hundred meters away from each other. One of the teams was hit hard, with three Marines killed, including Dewayne Williams, who would later receive a Medal of Honor posthumously for jumping on a grenade and absorbing the blast and protecting his comrades. When Dewayne's team was hit, it was just about dark and we were twenty minutes away through a newly marked booby trap area. We made it as fast as we could and a long firefight ensued until the other team could be pulled out. Our team stayed out there and the firefight went on for another four hours or so. We had several more close calls that night as there were just five of us and we were later told that there were between 50 and 100 enemy soldiers in the fight. Helicopters refused to land in the hot LZ that they described as an "anthill of bad guys." In one instance, I was putting in a claymore in the dark when a pair of legs showed up right in front of my nose and I had a very large NVA type on top of me. I pulled away his rifle and he decided to punch it out with me. We slapped each other around while rounds and explosions were going off around us from a mortar barrage that our Skipper had called in close to our area. Charles then pulled out a knife and I grabbed mine as well. We danced and nicked each other a bit. He then made a move. I pulled him down and he locked his teeth on my right hand between my thumb and forefinger. I then stabbed his kidney and slit his throat with my K-bar in my left hand. He died in my arms. I still have the scar. The corpse would soon save me from a shotgun blast from another gook. I shot him with the M-79 and hit him in the chest and he fell down hard, but it was too close for the round to explode. He was one tough bastard and while he was reaching for his shotgun, I rammed my .45 into his left eye and shot him. The firefight went on for a few more hours. We were called to come back in, in the pre-dawn hours, which I still feel was a dangerous and nutty move, but we made it in. We rested a day and then went right back out on the next patrol, and the next and the next! We were just plain crazy back in those days.[11]

* * * *

Later, my luck still held. A round cracked like a bullwhip by the bridge of my nose, close enough for me to feel the heat. We were crossing a river to a "little slice of heaven" that our Skipper, in a whimsical mood, named "Grenade Hill." One time a guy emptied a magazine on me as I ran towards him. He ran out of bullets just as my two rounds hit him in the face. Some other lousy shooter hit my backpack just behind my neck and spun me around but I was not hit. We were hit several times on Grenade Hill. One time there was a blizzard of rounds, and yet, somehow, I was among those who walked out and fired back with buzzes all around us. Once more, I did not get a scratch. This time, however, The Boss took a hit in the same leg that he had been wounded previously at Khe Sahn. Somehow, I feel that all of my close calls were, in hindsight, very lucky.[12]

Postlude

In December 1968, Jay returned to the United States on a Red Cross family emergency leave. It would be years later that Jay once again made contact with his old Hotel, 2/1 Marine brothers. He still stays in contact with quite a few of them and, along with his former captain and platoon sergeant, he was instrumental in making sure many of his former teammates received military awards for valor in 1998 that had been lost in a paperwork jungle years before. In return, his teammates are now trying to ensure that he is awarded his numerous Purple Hearts and both a Silver Star and Navy Cross, which he well deserved during his time on the battlefields of Vietnam.[13]

Postscript

Previously mentioned, Dewayne Williams earned his Medal of Honor on his nineteenth birthday, 19 September 1968. Dewayne was a highly regarded member of the author's personal squad from June to August 1968, when they both served together with Company I, 3rd Battalion, 27th Marines. His loss is still deeply felt.

I received an e-mail from Jay on 18 July 2006 after he noticed that I had left a request for close call stories on the Hotel, 2/1 guest book. He was first feeling me out, determining my intentions and credibility, and making sure I would treat Marines in only the best possible light. For the next several days, we exchanged several e-mails dated 18, 19, 26 and 27 July 2006. We found out we had a few common Marine Corps friends and had operated in the same area in Vietnam. His unit took over my unit's TAOR in September 1968. He sent me his close call stories, but was very hesitant, as he would rather talk about his former Marine comrades than himself. He never did answer my questionnaire for more personal information, both before and after his Marine Corps life, which I fully respect.

He also referred me back to the Hotel, 2/1 website for additional information on both himself and his unit.

38

USMC Private First Class Mike Stagner

> Luck is being ready for the chance.
> —J. Frank Dobie

Prelude

Mike Stagner was born in the Southern California city of Altadena on 3 September 1949. Mike came from a broken family; his father left when he was just a baby and his mother could not take care of him properly, so his maternal grandparents raised him. His grandparents were hard-working poor people; his grandfather was a welder and his grandmother was a seamstress. He was an only child and really did not have any close family. As a child, Mike played Little League and enjoyed roller skating and bowling.

He was a rebellious youth and was kicked out of high school at the age of 16. He then went to continuation school and managed to pass his GED, but his troubles continued. He ran the streets and got into drinking, along with a few minor problems with the police. He never stole or did anything seriously wrong, but he finally realized he was headed down the wrong path.

In the summer of 1968, he enlisted in the Marine Corps. Just prior to entering boot camp in San Diego, California, he married his wife, Linda. He kids and says he got married so he had someone to whom he could write. He landed on the famous yellow footprints at MCRD on 14 October 1968. "I knew the Marine Corps meant Vietnam and I was willing to take the challenge."

He graduated from boot camp in December and went to Camp Pendleton, California, for infantry training and artillery school. Artillery was to be his primary specialty. Following these schools, he was shipped to Okinawa and later arrived in Da Nang, Vietnam, in March 1969. From there, he went by truck up to Dong Ha, in the northeastern part of the country and south of the DMZ. He was assigned to Battery A, 1st Battalion, 12th Marines (1/12), 3rd Marine Division. He shortly joined his battery at Cua Viet near the South China Sea. Mike soon earned the nickname of "Orange" because his hair was the color of a goldfish.[1]

A Brief History of the 1st Battalion, 12th Marines

The 1/12 is an artillery support battalion that came into existence during the Second World War when it was activated on 1 September 1942 at San Diego. From California, the unit first deployed to Auckland, New Zealand, and then to Guadalcanal in July 1943. It participated in numerous Pacific campaigns, including Bougainville, Guam and Iwo Jima.

It was relocated back to Camp Pendleton in December 1945 and deactivated on 8 January 1946. The Battalion was activated again during the Korean War and sent to Japan. During March and April 1965, the Battalion was deployed to Vietnam and participated in the war from 1965 through 1969, operating from I Corps bases at Phu Bai, Da Nang, Cam Lo, Khe Sanh and Camp Carroll. In the 1990s, 1/12 would participate in the war in Iraq.[2]

May 1969
Alpha Battery, 1/12
Northern I Corps, South of the DMZ

From 1 to 3 May 1969, Alpha Battery was positioned at Fire Support Base (FSB) McClintock. Later, from 4 to 8 May, the unit was sent to Cua Viet for rehabilitation. From 9 May through the end of the month, they were relocated to FSB Fuller on top of Dong Ha Mountain. This FSB was located east of both Razor Back and Mutters Ridge and northeast of the rocky outcrop known as the Rockpile.

During May 1969, 1/12 fired 624 separate fire missions and expended nearly 12,000 rounds, of which 11,395 were high explosive (HE) shells. They were credited with 66 enemy KIAs and destroyed countless bunkers and other enemy fortifications.[3]

26 May 1969
Alpha Battery, 1/12
Fire Support Base Fuller

The Battery had been moved up to the top of Dong Ha Mountain for a few weeks now. Battery A had built a position for their six 105mm howitzers on the top of a high peak and was capable of providing close artillery support in any direction. The work was very hard. All materials, including ammo, supplies and equipment had to be man-carried and placed. There were no trucks, just an initial placement by helicopters

(CH-53s and 46s) and the guns tended to sink in the mud. Thousands of sandbags had to be filled with mud and assembled into gun pits and hooches. The wind and rain chilled us to the bone. The fire missions were long and everybody was worked into a trance. The Marines in the Battery were very close to each other. We humped ammo and worked together to accomplish our mission. Many lifelong friendships were born and many lives were forever changed.

As a battery, the troops worked as a unit to accomplish the common tasks such as humping ammo, building fortifications and doing whatever was necessary. The very close relationships came within the various gun crews. When your gun had duty, time off, chow or guard, it was only your crew, as all others were sleeping, eating or on work parties. The five Marines on your gun were yours. The duties within the gun pits were interchangeable. New guys usually prepped the rounds and loaded. Seasoned veterans were mainly gunners and assistant gunners and the section chief would always be on the phone receiving directions. On Dong Ha Mountain, the guns were arranged in line connected by common pit walls. I was on Gun #1 and shared some personal moments with Gun #2 and #3, but the farther down the line towards the CP [command post], the closeness seemed to fade a little. The firebase was also a night rest stop for various infantry platoons who would hump in and out daily. I don't recall even speaking to these Marines but their presence was always appreciated.

"Dee Dee" Dias and Harris were members of my gun team. In the next pit (#2) was Pfc Robert Van Vleet, a skinny kid from Utah, who was a hard worker, friendly and knew how to stay out of the sergeant's ire. Also in #2 was Corporal Raymond Gutierrez, a slightly built Marine also from California. I do not ever recall talking to him about California but I do remember that he was also a hard worker.

On the day I can never forget, the call rang out, "Battery adjust, enemy contact, rounds, charge, azimuth, deflection." All Marines scrambled. I was helping to prepare rounds. It was wet and almost dark. I was standing behind the #1 gun, loading powder bags into a canister. Dee Dee was next to me, setting a fuse, when I swear that it went completely quiet and then I heard for the very first time in my life the words "short round!" For some reason that hopefully I will understand some day, I immediately crouched down. There was a loud snap sound and then screams! Van Vleet and Gutierrez were on high ground when either the round hit or air-bursted directly between Guns #1 and #2. They died and six other Marines were wounded. I was unhurt. Out of the two gun crews, only two people were not killed or wounded. Death, pain, blood, sadness and the realization of mortality was the lesson of that day.

I am a United States Marine veteran but I must admit that at that moment I was a child. The gallant efforts displayed by other Marines inspired me. The Doc worked and the men held the victims down and carried them to the LZ, while the fire mission was completed. There was no shortage of leadership and courage. After it was all over and quiet again, I became overwhelmed and jumped into a bunker. I think I was scared. I remember thinking to myself, "What in the f*** are you doing? There is no danger now." The fact is that I was forever changed.[4]

Postlude

Five months later, in October 1969, the 12th Marines left Vietnam for good. Most of the Marines went home on the USS *Whetstone*, but Stagner was assigned to Fox Battery, 2/12 in Okinawa, where he finished his 13-month overseas deployment. He returned to the United States in April 1970 and took a 30-day leave. He then received orders for Camp Lejeune, North Carolina, and was offered two choices: a promotion to sergeant if he extended his enlistment or an "early out" of the service. He took the latter choice and left the Marines in May 1970.

Mike went to work for Pacific Telephone and attended Pasadena City College, where he earned an associate degree in 1973. He then attended California State University and received a Bachelor of Science degree in 1979. He started working at a small CPA firm and eventually passed the CPA exam and obtained a CPA license in 1983. He started his own practice in Covina, California. In 2004, he semi-retired and moved to Bullhead City, Arizona, where he obtained his Arizona CPA license. He works very hard during tax season and spends the rest of the year fishing and traveling with his wife of 38 years and the family dogs.

He and Linda had two children, Charles and Amy, and now have two beautiful grandsons, Seth and Tyler. "I love fishing and spending time with old Marines. I just get along with them better than civilians, doggies or other service guys." Every two years he attends reunions with his old Vietnam battery. He also belongs to the American Legion and the First Marine Division Association, and is now considering joining the Veterans of Foreign Wars.

Just recently, during the summer of 2006, I vacationed with two of my old Battery friends, Dias and Harris, in Puerto Vallarta, Mexico. Dias had been wounded on that fateful 26 May 1969 day, but both Harris and I had not been injured. I asked the now Colonel Harris (JAG officer) why the two of us had not been killed or hit when everybody was. He simply said, "It just was not our time, Mike."[6] I often think about Van Vleet and Gutierrez. God bless them both. They were taken at just nineteen years.

They are forever nineteen, while those of us who survived are now old. They missed what we were given and I will probably never understand why. I will never forget those two Marines. They gave all so we can be free. When I hear people speaking of gallant war heroes with medals and citations, I'll remember those two Marines who made the ultimate sacrifice with little, if any, recognition. They were the gallant heroes that I knew.[7]

Patriot Mike Stagner offers the following from an unknown author: "All Marines die in either the red flash of battle or the white cold of the nursing home. In their vigor of youth or the infirmity of age, all will eventually die, but the Marine Corps lives on. Every Marine who ever lived is living still, in the Marines who 'claim the title' today. It is that sense of belonging to something that will outlive our own mortality. It is belonging to something which gives people a light to live by and a flame to mark their passing."[8]

I received an e-mail from Mike Stagner, dated 4 April 2006, describing his "One day I can never forget." I enjoyed the story but put it on hold for a while, promising myself to revisit it a later date. During a lull in writing, I did review the story and sent out a questionnaire, which Mike immediately responded to in two e-mails, both dated 6 July 2006.

39

USMC Sergeant Ralph Bohannon

> Luck can often mean simply taking advantage
> of a situation at the right moment.
> — Michael Korda

Prelude

I was born in Burnside, Kentucky, on 3 January 1947. I had what might be classified as a typical life for a young boy raised in the South in the 1950s and '60s. My dad was a blue-collar worker and my mom was a housewife. Dad had a high school education and mom attended two years of college. Dad served with the Army Air Corps during World War II and was with Claire Chennault's Flying Tigers in Burma as a radio operator. Mother worked on a military base handing out airplane parts as her contribution to the war effort.

Activities during my youth included swimming with friends at the nearest creek, hunting, fishing and camping. I had my first BB gun when I was five and my dad gave me my first rifle, a Remington Nylon 66, at age sixteen. I spent many hours in the field enjoying that rifle and I still have it to this day. I mainly attended grades 1–12 at a small country school, Chumuckla School, which had a graduating class of only eleven students. I did not graduate from this class, as I had transferred to another school so I could be with my then girlfriend and now wife. During my senior year, I lived with my paternal grandmother and helped my uncle on his farm to earn money for school clothes and supplies. I had wonderful, loving parents and my youth was full and enjoyable.

I was exposed to the Marine Corps early in life. My mother had several college and childhood friends who joined the Marines shortly after Pearl Harbor and most were involved in well-known campaigns during the war. Many did not survive and she often spoke of them and their sacrifices. I cherished those stories of brave men and the name Marine was one that epitomized bravery and sacrifice to me. I began to develop a real interest in the Marines about my sophomore year in high school, reading anything I could find about them. In 1964, the Marines were committed to the Dominican Republic and their service was in the news daily. I briefly considered quitting school and joining the Marines at that time, but my dad quickly put an end to that thought! By this time I was fired up to be a Marine and joined under the 120-day delayed enlistment program on 10 May 1965, just weeks before graduating from high school.

Jeff, as he prefers to be called (his middle name is Jefferson), entered boot camp in September 1965 at Parris Island, South Carolina. After graduating from boot camp, he was assigned to the 1st Military Police (MP) Battalion at Camp Pendleton, California. This was the first unit of its kind since the Korean War and was intended to handle security and POWs, conduct patrols, engage in basic law enforcement procedures and manage military traffic. He deployed with the 1st MPs aboard the USS *Upshur* on 7 May 1966 and arrived in Da Nang on 1 June 1966. During this first tour in Vietnam, he was initially assigned to security around the Da Nang airstrip, manning a perimeter and conducting patrols. He later requested a transfer to an infantry regiment, which was granted in August, when he was assigned to the 1st Battalion, 3rd Marines (1/3). In June 1967, Jeff rotated back to the United States and was reassigned to the Marine Barracks, Naval Ammunition Depot in McAlester, Oklahoma.

In September 1967, Jeff married his high school sweetheart, Nita. They had met when he had crashed her sixteenth birthday party on 10 June 1963 and started dating later that September. He had actually carried her rings in his pack in Vietnam for 8 months. In April 1969, he was given an "early out" of the Marines, which was being offered to Vietnam veterans. "I remained out of the Corps for approximately one and a half months and, missing it more than I could have ever imagined, I reenlisted on 18 May 1969. Just a few months later, I was sent back to Vietnam, where I was assigned to a Combined Action Platoon [CAP] unit."[1]

A Brief History of CAP Units

In 1965, Marine and Army generals differed in their opinions on the direction of the war. Army General William Westmoreland wanted to ignore the local populace and bring the war out in the open to combat the enemy in large-scale operations, which would place the Americans at an advantage with their air and artillery superiority. Marine General Lewis Walt believed that there was a need to protect the villages and develop a rapport with the local population; otherwise, the war would go on forever. Walt stated, "The struggle was in the rice paddies, in and among the people, not passing through, but living among them, night and day and joining with them in steps towards a better life, long overdue." One Navy corpsman said, "Until we start to treat these people like human beings, they aren't going to want to help us."

In the summer of 1965, the Civic Affairs Officer for the 3rd Battalion, 4th Marines (3/4) saw an opportunity for Marines to work closely with the Vietnamese Popular Force (PF) soldiers, a poorly trained local militia, and turn them into an aggressive fighting force defending the villages. His plan was to combine a squad of 14 Marines with a Navy corpsman and a platoon of PFs (a total force of about 50 men).

Called a Combined Action Platoon (CAP), these units comprised a special breed of Marines. They had to be highly motivated volunteers and sympathetic to the Vietnamese people. One Marine said, "These men really believed they could help the Vietnamese people, and by doing so, help win the war."

General Walt believed PF soldiers could be a valuable fighting force. "He was defending his own home, family and neighbors. He knew each paddy, field, trail, bush or bamboo clump, each family shelter, tunnel and buried rice urn."[2]

Eventually there were four Combined Action Groups (CAGs) in the Marines' I Corps region, from Chu Lai to Dong Ha. Each CAG had several Combined Action Companies (CACOS), which in turn had numerous CAPs under their control. At its height, there were 4 CAGs, 19 CACOS and 114 CAPs, with an estimated strength of 2,000 Marines and 3,000 PFs.[3]

August 1969
2nd CAG, CACO 2-1, CAP 2-1-3,
3rd Marine Division
Tuy Loan, Hieu Duc District

Sergeant Jeff Bohannon was assigned to CAP 2-1-3 within the village of Tuy Loan, near Hill 10, approximately 20 miles southwest of Da Nang. It was near "Charlie Ridge" and Liberty road, which was the main supply route to An Hoa and Hill 55. It was in the Hieu Duc District, Quang Nam Province. He was the CAP commander of 8–12 Marines and oversaw the PF's strength of 30–35 men. His TAOR (tactical area of responsibility) covered several hamlets. His 2nd CAG was headquartered several miles to the east at Hoi An.

Our mission in CAP was to live among the populace and to work with the local South Vietnamese soldiers. These soldiers were similar to our National Guard troops, in that they were local, and lived and served in the area of their own villages. They were called Popular Force soldiers. They were not especially well trained and it was our mission, at least on paper, to train them in patrolling, ambushing, weapons, etc., with the intent of turning the villages over to them eventually to defend, with us moving on to do it again in another village.

A platoon of these PFs, led by a South Vietnamese sergeant, was assigned to each Marine CAP squad, and their sergeant was subordinate to me from an operational standpoint. He handled the discipline and conducted his platoon in daily matters, but I handled all the tactical aspects of our relationship. I was called Trung Si (Sergeant) Bo, which was short for Bohannon.[4]

Spring 1970
CAP 2-1-3
Tuy Loan Village, Hieu Duc District

Each year, the PF platoon was pulled back for retraining at Da Nang, essentially a month of boot camp. When this happened to our platoon, a platoon from a refugee camp replaced our PFs, and I believe most were either Viet Cong or sympathizers. When I first met with their sergeant, he was arrogant and uncooperative. He and his platoon were on easy street in the refugee village, never having to patrol or do anything they didn't want to, so I believe he may have been a little upset that he had been assigned to us. We managed to progress for a time, but our efforts to get the PFs to participate in the patrols and ambushes became increasingly difficult.

About two weeks into our relationship, my CAP had completed night activities and moved into our "day haven site." This particular day haven consisted of three small huts on an island in the middle of rice paddies. It had clear fields of fire for roughly 200 yards in all directions and was nicknamed by us as the "three-house island." At approximately 1000, a patrol consisting of three Marines was dispatched to the village to get the PF contingent. I later found out that when the patrol leader approached the assigned PFs, things deteriorated rather quickly. The PFs stated they did not feel like going out on patrol and, after an escalating angry exchange, their Bac Si (corpsman) got especially nasty with my patrol leader by spitting in his face. My patrol leader commenced by putting the errant Bac Si through the side of the small hut he was residing in and left the site to continue the patrol without PF participation.

Meanwhile, we on "three-house island" had no clue of the proceedings, as my patrol leader did not think it necessary to inform me of the incident or his decision to continue the patrol without the PFs. The first clue we had that not all was well was when my security informed me we had the entire platoon of PFs approaching our position on line, with weapons at the ready. Then to our amazement, they started firing their weapons in unison at us, but the rounds were going over our head. Given our experience with PF marksmanship, we were not at all sure it was intentional, so I immediately deployed my unit.

The PFs stopped behind a small paddy dike about one hundred yards from our position. I deployed my M-60s and M-79s to cover the PFs and called my patrol back to cover the rear. It did not take long for the PFs to realize they were not in the most advantageous position so they ceased firing. At this time, the PF sergeant approached our position with an interpreter who spoke English. The sergeant walked right up to me with his cocked .45 pistol in his hand and proceeded to stick the bore, rather aggressively, into my abdomen at the belly button position. He started yelling at me about the incident with my patrol leader and his Bac Si. He further stated he didn't like Americans and didn't want us in his area.

I didn't know if this idiot was going to shoot me, but I assure you that was foremost in my mind, and I was scared to death! In addition, knowing the accidental discharge history of the good old .45 caused me further concern. When he stopped his diatribe, I took my turn. I figured if I went, I was taking this scumbag with me and I pushed my M-16 right up under his little chin. I then clicked the safety to full automatic, a very audible, distinctive two clicks from safe to auto that was recognized by all present. The PF sergeant immediately realized his choice of weapons and aim point may not have been the best. His beady little eyes were now wide open and full of fear.

I then told him that if any of my Marines were injured in any way, even by accident, I was going to kill all of his PFs and burn down his village. He didn't have to think long before he removed his pistol and proceeded back to the refugee village with his platoon. After checking my trousers to see if I had pissed myself, which I hadn't, I got on the radio, and called our rear to report the incident and informed them we no longer required the services of this platoon. The platoon was pulled out that day and later replaced with another more cooperative unit. To our knowledge, we never saw that platoon again, but in reality, we probably ambushed some of them in later actions.

I had been in several firefights, both before and after this incident, but nothing as close up and personal as this was. I consider this was the closest that I came to being killed in my two tours in Nam.[5]

Postlude

Jeff finished his second Vietnam tour and returned to the United States in July 1970. He decided to make the Marines his career and spent a wonderful 24 years, retiring in 1989 as a first sergeant. He held numerous positions at duty stations around the country and the world, including Quantico, Virginia; Fort Dix, New Jersey; JFK International Airport, New York (where he served as a sky marshall); Okinawa, Japan; Parris Island, South Carolina (as a drill instructor); Washington, D.C.; Kaneohe Bay, Hawaii; Camp Lejeune, North Carolina; Mobile, Alabama; and Naples, Italy.

Whenever possible, his wife and two children accompanied him to his duty assignments. He is proud of both of his successful children and they have blessed him and Nita with three beautiful grandchildren. In September 2006, he and his wife celebrated 39 years of marriage together.

Upon military retirement, Jeff worked in a series of odd jobs while going to college at the University of West Florida, eventually earning a B.S. in 1995. "I would work a semester or two and then attend school for a while, trying to keep our heads above water. Thank God for my wonderful wife who carried the family during these hard times." Upon earning his degree, he became the assistant commandant of the Marion Military Institute in Marion, Alabama. Since his wife did not want to live in Alabama, he took another position, where he is still employed, as the Superintendent (Warden) of the Escambia County Road Prison, near Pensacola, Florida.

Jeff still enjoys hunting and fishing, along with anything he can do with the grandchildren. "We swim a lot and my grandson likes to shoot, fish, camp and canoe. I still scuba and snorkel and my daughter loves to join me in that. I hope to get the grandkids interested in that too."

Jeff maintains a membership in the local Marine Corps League chapter. He hopes one day to attend the CAP reunions and the Khe Sanh Veterans reunion, but at the present, there just does not seem enough time for travel. He believes this will all change in a few years when he retires for good. He does communicate with several Marines that he served with during his two Vietnam tours.[6]

In April 2006, I received an e-mail from Jeff Bohannon relating an experience he had in a CAP unit. Initially, I did not feel that it fit my "close call" criteria and filed the story away. Upon rereading it July 2006, I put myself in Jeff's position during the incident, when the PF soldier stuck his pistol in his stomach, and realized it does not get much closer than that that to a potential life-ending event. I sent Jeff an e-mail questionnaire and he responded with two e-mails, both dated on 11 July 2006.

Part Four: The Wars Against Terrorism

> I do not know beneath what sky
> Nor on what seas shall be thy fate;
> I only know it shall be high,
> I only know it shall be great.
> — Richard Hovey

40

Beirut: Bombing of the Marine Barracks

> For rarely man escapes his destiny.
> — Ludovico Ariosto

Prelude

On 23 October 1983, 241 Americans perished in what many consider to be one of the first instances of a suicide bombing, at the four-story Marine Corps headquarters barracks in Beirut, Lebanon. Rescue efforts continued for days, at times hindered by sniper fire, but eventually, nearly 80 fortunate Marines were found alive in the rubble. This chapter tells the story of one Navy corpsman and three lucky Marines, who served with the 1st Battalion, 8th Marines, 2nd Marine Division, and survived their close call with death.

A Brief History of the 1st Battalion, 8th Marines (1/8)

The 1/8 is an infantry battalion that was first activated at San Diego, California, on 1 April 1940, when it was assigned to the 2nd Marine Brigade. On 1 February 1941 the 2nd Marine Brigade was redesignated as the 2nd Marine Division. By December of this same year, the Battalion was assigned to the 2nd Marine Brigade, 2nd Marine Division. After several more subtle designation changes, it was assigned to the 2nd Marine Division and participated in the World War II campaigns of Guadalcanal, Saipan, Tinian and Okinawa. Following the war, it was sent to Japan for occupation duty and was finally relocated to Camp Lejeune, North Carolina, in July 1946. It was deactivated on 18 November 1947.

On 1 November 1950 the Battalion was reactivated as the 1st Battalion, 8th Marines, 2nd Marine Division and has been based at Camp Lejeune ever since. From the 1950s through the 1980s, they have been deployed numerous times to such places as the Mediterranean, Caribbean and Lebanon in 1958 and again in 1983. In 1990-91 the unit participated in Operation Desert Shield and Desert Storm in Southwest Asia. Its Marines have been involved in Operation Iraqi Freedom in Iraq on four separate tours: April 2003; June 2004-January 2005; June-October 2006; and September 2007. During July 2006 they were sent to Lebanon for the third time in their history to help in the evacuation of American citizens. No wonder the Battalion's nickname is the "Beirut Battalion."[1]

A Brief History of the Turmoil in Lebanon 1975-1985

Constant strife and civil war were evident during the period of 1975-1985 and, in fact, continue to this day. The conflicts arose from a country divided by religion (Christianity and Islam), Israeli and Syrian intervention, and a large contingent base of the Palestine Liberation Front (PLO). There were also numerous terrorist factions of every kind and size to further disrupt the countryside. By 1975, it was estimated that the PLO had over 300,000 people living mainly in the southern portion of Lebanon. Political tensions turned into military conflict, with a full-scale civil war beginning in April 1975. International intervention ultimately became necessary. By June 1982, a multinational peace force (MNF) consisting of United States Marines, French and Italian units were brought in to ensure the departure of the PLO and to protect the many defenseless citizens. By September nearly 15,000 Palestinian militants had been evacuated. Lebanon President Bashir Gemayel was assassinated on 14 September and his Christian Phalange militia entered some of the remaining PLO camps and massacred 700-800 Palestinians.

Amine Gemayel succeeded his brother and planned to force the withdrawal of both Israeli and Syrian forces from his country. On 17 May 1983, an agreement among Lebanon, Israeli and the United States arranged for an Israeli departure, contingent on the withdrawal of Syrian troops. Syria opposed this arrangement and refused to cooperate. Resistance against the United States and the other Western forces had been increasing with the U.S. Embassy bombings in 1983 and 1984. In between these two terrorist bombings, one of the more horrific attacks occurred at the Marine and French barracks located in Beirut in October 1983.[2]

23 October 1983
1st Battalion, 8th Marines, 24th Marine Amphibious Unit
Marine Barracks Headquarters, Beirut International Airport

At approximately 0622 on Sunday, 23 October 1983, the Battalion Landing Team (BLT) headquarters building in the Marine Amphibious Unit compound at the Beirut International airport was destroyed by a terrorist bomb. The bombing was carried out by one lone terrorist driving a yellow Mercedes Benz stake-bed truck that accelerated through the public parking lot south of the BLT headquarters building. The truck drove over the barbed and concertina wire obstacles, passed between two Marine guard posts without being engaged by fire, entered an open gate, passed around one sewer pipe barrier and between two others, flattened the Sergeant of the Guard's sandbagged booth at the building's entrance, penetrated the lobby of the building and detonated while the majority of the occupants slept. The force of the explosion, nearly 12,000 pounds of TNT, ripped the building from its foundation. The building then imploded upon itself. Almost all of the occupants were crushed or trapped inside the wreckage.

A total of 241 American service members (220 Marines, 18 Navy personnel and 3 Army soldiers) were killed. Nearly 80 were rescued from the collapsed building, 60 of them injured. This was the deadliest single-day death toll for the United States Marine Corps since the battle of Iwo Jima in World War II.

Approximately 20 seconds later, a similar attack occurred against the barracks of the French 3rd Company of the 6th French Parachute Infantry Regiment. Another truck-bomb terrorist drove down a ramp and into the building's underground garage, exploding and leveling their barracks. The French losses were 58 killed and 15 wounded.[4]

USN Hospital Corpsman Third Class Pedro Alvarado

Twenty-eight-year-old Navy corpsman Pedro Alvarado, of Ponce, Puerto Rico, usually slept on the fourth floor of the barracks. For some reason, and he is not sure why, he chose to sleep that night in the basement where medical supplies were kept and the Marines were treated for injuries or illnesses. "Something told me to go to that corner in the basement and you'll be safe. There was just a feeling."

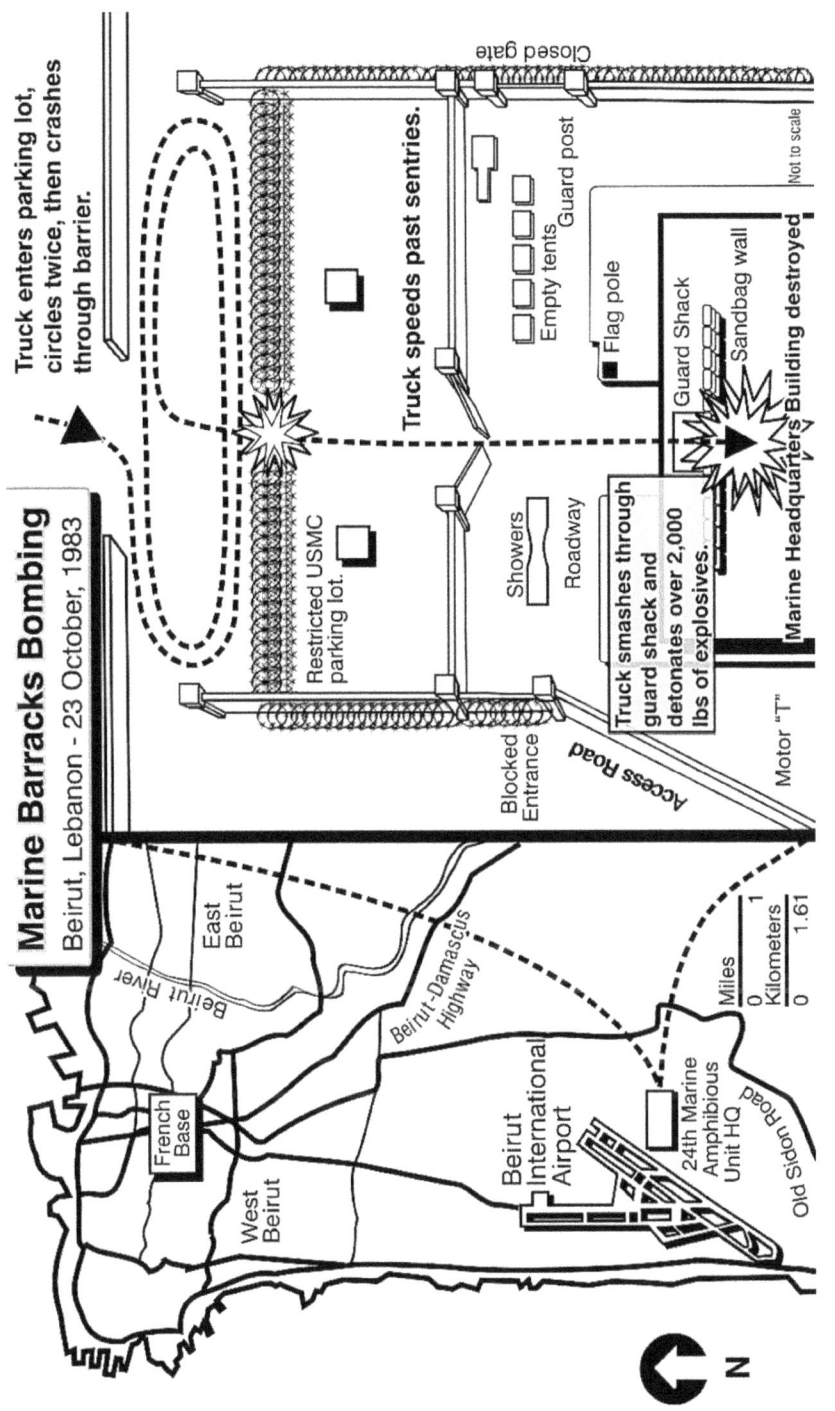

He did not hear the explosion. His first thought was that a rocket had hit the building. He yelled through a hole in the wreckage, blacked out and awoke later in a Lebanese hospital. He said he was afraid to ask about his friends and the other Marines that he worked with. He had a lot of affection for the Marines. "They didn't call you corpsman. They didn't call you by your last name. They called you Doc."

One bright light in his experience, however, was the news that his wife, Anilda, was expecting their first baby. "It helped take me out of this nightmare." Alvarado had just returned to Lebanon in early October after accompanying home the body of a friend killed in Beirut. He had no regrets about returning after the funeral. "I'm a serviceman. My unit was assigned to Lebanon and I had to be with my people. It would now be a little difficult to return to Beirut, but I would go."

When asked what he thought of the people responsible for the truck bomb attack on the Marine headquarters, he searched for the word. "I don't know the word in English but it is spelled C-o-w-a-r-d!"[5]

USMC Lance Corporal Steven Diaz

Lance Corporal Steven Diaz, from Chicago, Illinois, was walking adjacent to the building when the powerful bomb went off. The 20-year-old Marine was immediately thrown to ground. "I was crawling along the ground, scratching to get some cover. I couldn't get up. I was knocked down silly." Diaz was rescued and sent to a hospital in Wiesbaden, Germany, where he was treated for internal injuries. "I'm just worried about a lot of people. If you saw the blast, you would know why they can't find some of the guys."

Diaz also called the attack the action of a coward. "We were a peacekeeping force. We tried to keep our noses clean. They're in a war situation. They can shoot. We're not in a war. We're trying to keep the peace. The first thing that I am going to do when I get home is to grab my wife and son and never let go. I'm going to give them all I got."[6]

USMC Lance Corporal Renard Manley and USMC Lance Corporal Morris Dorsey

Lance Corporal Renard Manley, 25, of Panama City, Florida, was asleep on the top floor of the headquarters building. "The first thing I remembered was there was a giant concrete slab looming six inches above me. It was like a dream, like a coffin. I didn't know what happened." Lance Corporal Morris Dorsey of Poughkeepsie, New York, was also trapped in the wreckage.

They talked and yelled to each other for an hour. They tried humoring each other to keep awake. Dorsey said, "Do they have you out yet, man?" Manley replied, "I haven't seen anyone yet."

According to Manley, "One of my biggest fears was that the rescuers would dig from on top of me, and the concrete slab would fall. I gave them play-by-play instructions for how to get me. The first thing I told them after they got me out was to get Dorsey out next." Manley suffered bruised ankles and knees and a strained neck. "When I think of the other guys who didn't make it, I realized just how very, very lucky I was."[7]

Postlude

The identity of those responsible for the bombing is uncertain to this day; however, most believe it was the work of the Hezbollah militant group, backed by Iran and Syria. Hezbollah, Iran and Syria, all staunch opponents of a Western presence in Lebanon, denied any involvement. Several Shia militant groups claimed responsibility for the attacks.

In retaliation for the attacks, France launched an air strike in the Bekaa Valley against Iranian Revolutionary Guard positions. The Americans, afraid of upsetting relations with other Arab nations, failed to put together any retaliatory responses. The Marines were moved offshore where they could no longer be targeted. By 26 February 1984, all Marines were withdrawn from Lebanon and the rest of the MNF left by April.[8]

Today, a Cedar of Lebanon stands tall over a small memorial in the Arlington National Cemetery in section 59. This tree marks the location of 21 graves out of the 241 American military personnel who perished during the Beirut Marine barracks attack. Every year, a memorial service is held on the anniversary date of 23 October to honor their memory.[9]

On 20 June 2006, I imagined that there must be several near-death experiences as the result of the 1983 bombing of the Marine Barracks. I found my first stories from the online archives of *Stars and Stripes* and then proceeded with a more intense search.

Information obtained from *Star and Stripes* was authorized on 31 October 2007 (used with permission from the *Stars and Stripes*. ©1983, 2005, 2006, 2007 *Stars and Stripes*).

41

Iraq: Female Search Force

> Fate is what happens to you when your luck runs out.
> — Michael Garrett Marino

Prelude

By early June 2005, a group of about 20 female Marines had been working together for over three months, as part of a newly formed volunteer "Female Search Force," in the area of Fallujah, Iraq. Marines had the responsibility for providing security and sensitivities were a major concern of the Marines of the 3rd Battalion, 4th Marines, Regimental Combat Team-8 (RCT-8).

Female Marines had taken on a critical role in the RCT-8's mission in an effort to show respect for the Iraqi culture. At entry control points (ECPs) throughout the city, the female teams searched women and children for contraband in areas protected from the view of male Marines and civilians. A Marine captain said, "In this society, men and women don't associate as freely as we do back in the States. The women have a keen understanding of what their role is and they go about their job as professionals."

The female searchers also assist in the search of vehicles coming through the ECPs. Although not their regular job, the female Marines enjoy their temporary role in the city's security and the opportunities to work in support of a Marine infantry battalion. In early June 2005 Lance Corporal Christina Humphrey, a 22-year-old motor transport operator, stated, "It's great to interact with the infantry Marines. We will continue to stand our posts with a bolstered pride, recognizing the necessity of our role in this environment."[1]

The women had some close calls while standing duty. Humphrey said she was once pinned down during a firefight at one of the points with bullets striking the ground a foot away on both sides of her. Another close call came several days later, she said, when a man attempted to pull her into a frenzied crowd by the barrel of her rifle.[2]

23 June 2005
Female Search Force (FSF)
Fallujah, Iraq

On 23 June, the team's good luck finally ran out. As they left their day ECP positions, they joined a 16-truck convoy headed for their home base. The FSF boarded one of the seven-ton trucks. Along the way, Humphrey, who was sitting in the back of the truck, noticed a vehicle with a driver that she had seen before in the area. "He didn't fit the profile of a suicide bomber. The man had a woman and a child riding with him. Most suicide bombers are alone." Unfortunately, the vehicle had been rigged with bombs and it rammed right into their truck!

"I don't remember a lot. I don't know if I blacked out, or my subconscious won't let me, but I don't remember everything that happened," said Lance Corporal Lynn Beasley. "I do remember opening my eyes and the flames were right there. I thought to myself, I hope I'm not burning, but I knew I was."

Humphrey reported that the truck rolled onto its side. "I remember tucking and rolling as the truck flipped over. Then there was a second explosion from the gas tank."[3]

After the explosion, the Marines in the convoy began receiving sniper fire. "I grabbed the first weapon I saw, but the explosion rendered it unserviceable," Humphrey continued. "All of the weapons were scattered everywhere and the blast blew most of them apart."[4]

Humphrey said the survivors of the blast gathered at a wall when another truck in the convoy, full of infantry Marines, pulled up and loaded the wounded on a trailer. "Some people were so bad their skin was coming off their arms. One girl's face was burned so bad you could see her skull and one girl's hands had no skin." Humphrey received several minor burns, a concussion, an injured back and a temporary loss of sight in her right eye. She said her sight has improved but is poor when she's stressed out and she now has migraine headaches.[5]

"After the firefight, we started giving first aid to the casualties," Humphrey recalled. "Everyone was in shock and six Marines had to be air-lifted out." Six people died that day, including two female Marines and a female Seabee. Nineteen others from the convoy were wounded, including eleven females. A male Marine remembers getting the call about the convoy attack and hoping none of the women were involved. Corporal Anthony Rodriguez stated, "It was about 2100 when we got the word so we knew the females were in the convoy. When the trucks arrived carrying the body bags, I looked to see who was killed, to see if it was any of our females."[6]

Corporal Beasley's injuries were more serious than those of Humphrey.

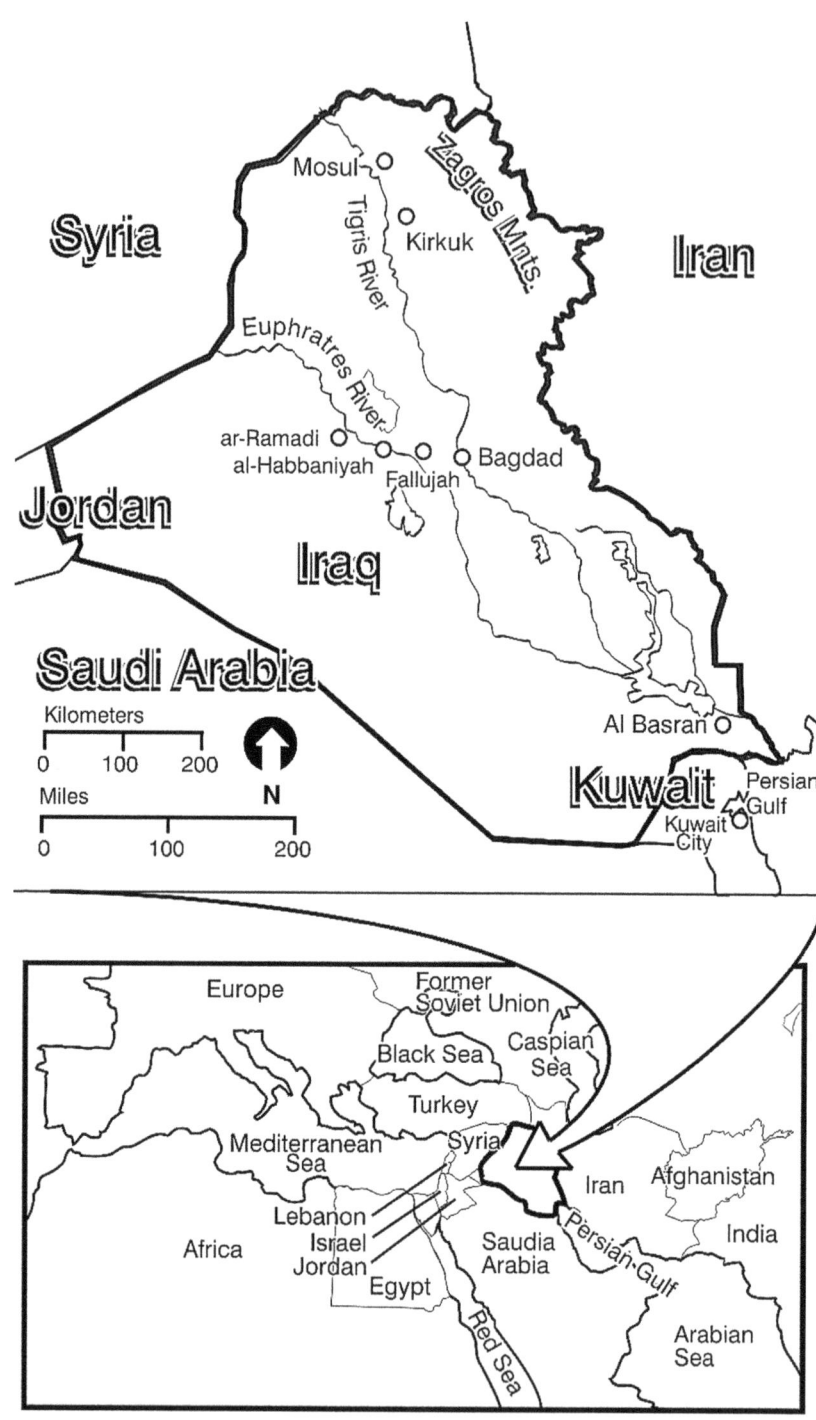

Iraq in relation to the Middle East

She had burns to her face and legs, bruised ribs, perforated eardrums and several shrapnel wounds. She was evacuated out along with several other women and ended up at Brooke Army Medical Center in San Antonio, Texas. She spent about three weeks there before going home to Illinois for a month to recuperate.[7]

"Everyone worked together as a team that day," Humphrey concluded. "The Marines died being Marines. I don't think the females got more attention. No matter what gender someone is, the pain and loss is still the same."

The two women Marines who were killed that evening were the first female Marines of the Iraqi War to die. As of 28 September 2005, a total of 46 out of 1,933 deaths during Operation Iraqi Freedom had been women.[8]

Just prior to being evacuated from Iraq, Corporal Beasley gave Corporal Humphrey a special necklace and told her not to take it off until they saw each other again.[9]

Postlude

When Humphrey returned from Iraq, a friend from boot camp spoke with her about her experiences. "I was shocked when she told me about the attack in Iraq," said Lance Corporal Rebecca Ide. "The attack gave her a different perspective on life. She values life more now because she almost lost hers."[10]

By October 2005, Humphrey and Beasley were reunited at Camp Hansen on Okinawa, where they resumed their original jobs in motor transport. When they met for the first time Corporal Humphrey proudly showed off the necklace that she had worn since Beasley had given it to her months before. The two lucky women both received Purple Hearts for their injuries and Humphrey was awarded a Navy-Marine Corps Achievement Medal with combat "V" for the checkpoint firefight.

"It's not like I'm proud of it. It's not a medal you really want to get, but if you do, you accept it and move on," Beasley said. "It doesn't matter what medals you have on," Humphrey said. "I'd give all those medals back just to get my friends back."

Beasley continues to have some lingering effects from her injuries. "I have special garments I have to wear on my legs for the next two years and I can't be exposed to direct sunlight. I also still have some shrapnel that will eventually work its way out."[11]

All of the FSF team members who survived the 23 June close call incident considered themselves to have been extremely lucky that they did not perish during the truck suicide bombing attack.

Postscript
August 2006
The Lioness Program

Over a year after the 23 June 2005 car bombing attack against the FSF team, the Marines remained undeterred in utilizing female Marines to help in the war on terrorism. Similar groups are now being used all around Iraq. One of the more recent ones is called the Lioness Program, initiated by the 3rd Marine Air Wing to conduct searches along the Iraqi borders to stop insurgents from using women smugglers to gain funds or weapons. The Lioness Program consists of eight female volunteer Marines from different units who each serve a 30-day rotation. The female Marines first receive briefs and appropriate training from Regimental Combat Team-7 personnel, before going to their temporary base at Camp Korean Village, Iraq. Once at the base, they are given more intense classes on procedures and how to properly handle themselves in various situations. This includes everything from proper search techniques to shooting from supported firing positions.

"The training puts you in the combat mindset that every Marine is a rifleman, regardless of gender," said Lance Corporal Hollye Meeks, a motor transport vehicle operator. "It was realistic training to help familiarize you with your gear and your weapon. I don't know what to expect, but I'll expect the worst, hope for the best and rely on my training."

"I wanted to do something different," said Sergeant Alice Dunne, an electrical equipment repair specialist. "In Al Asad, you never felt like you're in the fight; you were just doing your job."

"I wanted to see a different part of the Marine Corps," said Lance Corporal Katheryn Saldarriage, a nuclear, biological and chemical defense specialist. "I wanted to see the culture and the people."

Although most of the volunteers are from different units and military occupations, they have bonded as a tight-knit team and have learned to count on each other in the short time they have trained together. "I have confidence in the rest of the team," said Corporal Valerie Gavaldon, a combat engineer. "I'm confident they can handle the mission. We're showing people that females have a special mission in this war as well."[12]

As of 6 November 2007, female fatalities in the Iraqi Coalition had reached 99 out of the overall total of 4,164 deaths. This includes both combat and non-combated related casualties.[13]

On 7 July 2006, I ran across an interesting story from the online *Stars and Stripes* archives about the deadliest incident involving women in Iraq. Three were killed and eleven wounded. All of the survivors were extremely lucky. I then did a complete online search for the Female Search Force.

Information obtained from *Star and Stripes* was authorized on 31 October 2007 (used with permission from the *Stars and Stripes*. ©1983, 2005, 2006, 2007 *Stars and Stripes*).

42

Afghanistan: "The Nightfighters"

> Fortuna Fortes Juvat (Fortune Favors the Brave).
> — Latin proverb

Prelude

This chapter relates three stories about one Navy corpsman and two Marines, who were part of the same unit (Company E, 2nd Battalion, 3rd Marines) in Afghanistan in 2005. Each close call incident is unique, though the reader will see a link to one of the stories.

The 2nd Battalion, 3rd Marines (2/3), 3rd Marine Division is based out of the Marine Corps Base Hawaii located at Kaneohe Bay, Hawaii. The unit's nickname is the "Nightfighters," and their motto is "Fortune Favors the Brave." The Battalion has had a notable history in America's wars. The 2/3 participated in the battles for Bougainville and Guam during World War II, then saw action in the Vietnam War, Operation Desert Storm in Kuwait, Operation Enduring Freedom in Afghanistan and Operation Iraqi Freedom. The Battalion consists roughly of 1,000 Marines and sailors.[1]

A Brief History of the United States/Coalition War in Afghanistan

Since 1996, Osama bin Laden had been living in Afghanistan along with other members of al-Qaeda, operating terrorist training camps in a loose alliance with the ruling Afghanistan Taliban Party. Following the 1998 U.S. Embassy bombings in West Africa, the Clinton administration fired cruise missiles at these camps with limited effect on their overall operations. After the 11 September 2001 attacks on the World Trade Center in New York, the Pentagon, and an airliner that crashed in Pennsylvania, investigators quickly amassed evidence implicating bin Laden and his organization.

The George W. Bush administration delivered ultimatums to the Taliban that they needed to turn over al-Qaeda leaders and close all of the terrorist camps in Afghanistan. The Taliban made some minor responses but President Bush rejected them as insincere. The UN Security Council had also issued a resolution to the Taliban making similar demands.

On 7 October 2001, American and British forces began an aerial bombing campaign targeting Taliban forces and al-Qaeda. Just prior to the attack, Osama bin Laden called for a jihad, a war of Muslims against the entire non–Muslim world. A coalition of tribes known as the Northern Alliance, assisted by U.S. Special Forces, undertook the ground war against the Taliban. Several other countries contributed men and equipment for the fight against the terrorists under a Coalition of Nations.

By the end of the year, most large-scale resistance ended and surviving Taliban and al-Qaeda leaders, including Mullah Omar and bin Laden, were forced into hiding, most likely in the mountains of northwestern Pakistan. Fighting on a smaller scale continues to this day, mainly in the form of ambushes and improvised explosive devices (IEDs). The U.S. still maintains a presence of nearly 10,000 troops in Afghanistan, providing security and searching for the elusive terrorists. As of June 2006, Coalition forces had suffered 393 killed and 718 wounded.[2]

June 2005
2nd Battalion, 3rd Marines
Camp Blessing, Kunar Province, Afghanistan

The 2/3 arrived in Afghanistan in June 2005 and began operations in the surrounding area of the Kunar Province. This province, one of 34, is situated in the northeastern portion of the country along the Pakistan border. Its capital city is Asadabad.

By July, average temperatures exceeded 100 degrees in the province, greatly hampering day-to-day activities of the 2/3 Marines. One Marine said that they drank a case of water every time they went out on a patrol. Another stated, "Your head pounds and your cammies are completely soaked like you just took a shower in them."[3]

Corporal Andrew Lowe
September 2005
Company E, Mortars, 2nd Battalion, 3rd Marines
Camp Blessing, Kunar Province

In early September 2005, Afghan contractors were tasked to construct a base for a flagpole at Camp Blessing. Initially, this base was intended to be a

Afghanistan in relation to the Middle East

small structure, but the Afghans built one much larger than expected. Corporal Andrew Lowe of San Diego, California, was a mortar-man with Company E at Camp Blessing. About a week after the base for the flagpole had been built, enemy mortar rounds landed inside the camp, killing Lance Corporal Steven Valdez. During the attack, one round landed near the flagpole and most of the shrapnel hit the structure instead of nearby Marines. Lowe was temporarily deafened by the blast and was so close to the explosion that smoke steamed out from underneath his helmet. "That flagpole saved my life! You think it would be the scariest moment in your life. It was just weird with it landing so close."[4]

A simple thing like a flagpole provided a close call for this Marine, but soon, more Company E, 2/3 personnel would also experience near-death events.

Hospital Corpsman Third Class Robert Maldonado
30 September 2005
Company E, 2nd Battalion, 3rd Marines
Korengal Valley, Kunar Province

Twenty-five-year old Los Angeles native Robert Maldonado was on his first combat deployment. On 30 September 2005, Maldonaldo's unit was on a convoy through the Korengal Valley, appropriately called "bad guy central." The corpsman and three Marines brought up the rear of the convoy in their armored Humvee, when suddenly an IED exploded directly underneath them. The explosion blew the doors off their vehicle and both the gunner and relief driver were sent flying outside. The Marine driver took the brunt of the blast, but miraculously, Maldonado received only minor shrapnel in his arms and legs. "I was the lucky one! My ears were ringing and I was throwing up. I think it was radiator fluid; my mouth tasted like chemicals."

Maldonado lurched out of the Humvee, pulling the unconscious driver with him. The driver's lower leg was blown open with bones sticking out of the large wound. "The blood was so bright it looked almost pink. It was spurting rhythmically into the air. I thought, oh God, this is arterial bleeding, which could cause death in minutes. I put a tourniquet on him, tightened it as much as I could, and then wrapped and stabilized the sergeant's leg using his rifle as a brace."

Maldonaldo, still puking and stumbling, next went to the aid of the machine gunner, who was out in the road and unprotected against potential enemy fire. The gunner also had a shattered lower leg, which the corpsman splinted and bandaged after dragging him to safety behind the Humvee. He also applied a tourniquet because of all the blood he observed.

Finally, he began looking for the third Marine. He located him on the other side of the vehicle, half-hanging off a cliff. Inspecting the injured man he found the same sort of injury the other two Marines had suffered. He had a splintered lower leg with bones sticking out as well. As Maldonado finished bandaging his third patient and was checking the driver again, other Marines from the convoy showed up and were surprised that all of the injured had been taken care of already. The three Marines and Maldonado were evacuated by helicopter to the combat support hospital at Bagram Air Base.

At the hospital, a military doctor told the corpsman that his quick action had saved the driver's life. "I just thank God he was the closest one to me and, therefore, the first one that I helped. The doctor also told me I might have saved the machine gunner too, because he also had arterial bleeding."

Not only was Maldonado lucky to have escaped the same serious injuries of his Humvee companions, but they too were fortunate that he was able to provide life-saving first aid on the spot. Within days, Maldonado was back in the field and would soon play a role in the next Company E close call. For his quick and appropriate actions that day, he was awarded the Navy Achievement Medal with "V" for Valor.[5]

Lance Corporal John McClellan
11 and 17 October 2005
Company E-Antitank Team, 2nd Battalion, 3rd Marines
Asadabad to Camp Blessing, Kunar Province

On 11 October 2005, 19-year-old Lance Corporal John McClellan of Columbia, Missouri, was part of an armored convoy traveling from Forward Operating Base Asadabad to Camp Blessing. Along the way, the convoy received enemy rifle fire. McClellan did not feel it when he was hit with a ricochet from a 7.62mm bullet. His reaction was to rock back the M-79 grenade launcher from his Humvee turret and return fire. When he did finally notice his wound, he looked around his body for other holes and saw blood coming from his wrist.

The firefight lasted about five minutes, during which time another Marine was critically wounded. Only when the convoy resumed its journey to Camp Blessing did McClellan begin to ponder his injury. "It was just like, WOW! I got hit but was OK. I wondered how my fellow Marine was doing the rest of the way there. My wound never really hurt. I just got lucky." A day later, McClellan learned a bullet fragment was lodged in his wrist. He underwent surgery to have the piece removed and required a few stitches to close the wound.[6]

* * * *

Only six days later, on 17 October, McClellan was on another convoy along the same route as 11 October. It was his second time outside the wire since he was shot. By this time, his fellow Marines were already starting to give him grief. Lance Corporal Chris Acey said, "Before we left, we were joking around saying that we were going to get shot at because he was with us."

Along the route, Marines stopped to inspect a suspected roadside IED when a barrage of enemy rocket-propelled grenades, mortars and machine gun fire rained down on the convoy from a nearby ridgeline. Once again, McClellan was in a Humvee turret and he responded by firing his M-240 machine gun. "The only reason I knew I got hit was because I felt pressure on my arm and heard a 'tink' on the back of the turret shield. I yelled, 'I got hit. I think I'm hit.' I looked at the back of my arm and saw blood running down."

McClellan ducked down in his Humvee and another Marine took his position in the turret. John assessed his wound and rationalized that he had to get back into the fight. He got out of the vehicle and began returning fire. "I grabbed my M-16 and started shooting. I figured the enemy was not going to stop firing just because I was shot, so I started shooting to help gain fire superiority."

Navy Corpsman Robert Maldonado, arrived on the scene to cut open McClellan's uniform to treat his wound. "He asked me if it was bad and I told him, 'It's not bad, but not good either.'"

After a nearly 25-minute firefight, the Marines made their way to Camp Blessing, where McClellan received an IV and had his wound cleaned. It was later X-rayed to make sure the bullet had exited and had not caused additional damage. "When a round penetrates the body, it normally bounces around and can do a lot more damage," Maldonado said. "I thought it bounced around. I thought it was still inside him. When we got back to Blessing, we found out it went in and out. He was extremely lucky."

By now, the lance corporal was really being harassed. He earned many nicknames, including "Bullet Sponge" and "Lucky." Despite being shot twice in the same arm in one week, McClellan was soon walking around and had full use of his limb. He heard rumors that he might not be allowed outside the base again, but he wanted to be with his fellow grunts. "I don't like sitting on the bench. If my team is going to be out there, I want to be there with them." However, if he did head out again, he wanted to avoid earning the latest nickname that is floating around Asadabad: "Third time's a charm!" "They say I'm going to get shot again, but hopefully I won't."[7]

Postlude

The Marines at Camp Blessing have been credited with uncovering the most weapon caches, taken the most enemy indirect-fire attacks inside their camp and killed the most enemy of any unit from 2/3, 3rd Marine Division during its deployment in Afghanistan. Through intelligence gathered from local sources, the Marines uncovered 29 weapon caches, including 10,000 pounds of ordnance, 600 rounds of 82mm mortars rounds and 200 rocket-propelled grenades. As of the end of October 2005, they had suffered three Marines killed and 14 wounded.[8]

Postscript

Nearly one year later, just shortly after midnight on 27 September 2006, the parents of John McClellan received a call that a sniper had seriously wounded their son during his first month on a new deployment to Iraq. The "third time's a charm" proved, unfortunately, to be accurate. He had been shot by a sniper's bullet that missed his carotid artery by the thickness of two sheets of paper, his mother said, but it appears the bullet severed a nerve that controls the left side of his face. Operating in Haditha, Iraq, surgeons found that the bullet entered over his left ear and exited through the back of his neck. His doctors say he was lucky not to have any brain damage. He still may have to wear a hearing aid but his vision is fine. He first received care at the military hospital in Bethesda, Maryland, and was taken out of intensive care in early October. He was next sent to a hospital in Tampa, Florida, to undergo rehabilitation work.[9]

"He looked at me square in the eye and told me, 'I am so glad to be alive,'" said Connie McClellan, the Marine's mother. She said, "'About half as much as I am.' It just told me how determined he is going to be to get well." The lance corporal faces several more surgeries in the future and it is hoped that his ultimate recovery will be a total success.[10] By early 2007, John had made tremendous progress, but still suffers a few permanent disabilities. According to his mother, "One by one, God has answered the prayers of the thousands of people praying for John."[11]

On 18 April 2006, on a search through *Stars and Stripes* for "lucky Marines," I found an article about Lance Corporal John McClellan, who had been shot twice in one week in the same arm. I filed the story away, not sure if I was going to use it or not. Then, on 20 June 2006, I located another story of a Navy corpsman who also had a close call and found out that not only did he serve in the same unit (2/3) as

McClellan, but he had actually treated this same Marine several weeks after his own incident. Just prior to writing this chapter, while looking for more information on their 2/3 unit, I found my third close call 2/3 story. The chapter title, Nightfighters, is the motto of the 2nd Battalion, 3rd Marines.

On 1 November 2006, I learned of McClellan's third injury, this time in Iraq, by coming across an online article from the Marine Corps News Room.

Information obtained from *Star and Stripes* was authorized on 31 October 2007 (used with permission from the *Stars and Stripes*. ©1983, 2005, 2006, 2007 *Stars and Stripes*).

43

USMC Gunnery Sergeant Michael Burghardt

> Luck is what happens when preparation meets opportunity.
> — Elmer G. Letterman

Prelude

A native of Fountain Valley, California, Michael Burghardt was born in 1970 to a former Marine hero. His father, Josef Burghardt, served three combat tours in Vietnam, earning three Bronze Stars for bravery and three Purple Hearts for wounds received in action. His last wound ended his career when an enemy sniper shot and permanently paralyzed him from the waist down. Not deterred, Michael joined the Marine Corps in 1988, right out of high school at the age of 18. After attending boot camp in San Diego, he entered the Marines, which would become his life's chosen profession. After 3 years in the Corps, he was assigned to the field of explosive ordnance disposal (EOD), which, as of 2007, is what he is still doing some 15 years later. The wars in Afghanistan and Iraq were the perfect place for Burghardt to continue to hone his EOD skills on the numerous IEDs (improvised explosive devices) and various unexploded ordnance found all over these countries.[1]

February 2005
Headquarters and Service (H & S) Company,
8th Engineer Support Battalion, 2nd Force
Service Support Group
Marine Corps Base Camp Lejeune, North Carolina

By February 2005, Gunnery Sergeant Burghardt had recently returned from his second combat tour in Iraq. While there, he was a team leader with H & S Company, 8th Engineer Support Battalion, 2nd Force Service Group, which is based at Camp Lejeune, North Carolina. His EOD Team was attached to the Task Force-2nd Battalion, 7th Marines (2/7). He was credited for approaching 64 IEDs, discovered and cleared an IED manufacturing house, and destroyed 1,548 pieces of ordnance, two heavy machine guns, a 60mm mortar and a recoilless antitank gun. The fact that this was all done without a single injury to his team, himself or 2/7 is testimony to the gunny's superior skill, training, professionalism and valor. For his heroic action, day in and day out, he was awarded the Bronze Star with a combat "V" device for valor, thus becoming the second in his family to earn this medal.

The Talon, a robot used to defuse bombs, broke down during the second call that Burghardt's EOD team received. Even without this technology, his team was forced to push on. He gave credit to his team for their willingness to trust and never question him.

> I had a great team. They knew that we had a job to get done and this was the way we had to do it. I would never put my team in danger. My team members are also being recognized for what we did. Staff Sergeant Victor Levine is receiving a Bronze Star and Sergeant John Camara is getting a Navy and Marine Corps Commendation Medal.

During one incident on his second tour in 2004, Burghardt's EOD Team was able to locate and destroy 26 IEDs in a six-hour period along a treacherous 13-kilometer stretch of road, named Alternate Supply Route Lincoln. Convoys traveling along this route had been facing a heavy insurgency for quite awhile.

Burghardt said the team had now begun searching for IEDs, which is something the team did not normally do.

> I would sit on top of a light-armored vehicle looking for what I call a "trail of ants." As soon as I saw one, I would get the vehicle to stop and take my K-bar [Marine fighting knife] and wire cutters, and then approach the IED from a different angle to render it safe. Then my team would blow it up. A trail of ants is what looked like somebody had tried to hide wires by burying them. I would locate the route that the insurgents had taken to place the IEDs and then low crawl along their footsteps until I found the receiver.

Later, on 23 April 2004, Gunny Burghardt and his Team returned to Alternate Supply Route Lincoln to clear four more IEDs, some of which had been placed in the same location within the past 12 hours. Despite the fact that some of the IEDs were probably secondary devices designed specifically to kill his team, they proceeded to the site and destroyed the enemy traps.

Although he received the Bronze Star, the modest Burghardt feels that he was just doing his job. "I'm supposed to be great, that's why I'm the team leader." The gunnery sergeant earned his nickname of "Clark Kent" (a.k.a. Superman, the Man of Steel) during his first two EOD tours of duty in Iraq.

After returning to Camp Lejeune from their Iraqi deployment, Burghardt and his team put together training packages with the real-world experiences they gained overseas for Marines and sailors getting ready to head into the war zones.[2]

Within the year, Gunny Burghardt would return once more to Iraq for his third combat tour and to what not only would be a very close call experience, but which would also draw attention to his exploits from throughout the world.

September 2005
USMC EOD Team supporting the Army's 2nd Brigade, 28th Infantry Division
Ramadi, Iraq

Gunnery Sergeant Burghardt's new EOD team was composed of younger and more inexperienced Marines and he felt an even greater need to train and protect his men. Instead of being assigned to a Marine unit, his team was attached to an Army unit operating near the Sunni city of Ramadi. Burghardt described Ramadi as "the scariest place on Earth."[3]

Quite often, there is intra-service rivalry and lots of kidding between the Marines and Army soldiers, but these two groups worked well together and supported each other. The Army provided the needed security while the Marines went about their dangerous bomb-disposal work. One Army lieutenant said, "The biggest threat to us in Iraq is IEDs. We loved working with the Marines. They made us better soldiers." Burghardt responded by saying, "I feel part of this Army team. They take care of us like brothers."[4]

When Burghardt returned for his third tour in Iraq, he not only found more IEDs than he had previously, but they were also becoming more sophisticated and innovative. He shakes his head in wonder at the variety and evolution of the roadside bombs he has encountered and the relentlessness with which they are planted. Washing machine timers, cordless telephone docking stations, battery acid, shaped charges and artillery rounds scrounged from all corners of the globe were the insurgent's currently preferred tools.

> It's only a matter of time before they move on to newer and deadlier devices. It's a big game of chess. They're thinking their steps through on how to beat us and we're doing the same thing. In the hierarchy of roadside bombers, the insurgents are divided into three groups: those who plant the bombs, those who design them and those who finance the

process. The lowest rungs, those who plant the IEDs, are most likely doing it for financial reasons as opposed to ideology. It's almost like a drug habit. There are the guys on top who have the money and do the planning, and then there are the crack addicts down below. They make their living planting IED after IED until somebody puts a bullet in them![5]

19 September 2005
USMC EOD Team attached to the 1st Platoon,
167th Calvary of the Nebraska National Guard
Tammim Neighborhood in Western Ramadi

Early in the morning, on 19 September 2005, Gunny Burghardt extended his third combat tour by an additional three months. He did this with the knowledge that five EOD technicians that he had worked with had recently been killed, including one death that had occurred just three weeks previously. This technician had sunk his knife into a dirt berm and activated the pressure switch on a buried bomb. Also, surely on his mind was one larger bomb that had destroyed a 25-ton amphibious assault vehicle and killed 14 fellow Marines. "Pink mist" is how Burghardt and his fellow bomb defusers describe what they turn into if they make a mistake.

Later that morning, a bomb had gone off in the wild Tammin neighborhood of western Ramadi, a Sunni Triangle city of 400,000, west of Fallujah and on the main road to Syria. The explosion had destroyed a vehicle and killed four soldiers. Burghardt, who was looking to clear an evacuation route for the vehicles, noticed an odd piece of shrapnel in what he thought was a recent bomb crater. The hole was roughly 4½ feet deep and he want to investigate the situation. As he took a closer look, the shattered gravel beneath his foot suddenly shifted, revealing a package wrapped in orange plastic and a cordless telephone base station.

Realizing that he had just stumbled onto a primed explosive, Burghardt stuck his knife in the dirt and dredged up a red detonating cord that led to a pair of 122mm artillery shells. He cut the cord with scissors and told the rest of his team to stay back. "I thought I had done well," Burghardt said.

What he had not noticed was a second detonating cord that ran from the same base station to a third artillery shell buried behind him. The triggerman, probably observing from a distance with binoculars and figuring he would not lure anyone else in, placed the potentially deadly phone call. "That's when I heard the distinct crack of that artillery shell."

The explosion hurled Burghardt ten feet into the air. His limp body frame came smashing down, face first, on the roadway, as his team watched in horror. "All I remember is opening my eyes and hearing a ringing in my ears. They all thought I was dead, but when I moved, I could hear them yell, 'He's alive.'" After hitting the ground, he was initially unable to feel anything from the waist below. "I was lying there thinking I didn't want to be in a wheelchair next to my dad and for him to see me like that."

Relief came quickly and he was soon able to wiggle his toes. Medics cut away his bloody pants to reveal that the backs of his legs had been studded with shrapnel and bruised from the top of his boots to the waist. As they prepared to place him on a stretcher, Burghardt shouted, "No." He didn't want his teammates or the insurgents to see him carried from the scene. He was going to walk.

As he was helped to his feet, he felt a wave of anger and adrenaline flow through his system. He had just extended his tour that morning and he was livid that he had been bested by the bomber. "I was really pissed off that they got me, that after all this time, they got me! I figured the triggerman was still watching, so I flipped him off and yelled, f*** you! I'll be out here next week!"

Photographer Jeff Bundy of the *Omaha World-Herald* captured Burghardt's gesture. Soon, it would be seen around the world in newspapers and on Web sites, office walls, refrigerators and screensavers.[6]

Postlude

Gunnery Sergeant Burghardt recuperated for three weeks at his unit's headquarters. His main injuries were wounds and burns on his legs, back and backside. He described these weeks as "among the most difficult in his career."

Since returning to the field, Burghardt has had plenty of other experiences with exploding roadside bombs, but they have been from the relative safety of a heavily armored mine-clearing vehicle called a Buffalo. The vehicle, which deactivates explosives using a long, hydraulic arm, is also outfitted with ballistic glass windows that give occupants an up-close view of the explosives. Burghardt rides along with other technicians to give advice to the arm operator on how to deal with the explosives. He describes the experience of riding in a Buffalo and getting close to bombs akin to visiting an "IED petting zoo."

There will be no amusement park ride back in the States that can compare with the Buffalo. You will never get a chance to get that close to an IED and feel all of those emotions, happiness, suspense and adrenaline.

So far, Burghardt has seen at least 20 roadside bombs explode while riding in the Buffalo. Each time the vehicle rolls up to a suspected IED, Burghardt states, "The emotions are the same. It's back to the chess game. You're in suspense! What is going to happen? You have control, but don't know what the bomb builder has in store for you. You don't know what else he's putting out there. That's where it's a chess game. You're out there and you're waiting for that queen to come sliding across the board."[7]

Postscript

As of June 2007, Burghardt had been promoted to master sergeant and was stationed at Camp Fuji, Okinawa. His new job description title was Combined Arms Training Center EOD Chief, in charge of a corporal's NCO course. Burghardt made sure that IED familiarization training played an important part of the course.[8]

On 14 June 2006, I received a group e-mail from Gregory Romeu in a distribution for former Marines. Attached to the e-mail was an AOL story about Michael Burghardt, which proved to be very interesting. Upon a more thorough online search for more information, I was able to locate several stories about this very lucky Marine hero.

Information obtained from *Star and Stripes* was authorized on 31 October 2007 (used with permission from the *Stars and Stripes*. ©1983, 2005, 2006, 2007 *Stars and Stripes*).

44

Iraq: Combat Train One

> Everything in life is luck.
> — Donald Trump

Prelude

This chapter describes the events surrounding how four extremely lucky Marines with the 1st Battalion, 1st Marines, 1st Marine Division survived a very unusual close call incident while just sitting in their armored vehicle at a combat observation outpost. They felt totally safe, as they were not on the road or in an Iraqi city where they could expect danger at any time.

A Brief History of the 1st Battalion, 1st Marines

By the time the 1st Battalion, 1st Marines (1/1) arrived in Iraq in early February 2006, they had brought with them an illustrious history of defending America and other nations around the world. The Battalion was initially activated on 1 March 1941 at Guantanamo Bay, Cuba, as part of the 1st Marine Division. The 1/1 deployed to Wellington, New Zealand, in 1942 in preparation for combat in the Pacific during the Second World War. The Battalion participated in the island campaigns of Guadalcanal, New Britain, Finschhafen, Peleiu and Okinawa. During the Korean War, they fought with distinction at Inchon-Seoul, the East Central Front, Chosin Reservoir, and the Western Front. They also defended the Korean DMZ after the war from 1953 to 1955.

In 1965, they deployed to Vietnam and operated against the communist forces from Da Nang, Dong Ha, Hue, Con Thien, Quang Tri, Phu Bai and Khe Sanh. They returned to the United States at Camp Pendleton in 1971. Their next war assignment came in Operations Desert Shield and Desert Storm in Saudi Arabia, Kuwait and Iraq. In the 2000s, they have continued the battle in the Wars against Terrorism in Operation Iraqi Freedom (OIF).

The mottos of 1/1 remain "First of the First" and "Ready to Fight."[1]

20 January–3 February 2006
1st Battalion, 1st Marines, 1st Marine Division
Camp Fallujah, Iraq

The Battalion began its latest deployment from Camp Pendleton, California, to Camp Fallujah, Iraq, on 20 January 2006. By early February most of the unit's assets, both men and equipment, had settled into their new environment. In a small ceremony on 3 February, 1/1 took over control of their new area from the outgoing 2nd Battalion, 2nd Marines (2/2). Lieutenant Colonel David J. Furness, the battalion commander, officially posted the colors and established 1/1's Iraqi mission. He stated, "Our first mission is to train, mentor, coach and work with the Iraqi Army; second, is to fight the insurgency operations combined with them and third, conduct independent insurgency operations."

The Battalion designated their new area of operations (AO) "Chromite," a name dating back to the famous landing at Inchon, Korea, in 1950. 1/1 played an important role in this Korean operation named "Chromite." Fallujah is a city west of Baghdad and the new AO was north of Fallujah, near the city of Karma. The Battalion positioned several outposts throughout their operational area, where they could best serve their Marines, the Iraqi Army and the Iraqi civilians.[2]

2 April 2006
Combat Train One
1/1 Operational Area

In order to keep 1/1's outlying posts constantly supplied with "bullets, beans and bandages," convoys were constantly on the roads delivering needed supplies, along with the all-important mail for their Marines and sailors. A group, designated as Combat Train One, commanded in the field by Staff Sergeant Alberto PerezTorres, undertook these convoys. The convoys consisted of several seven-ton supply trucks, supported by Humvees with mounted machine guns. Their main concern was IEDs and occasional sniper fire during their day and nighttime runs. "As of 2 April, we have been lucky. None of the combat trains have hit an IED while on missions," said the 38-year-old PerezTorres from Culver City, California. "We have encountered a few, but we have been able to call out EOD Teams to take care of them."

The Combat Train One missions begin hours, and even days, before they actually start up the engines on their Humvees and trucks. They decide what supplies need to go out, ranging from spare parts and ammunition to mail. Map studies and routes are then selected. Next, security is discussed and then the plans are reviewed repeatedly. Running supplies is a constant on-the-go mission for the Marines, despite any type of conditions. Nearly every day, a combat train takes to the road, keeping supplies moving forward.

"In the two months the Battalion has been in country we have been on a total of 108 missions," said Warrant Officer Jeromie A. Rogers, the 32-year-old officer-in-charge of the supply operations. "Depending on the mission and what we encounter, we can drive anywhere from 10 to 60 miles. In addition to resupplying and transportation, the teams set up vehicle checkpoints and provide a quick reaction force for the Battalion."

The Marines driving the supplies forward bring with them a hodge-podge of different skills. They comprise the Battalion's Marines and attachments, all working together to keep the wheels rolling. "In the teams we have a mixture of motor transport, infantry and communication Marines," PerezTorres said. "All of the Marines are outstanding and perform their jobs well." The Marines know the value of the job they perform for the Battalion. They realize that without them, the Battalion's Marines would not be able to perform their role in operations.

"Like any other job here, there are risks," PerezTorres stated. "We look forward to the missions we are given. We are happy to do our job." Little did the staff sergeant know, on this 2 April date, that in just eight days, those risks would increase dramatically.[3]

10 April 2006
Combat Train One
Observation Post Four, Karma, Iraq

On 10 April 2006, Staff Sergeant PerezTorres once again commanded the Combat Train One convoy, a day excursion to the Battalion's Observation Post Four (OP-4), located at a former Iraqi government morgue in the city of Karma. Riding with PerezTorres in his Humvee were the driver, Lance Corporal Jeremy Newby, the machine gunner, Corporal Hari-Das Felix, and the radio operator, Corporal Ernesto Mangual.

"My attitude is that we know we're going to get hit but we just don't know when," reported PerezTorres. Yet, even after racking up hundreds of miles of resupply missions, his Humvee crew really did not expect the biggest threat of their tour to come plummeting in from the skies above. On this particular afternoon, Combat Train One was just wrapping up a visit to OP-4 in Karma. It had taken roughly 45 minutes to unload the convoy's seven-ton trucks and a company of grateful Marines was busy tearing into boxes of mail, as well as their first hot meal in days.

Not too far off, however, enemy insurgents were observing what the

Marines were doing and saw that the convoy and Marines were bunched up, providing a perfect target for their 82mm mortars.[4] These mortars were designed to hit targets between 80 and 3,200 meters away, delivering a 3.1 kilogram (6.82 pounds) explosive round. The rounds were constructed to explode on impact.[5] The Soviets first developed the 82mm mortar, which was just slightly larger than the standard NATO 81mm mortars. This gave them a tactical advantage: they could use our 81 mm rounds, but we could not use theirs. This was first used to a great extent during the Vietnam War.

The Humvee crew was just waiting around to get the word to move out. Newby was sitting in the driver's seat, resting his head against the thick, layered-glass side window. "I came back to the truck and said, hey gents, we're Oscar Mike [On Mission], get ready to go," the staff sergeant said. Newby lifted his head off the glass and put on his helmet. At that instant, an explosion just outside Newby's door jerked the vehicle sideways. Dirt, glass and metal flew through the Humvee.

"I was in the back messing around with the radio," said Corporal Mangual of Miami, Florida. "I heard a BOOM and the next thing I knew, I'm lying against the seat and I saw smoke everywhere." Corporal Felix, from Omaha, Nebraska, was sitting in the gun turret and found himself knocked down into the vehicle. PerezTorres shouted, "Incoming!"

While it was apparent that OP-4 was under a mortar attack, the crew did not know what happened until much later. Evidently, an 82mm mortar round had punched through the metal roof of their vehicle, directly over Newby's seat. It then went through the driver's side window and embedded itself in the dirt outside the Humvee, where it exploded. The blast knocked Newby and Mangual unconscious. They awoke moments later to the noise of shouting. "I saw the bright light of the explosion and then I was out," Newby said. "Everything was blurred until I was in the outpost's COC [command operation center] lying on my back and getting checked out."

Fortunately, none of the Marines suffered life-threatening injuries, although Newby and Mangual were treated for concussions. The driver also suffered cuts to his face and hand. When the Marines finally realized what happened, they were speechless. "Mortars are supposed to explode on impact," Mangual said. "This one had two impacts and didn't explode until it hit the ground outside the Humvee. I figured the most I had to fear about was from roadside bombs. IEDs are what you're thinking about most of the time. You're not thinking you're going to get hit by a mortar round."

PerezTorres said that the episode was an eye-opener. "We realized then that we weren't untouchable. Things can be quietly scary out there. There are many aggressive individuals here and there is always danger. We can't take the quietness for granted."

The four lucky Marines now realize that that had escaped death with what they call "a million-to-one close call." Their unit, 1/1, returned to the United States in August 2006 and would be deployed back again in 2007.[6]

On 28 July 2006, while searching for more online close call stories, I came across an interesting story from a 15 July 2006 *Stars and Stripes* article. I then proceeded to do a more detailed online search for additional information.

Information obtained from *Star and Stripes* was authorized on 31 October 2007 (used with permission from the *Stars and Stripes*. ©1983, 2005, 2006, 2007 *Stars and Stripes*).

45

Iraq: Kevlar Helmet Headshots

> Fortuna Favet Fortibus (Fortune Favors the Strong).
> — Latin proverb

Prelude

This chapter describes two incidents of young lucky Marines in Iraq who were shot in the head and were both saved by their Kevlar helmets. The two separate close call stories occurred within three weeks of each other and further shows how innovative technology is saving the lives of our American men and women while they fight the War against Terrorism. Prior to the actual battle descriptions, a short history of Kevlar and then a brief history of the military units involved are presented.

A History of Kevlar

Due to technology first developed in 1965, coalition forces in Iraq and Afghanistan now have a better chance of surviving being hit by bullets and shrapnel than ever before. Although not totally bullet-proof, helmets lined with Kevlar have reduced the number of serious head injuries. Layers of Kevlar, a fiber developed by chemical giant DuPont, do a great job of stopping shots from low-velocity guns.

Ironically, DuPont, the Delaware manufacturer of Kevlar, began making gunpowder and explosives in 1802. A DuPont chemist, who was experimenting with polymers to find a new way to reinforce automobile tires, invented Kevlar in 1965, while another chemist developed the process that helped in the mass production of Kevlar in 1970. The lightweight Kevlar fiber is five times stronger than steel and can help stop or reduce injuries from bullets.

American troops in the Mideast are using the new Kevlar helmets. The 4.1-pound helmets are 20 to 40 percent more resistant to shrapnel than the old Vietnam era steel helmets used in the 1960s and 1970s.

Kevlar can trap a bullet in a layered web of woven fabrics which absorbs the impact and disperses it to other fibers in the weave. This dispersal of the energy from the impact protects the body from blunt head trauma.[1]

A Brief History of the 3rd Battalion, 8th Marines (3/8), 2nd Marine Division

The 3rd Battalion, 8th Marines was first activated on 1 November 1940 at San Diego, California, and became part of the 2nd Marine Division in early 1941. During World War II, the unit participated in the battle campaigns of Guadalcanal, Tarawa, Saipan, Tinian and Okinawa. After a short stint of occupation duty in Japan, they relocated to Camp Pendleton, California, from February to March 1946, when they were deactivated.

During the Korean War, on 15 January 1951, 3/8 was reactivated at their current home base of Camp Lejeune, North Carolina. In the 1950s through the 1980s, 3/8 was deployed to numerous parts of the Mediterranean, Caribbean and North Atlantic areas for the Cuban Missile Crisis and service in the Dominican Republic and Liberia. The 1990s found the Regiment in Iraq, Bosnia, Liberia and the Central African Republic.

In the 2000s, 3/8 was committed to the War against Terrorism and operated in Afghanistan from December 2001 through September 2002; Haiti from February through July 2004; and Iraq from January through August 2005. In early March 2006, they deployed once more to Iraq. The 3/8's motto is "Fortune Favors the Strong."[2]

Lance Corporal Richard Caseltine
14 April 2006
Company I, 3rd Battalion, 8th Marines
Ramadi, Iraq

On the morning of 14 April 2006, Richard Caseltine, from Aurora, Indiana, was part of a joint Iraqi army and Marine foot patrol through the dangerous and battle-scarred downtown streets of Ramadi, Iraq. The Marines provided a two-squad team, roughly 15 to 20 men, from India (I) Company, 3/8. The patrol was basically making their presence known and helping to maintain the peace in a city where terrorists still operated.

Caseltine and three other Marines surreptitiously slipped away from the main group to locate a spot where they could oversee the patrol, identify problem areas and possibly locate enemy positions. They entered the front gate of a two-story villa and convinced the occupant family to hide out in one of their rooms while the four Marines moved up to the roof. The rooftop was enclosed with shoulder-high walls, so the Marines positioned themselves in the four corners to give them a 360-degree observation of the surrounding area.

Within 30 minutes, one of the Marines, Lance Corporal Benjamin Congleton of Lexington, Kentucky, observed a man dressed in black, crouching next to a light pole. He appeared to be nervous as he held a bundle of electrical wires and kept looking all around him. Congleton called Caseltine over to get a second opinion and they both agreed this man was a terrorist who was probably planting an IED with hopes of killing some of the men in the joint patrol. Congleton brought up his M-16, fired, perhaps too hastily, and missed his first shot. Caseltine took the next shot with his M-4 carbine as the man rose and began to run. His shot stuck the terrorist in the leg and immobilized him, allowing Congleton a second opportunity and this time his shot had a deadly result.

Caseltine then turned around and began heading back to his designated corner, when, after three or four steps, he felt something hit the top backside of his Kevlar helmet. "It felt like someone came from behind and punched me in the back of the head as hard as he could. It just rocked me. I went forward and my ears started ringing really badly. I couldn't hear anything!"

Initially the Marines were not sure if one of them had misfired one of their own weapons, but it did not take long for them to learn that it had been a lone enemy sniper bullet, probably shot by the person protecting the man placing the IED. Ducking under the walled edge, the rooftop Marines raced over to assist Caseltine, who was now yelling, "I got hit! I got hit!"

A quick check revealed blood at the back of his neck but no probable serious injury. Caseltine was able to extract himself to the relative safety of one of the rooms below where a Navy corpsman checked him over. The back of his neck burned but otherwise he felt fine. "He had this big smile on his face," said Lance Corporal Jefferson Ortiz of Miami, Florida. "He knew he'd gotten very, very lucky."

Smoke grenades were tossed and a Humvee arrived to evacuate Caseltine. While he was being extracted, insurgents attacked the patrol. "We were taking fire from every street corner," Congleton said. "It seemed like we were fighting the entire city."

In the meantime, Caseltine was flown by helicopter to a nearby hospital at the Balad Air Base. Medics treated him by removing bullet fragments that had lodged a quarter-inch into his neck. "They said I was lucky it didn't go in deeper. My luck was running pretty good that day. If I had bought a lottery ticket, I probably would have won."

Three days later, Caseltine was back at his base and only hours away from rejoining his squad at an outpost in Ramadi. Richard still cherishes a picture of his wife that he had placed in the top of his Kevlar helmet that had been split in half by the sniper's bullet. It was how he kept his wife close to him.

> You expect that when somebody gets shot in the head, they're dead. I consider myself lucky. They always tell us not to throw our Kevlars around or bang them on the ground. I usually did, but I ain't gonna be throwing my new one down. I ain't gonna take it for granted anymore because I know they work.[3]

Back home, Richard's mother Joni stated, "In one day, I received the worst phone call any mother could and then later was able to hear that my son was alive and talking. He was able to get up, walk and even grin. When I spoke with him, he told me he was fine and waiting to go back to Ramadi. May God bless all in uniform and may he continue to bless them and their families. Rich, I love you and I am so very proud of you."[4]

A Brief History of the 1st Battalion, 25th Marine (1/25), 4th Marine Division

On 1 May 1943, the 1st Battalion, 25th Marines was formed at Camp Lejeune, North Carolina, and was then shipped off to Camp Pendleton, California, to be assigned to the 4th Marine Division. During World War II, 1/25 saw action in the island-hopping campaigns of Kwajalein, Saipan, Tinian and Iwo Jima. The Battalion played a critical role in the seizure of Hill 382 (Turkey Knob) in an area that Marines on Iwo Jima called the "meat grinder." For its actions, 1/25 received a Presidential Unit Citation. The Battalion saw no further action during the war due to having to rebuild after heavy losses on Iwo Jima. They were deactivated on 31 October 1945.

On 1 July 1962, the Battalion was reorganized and redesignated in conjunction with the new concept and mission of the Marine Corps Reserve as the 1st Battalion, 25th Marines, 4th Marine Division, Fleet Marine Force (FMF), Massachusetts. On 30 September 1977, the headquarters was relocated to Camp Edwards, Cape Cod, Massachusetts. They have been awarded the General Harry Schmidt Trophy for being the most combat-ready battalion in the 4th Marine Division on three separate years.

On 25 November 1990, 1/25 was again called to active duty to serve in the Gulf War against Iraq. They mobilized at Camp Lejeune and then promptly moved to Kuwait on 29 December where they were assigned to the 1st Marine Division. They were one of the few reserve units to be with the front-line units during the war. They had the responsibility of controlling over 8,500 Iraqi POWs. In April 1991, the Battalion returned to the United States and was deactivated at Camp Edwards, Massachusetts. The Reserve Battalion is spread throughout New England, with H&S and the Weapons Company in Devens, Massachusetts; Company A in Topsham, Maine; Company B in Londonderry, New Hampshire; and Company C in Plainville, Connecticut. They are commonly known as "New England's Own."

The Connecticut unit, Company C, has a primary mission "to locate, close with, and destroy the enemy by fire and maneuver, or repel his assault by fire and close combat." Their additional specialty mission is "to conduct offensive operations against forces in cold weather and mountainous environments."

In early April 2006, 1/25 was again activated and sent to Fallujah, Iraq, for a seven-month deployment. They became part of Regimental Combat Team-5 (RCT-5). Their main focus was to train the Iraqi Security Forces and to conduct counterinsurgency operations.[5]

USMC Private First Class Fred Linck
5 May 2006
Company C, 1st Battalion, 25th Marines
Fallujah, Iraq

When 19-year-old Private First Class Fred Linck from Westbrook, Connecticut, arrived in Fallujah, he had only been part of 1/25 for just a few months. An infantryman assigned to Company C, he began 5 May 2006 on a security post but was soon tasked to be part of a reaction force going into Fallujah to respond to a call to check out a possible IED. "It seemed just like any other day, but everything soon changed for me. We got some intelligence stating that there was a possible improvised explosive device on the corner of the main street in Fallujah. My team of Marines reacted to the call and showed up on the site. We immediately dismounted our vehicles and set up a cordon of the area."

Some of the men in the team did not believe that this was a normal mission, instead fearing it might be a possible trap. Teammate Lance Corporal Randon Hogen stated, "Something told me this was a setup, a pretty usual tactic for the insurgents to use against us." Hogen's gut feelings proved to be right. Somewhere in the shadows of the surrounding buildings, an enemy was waiting for the Marines to come into view.

"I was running back across the street after we had confirmed that the IED we responded to was in fact not one, when I heard the shot," reported Lance Corporal Kelvin Grisales, Linck's fire team leader and friend. A single shot exploded through the air, disrupting the silence. Everyone instinctively dropped and sought cover and not even Linck, who had been hit, knew what happened.

"After the shot rang out, I remembered hearing someone screaming, 'Man down! Man down!' I realized a second later that man was me. I was on the ground." It took a couple seconds for everything to appear clear to Linck. The sounds of Marines calling for help were not for anyone but him, but he was ready to get up and fight.

"I was pretty scared when I realized that I had just taken a round to the head, but the scariest part was that I was thinking about it and I felt fine. It felt as if I had fallen and hit my head, that's it."

Not knowing Linck's status, his team did not take any chances and followed their training by evacuating him out of the hostile area. "When we picked him up, he grabbed my hand and told me he was pretty nervous," said Grisales. "All I could do was to try to reassure him that he would be all right." Linck was transferred directly to the nearest hospital, where he was treated and released without even a stitch in his head.

His issued Kevlar helmet had stopped the majority of the round from penetrating. A small piece of fragmentation from the bullet pierced the headband inside his helmet, causing a slight laceration on his forehead. "It was such a relief for us when we pulled up to the hospital and we found out that he was okay," Grisales stated. Hogen added, "I thank God it happened the way that it did."

Linck does not discount Divine intervention or luck, but now trusts his gear more than ever. "I know for sure that if it wasn't for that helmet, I wouldn't be standing here right now. It pays to wear all the gear the way it is supposed to be worn. It is kind of like getting a second lease on life. I want to make sure I do everything right from now on." Linck was immediately returned to normal duty.[6]

I discovered the story about Richard Caseltine on AOL News on 15 April 2006, which prompted a further on line search for additional information. Almost one month later, I discovered the story on Fred Linck and realized I had the beginnings to a good developing chapter on Kevlar helmet headshots. I wrote both Marines in Iraq, but did not receive any replies.

Usage permission was granted from the AP on the Caseltine story by Todd Pitman on 16 November 2007. (Used with permission of the Associated Press. Copyright ©2007. All rights reserved).

46

Iraq: Body Armor Shots

> Angels deliver fate to our doorstep —
> and anywhere else it is needed.
> — Jessi Lane Adams

Prelude

This chapter highlights three Marines who, within a one-month period, were all hit in the upper body torso area by terrorist sniper bullets and were all saved by their body armor. Their lucky close calls could all have ended in serious or fatal injuries. What is even more unusual is that these three Marines were in the same unit: Company D, 3rd Light Armored Reconnaissance (3rd LAR) Battalion, assigned to Regimental Combat Team-5 (RCT-5) in Iraq.

A Brief History of the 3rd Light Armored Battalion

The 3rd LAR Battalion's nickname is the "Wolfpack" and their motto is "The strength of the pack is the wolf; the strength of the wolf is the pack." Their mission statement is to "conduct reconnaissance, security, and limited offensive and defensive operations as directed by the division or support commander." Their primary weapon system is the LAV-25 (Light Armored Vehicle-25) and they are now part of the 1st Marine Division and 1st Marine Expeditionary Force. The unit is based out of the Marine Corps Air Ground Combat Center in Twentynine Palms, California.[1]

In 1980, the Marine Corps identified a requirement to enhance the mobility and firepower of the units tasked with rapid deployment responsibilities. A family of six Light Armored Vehicles was determined to be the means of meeting this requirement. On 27 September 1982, a production contract for the LAV-25 and a companion development contract for five other LAV configurations (maintenance/recovery, logistics, mortar, antitank, and command and control) were awarded to General Motors of Canada. The LAV family of vehicles was highly mobile and able to move on land and water, thus providing a fighting capability previously unrealized.

The 3rd LAR Battalion evolved through several name changes after initially receiving their first LAV-25s in April 1984. On 1 October 1988, they were designated as the 3rd Light Armored Infantry Battalion and relocated to Okinawa, Japan. They returned to Twentynine Palms on 18 July 1991 as part of Regimental Combat Team 7 (RCT-7).

In August 1990, most of the unit deployed to Saudi Arabia in support of Desert Shield, as part of the 7th Marine Expeditionary Brigade, Task Force Lima. Once the ground war in Kuwait and Iraq began, they found themselves at the forefront of the action. They were part of the first coalition force to enter Kuwait City and helped capture the Kuwait International Airport.

From December 1992 to April 1993, part of the Battalion supported Operation Restore Hope in Somalia. Their mission consisted of convoy escorts, delivering some 4,000 metric tons of grain to outlying areas.

On 1 March 1994, the unit received its current official name as the 3rd Light Armored Reconnaissance Battalion. They participated in counter-drug operations in support of Joint Task Force 6 in Arizona throughout 1994. It was during the early 1990s that the Battalion's nickname and radio call sign became "Wolfpack."

In late January through February 2003, the Battalion deployed with the 1st Marine Division to Kuwait in support of Operation Enduring Freedom. On 21 March, the 3rd LAR Battalion and its attachments crossed into Iraq with the beginning of Operation Iraqi Freedom. The Wolfpack helped lead the way for the Division's lightning attack northward towards Baghdad. On 13 April, the Battalion's Company D received national recognition when they rescued seven Americans who had been taken prisoner early in the war, including two Army pilots and Shoshana Johnson, a female soldier from the same unit as Jessica Lynch. By mid-June, the Battalion returned to their Twentynine Palms base.

Their second deployment to Iraq began in August 2004, and they were again assigned to the RCT-7 and fought mainly in the Fallujah area. In one battle in the Fallujah Peninsula, they suffered 1 KIA and 62 WIAs while taking the North and South Bridges and the Fallujah Hospital. In early April 2005, they returned to the United States.[2]

In the beginning of 2006, the 3rd LAR Battalion redeployed to Iraq for the third time in as many years. They were responsible for the western portion of the Al Anbar province, including the Iraqi-Jordanian border and the southern portion of the Iraqi-Syrian border. They were assigned to the Regimental Combat Team-5 (RCT-5).[3]

A Recent History of Body Armor

An internal Pentagon report that was first published by the *New York Times* found that up to 80 percent of fatal torso wounds suffered by Marines in Iraq could have been prevented by better body armor.

Several months after a military study found that Marine Corps deaths could be reduced by wearing side insert plates in the body armor, all Marines in the Anbar province were issued this gear. The average Marine's combat load includes around 50 pounds of protective equipment and the two extra plates added about 8 pounds. According to Captain James Le, RCT-5 supply officer, by mid-January 2006, almost all line companies in the Regiment had been issued the new plates. The side plates, along with the other body armor (flak jackets and Kevlar helmets) became required gear for everyone operating under the Marine command in western Iraq. Although some Marines complained about the requirement, "If it saves lives, it's worth the weight," Le stated. Quoting another Marine, "When you've got all this weight on already, what's a few extra pounds going to hurt?"

Marines are now equipped with the interceptor body-armor system, which consists of an outer tactical vest (OTV), made of Kevlar and the small arms protective insert plates (SAPI). The OTV and the associated neck, throat and groin protectors were designed to offer protection from fragmentation weapons. The ceramic SAPI plates help to deflect multiple hits from assault rifles common on the current battlefield.

Simula Incorporated of Tempe, Arizona, produces the SAPI plates. As of 2003, Simula had sold about 150,000 plates to the military since 1998, and this production has more than tripled in recent years. The plates cost over $400 each.[4]

Lance Corporal Robert Dean
14 May 2006
Company D, 3rd LAR Battalion
Gharmah, Iraq

While operating in the area of Gharmah, Iraq, on 14 May 2006, Lance Corporal Robert Dean, an LAV crewmember with Company D, 3rd LAR Battalion, was shot by a sniper from roughly 500 meters away. "We had an area cordoned off and the scouts were out searching the area," recalled Corporal Dustin Nelson, Dean's vehicle commander. "I reached down to give Dean some water and as he popped out of his hatch to take it from me, I heard a crack." Dean reported, "I thought at first that someone had thrown a rock at me before I realized a bullet had hit me."

The Marines immediately responded to the attack by returning a large volume of fire in the direction of the insurgent. "The bullet would have hit his femoral bone and possibly gone through and hit his femoral artery," said Chad Kenyon, the Navy corpsman who treated Dean after the incident. "If that happened, he could have bled to death within a few minutes. It would have been a sticky situation, but the plates did their job and stopped the bullet."

"The round hit the very bottom of the plate, shattering some of the ceramic, but the fiber paper that backed the plate, caught the round like a baseball mitt," added Nelson, from Grand Junction, Colorado. "Now even our Iraqi interpreter wants the side SAPI plates, despite the fact that he previously was complaining that his flak vest was too heavy."

Twenty-year-old Dean, from Spring, Texas, stated, "They make it harder to get in and out of the vehicle, but without them, I would probably be in bad shape. It was a good thing that they made us wear them."

When the gear became mandatory for the Marines, many complained, but most have now rescinded their objections after seeing the plates in action. Thanks to the side SAPI plates, a life was perhaps saved and a serious injury was definitely prevented.[5]

Private First Class Jason Hanson
June 2006
Company D, 3rd LAR Battalion
Habbaniyah, Iraq

Several weeks after Lance Corporal Dean's incident, Private First Class Jason Hanson's Company D unit was operating in support of the 3rd Battalion, 5th Marines (3/5) to complete counterinsurgency and humanitarian operations in the town of Habbaniyah. Twenty-one-year-old Hanson, from Forks, Washington, was the lead scout on a patrol looking for roadside bombs on the main highway when a sniper shot him in the chest. "I was checking my side and when I looked forward, I got shot and it knocked me down."

"I saw him on the ground, ran up to him and rolled him over," said Navy corpsman Chad Kenyon from Tucson, Arizona. Kenyon was the same corpsman who had previously attended to Lance Corporal Dean, weeks earlier. "I saw that the round had gone through the front of his flak jacket, so I opened it up and saw no bleeding. Then he looked up at me and said I'm fine, Doc."

The 7.62mm enemy bullet went through Hanson's rifle but was stopped by the Marine's SAPI plate, leaving him with just some bruising on his chest. It could have been much worse.

"The round definitely would have hit him in the diaphragm, which is a muscle that assists in breathing," said Hospital Corpsman Third Class Jose Mata Jr., the Company's senior corpsman from Hialeah, Florida. "It's not a good day when that happens because he probably wouldn't have lived."

According to Hanson, "They are bulky, heavy and hot in the already soaring temperatures, but I now have a different perspective on the ceramic plates that I'm toting around my body. I'm happy to carry the extra weight!"[6]

Sergeant Joshua Adams
June 2006
Company D, 3rd LAR Battalion

Just a few days later, Sergeant Joshua Adams, an LAV commander from Bowling Green, Missouri, was shot while cordoning off an area after discovering an improvised explosive device (IED).

"We were blocking off a road and one car pulled up from a side street and the guy in the back of the vehicle started moving around to face us," said Lance Corporal Kyle Lyons, an LAV gunner from Houston, Texas. "I was telling Sergeant Adams about this guy when he got hit. He dropped down and then said he was fine."

"My gunner took over while I assessed my wounds and pulled some shrapnel out of my arm. The round went into my SAPI but when it hit, the round shattered and some of it went into my wrist. We then chased down the vehicle and detained the two men."

"The round would have hit him in the liver, causing massive internal damage," Corpsman Mata reported. "It could have been bad. The SAPI plates did their job."[7]

Postlude

Although the American public has heard many reports over the years that our Marines and Army troops are not well protected, it would seem that they are better equipped and protected than in any previous war. The government, however, continues to conduct research for better and lighter protective devices that will ensure the maximum amount of survival for our men and women sent out in harm's way.

Postscript

Private First Class Jason Hanson was killed while conducting combat operations in the Anbar Province, Iraq, on 29 July 2006.

Navy Hospital Corpsman Chadwick Kenyon, the corpsman who first went to the aid of both Lance Corporal Robert Dean and Private First Class Jason Hanson, was killed on 20 August 2006 when his vehicle was hit by an explosive in the Anbar Province.[8]

I first came across an online story about Sergeant Adams and Private First Class Hanson while web surfing on 23 June 2006. Several days later, on 26 June, while looking for more input concerning the two above Marines, I found a third story about Corporal Dean and could not believe all of the similarities and coincidences that tied the three incidents together.

On 23 August 2006, in the *Riverside (California) Press Enterprise*, I learned of the unfortunate death of Corpsman Chad Kenyon, who had provided aid for two of the Marines highlighted in this chapter. Later, I also leaned that Pfc Jason Hanson had been killed in an earlier incident.

I received permission to reprint from *Body Armor News*, on 29 October 2007.

Information obtained from *Star and Stripes* was authorized on 31 October 2007 (used with permission from the *Stars and Stripes*. ©1983, 2005, 2006, 2007 *Stars and Stripes*).

47

Iraq: Combat Photographers

> They, who await no gifts from
> chance, have conquered fate.
> — Matthew Arnold

Prelude

Two combat photographer Marines in the Iraqi War, Corporal Brian Henner and Lance Corporal Shane Keller, have had several close calls performing their duties. They are representatives of hundreds of combat photographers before them, during many of our nation's wars, who have faced dangerous situations and challenges.

A Brief History of Combat Photographers

Photographic records of war began soon after the camera's invention, probably beginning with the Crimean War in 1855 and the American Civil War in the 1860s. As new camera developments were invented, including faster film and smaller and lighter cameras, better pictures were produced in the First and Second World Wars, especially with the introduction of 35mm film. The Vietnam War brought the photographic history right into the living rooms as television provided nearly instant images of the war.[1]

Today's Marine Corps combat photographers are required to have normal color vision, a GT score of 100 or higher, and a security clearance, and to complete a basic still photography course or pass an MOS (military occupation specialty) proficiency by completion of appropriate civilian schooling. There are currently 177 combat photographers and 120 motion picture technicians in the Marine ranks. These Marines also receive training in handling combat situations. Subjects such as reloading film and rifle ammunition under fire are taught at several different schools.[2]

From Pickett's Charge upon Cemetery Ridge at Gettysburg to the raising of the American flag over Mount Suribachi at Iwo Jima and beyond, combat photographers have captured great moments in American combat history. The camera lens has played an important role, and many military men and women have risked their lives and exhibited their talents to preserve our battlefield heritage on film.[3]

The ability to capture moments that remain etched in the archives of Marine Corps lore, as well as the less extravagant happenings that occur on a daily basis, makes the combat cameraman of the Marines a unique and valuable asset, as well as the torchbearer of a profession with a lengthy history. The Marines' combat camera mission is a diverse one that requires initiative and drive to accomplish.

Private First Class Andrew Pendracki, a combat videographer, states, "In Iraq, all of the training missions we've done in the past come into effect because we have to know exactly what we are videotaping and photographing in order to get the best angles and camera shots to tell the story through video or images."

Marine Lieutenant Colonel David S. Heesacker stated, "Having a combat camera section has been very valuable, especially in the explosive ordnance disposal field. They've been able to capture some things with photography that have allowed us to go back and examine them in order to identify dangerous situations we didn't know were there and possibly save lives."

Combat photographers also need a secret clearance because of some of the work that they do. They may be attached to reconnaissance units to take photographs from the air that cannot be made public to ensure the safety of American troops.[4]

Lance Corporal Shane Keller
Late February 2005
Regimental Combat Team-2 (RCT-2)
Haqlayniah, Iraq

In late February 2005, 26-year-old Lance Corporal Keller, a native of Harrisburg, Pennsylvania, was deployed in the western part of the Anbar Province, Iraq, near the end of his oversea tour. Keller, a combat photographer, had been supporting Marines and Iraqi forces for several months documenting their security and stabilization operations for the RCT-2's historical, training and intelligence purposes. He had been attached to various infantry units during his year-long deployment. Most of his time in Iraq had been spent within towns and villages.

I witnessed many changes in Iraq while I was there, but none more evident than the abilities of the Iraqi Security Forces and Iraqi Army. When I first got to Iraq, I was only working alongside Marines, but over time, the Iraqi forces began to get more involved. They now seem to be doing a better job.

The Iraqi forces were not the only ones improving at their jobs. Keller explained that he grew both professionally and personally. The 5-foot-4-inch Marine also said he was able to work better with the equipment he was required to carry.

I'm not a big guy and I still had to carry a rifle, pistol, camera, flak jacket and helmet in 130-degree weather, so being there definitely got me used to carrying all the gear combat photographers are required to have.

Keller's gear came in handy during some close calls in combat. He recalled one event that almost took his life. "I was in the town of Haqlayniah with 3/25 when we found a weapons cache inside a house. The people who owned the building said that they didn't know about the weapons and that they rented the building out to another person." The Marines and the owner of the house then traveled in military vehicles to meet the renter of the house for questioning. When Keller's vehicle reached an intersection on the way, one of the antennas was caught on a low power line.

Keller stood up in the back of the vehicle to untangle the line, when a rocket-propelled grenade (RPG) was shot into the building wall about five feet away from him. The blast knocked him back into the vehicle, breaking his camera. Reacting to the attack, Keller assumed the role of rifleman.

After the RPG hit, we began taking AK-47 fire from down the road. I stood up and Corporal Erik Ely, another combat photographer, and I fired back. We then dismounted and began searching the area for the person who shot the RPG. A few minutes later, another RPG was shot and landed about ten feet away from me. I was lucky to escape from that situation and it changed my outlook on things in life.

After returning to Camp Lejeune, North Carolina, Keller explained how a year in a combat zone affected him and will continue to affect him in the future.

Being in Iraq for that long helped me learn to be able to do more with less and survive with the bare minimum. This experience has taught me the importance of living every day to the fullest and to never take things in life for granted.[5]

Corporal Brian Henner
23 July 2006
Regimental Combat Team-7 (RCT-7)
Haqlaniyah, Iraq

Corporal Henner was a Marine combat photographer with Regimental Combat Team-7, based out of Camp Al Asad. The incident took place in Haqlaniyah, Iraq, one of three Euphrates River valley cities in the western portion of Al Anbar Province which make up the Haditha Triad region.

As a combat photographer, and on his second Iraqi tour, Henner has taken thousands of pictures of Marines, soldiers and Iraqi security forces, conducting operations in the Al Anbar Province. He has spent countless hours in the field, documenting the war through photos.

On 23 July 2006, Henner was snapping pictures of Marines searching Iraqi vehicles at an inspection checkpoint. All of a sudden, the Marines began receiving gunfire from a tree line across the street. The Marines immediately took cover behind a car, but Henner was caught in the open, adjacent to the small center median. As the enemy fire continued, he lay on his belly behind the median and returned fire with his rifle. Eventually he was able to start crawling away along the median. It was at this time that an insurgent's bullet hit his Kevlar helmet, taking a chunk out of the top of the protective device. "I saw a flash and then wham, something hit me hard! I knew it wasn't a rock, and I thought, damn, I think I just got shot in the head."

With other the Marines yelling at him to move, the corporal sprang to his feet, ran for the car and slid across the hood to safety. In doing so, he broke his camera lens. He then used his personal camera to record short video clips of the ongoing battle, which lasted nearly 30 minutes.

Although a religious man, Corporal Henner does not attribute Divine intervention, luck, fate or destiny to the fact that he is still alive after taking an enemy bullet to the head. The 22-year-old Marine from Rochester, New York, says it was his Kevlar helmet that saved his life. "If I didn't have it on, it probably would have gone into the top of my head. It didn't just graze; it dug into the helmet, but that's why we wear them. This was my first bona fide firefight. I am now a bit more aware of what's going on around me and I carry more rifle magazines."

His parents were relatively calm about the incident after Henner called them by phone to tell them what had happened. "My mom has taken credit for this with all of the prayers that she says for me."

Henner joined the Marines after the terrorist attacks on the World Trade Center in 2001. "It makes me mad that people don't remember that anymore. That was a big recruiting drive for the United States military." He now has less than six months left in the Marine Corps and plans on leaving the military to pursue a college education.⁶

> You and I have a rendezvous with destiny.
> — Ronald Reagan

On 6 October 2006, I came across an article in the *Marine Corps News* submitted by the 2nd Marine Division on 2 March 2006 which told the close call story of Lance Corporal Keller. Keller had been a combat photographer in Iraq and this clicked with another story in one of my previous chapters that involved another combat photographer, Corporal Brian Henner. I decided to remove Henner's story from that chapter and add it to a new one where these two could be highlighted and the history of combat photographers could be told.

Chapter Notes

Chapter 1

1. Mickey Gold, "John," unpublished biography of John Egan (1992), 2.
2. Commander Naval Forces Marianas, USS *San Francisco* (CA-38) website, http://www.geocities.com/mariwether.geo/sfa.html.
3. Letter to the author, 26 April 2006.
4. Memorial Service: USS *San Francisco* (CA-38), "The Naval Battle of Guadalcanal: Twenty-Four Minutes of Thundering Hell on Iron Bottom Bay," USS *San Francisco* Memorial Foundation (28 May 2006).
5. Letter, 26 April 2006.
6. Memorial Service: USS *San Francisco* (CA-38).
7. Ibid.
8. Letter, 26 April 2006.
9. *Dictionary of American Naval Fighting Ships*, Office of the Chief of Naval Operations, Naval History Division, Washington, D.C.; USS *San Francisco* II (CA-38) website, http://www.iibiblio.org/hyperwar/USN/ships/dafs/CA/ca38.html.
10. Memorial Service: USS *San Francisco* (CA-38).
11. Warrant Officer 1 John Garvey, Oral History Tape 2 of 2, "Sergeant John Egan, USMC, World War II Veteran-Pearl Harbor Survivor, USS *San Francisco* CA-38," California State Military Reserve Center for Military History, Concord, California, (19 May 2003).
12. Mickey Gold, "John," 3–4.
13. Questionnaire returned to the author, 6 May 2006.

Chapter 2

1. Al Zdon, "The First Invasion: Guadalcanal," *War Stories: Accounts of Minnesotans Who Defended Their Nation* (Minnesota: Moonlit Eagle Productions, 2002), 81–82.
2. Lineage of the Second Marine Division, Second Marine Division Association website, http://www.2marine.com/main.html.
3. Al Zdon, "The First Invasion: Guadalcanal," 85.
4. Ibid., 82–83, 85.
5. Ibid., 83.
6. Ibid., 81, 84.

Chapter 3

1. Questionnaire returned to the author, 22 August 2006.
2. "The President's Own," Marine Corps Band website, http://www.marineband.usmc.mil/learning_tools/our_history/index.htm.
3. "Marine Corps Band," Marine Corps website, http://marines.com/page/usmc.jsp?pageId=/page/Detail-XML-Conversion.jsp?pageName=Marine-Corps-Band&flashRedirect=true.
4. Questionnaire, 22 August 2006.
5. "The Battle of Tarawa," Wikipedia website, http://en.wikipedia.org/wiki/Battle_of_Tarawa.
6. Ibid.
7. Letter to the author, 11 August 2006.
8. "The Battle of Tarawa," Wikipedia website.
9. Letter, 11 August 2006.
10. Questionnaire, 22 August 2006.
11. Don Bedwell, "Marine Bands: Bandsmen Give Performance of their Lives in Iraq," *Leatherneck* 88, no. 10 (October 2005): 22–25.

Chapter 4

1. Questionnaire returned to the author, 2 September 2006.
2. "The Battle of Saipan," Wikipedia website, http://en.wikipedia.org/wiki/Battle_of_Saipan.
3. Ibid.
4. Letter to the author, 24 August 2006.

5. "The Battle of Saipan," Wikipedia website.
6. Questionnaire, 2 September 2006.

Chapter 5

1. Letter to the author, 26 July 2006.
2. "4th Marine Division," Military Global Security website, http://www.globalsecurity.org/military/agency/usmc/4mardiv.htm.
3. Letter, 26 July 2006.
4. "4th Marine Division."
5. "The Battle of Tinian," Wikipedia website, http://en.wikipedia.org/wiki/Battle_of_Tinian.
6. "Tinian ... Home of the Enola Gay," 4th Marine Division website, http://www.fightingfourth.com/tinian.htm.
7. Letter, 26 July 2006.
8. Ibid.
9. "Tinian ... Home of the Enola Gay," 4th Marine Division website.
10. "The Battle of Tinian," Wikipedia website.
11. Ibid.
12. "Tinian Landing Beaches, Ushi Point and North Fields, Tinian Island," Aviation: From Sand Dunes to Sonic Booms, National Park Service website, http://www.cr.nps.gov/nr/travel/aviation/tin.htm.
13. "USS *Indianapolis* (CA-35)," Wikipedia website, http://en.wikipedia.org/wiki/ USS_Indianapolis_%28CA-35%29.
14. Letter, 26 July 2006.

Chapter 6

1. Questionnaire e-mailed to the author, 15 July 2006.
2. "History of the Third Marine Division," The Third Marine Division Association website, http://www.caltrap.org/ap/history.html.
3. Questionnaire, 15 July 2006.
4. Ibid.
5. Ibid.
6. Ibid.
7. "Tank Landing Ship," Wikipedia website, http://en.wikipedia.org/wiki/LST.
8. E-mail to the author, 8 July 2006.
9. "About LCI's," USS Landing Craft Infantry National Association website, http://www.usslci.com/html/aboutlci.html.
10. E-mail, 8 July 2006.
11. David Llewellyn, "Nakajima B6N Tenzen," website, http://compass.dircon.co.uk/Tenzen.htm (no longer an active URL).
12. Questionnaire, 15 July 2006.
13. E-mail, 8 July 2006.
14. "Battle of Guam," Wikipedia website, http://en.wikipedia.org/wiki/Battle_of_Guam.
15. Questionnaire, 15 July 2006.
16. "Battle of Guam," Wikipedia website.
17. Questionnaire, 15 July 2006.

Chapter 7

1. Questionnaire returned to the author, 12 May 2006.
2. Letter to the author, 9 May 2006.
3. "The Battle of Peleliu," Wikipedia website, http://en.wikipedia.org/wiki/Battle_of_Peleliu.
4. "U.S. 1st Marine Division," Wikipedia website, http://en.wikipedia.org/wiki/US_1st_Marine_Division.
5. Jeremy Gypton, "Bloody Peleliu: Unavoidable Yet Unnecessary," Military History Online.com website, http://www.militaryhistoryonline.com/wwii/peleliu/default.aspx.
6. Letter, 9 May 2006.
7. Jeremy Gypton, "Bloody Peleliu."
8. Ibid.
9. Letter, 9 May 2006
10. Ibid.
11. Ibid.
12. Ibid.
13. Jeremy Gypton, "Bloody Peleliu."
14. Letter, 9 May 2006.
15. "Battle of Peleliu," Wikipedia website.
16. Questionnaire, 12 May 2006.

Chapter 8

1. Letter to the author, 21 August 2006.
2. "Fleet Marine Force Corpsman," Marine Corps Brotherhood website, http://marinecorpsbrotherhood.usmchq.com/whats_new.html.
3. "Navy Corpsmen & the Navy Hospital Corps," Essortment website, http://pa.essortment.com/navycorpsmen_rwoy.htm.
4. Letter, 21 August 2006.
5. Beryl Bonacker, "Peleliu Remembered," *Military* 22, no.8 (January 2006): 6–8.
6. Letter, 21 August 2006.
7. Ibid.
8. Beryl Bonacker, "Peleliu Remembered," 12–13.

Chapter 9

1. Letter to the author, 3 June 2006.
2. "3rd Battalion, 1st Marines," Military

Global Security website, http://www.globalsecurity.org/military/agency/usmc/3-1.htm.
3. Letter, 3 June 2006.
4. "Battle of Okinawa," Wikipedia website, http://en.wikipedia.org/wiki/Battle_of_Okinawa.
5. Letter, 3 June 2006.
6. "Battle of Okinawa," Wikipedia website.
7. Colonel Joseph H. Alexander, USMC (Ret), "The Final Campaign: Marines in the Victory of Okinawa," *Marines in World War II Commemorative Series* (History and Museums Division, Headquarters, U.S. Marine Corps, Washington, D.C.), http://www.nps.gov/wapa/indepth/extcontent/usmc/pcn-190-003135-00/index/htm.
8. Kent Roberts Greenfield, Editor, "Okinawa: The Last Battle," *The U.S. Army in World War II—The Pacific War*, Washington D.C., Center of Military History, U.S. Army (1948): Chapter XIV, 365, located online at: http://army.mil/cmh-pg/books/wwii/okinawa/chapter14.htm#b2.
9. Colonel Joseph H. Alexander, USMC (Ret).
10. Letter, 3 June 2006.
11. Colonel Joseph H. Alexander, USMC (Ret).
12. "Battle of Okinawa," Wikipedia website.
13. Letter, 3 June 2006.
14. Ibid.

Chapter 10

1. Al Zdon, "K-3-5: The Proud and the Few," Minnesota American Legion online "War Stories" link, http://www.mnlegion.org.

Chapter 11

1. Benton F. Corry, "War Memories," unpublished and undated memoirs sent to the author on 17 August 2006, 1–8.
2. Ibid., 7–12.
3. Ibid., 11.
4. Ibid., 11–12.
5. Ibid., 12.
6. Ibid., 12.
7. Ibid., 13.
8. Ibid., 17–20.
9. Ibid., 20–26.
10. Ibid., 26.
11. Ibid., 26.
12. Ibid., 29.
13. Ibid., 29.
14. Ibid., 30.
15. Ibid., 30.

16. Ibid., 31.
17. Ibid., 31–32.
18. Ibid., 32.
19. Ibid., 34–35.
20. Ibid., 35–37.
21. Ibid., 37, 41.
22. Ibid., 43–44.
23. Ibid., 62–63.

Chapter 12

1. Questionnaire/letter to the author, 27 November 2006.

Chapter 13

1. Questionnaire to the author, 5 September 2006.
2. Letter to the author, 17 August 2006.
3. Ibid.
4. Ibid.
5. Ibid.
6. "Battle of Iwo Jima," Wikipedia website, http://en.wikipedia.org/wiki/Battle-Iwo_Jima.
7. Ibid.
8. Letter, 17 August 2006.
9. Ibid.
10. Ibid.
11. Ibid.
12. Ibid.
13. Ibid.
14. Ibid.
15. "Battle of Iwo Jima," Wikipedia website.
16. "Tadamichi Kuribayashi," Japundit website, http://japundit.com/archives/2006/08/17/3333/.
17. "Battle of Iwo Jima," Wikipedia website.
18. Letter, 17 August 2006.
19. Questionnaire, 5 September 2006.

Chapter 14

1. Questionnaire to the author, 11 October 2006.
2. George Green, "Compilation of Memoirs," unpublished, undated and unpaged, sent to the author 18 September 2006.
3. Anthony Staunton, "The Bougainville Campaign 1944–1945," Digger History website, http://www.diggerhistory2.ingo/hardnbold/pages/bougainville/htm.
4. George Green, "Memoirs."
5. 1st Lt. Robert Arthur and 1st Lt. Kenneth Cohlmia, *The Third Marine Division* (Washington D.C.: Infantry Journal Press, 1948).

6. George Green, "Memoirs."
7. Ibid.
8. Ibid.
9. Ibid.
10. Ibid.
11. Ibid.
12. Ibid.
13. Ibid.
14. Ibid.
15. Ibid.
16. Ibid
17. Ibid.
18. Questionnaire, 11 October 2006.
19. Ibid.
20. Letter to the author, 11 October 2006.
21. E-mail to the author, 21 November 2006, including article by Bob Dart, "Marines See Museum Dedicated," Cox News Service, 11 November 2006.

Chapter 15

1. Eileen Smyth Judd, "George Joseph Smyth," unpublished biography e-mailed to the author 1 June 2007.
2. George Smyth's official USMC military service record, serial number 563813, provided to the author by Eileen Judd.
3. Mark Flowers, "The Bazooka in Marine Corps Service," World War II Gyrene website, http://www.ww2gyrene.org/weapons_bazooka.htm.
4. USMC military service record.
5. "Uncommon Valor: The 60th Anniversary of the Battle of Iwo Jima," (Florida: Faircount LLC, 2005), 44–45.
6. "Eagle Carrier Boy is Iwo Hero," *Brooklyn Eagle* (April 1945).
7. Ibid.
8. Ibid.
9. "Uncommon Valor," 45.
10. "Eagle Carrier Boy is Iwo Hero."
11. Ibid.
12. George Smyth, "You Gave Me Blood," *New York Sunday Mirror* (27 January 1952).
13. "Marine Photo in Blood Drive Identified Here," *New York Herald Tribune* (24 January 1952).
14. George Smyth's official USMC casualty report, casualty number 024545, dated 30 March 1945, provided to the author by Eileen Judd.
15. USS *Lowndes* (APA-154) Deck Log entries for February-March 1945, http://dobrinkman.net/lowndes/decklog/html.
16. USMC casualty report.
17. "Chronic subdural hematoma," MedlinePlus Medical Encyclopedia website, http://nlm.nih.gov/medlineplus/ency/article/000781.htm.

18. George Smyth, "You Gave Me Blood."
19. USMC military service record.
20. Eileen Smyth Judd, "George Joseph Smyth."
21. George P. Oslin, Publicity Director, Western Union Telegraph Company, news release, New York (22 January 1952).
22. Eileen Smyth Judd, "George Joseph Smyth."
23. George P. Oslin, Western Union news release.
24. "Gives 7th Pint, 'Owes' 6," *Levittown Daily News* (27 February 1952).
25. Rhoda Amon, "Marine Hero 'Died' on Iwo — Lived to Tell of Bloodiest Battle," *Long Island Daily News* (9 September 1955).
26. E-mail sent to the author by Eileen Judd, 8 July 2007.
27. Rhoda Amon, "Marine Hero 'Died' on Iwo."

Chapter 16

1. William Byrd, *By the Dawn's Early Light: From the Cotton Fields of Mississippi to the Beaches of Iwo Jima* (Mississippi: Self-published and edited by Marvin D. Veronee, 2005), 1–10.
2. "U.S. 5th Marine Division," Wikipedia website, http://en.wikipedia.org/U.S._5th_Marine_Division.
3. "The 5th Marine Division," World War II Gyrene website, http://ww2gyrene.org/spotlight5_5thmardiv.htm.
4. William Byrd, *By the Dawn's Early Light*, 11, 13.
5. Ibid., 13, 15.
6. Ibid., 18.
7. Ibid., 19
8. Ibid., 19
9. Ibid., 20.
10. Ibid., 20.
11. Ibid., 26.
12. Ibid., 28.
13. "U.S. 5th Marine Division," Wikipedia website.
14. "The 5th Marine Division," World War II Gyrene website.

Chapter 17

1. Questionnaire e-mailed to the author, 15 August 2006.
2. "The Philippines," National Archives Learning Curve website, http://www.spartacus.schoolnet.co.uk/2WWphilippines.htm.
3. Lee Burgee, e-mail sent to the author, 14 August 2006.

Chapter 18

1. Questionnaire sent to the author, 29 July 2006.
2. Gordon Rottman, *Korean War Order of Battle: United States, United Nations, and Communist Ground, Naval and Air Forces, 1950–1953* (Louisiana: Brown Mouse Publishing, December 2002). Excerpts were located at the following website: http://www.korean-war/USMarines/us-marines.html.
3. Questionnaire, 29 July 2006.
4. Don Knox, *The Korean War: Pusan to Chosin, An Oral History* (Florida: A Harvest Book: Harcourt Brace, 1987), 89.
5. Ibid., 92.
6. Ibid., 119–120,130.
7. Ibid., 138–140.
8. Ibid., 140–141.
9. Ibid., 143–144.
10. Questionnaire, 29 July 2006.
11. Don Knox, 145–146.
12. Ibid., 147.
13. Ibid., 162–163.
14. Ibid., 163.
15. Questionnaire, 29 July 2006.

Chapter 19

1. Al Zdon, "A machine gunner in the Marines took part in three Korean landings, was wounded, rehabilitated, and rejoined his unit — all in eight months," Minnesota American Legion online "War Stories" link, http://www.mnlegion.org.

Chapter 20

1. Questionnaire e-mailed to the author, 15 August 2006.
2. Dan Prindible III, interviewer, "Proud Survivor of the 'Chosin Few,'" Eyewitness to War, Special Edition, *Military History Magazine* (December 1995), 76.
3. Questionnaire, 15 August 2006.
4. Don Knox, *The Korean War: Pusan to Chosin, An Oral History* (Florida, A Harvest Book — Harcourt Brace & Company, 1987), 266–268.
5. Questionnaire, 15 August 2006.
6. Dan Prindible III (interviewer), 73–74, 76.
7. Ibid., 76.
8. E-mail sent to the author, 14 August 2006.
9. Dan Prindible III (interviewer), 76.
10. Ibid., 74.
11. Questionnaire, 15 August 2006.
12. Don Knox, *The Korean War*, 611.
13. Questionnaire, 15 August 2006.
14. Dan Prindible III (interviewer), 73.
15. Ibid., 75.
16. Questionnaire, 15 August 2006.
17. E-mail, 14 August 2006.
18. Dan Prindible III (interviewer), 76.

Chapter 21

1. Al Zdon, "Anything but a Forgotten War," *War Stories: Accounts of Minnesotans Who Defended Their Nation* (Minnesota: Moonlit Eagle Productions, 2002), 135–136.
2. Ibid., 136–137.
3. Ibid., 137.
4. Ibid., 137–138.
5. Ibid., 138.

Chapter 22

1. Bud Valkenburg, short biography sent to the author, dated 14 June 2006.
2. Bud Valkenburg, "Close Calls in Korea," *Depoe Bay Beacon* newspaper, (19 May 2006), 18–19.
3. Bud Valkenburg, short biography, 14 June 2006.
4. Bud Valkenburg, "Close Calls in Korea," 19.

Chapter 23

1. John Bastian (editors: Arthur Wilson and Norman Strickbine), "Frozen Zipper," *Korean Vignettes: Faces of War* (Oregon: Artwork Publications, 1996), 71.
2. "2nd Battalion 7th Marines," Wikipedia Website, http://en.wikipedia.org/wiki/2nd_Battalion_7th_Marines.
3. "Sudong-ni and a New Enemy," A Brief History of Dog Company, 2nd Battalion 7th Marine Regiment, First Marine Division, Korea 1950–1955, Marzone website, http://marzone.com/dog2-7/Hist-1.htm.
4. John Bastian, "Frozen Zipper," 71.

5. Ibid.
6. "Sudong-ni and a New Enemy."
7. John Bastian, "Frozen Zipper," 71.

Chapter 24

1. "Battle of Chosin Reservoir—'Task Force Drysdale,'" Wikipedia website, http://en.wikipedia.org/wiki/Battle_of_Chosin _Reservoir.
2. Charles Suplee (editors: Arthur Wilson and Norman Strickbine), "It was a Dud," *Korean Vignettes: Faces of War* (Oregon: Artwork Publications, 1996), 163.
3. Charles Fieldson (editors: Arthur Wilson and Norman Strickbine), "A Marine Never Quits," *Korean Vignettes: Faces of War* (Oregon: Artwork Publications, 1996), 167.
4. "Battle of Chosin Reservoir," Wikipedia website.

Chapter 25

1. Elbert Koonce (editors: Arthur Wilson and Norman Strickbine), "The Sausage Grinder and Jochum's Ear," *Korean Vignettes: Faces of War* (Oregon: Artwork Publications, 1996), 175.

Chapter 26

1. Forest Heistermann, (editors: Arthur Wilson and Norman Strickbine), "Click," *Korean Vignettes: Faces of War* (Oregon: Artwork Publications, 1996), 229.
2. "Battle of Chosin Reservoir," Wikipedia Website, http://en.wikipediia.org/Battle_of_Chosin_Reservoir.
3. Gina DiNicolo, "Chosin Reservoir," *The Retired Officers Magazine* 56, no. 11 (November 2000).
4. Forest Heistermann, "Click," 229.
5. Ibid.
6. Gina DiNicolo, "Chosin Reservoir."
7. "Battle of Chosin Reservoir," Wikipedia website.
8. Forest Heistermann, "Click," 229.

Chapter 27

1. William Palizzolo (editors: Arthur Wilson and Norman Strickbine), "Fate Flips the Coin," *Red Dragon: Faces of War II,* (Oregon: Artwork Publications, 2003), 173.
2. Ibid.

Chapter 28

1. Richard Aiple (editors: Arthur Wilson and Norman Strickbine), "The Water Hole Stickup," *Korean Vignettes: Faces of War* (Oregon: Artwork Publications, 1996), 351.

Chapter 29

1. John Graham (editors: Arthur Wilson and Norman Strickbine), "Escape from Manpojin," *Korean Vignettes: Faces of War* (Oregon: Artwork Publications, 1995), 281.
2. "U.S. Military Korean War Statistics," All POW-MIA Korean War U.S. Casualties Including POWs and MIAs website, http://www.aiipowmia.com/koreacw/kwkia_menu.html.
3. "Korean War," Wikipedia website, http://en.wikipedia.org/wiki/Korean_War.
4. John Graham, "Escape from Manpojin," 281.

Chapter 30

1. Questionnaire sent to the author, 1 October 2006.
2. Master Sergeant Robert Fugate, "Vegas, Reno and Carson," *Leatherneck* magazine, 17.
3. Letter to the author, 22 September 2006.
4. Al Hemingway, "Highest damn beachhead in Korea: at Reno, Carson and Vegas—dubbed the Nevada Cities—Marines once again defeated the Chinese in March 1953—Korean War, *VFW Magazine* (March 2003).
5. "Navy Cross Citation for Kenneth Edwin Taft, Jr.," located online at http://www.homeoftheheroes.com/valor/1_Citations/05_Koreasnc/nc_08korea_usmcMZ.html#S.
6. Al Hemingway, "Highest damn beachhead in Korea."
7. "Western Korean Front 1952–1953, First Marine Division Sector, The Jamestown Line and Major Outposts," located at http://ourragegis.com/korea/final-2d.jpg.
8. Questionnaire, 1 October 2006.

Chapter 31

1. Melvin Boland (editors: Arthur Wilson and Norman Strickbine), "When Ya Gotta Go, Ya Gotta Go," *Red Dragon: Faces of War II* (Oregon: Artwork Publications, 2003), 131.
2. Robert Wickman (editors: Arthur Wilson and Norman Strickbine), "Last Days of War," *Red Dragon: Faces of War II* (Oregon: Artwork Publications, 2003), 395.

3. "Western Korean Front 1952–1953, First Marine Division Sector, The Jamestown Line and major Outposts," http://ourragegis.com/korea/final-2d.jpg.
4. Robert Wickman, "Last Days of the War," 395.
5. "Korean War," Wikipedia website, http://en.wikipedia.org/wiki/Korean_War.
6. Dan Prindible III (interviewer), "Proud Survivor of the 'Chosin Few,'" Eyewitness to War, Special Edition, *Military History Magazine* (December 1995), 74.

Chapter 32

1. Questionnaire sent to the author, 2 June 2006.
2. "1st Battalion 9th Marines," Wikipedia website, http://en.wikipedia.org/wiki/1st_Battalion_9th_Marines.
3. "Operation Buffalo," 1st Marine Division Association website, http://1stmarinedivisionassociation.org/operations-history-folder/buffalo.htm.
4. Ibid.
5. Letter to the author, 19 January 2006.
6. "Operation Buffalo," 1st Marine Division Association website.
7. Ibid.
8. Letter, 19 January 2006.
9. Questionnaire, 2 June 2006.

Chapter 33

1. E-mail sent to the author, 1 June 2006.
2. Ibid.
3. Resume sent to the author, 1 June 2006.
4. E-mail, 1 June 2006.
5. Resume, 1 June 2006.
6. E-mail, 1 June 2006.
7. Resume, 1 June 2006.
8. USMC Monthly Command Chronology for the 3rd Battalion, 4th Marines, May 1968.
9. John A. Hudson, 3/4 message board, 12 May 2006, http://groups.yahoo.com/group/ThirdBnFourthMarines/message/3691.
10. E-mail, 1 June 2006.
11. John A. Hudson, 3/4 message board, 14 May 2006, message 3704.
12. E-mail, 1 June 2006.
13. USMC Command Chronology.
14. E-mail, 1 June 2006.

Chapter 34

1. Robert Simonsen, "Insights of a Vietnam Bound Marine," unpublished short story (1972).
2. James S. Santelli, "A Brief History of the 27th Marines," Marine Corps Historical Center, Washington, D.C. (August 1968).
3. Robert Simonsen, "An Unforgettable Experience," unpublished short story (June 1968).
4. USMC Monthly Command Chronology for the 2nd Battalion, 7th Marines, May 1968.
5. Robert Simonsen, "An Unforgettable Experience."
6. Ibid.
7. Ibid.
8. Ibid.
9. Robert Simonsen, *Every Marine-1968 Vietnam: A Battle for Go Noi Island* (Maryland: Heritage Books, Inc., 2005), 381–382.

Chapter 35

1. Letter to the author, 14 December 2006.
2. Letter to the author, 5 December 2006.
3. Ibid.
4. Ibid.
5. Letter, 14 December 2005.

Chapter 36

1. Questionnaire e-mailed to the author, 28 April 2006.
2. E-mails sent to the author, 14 April, 25 and 27 July 2006.
3. "History of Bravo Company 3rd Tank Battalion," http://usmcvta.org/3rdtanks/historybco3rdtanks.htm.
4. USMC Monthly Command Chronology for the 3rd Tank Battalion, July 1968.
5. Lieutenant Colonel Faris R. Kirkland (retired), "Thor: A Case Study in Multi-Service Coordination," *Field Artillery* (February 1993): 11–13.
6. USMC Monthly Command Chronology, July 1968.
7. E-mails, 14 April, 25 and 27 July 2006.
8. Lieutenant Colonel Faris Kirkland (retired), "Thor," 11.
9. E-mails, 14 April, 25 and 27 July 2006.

Chapter 37

1. "Lance Corporal Jay Vincens," Hotel Company, 2nd Battalion, 1st Marines' website, http://www.hotel-marines.org.
2. E-mail sent to the author, 19 July 2006.
3. Ibid.
4. Ibid.
5. Bobby Hingston, "Incident," Hotel, 2/1 website.

6. E-mail, 19 July 2006.
7. Bobby Hingston, "Incident," Hotel, 2/1 website.
8. E-mail, 19 July 2006.
9. Bobby Hingston, "Alpha Squad," Hotel, 2/1 website.
10. E-mail, 19 July 2006.
11. Ibid.
12. Ibid.
13. "Lance Corporal Jay Vincens," Hotel, 2/1 website.

Chapter 38

1. Questionnaire e-mailed to the author, 6 July 2006.
2. "1st Battalion, 12th Marines," Global Security website, http://www.globalsecurity.org/military/agency/usmc/1–12.htm.
3. USMC Monthly Command Chronology for the 1st Battalion, 12th Marines, May 1969.
4. E-mail to the author, 14 April 2006.
5. Questionnaire, 6 July 2006.
6. E-mail to the author, 6 July 2006.
7. E-mail, 14 April 2006.
8. Ibid.

Chapter 39

1. Questionnaire e-mailed to the author, 11 July 2006.
2. Terrance Maitland and Peter McInery, *The Vietnam Experience: A Contagion of War* (Massachusetts: Boston Publishing, 1983), 60, 62.
3. "Combined Action Force," Angel Fire website, http://angelfire.com/tx3/capmarine/images/CAF1970.jpg.
4. E-mail sent to the author, April 2006.
5. Ibid.
6. Questionnaire, 11 July 2006.

Chapter 40

1. "History of the 1st Battalion, 8th Marines," USMC Public Website News, http://iimefpublic.usmc.mil.
2. "History of Lebanon, The Lebanese Civil War: 1975–1990," Wikipedia website, http://en.wikipedia.org/wiki/History_of_ Lebanon.
3. "Beirut Memorial On Line — History," Department of Defense Report, http://beirut-memorial.org/history/dod.html.
4. "1983 Beirut barracks bombing," Wikipedia website, http://en.wikipedia.org/1983_Beirut_barracks_bombing.

5. Judy Sarasohn, "It was like a dream, like a coffin, trapped in rubble," *Stars and Stripes* European edition, Weisbaden, Germany (29 October 1983).
6. Ibid.
7. Ibid.
8. "1983 Beirut barracks bombing," Wikipedia website.
9. "Terrorist Bombing of the Marine Barracks, Beirut Lebanon," Arlington National Cemetery website, http://www.arlingtoncemetery.net/terror.htm.

Chapter 41

1. "Female Marines Add to Cultural Sensitivities," Department of Defense, Fallujah, Iraq, 13 June 2005, http://defendamerica.mil.articles/june2005/a061305pj1.html.
2. Fred Zimmerman, "Marines receive Purple Hearts, recall brush with death," *Stars and Stripes* Pacific edition, Camp Hansen, Okinawa (12 October 2005).
3. Ibid.
4. Lance Corporal Cathryn Lindsay and Sergeant Ethan Rocke, "Insurgent attacks hit close to home — Truck Company involved in convoy, first female Marines' lives lost during OIF," *Marine Corps News*, Camp Butler, Okinawa (October 2005).
5. Fred Zimmerman, "Marines receive Purple Hearts."
6. Lindsay and Rocke, "Insurgent attacks."
7. Fred Zimmerman, "Marines receive Purple Hearts."
8. E-R Staff, "Chico Marine receives Purple Heart for injuries in Iraq," Marine Corps Newsroom (1 October 2005).
9. Fred Zimmerman, "Marines receive Purple Hearts."
10. Lindsay and Rocke, "Insurgent attacks."
11. Fred Zimmerman, "Marines receive Purple Hearts."
12. Staff Sergeant Raymie Cruz, 3rd Marine Aircraft Wing, "Female Marines train for Iraq border security," *Marine Corps News*, Camp Korean Village, Iraq, Story ID # 2006814162041 (13 August 2006).
13. "Iraq Coalition Casualties: Female Fatalities," 6 November 2007, http://icasualities.org/oif/Female.aspx.

Chapter 42

1. "2nd Battalion 3rd Marines," Wikipedia website, http://en.wikipedia.org/wiki/2nd_Battalion_3rd_Marines.

2. "United States War in Afghanistan," Wikipedia website, http://en.wikipedia.org/wiki/U.S._invasion_of_Afghanistan.
3. Sergeant Robert M. Storm, MCB Hawaii, "Marines and Sailors endure heat wave in Afghanistan," *Marine Corps News*, Jalalabad, Afghanistan, Story ID # 200581155842 (11 August 2005).
4. Steve Mraz, "Marines learn how to win over Afghan town with aid, respect, sensitivity," *Stars and Stripes* Mideast edition, Camp Blessing, Afghanistan (29 October 2005).
5. Lisa Burgess, "Heroes 2006: I was actually the lucky one—Corpsman saved two Marines after IED blasted Humvee," *Stars and Stripes* (14 June 2006).
6. Steve Mraz, "Shot twice in a week, Marine dubbed 'Lucky,'" *Stars and Stripes* Mideast edition, Asadabad, Afghanistan (26 October 2005).
7. Ibid.
8. Steve Mraz, "Marines learn how to win over Afghan town."
9. Leo Shane III, "Thrice-wounded Marine shows his teammates what luck really is," *Stars and Stripes* Mideast edition (3 November 2006).
10. "Local Marine leaves intensive care," Marine Corps News Room (October 2006), http://www.marine-corps-news.com/2006/10/.
11. "By the Grace of God, Still a Marine," Marine Corps News Room (July 2007), http://www.marine-corps-news.com/2007/07/.

Chapter 43

1. Monte Morin, "Marine bomb expert shaken but not deterred by IED," *Stars and Stripes* Mideast edition (15 January 2006).
2. Corporal C.J. Yard, "No Injuries, 64 IEDs Rendered Safe," *Marine Corps News*, MCB Camp Lejeune, N.C. (10 February 2005).
3. Monte Morin, "Marine bomb expert."
4. C. David Kotok, "Injured Marine Defies Attackers (1 finger salute)," *Omaha World-Herald*, Ramadi, Iraq (24 September 2005).
5. Monte Morin, "Marine bomb expert."
6. Ibid.
7. Ibid.
8. Corporal Warren Peace, "Camp Fuji corporal's course receives explosive overhaul," *Marine Corps News*, Camp Fuji, Okinawa (8 June 2007).

Chapter 44

1. "1st Battalion, 1st Marines Lineage," 1st Marine Division website, http://www.imef.usmc.mil/msc/1mardiv/1BN1MAR/lineage.htm.

2. "1st Battalion, 1st Marines officially take over AO," *Marine Corps News*, Camp Fallujah, Iraq (22 February 2006).
3. Corporal William Skelton, 1st Marine Division, "Combat Train keeps wheels rolling for 1st Battalion, 1st Marine Regiment," *Marine Corps News*, Abu Ghraib, Iraq, Story ID # 2006 434749 (2 April 2006).
4. Monte Morin, "Mortar-ized Humvee shook up Marines in supply convoy," *Star and Stripes* Mideast edition (15 July 2006).
5. "82 mm Mortar ARCUS M-82," Arcus Company website, http://www.arcus-bg.com/products/closesupport/4_82_mm_mortar_arcus_m_82/print.html.
6. Monte Morin, "Mortar-ized Humvee."

Chapter 45

1. Benny Evangelista, "Kevlar saving lives, minimizing wounds in Iraq—Technology first developed in 1965," *San Francisco Chronicle* Archives, (7 April 2003).
2. "3rd Battalion 8th Marines History," Marine Corps Base, Camp Lejeune website, http://www.lejeune.usmc.mil/2dmarine/38/HISTORY.htm.
3. Todd Pitman, "Lucky Marine Survives Sniper's Shot to Back of Head," Associated Press, Ramadi, Iraq (14 April 2006).
4. James Joyner, "Marine Shot in Head, Walks Away," *Outside the Beltway* (14 April 2006).
5. "History: Charlie Company, 1st Battalion, 25th Marines, 4th Marine Division," Marine Forces Reserve website, http://www.mfr.usmc.mil/4thmardiv/.
6. Corporal Brian Reimers, 1st Marine Division, *Marine Corps News*, Fallujah, Iraq, Story ID # 20065954630, (7 May 2006).

Chapter 46

1. "3rd Light Armored Reconnaissance Battalion," Wikipedia website, http://en.wikipedia.org/wiki/3rd_Light_Armored_Reconnaissance_Battalion.
2. "Marine Air Ground Task Force Training Command," Marine Corps website, http://29palms.usmc.mil/fmf/3rdlar/Bn%20History.asp.
3. "3rd Light Armored Reconnaissance Battalion," Wikipedia website.
4. Joseph Giordino, "Body Armor Inserts Provide Extra Safety," *Stars and Stripes* (4 May 2006).
5. Corporal Graham Paulsgrove, "Side SAPI

plate saves lives," *Marine Corps News*, Gharmah, Iraq, Story ID # 200651755243 (14 May 2006).

6. "Body Armor Saves Marines," *Body Armor News* website, http://bodyarmornews.com/body-armor-saves-marines.htm.

7. Ibid.

8. Vijay Joshi, "Casualties from California," *Riverside (California) Press Enterprise* (23 August 2006). A10.

Chapter 47

1. "Combat Photography, 1918–1971," Eye-Witness to History website, http://www.eyewitnesstohistory.com (2000).

2. "Marine Corps (USMC) Enlisted Job Descriptions — MOS 4641, Combat Photographer."

3. "Alumnus Heads Combat Photography Unit: Chief Warrant Officer Lopez preserves visual battlefield history for Marine Corps," National University Alumni Newswire (20 February 2006).

4. Staff Sergeant Houston White Jr., 3rd Marine Aircraft Wing, "MWSS-273 Combat photographers capture history during OIF," *Marine Corps News*, Al Asad, Iraq, Story ID # 20048311719 (28 August 2004).

5. Lance Corporal Lucian Friel, 2nd Marine Division, "Harrisburg, Penn. Native experiences year in Iraq," *Marine Corps News*, MCB Camp Lejeune, Story ID # 20063215439 (2 March 2006).

6. Staff Sergeant Jim Goodwin, "Marine Photographer Saved by Helmet," *Marine Corps News*, Camp Al Asad, Iraq (31 July 2006).

Bibliography

Books

Byrd, William. *By the Dawn's Early Light: From the Cotton Fields of Mississippi to the Beaches of Iwo Jima.* Mississippi: Self published and edited by Marvin D. Veronee, 2005.

Knox, Don. *The Korean War: Pusan to Chosin, an Oral History.* Florida: Harvest Book-Harcourt Brace, 1987.

Maitland, Terrance, and Peter McInery. *The Vietnam Experience: A Contagion of War.* Massachusetts: Boston Publishing Company, 1983.

Rottman, Gordon. *Korean War Order of Battle: United States, United Nations, and Communist Ground, Naval and Air Forces, 1950–1953.* Louisiana: Brown Mouse, December 2002.

Simonsen, Robert. *Every Marine—1968 Vietnam: A Battle for Go Noi Island.* Maryland: Heritage, 2005.

Uncommon Valor—The 60th Anniversary of the Battle of Iwo Jima. Florida: Faircount, 2005.

Wilson, Arthur, and Norman Stickbine (editors). *Korean Vignettes—Faces of War.* Oregon: Artwork, 1996.

____, and ____ (editors). *Red Dragon—Faces of War II.* Oregon: Artwork, 2003.

Zdon, Al. *War Stories—Accounts of Minnesotans Who Defended Their Nation.* Minnesota: Moonlit Eagle, 2002.

Newspapers and News Services

"Alumnus Heads Combat Photography Unit: Chief Warrant Officer Lopez Preserves Visual Battlefield History for Marine Corps." *National University Alumni Newswire,* 20 February 2006.

Amon, Rhoda. "Marine Hero 'Died' on Iwo—Lived to Tell of Bloodiest Battle." *Long Island Daily News,* 9 September 1955.

Burgess, Lisa. "Heroes 2006: I Was Actually the Lucky One—Corpsman Saved Two Marines After IED Blasted Humvee." *Stars and Stripes,* 14 June 2006.

"By the Grace of God, Still a Marine." *Marine Corps News Room,* July 2007. http://www.marine-corps-news.com/2007/07/.

Cruz, Staff Sergeant Raymie 3rd Marine Aircraft Wing. "Female Marines Train for Iraq Border Security." *Marine Corps News.* Camp Korean Village, Iraq, Story ID # 2006814162041, 13 August 2006.

Dart, Bob. "Marines See Museum Dedicated." *Cox News Service,* 11 November 2006.

"Eagle Carrier Boy Is Iwo Hero." *Brooklyn Eagle Newspaper,* April 1945.

E-R Staff. "Chico Marine Receives Purple Heart for Injuries in Iraq." *Marine Corps Newsroom,* 1 October 2005.

"1st Battalion, 1st Marines Officially Take Over AO." *Marine Corps News.* Camp Fallujah, Iraq, 22 February 2006.

Friel, Lance Corporal Lucian, 2nd Marine Division, "Harrisburg, Penn. Native Experiences Year in Iraq." *Marine Corps News.* MCB Camp Lejeune, Story ID # 20063215439, 2 March 2006.

Giordino, Joseph. "Body Armor Inserts Provide Extra Safety." *Stars and Stripes,* 4 May 2006.

"Gives 7th Pint, 'Owes' 6." *Levittown Daily News*, 27 February 1952.

Goodwin, Staff Sergeant Jim. "Marine Photographer Saved by Helmet." *Marine Corps News*. Camp Al Asad, Iraq, 31 July 2006.

Joshi, Vijay. "Casualties from California." *Riverside, CA Press Enterprise*, 23 August 2006.

Joyner, James. "Marine Shot in Head, Walks Away." *Outside the Beltway*, 14 April 2006.

Kotok, C. David. "Injured Marine Defies Attackers (1 finger salute)." *Omaha World-Herald*. Ramadi, Iraq, 24 September 2005.

Lindsay, Lance Corporal Cathryn, and Sergeant Ethan Rocke. "Insurgent Attacks Hit Close to Home-Truck Company Involved in Convoy, First Female Marines' Lives Lost During OIF." *Marine Corps News*. Camp Butler, Okinawa, October 2005.

"Local Marine Leaves Intensive Care." *Marine Corps News Room*, October 2006. http://www.marine-corps-news.com/2006/10/.

"Marine Photo in Blood Drive Identified Here." *New York Herald Tribune*, 24 January 1952.

Morin, Monte. "Marine Bomb Expert Shaken But Not Deterred by IED." *Stars and Stripes*—Mideast edition, 15 January 2006.

Morin, Monte. "Mortar-ized Humvee Shook Up Marines in Supply Convoy." *Star and Stripes*—Mideast edition, 15 July 2006.

Mraz, Steve. "Marines Learn How to Win Over Afghan Town with Aid, Respect, Sensitivity." *Stars and Stripes*—Mideast edition. Camp Blessing, Afghanistan, 29 October 2005.

Mraz, Steve. "Shot Twice in a Week, Marine Dubbed 'Lucky.'" *Stars and Stripes*—Mideast edition. Asadabad, Afghanistan, 26 October 2005.

Oslin, George P., Publicity Director. *Western Union Telegraph Company*. News Release, New York, 22 January 1952.

Paulsgrove, Corporal Graham. "Side SAPI Plate Saves Lives." *Marine Corps News*. Gharmah, Iraq, Story ID # 2006517552 43, 14 May 2006.

Peace, Corporal Warren. "Camp Fuji Corporal's Course Receives Explosive Overhaul." *Marine Corps News*. Camp Fuji, Okinawa (8 June 2007).

Pitman, Todd. "Lucky Marine Survies Sniper's Shot to Back of Head." *Associated Press*. Ramadi, Iraq, 14 April 2006.

Reimers, Corporal Brian Reimers, 1st Marine Division. *Marine Corps News*. Fallujah, Iraq, Story ID # 20065954630, 7 May 2006.

Sarasohn, Judy. "It Was Like a Dream, Like a Coffin, Trapped in Rubble." *Stars and Stripes*—European edition. Weisbaden, Germany, 29 October 1983.

2nd Marine Division, "Harrisburg, Penn. Native Experiences Year in Iraq," *Marine Corps News*, MCB Camp Lejeune, Story ID # 20063215439 (2 March 2006).

Shane, Leo, III. "Thrice-Wounded Marine Shows His Teammates What Luck Really Is," *Stars and Stripes*—Mideast edition, 3 November 2006.

Skelton, Corporal William, 1st Marine Division. "Combat Train Keeps Wheels Rolling for 1st Battalion, 1st Marine Regiment." *Marine Corps News*. Abu Ghraib, Iraq, Story ID # 2006434749, 2 April 2006.

Smyth, George. "You Gave Me Blood." *New York Sunday Mirror*, 27 January 1952.

Storm, Sergeant Robert M. MCB Hawaii. "Marines and Sailors Endure Heat Wave in Afghanistan." *Marine Corps News*. Jalalabad, Afghanistan, Story ID # 2005 81155842, 11 August 2005.

Valkenburg, Bud. "Close Calls in Korea," *Depoe Bay Beacon* newspaper, 19 May 2006.

White, Staff Sergeant Houston, Jr., 3rd Marine Aircraft Wing. "MWSS-273 Combat Photographers Capture History During OIF." *Marine Corps News*. Al Asad, Iraq, Story ID # 20048311719, 28 August 2004.

Yard, Corporal C.J. "No Injuries, 64 IEDs Rendered Safe." *Marine Corps News*.

MCB Camp Lejeune, N.C., 10 February 2005.

Zimmerman, Fred. "Marines Receive Purple Hearts, Recall Brush with Death." *Stars and Stripes*— Pacific edition, Camp Hansen, Okinawa, 12 October 2005.

Periodicals

Bedwell, Don. "Marine Bands: Bandsmen Give Performance of Their Lives in Iraq" *Leatherneck*, October 2005, Volume LXXXVIII, No. 10.

Bonacker, Beryl. "Peleliu Remembered," *Military*, January 2006, Vol. XXII, No. 8.

DiNicolo, Gina. "Chosin Reservoir." *The Retired Officers*, November, 2000, Volume LVI, No.11.

Fugate, Master Sergeant Robert. "Vegas, Reno and Carson." *Leatherneck* (date unknown).

Gypton, Jeremy. "Bloody Peleliu: Unavoidable Yet Unnecessary," *Military History Online.com* website. http://www.militaryhistoryonline.com/wwii/peleliu/default.aspx.

Hemingway, Al. "Highest Damn Beachhead in Korea: At Reno, Carson and Vegas — Dubbed the Nevada Cities — Marines Once Again Defeated the Chinese in March 1953 — Korean War." *VFW*, March 2003.

Kirkland, Lieutenant Colonel Faris R. (retired). "Thor: A Case Study in Multi-Service Coordination." *Field Artillery*, February 1993.

Prindible, Dan, III, interviewer. "Proud Survivor of the 'Chosin Few,'" Eyewitness to War, Special Edition. *Military History* magazine, December 1995.

Personal Accounts

Bergee, Lee. E-mails set to author dated 14 and 15 August 2006.

Bohannon, Jeff. E-mails to author dated April 2006 and 11 July 2006.

Bonacker, Beryl. Letter to author dated 21 August 2006.

Drendall, Harry. Letters to author dated 11 and 22 August 2006.

Dunlap, Earl. Letter to author dated 26 July 2006.

Egan, John. Letters to author dated 26 April 2006 and 6 May 2006.

Green, George. Letter to author dated 11 October 2006.

Horton, Bruce. Letters to author 19 January 2006 and 2 June 2006.

Larkin, James. Letters to author dated 22 September 2006 and 1 October 2006.

Luster, Herbert. Letter to author dated 29 July 2006.

McLaughlin, John. E-mail to author dated 1 June 2006.

Nichols, Charles. Letter to the author dated 27 November 2006.

Peto, George, Jr. Letter to author dated 3 June 2006.

Porter, Jack. Letters to author dated 24 August 2006 and 2 September 2006.

Riordan, Art. Letters to author dated 5 and 14 December 2006.

Samo, Andrew. E-mails to the author dated 8 and 15 July 2006.

Seidler, James. Letters to the author dated 9 and 12 May 2006.

Stagner, Mike. E-mails to author dated 14 April 2006 and 6 July 2006.

Stevens, Kenneth. Letters to author dated 17 August 2006 and 5 September 2006.

Valkenburg, Bud. Letter to author dated 14 June 2006.

Vincens, Jay. E-mail to author dated 19 July 2006.

Wear, John, II. E-mails to author dated 14 and 28 April 2006, 25 and 27 July 2006.

Military-Government Sources

Alexander, Colonel Joseph H. USMC (Ret). *The Final Campaign: Marines in the Victory of Okinawa*. Marines in World War II Commemorative Series. History and Museums Division, Headquarters, U.S. Marine Corps, Washington, D.C.). http://www.nps.gov/wapa/indepth/extcontent/usmc/pcn-190-003135-00/index.htm.

Arthur, 1st Lt. Robert, and 1st Lt. Kenneth Cohlmia. *The 3rd Marine Division History*. Washington D.C.: Infantry Journal Press, 1948.

"Beirut Memorial On Line — History." Department of Defense Report. http://beirut-memorial.org/history/dod.html.

Commander Naval Forces. USS San Francisco (CA-38). http://www.geocities.com/mariwether.geo/sfa.html.

Dictionary of American Naval Fighting Ships, Office of the Chief of Naval Operations, Naval History Division. Washington D.C. USS San Francisco II (CA-38). http://wwwiibiblio.org/hyperwar/USN/ships/dafs/CA/ca38.html.

"Female Marines Add to Cultural Sensitivities." Department of Defense. Fallujah, Iraq, 13 June 2005. http://defendamerica.mil.articles/june2005/a061305pj1.html.

"1st Battalion, 12th Marines." Global Security website. http://www.globalsecurity.org/military/agency/usmc/1-12.htm.

Fleet Marine Force Corpsman. Marine Corps Brotherhood website. http://marinecorpsbrotherhood.usmchq.com/whats_new.html.

4th Marine Division. Military Global Security website. http://www.globalsecurity.org/military/agency/usmc/4mardiv.htm.

Greenfield, Kent Roberts, Editor. *Okinawa: The Last Battle. The US Army in World War II—The Pacific War*, Washington D.C. Center of Military History, US Army, 1948: Chapter XIV. http://army.mil/cmh-pg/books/wwii/okinawa/chapter14.htm#b2.

"History: Charlie Company, 1st Battalion, 25th Marines, 4th Marine Division." Marine Forces Reserve website. http://www.mfr.usmc.mil/4thmardiv/.

History of Bravo Company 3rd Tank Battalion. http://usmcvta.org/3rdtanks/historybco3rdtanks.htm.

"History of the 1st Battalion, 8th Marines," USMC Public Website News. http://iimefpublic.usmc.mil.

History of the Third Marine Division. The Third Marine Division Association website. http://www.caltrap.org/ap/history.html.

"Iraq Coalition Casualties: Female Fatalities." 6 November 2007. http://icasualties.org/oif/Female.aspx.

Lineage of the Second Marine Division. Second Marine Division Association website. http://www.2marine.com/main.html.

"Marine Air Ground Task Force Training Command." Marine Corps website. http://29palms.usmc.mil/fmf/3rdlar/Bn%20History.asp.

Marine Corps Band. Marine Corps website. http://marines.com/page/usmc.jsp?pageId=/page/Detail-XML-Conversion.jsp?pageName=Marine-Corps-Band&flashRedirect=true.

Marine Corps (USMC) Enlisted Job Descriptions — MOS 4641, Combat Photographer.

Navy Cross Citation for Kenneth Edwin Taft, Jr. Located online at: http://www.homeofheroes.com/valor/1_Citations/05_Koreas-nc/nc_08korea_usmcMZ.html#S.

"Operation Buffalo," 1st Marine Division Association website. http://1stmarinedivisionassociation.org/operations-history-folder/buffalo.htm.

The President's Own. Marine Corps Band website. http://www.marineband.usmc.mil/learning_tools/our_history/index.htm.

Santelli, James S. "A Brief History of the 27th Marines." Marine Corps Historical Center, Washington, D.C., August 1968.

"Terrorist Bombing of the Marine Barracks, Beirut Lebanon." Arlington National Cemetery website. http://www.arlingtoncemetery.net/terror.htm.

3rd Battalion, 1st Marines. Military Global Security website. http://www.globalsecurity.org/military/agency/usmc/3-1.htm.

"3rd Battalion 8th Marines History." Marine Corps Base, Camp Lejeune website. http://www.lejeune.usmc.mil/2dmarine/38/HISTORY.htm.

Tinian ... Home of the Enola Gay. 4th Marine Division website. http://www.fightingfourth.com/tinian.htm.

Tinian Landing Beaches, Ushi Point and North Fields, Tinian Island. Aviation: From Sand Dunes to Sonic Booms. National Park Service website. http://www.cr.nps.gov/nr/travel/aviation/tin.htm.

USMC Monthly Command Chronology for the 1st Battalion, 12th Marines, May 1969.
USMC Monthly Command Chronology for the 2nd Battalion, 7th Marines, May 1968.
USMC Monthly Command Chronology for the 3rd Battalion, 4th Marines, May 1968.
USMC Monthly Command Chronology for the 3rd Tank Battalion, July 1968.
U.S. Military Korean War Statistics. All POW-MIA Korean War US Casualties Including POWs and MIAs website. http://www.aiipowmia.com/koreacw/kwkia_menu.html.
USS *Lowndes* (APA-154) Deck Log entries for February–March 1945. http://dobrinkman.net/lowndes/decklog/html.
Warrant Officer 1 John Garvey. Oral History Tape 2 of 2, "Sergeant John Egan, USMC, WW II Veteran–Pearl Harbor Survivor, USS San Francisco CA-38," California State Military Reserve Center for Military History, Concord, California, 19 May 2003.

Websites

"About LCI's," USS Landing Craft Infantry National Association website. http://www.usslci.com/html/aboutlci.html.
"The Battle of Chosin Reservoir-'Task Force Drysdale.'" Wikipedia website. http://en.wikipedia.org/wiki/Battle_of_Chosin_Reservoir.
"The Battle of Guam." Wikipedia website. http://en.wikipedia.org/wiki/Battle_of_Guam.
"The Battle of Iwo Jima." Wikipedia website. http://en.wikipedia.org/wiki/Battle-Iwo_Jima.
"The Battle of Okinawa," Wikipedia website, http://en.wikipedia.org/wiki/Battle_of_Okinawa.
"The Battle of Peleliu." Wikipedia website. http://en.wikipedia.org/wiki/Battle_of_Peleliu.
"The Battle of Saipan." Wikipedia website. http://en.wikipedia.org/wiki/Battle_of_Saipan.
"The Battle of Tarawa." Wikipedia website. http://en.wikipedia.org/wiki/Battle_of_Tarawa.
"The Battle of Tinian." Wikipedia website. http://en.wikipedia.org/wiki/Battle_of_Tinian.
"Body Armor Saves Marines." *Body Armor News* website. http://bodyarmornews.com/body-armor-saves-marines.htm.
"Chronic Subdural Hematoma," MedlinePlus Medical Encyclopedia website. http://nlm.nih.gov/medlineplus/ency/article/000781.htm.
"Combat Photography, 1918–1971." EyeWitness to History website. http://www.eyewitnesstohistory.com (2000).
"Combined Action Force." Angel Fire website. http://angelfire.com/tx3/capmarine/images/CAF1970.jpg.
"82 mm Mortar ARCUS M-82." Arcus Company website. http://www.arcus-bg.com/products/closesupport/4_82_mm_mortar_arcus_m_82/print.html.
Evangelista, Benny. "Kevlar Saving Lives, Minimizing Wounds in Iraq — Technology first developed in 1965." *San Francisco Chronicle* Archives, 7 April 2003.
"The 5th Marine Division." World War II Gyrene website. http://ww2gyrene.org/spotlight5_5thmardiv.htm.
"1st Battalion, 1st Marines Lineage." 1st Marine Division website. http://www.imef.usmc.mil/msc/1mardiv/1BN1MAR/lineage.htm.
"1st Battalion 9th Marines." Wikipedia website. http://en.wikipedia.org/wiki/1st_Battalion_9th_Marines.
Flowers, Mark. "The Bazooka in Marine Corps Service." World War II Gyrene website. http://www.ww2gyrene.org/weapons_bazooka.htm.
"History of Lebanon, The Lebanese Civil War: 1975–1990." Wikipedia website. http://en.wikipedia.org/wiki/History_of_Lebanon.
Hotel Company, 2nd Battalion, 1st Marines' website. http://www.hotel-marines.org.
Hingston, Bobby. "Alpha Squad; Hingston, Bobby. "Incident"; "Lance Corporal Jay Vincens."
"Korean War." Wikipedia website. http://en.wikipedia.org/wiki/Korean_War.

Llewellyn, David. "Nakajima B6N Tenzen" website. http://compass.dircon.co.uk/Tenzen.htm (no longer an active URL).
"Navy Corpsmen & the Navy Hospital Corps," Essortment website. http://pa.es sortment.com/navycorpsmen_rwoy.htm.
"1983 Beirut Barracks Bombing." Wikipedia website. http://en.wikipedia.org/1983_Beirut_barracks_bombing.
"The Philippines." National Archives Learning Curve website. http://www.spartacus.schoolnet.co.uk/2WWphilippines.htm.
"2nd Battalion 3rd Marines." Wikipedia website. http://en.wikipedia.org/wiki/2nd_Battalion_3rd_Marines.
2nd Battalion 7th Marines. Wikipedia Website. http://en.wikipedia.org/wiki/2nd_Battalion_7th_Marines.
Staunton, Anthony. "The Bougainville Campaign 1944–1945," Digger History website. http://www.diggerhistory2.ingo/hardnbold/pages/bougainville/htm.
"Sudong-ni and a New Enemy: A Brief History of Dog Company, 2nd Battalion 7th Marine Regiment, First Marine Division, Korea 1950–1955." Marzone website. http://marzone.com/dog2-7/Hist-1.htm.
"Tadamichi Kuribayashi." Japundit website. http://japundit.com/archives/2006/08/17/3333/.
"Tank Landing Ship." Wikipedia website. http://en.wikipedia.org/wiki/LST.
"3rd Light Armored Reconnaissance Battalion." Wikipedia website. http://en.wikipedia.org/wiki/3rd_Light_Armored_Reconnaissance_Battalion.
"United States War in Afghanistan." Wikipedia website. http://en.wikipedia.org/wiki/U.S._invasion_of_Afghanistan.
"U.S. 1st Marine Division." Wikipedia website. http://en.wikipedia.org/wiki/US_1st_Marine_Division.
"U.S. 5th Marine Division." Wikipedia website. http://en.wikipedia.org/U.S._5th_Marine_Division.
"USS *Indianapolis* (CA-35)." Wikipedia website, http://en.wikipedia.org/wiki/USS_Indianapolis_%28CA-35%29.
"Western Korean Front 1952–1953, First Marine Division Sector, The Jamestown Line and Major Outposts." Located at: http://ourragegis.com/korea/final-2d.jpg.
Zdon, Al. "A Machine Gunner in the Marines Took Part in Three Korean Landings, Was Wounded, Rehabilitated, and Rejoined His Unit — All in Eight Months." Minnesota American Legion online "War Stories" link. http://www.mnlegion.org.
_____. "K-3-5: The Proud and the Few." Minnesota American Legion online "War Stories" link. http://www.mnlegion.org.

Miscellaneous

Corry, Benton. *War Memories*. Unpublished and undated memoirs sent to the author on 17 August 2006.
Gold, Mickey. *John*. Unpublished biography of John Egan, 1992.
Green, George. Unpublished and undated memoirs sent to the author 18 September 2006.
Hudson, John A. 3/4 message board, 12 May 2006. http://groups.yahoo.com/group/ThirdBnFourthMarines
Judd, Eileen Smyth. *George Joseph Smyth*. Unpublished and undated biography e-mailed to the author 1 June 2007.
Memorial Service Pamphlet: USS San Francisco (CA-38). "The Naval Battle of Guadalcanal — Twenty-Four Minutes of Thundering Hell on Iron Bottom Bay." USS San Francisco Memorial Foundation, 28 May 2006.
Simonsen, Robert. *Insights of a Vietnam Bound Marine*. Unpublished short story, 1972.
_____. *An Unforgettable Experience*. Unpublished short story, June 1968.

Index

Abe, Vice Admiral Hiroaki 8
Acey, Chris 277
Adams, Jessi Lane 297
Adams, President John 19
Adams, Joshua 301–302
Advanced Infantry Training (AIT) 203
Afghanistan 2, 34, 39, 80, 159, 224, 272–280, 291, 292
Ahwahnee Hotel, Yosemite, CA 11
Aiple, Richard 180–181
Akron, OH 56
Alabama 255
Al Anbar Province 298–299, 301–302, 304, 306
Al Asad, Iraq 270
Almond, Major General Ned 172
al-Qaeda 272–273
Altadena, CA 245
Alternate Supply Route Lincoln, Iraq 281
Alvarado, Pedro 262–264
American Airlines 231
American Legion 17, 25, 67, 90, 143, 152, 245
American University, Mexico City, Mexico 12
Amnesca, Steven 215
Anderson, Jim 64–67
Andong, South Korea 157
An Hoa, Vietnam 160, 252
Anoka, MN 14, 17
Apra Harbor, Guam 107
Archambault, Lieutenant Raoul J. 98
Ariosto, Ludovico 259
Arizona 248, 298
Arkadelphia, AR 135
Arkansas 27, 131, 134
Arlington National Cemetery 265
Armstrong College, GA 32
Army of the Republic of Vietnam (ARVN) 239
Arnold, Matthew 303
Artworks Publication 164
Asa River, Okinawa 60
Asadabad, Afghanistan 273, 276–277
Ascome City, South Korea 144
Aslito Airfield, Saipan 29
Assan Beach, Guam 95

Associated Press (AP) 296
Atoka, TN 212
Auburn, MA 33
Auckland, New Zealand 39, 246
Aurelius, Marcus 149
Aurora, IN 292
Australia 48, 119
Awacha Draw, Okinawa 73

B-17 bomber 55
B-29 bomber 28, 31, 36, 41, 84
B-52 bomber 234
Bagdad, Iraq 287, 298
Bagram Air Base, Afghanistan 276
Balad Air Base, Iraq 293
Balboa Park, San Diego, CA 69
Bangladesh 44
Bankhead, Will 68
Bastian, John 160–164
Bataan Memorial Museum, Santa Fe, NM 147
Bataan Peninsula, Philippines 119
Bath, ME 78
Bay of Pigs, Cuba 213
Beasley, Lynn 267, 269
Beirut International Airport 262
Beirut, Lebanon 2, 259–265
Bekaa Valley, Lebanon 265
Belleau Wood, France 38, 44
Ben Hai River, Vietnam 207, 210
Bergee, Lee 118–121, 144–148, 199
Bethel College, McKenzie, TN 212
Bethesda Hospital, MD 278
Betio Island, Tarawa 20–22
Big Springs, TX 135
bin Laden, Osama 272–273
Black, Shirley Temple 226
Blewitt, Kenneth 54
Bloody Nose Ridge, Peleliu 48, 65, 78–79
"Bock's Car" 36
Body Armor News 302
Bohannon, Ralph 250–258
Bohol, Philippines 119
Boland, Melvin 195–197
Bonacker, Beryl 50–55
Bonacker, Marlyn 55

326 INDEX

Bosnia 292
Boston Chelsea Hospital, MA 80
Boston, MA 33, 177
Botes, George 228
Bougainville Island 38–39, 94–95, 104, 205, 246, 272
Boulder City area, Korea 198–199
Bowling Green, MO 301
Boxer Rebellion, China 169
Boy Scouts 18, 68, 92, 232
Brady, John 51
Bronx, NY 185
Bronze Star 23, 51, 66, 100, 176, 280–281
Brooke Army Medical Center, TX 269
Brooklyn Eagle newspaper 103, 108
Brooklyn, NY 103, 106, 109
Brown, H. Jackson, Jr. 160
Bryon, Lord 238
Buckner, Lieutenant General Simon Bolivar 58, 62
Buffalo 284
Buise, William 115
Bullhead City, AZ 248
Bulwer-Lyton, E.G. 18
Bumps, Private First Class 87
Bundy, Jeff 284
Burghardt, Joseph 280
Burghardt, Michael 280–285
Burke, Private First Class Robert 222
Burke, SD 203
Burma 250
Burns, Bob 104
Burnside, KY 250
Burnside, MN 143
Bush, President George W. 272–273
By the Dawn's Early Light 117
Byrd, William 113–117
Byron, Lord 238

C-47 aircraft 141
C-141 cargo/troop carrier 227
California 134, 247
California Center for Military History 13
California State University, L.A. 224, 248
Callaghan, Rear Admiral Daniel J. 9, 11
Caltrap newsletter 42, 90
Ca Lu, Vietnam 57
Camara, John 281
Cambodia 39
Cameron, WI 67
Cam Lo, Vietnam 246
Camp Al Asad, Iraq 306
Camp Blessing, Afghanistan 273, 275–278
Camp Carrol, Vietnam 246
Camp Del Mar, CA 197
Camp Dunlap, Niland, CA 94
Camp Edwards, Cape Cod, MA 294–295
Camp Elliot, CA 14, 27, 38, 50, 64, 69, 82, 94, 233
Camp Fallujah, Iraq 287

Camp Fuji, Okinawa 285
Camp Geiger, NC 226
Camp Hansen, Okinawa 269
Camp Korean Village, Iraq 270
Camp Las Flores, CA 232
Camp Lejeune, NC 15, 25, 32–33, 94, 103, 118, 127, 144, 185, 193, 213, 216, 226, 248, 255, 259, 280–281, 292, 294, 305
Camp Otsu, Japan 154
Camp Pahatanmui, New Zealand 28
Camp Pendleton, CA 7, 33–34, 44, 57, 82, 113–114, 118, 127, 136, 144, 149, 154, 160, 167, 177, 182, 197, 203, 210, 216, 218–220, 226, 232–233, 237, 245–246, 251, 286–287, 292, 294
Camp Shelby, MS 113
Camp Tarawa, HI 113–114, 117, 219
Camp White Museum, OR 54
Cam Sa, Vietnam 242
Canal Zone, Panama 238
Cape Esperance, Guadalcanal 8
Cape Glouchester, New Britain 51–52, 56, 64–65, 78
Caribbean 260, 292–294, 296
Caroline Island Group 28
Carriveau, Orville 116
Caseltine, Richard 292–294, 296
Cau Ha, Vietnam 220, 227, 230
Cebu, Philippines 119
Cemetery Ridge, Gettysburg, PA 303
Central African Republic 292
Central America 238
CH-46 helicopter 247
CH-53 helicopter 227, 247
Ch'angch'on, South Korea 128
Ch'angwon, South Korea 128
Charan Kanoa, Saipan 29
Charlie Ridge, Vietnam 252
Chateau Thierry, France 44
Chennault, Clair 250
Chicago, IL 7, 63, 92–94
Chicago Tribune newspaper 93
Chidester, Lieutenant Colonel 168–169
China 57, 67, 76, 125, 161–162, 169, 199
China Wall, Peleliu 48
Chindong-ni, South Korea 128
Chinese Communist Forces (CCF) 44, 140, 145–147, 156, 158, 162–163, 165, 168–171, 174–176, 178, 183, 186, 188, 190, 192–193, 195–196
Chinhung-ni, North Korea 168, 174–175
Chosen Few 148, 176
Chosin (Changjin) Reservoir, North Korea 44, 55, 140, 142, 144–145, 147, 151, 156–157, 160–162, 165, 173–174, 176, 286
Christian Phalange 260
Chu Lai, Vietnam 57, 160, 252
Chunchon, Korea 195
Cicero, IL 63
Civilian Conservation Corps (CCC) 56

Clauson, George 185
Cleveland, OH 56
Clifton, NJ 153
Clinton KY 27
Coast Guard Auxiliary 42
Coates, Captain Sterling 206
Coleman, Langston 33
Coles, Vincent 222
Colfax, WI 67
Collier, Robert 201
Columbia, MO 276
Columbus, OH 63
Combat Action Ribbon 25
Combat Photographer 107–108, 110, 303–307
Combat Train One 286–290
Concord, CA 13
Confucius 43
Congleton, Benjamin 293
Connecticut 238
Con Thien, Vietnam 205–206, 233–234, 241, 286
Corpus Christi, TX 42
Corregidor, Philippines 119
Corry, Benton 68–77
Corsair aircraft 132, 169, 171, 184
Cox News Service 101–102
Craig, Brigadier General Edward 127
Crimea War 303
Cua Viet, Vietnam 57, 234, 241, 245–246
Cua Viet River, Vietnam 34
Cub Scouts 232
Cuba 160
Cuban Missile Crisis 15, 57, 213, 292
Culver City, CA 287

Dai Loc, Vietnam 160
Dakeshi Ridge, Okinawa 60
Dallas, WI 64
Da Nang, Vietnam 57, 160, 220, 224, 227, 230, 233, 239, 241, 245, 246, 251–252, 286
Dart, Bob 101
Dean, Robert 299–300, 302
de La Tochefoucauld, Duc 103
Deleware 291
Depoe Bay, OR 159
Depoe Bay Beacon newspaper 159
Devens, MA 295
Diaz, Steven 264
Disabled American Veterans (DAV) 12, 135, 210
Distinguished Service Medal 51
DMZ (Korea) 57, 286
DMZ (Vietnam) 57, 205–206, 234, 236, 245–246
Dobie, Frank J. 245
Dominican Republic 15, 151, 292
Dong Ha, Vietnam 205–206, 233–234, 245, 252, 286
Dong Ha Mountain, Vietnam 246–247
Dorsey, Morris 264–265

Drendall, Harry 18–26
Drysdale, Douglas, Lieutenant Colonel 165–166, 169
Dunlap, Earl 33–37
Dunne, Alice 270
Duplantis, Lieutenant Colonel Wendell H. 105
DuPont 291

Eastwood, Clint 101
Egan, John 7–13
Eliot, George 5
El Toro, CA 230
Ely, Erik 305
Empress Augusta Bay, Bougainville 95, 233
England 12, 55
English Army: 41st Independent Commando Royal Marines 161, 165–166, 168–169, 172
Enola Gay 36
Erskine, Major General Graves 104
Euphrates River, Iraq 306
Europe 92
Evans, Tom 77
Evansville, IN 170
Every Marine 224–225, 231

Fallujah Hospital 298
Fallujah, Iraq 266–269, 283, 287, 295, 298
"Fat Man" 36
Felix, Hari-Das 288–289
Female Search Force (FSF) 266–271
Fieldson, Charles 167–169
Fiji Island 11
Finschhafen, Papua, New Guinea 286
Fire Support Base, Fuller (FSB), Vietnam 246–248
Fire Support Base, McClintock, Vietnam 246
First Marine Division Association 12, 49, 54, 63, 76, 194, 248
First Naval Battle of Guadalcanal 10–11
Five Brothers, Peleliu 65
Five Sisters, Peleliu 65
Flags of Our Father 101
Florida 231
Florida Island, Guadalcanal 9
Flying Tigers 250
Follow Me newsletter 26, 32
Ford Island, Pearl Harbor, HI 154
Forest Park, IL 216
Forks, WA 300
Fort Belvoir, VA 218
Fort Bragg, NC 213
Fort Dix, NJ 255
Fort Madison, IA 118
Fort Sheridan, IL 93
Fort Snelling, MN 151
Fountain Valley, CA 172, 280
France 113, 260, 265
Frankfurt, Germany 232

Franklin, Benjamin 68
French Army: 6th Parachute Infantry Regiment 262
Funchilin Pass, North Korea 168, 175
Furman University, SC 32
Furness, Lieutenant Colonel David 287

Garapan, Saipan 29
Garfield, President James A. 212
Garvey, Warrant Officer John 13
Gavaldon, Valerie 270
Geiger, Major General Roy 41
Gemayel, President Amine 260
Gemayel, President Bashir 260
General Electric 104
Germany 7, 55
Gerneral Motors, Canada 298
Gharmah, Iraq 299
G.I. Bill 12, 54, 76, 101, 224
Gilbert Island Group 20–22, 28
Go Noi Island, Vietnam 57, 220–225, 227–230
Gold, Mickey 13
Golden Gate Bridge, CA 31
Graham, John 182–184
Grand Junction, CO 300
Great Lakes, Chicago, IL 62, 67
Green, George 92–102
Green Berets 240
Gregory, SD 203
Grenada Island 15
Grenade Hill, Vietnam 243
Grimutter, Leslie 170
Grisales, Kelvin 295–296
Grobe, Private First Class 87
Guadalcanal Island 8–10, 15–16, 20, 28, 39, 44, 48, 65, 70, 94, 160, 246, 259, 286
Guam Island 23, 31, 34, 39–41, 80, 84–86, 87, 90–91, 95–96, 100, 104, 107–108, 136, 172, 205, 233, 246, 272, 292
Guantanamo Bay, Cuba 44, 286
Guest of the Emperor 147
Guinness Book of World Records 197
Gulf War 294
Gutierrez, Raymond 247–248

Habbaniyah, Iraq 300
Haditha, Iraq 278, 306
Hadnot Point, Camp Lejeune 100
Hagaru-ri, North Korea 140–141, 146, 156, 165–169, 173–174
Haiti 292
Hamhung, North Korea 147
Hammond, IN 7
Han River, South Korea 155
Hanson, Jason 300–302
Haqlayniah, Iraq 304–306
Harcourt, Inc. 135
Harris, Colonel 248
Harrisburg, PA 304

Harte, Brett 1
Hawaii 20, 28, 83, 111, 134, 150–151, 220
Hearne, TX 125
Heesacker, Lieutenant Colonel David 304
Heinze, Captain Rodney 97–98
Heistermann, Forest 172–176
Hell Fire Valley, Korea 165–169
Henderson, Jack 222
Henderson Field, Guadalcanal 8, 78
Henner, Brian 303, 306–307
Hezbollah 265
Hialeah, FL 301
Hiei (Japanese battleship) 8–9, 11
Hieu Duc District, Vietnam 252
Hill 10, Vietnam 252
Hill 55, Vietnam 252
Hill 81, Okinawa 75
Hill 123, Korea 155
Hill 148, Vietnam 221
Hill 150, Korea 188
Hill 153, Korea 188
Hill 190, Korea 188, 190
Hill 207, Korea 133
Hill 208, Korea 145
Hill 382 (Turkey Knob), Iwo Jima 294
Hill 552, Vietnam 213
Hill 673, Korea 178
Hill 689, Vietnam 213–216
Hill 698, Korea 162
Hill 758, Vietnam 214–216
Hill 1282, Korea 170
Hill 1310, Korea 180
Hingston, Bobby 240–241
Hiroshima, Japan 36, 62, 66, 80
Hitler, Adolph 93
Hoa Vang, Vietnam 57
Hoffer, Eric 38
Hogen, Randon 295–296
Hoi An, Vietnam 252
Hold Your Heads High Marines 77
Hollywood, CA 218
Homer 64
Honeywell Company 149
Hope, Bob 183
Horton, Bruce 203–211
Houston, TX 301
Hovey, Richard 257
Hue City, Vietnam 233, 286
Humphrey, Christina 266–267, 269
Humvee 275–277, 287–289, 293
Hungnam, North Korea 173–176
Hutchenson, Captain 207

I Corps, Vietnam 204–205, 233, 246
Iceland 15, 94
Ide, Rebecca 269
Iliad 64
Illinois 27
Inchon, South Korea 57, 138–139, 144–145, 150, 154, 183, 286–287

Index

Infantry Training Regiment (ITR) 203, 218, 226, 232
Iowa 83, 121
Iran 265
Iran Revolutionary Guard 265
Iraq 2, 25, 34, 39, 44, 57, 80, 159–160, 224, 233, 246, 265–271, 278, 280–307
Iraqi Army 287, 295, 305
Iraqi Coalition 270
Iron Bottom Sound, Guadalcanal 9
Israel 260
Italy 260
Iwo Jima Island 34, 37, 39, 41, 51, 84–91, 96–101, 104–108, 110–112, 114–117, 172, 205, 219, 233, 246, 294, 304
Iwo Jima Veterans 90

James, Shirley 232
Jamestown Line, Korea 185–186, 189, 198
Japan 15, 20, 31, 36, 39, 43, 62, 76, 90, 127, 141, 151, 162, 183, 232–233, 246, 259, 292
Japanese Army 20, 24, 28, 43, 58, 60; Kamikaze pilots 23, 40, 62, 72
Jasper, AL 68
Jefferson, President Thomas 19, 56
Jerue, Colonel George 206–207
JFK International Airport 255
Johnson, Bob 14–17
Johnson, President Lyndon B. 219, 227
Johnson, Shoshana 298
Jones, Eugene S. 107–108, 110
Jones Beach, Long Island, NY 228
Jordan 298
Judd, Eileen 111–112

Kaneohe Bay, HI 255, 272
Karma, Iraq 287–288
Keiji, Rear Admiral Shibaski 20
Keizer, OR 197
Keller, Shane 303–305, 307
"Kent, Clark" 282
Kentucky 27
Kenyon, Chad 300, 302
Kevlar 291–296, 299, 306
Khan, Genghis 186
Khe Sahn Combat Base, Vietnam 213, 216, 233, 239, 241, 243, 286
Khe Sahn Veterans Association 255
Kirishima (Japanese battleship) 8, 11
Kitano Point, Iwo Jima 89–90
Kito, Isao 67
Klamath Falls, OR 80
Klatt, Platoon Sergeant 9–10
Knox, Don 135
Kobe, Japan 57, 150, 154
Kokura, Japan 36
Koonce, Elbert 170–171
Korda, Michael 250
Korea 2, 57, 109–110
Korean Labor Corps (Chig-ee bearers) 180, 189

Korean Service Medal 163–164, 169
Korean Straights 128
Korean Vignettes — Faces of War 164, 169, 171, 187
Korean War 39, 44, 51, 57, 76, 109, 121, 123–199, 233, 246, 251, 286, 292
The Korean War: Pusan to Chosin, An Oral History 135
Korengal Valley, Afghanistan 275
Kosong, South Korea 131
Koto-ri, North Korea 145–147, 161, 165, 169, 173–174
Kroc, Ray 203
Kuebler, Diane 81, 117
Kunar Province, Afghanistan 273, 275–276
Kunishi Ridge, Okinawa 75, 80
Kuribayashi, Lieutenant General Tadamichi 84, 86, 90
Kuwait 44, 233, 286, 294, 298
Kuwait City, Kuwait 298
Kuwait International Airport 298
Kwajelein Atoll, Marshall Islands 33, 39, 294
Kyushu, Japan 16–17

Landing craft, vehicle and personnel (LCVP)/ Higgins boats 21, 29, 52–53, 86, 95–96
Landing ship, infantry (LCI) 40, 52–53
Landing ship, tank (LST) 40, 52–53, 66–67, 72, 114, 154, 156
Landing vehicle, tracked (LVT)/amtrac 29, 96, 154
Larkin, James 185–194
Las Vegas, NV 210
Le, Captain James 299
Leatherneck magazine 25, 211
Lebanon 15, 260–265
Lebanon Valley College 18
Lebonte, Lieutenant Commander 226
Legion of Merit 51
Letterman, Elmer G. 280
Levine, Robert 125
Levine, Victor 281
Levitttown, Long Island, NY 109–110
Lexington, KY 293
Leyte, Philippines 119
Liberia 292
Liberty Bridge, Vietnam 221
Liberty Road, Vietnam 252
Life magazine 108
Light Armored Vehicles (LAV) 297–299, 301
Linck, Fred 295–296
Lioness Program 270
"Little Boy" 36
Little Creek, VA 144
Little Rock, AR 125
Londonberry, NH 295
Long Prairie, MN 82
Los Angeles, CA 134, 224
Lowe, Andrew 273, 275
Luster, Herbert 125–135

Luzon, Philippines 119
Lynch, Jessica 298
Lyons, Kyle 301

MacArthur, General Douglas 28, 43, 118–119, 127, 134, 138, 140, 156, 161, 172–173
Majon-dong, North Korea 168
Malayan Archipelago 118
Maldonado, Robert 275–277
Manchuria, China 184
Mangual, Ernesto 288–289
Manhattan, NY 109, 226
Manila, Philippines 119
Manley, Renard 264–265
Manpojin, North Korea 184
Mare Island Yard, CA 7, 11
Mariana Island Group 16, 20, 23–24, 28–31, 33–37, 39–41, 84, 95, 104, 107
Marine Barracks, Beirut 259–265
Marine Barracks, Naval Ammunition Depot, McAlester, OK 251
Marine Barracks, Naval Operating Base, Norfolk, VA 31
Marine Barracks, Pearl Harbor, HI 127
Marine Corps Association 148, 194, 210
Marine Corps Heritage Foundation 194
Marine Corps League 12, 80, 109, 135, 255
Marine Corps Museum, Quantico, VA 101–102
Marine Corps News 307
Marine Corps Recruiting Depot (MCRD), Parris Island, SC 18, 33, 78, 103, 118, 177, 185, 226, 251,255
Marine Corps Recruiting Depot (MCRD), San Diego, CA 27, 31, 38, 64, 82, 93, 113, 125, 136, 154, 203, 218, 232, 245, 280
Marine Corps Tanker's Association 237
Marine Memorial Foundation 194
Marino, Michael Garrett 260
Marion, AL 255
Marshall Island Group 20, 28, 83
Masan, South Korea 134, 157, 175
Massachusetts 231, 294
Mata, Jose, Jr. 301
Matsoman (commercial liner) 14
Maui, HI 36
Mazur, Carl 78–80
McCandless, Commander Bruce 9
McCann 2nd Lieutenant Charles 87
McClellan, Connie 578
McClellan, John 276–279
McFee, William 144
McGregor, TX 125
McLaughlin, Captain John 212–217
Medal of Honor 11, 34, 51, 61, 87, 90, 151, 220, 222, 242, 244
Mediterranean 292
Meeks, Hollye 270
Memphis, TN 143, 217
Merchant Marines 153

Miami, FL 289, 293
Midway Island 8, 125
Military magazine 37, 55, 135
Military History magazine 121, 148
Milwaukee, WI 43
Mindanao, Philippines 119
Minneapolis, MN 136, 149
Miryang, South Korea 133
Mississippi 113
Mississippi River 27
Mitchum, Robert 182
Mobile, AL 255
Montana 83
Moonlit Eagle Productions 17, 152
Morotai Island, Maluka Island Group 28
Motoyama, Iwo Jima 105
Mount Balbi, Bougainville 94
Mount Everest 162
Mount Suribachi, Iwo Jima 86, 105, 107, 304
Mount Tapachau, Saipan 30–31
Mountaintop, PA 18
Mueller, Major General Paul 43
Mulligan, Sergeant 116
Multination Peace Force (MNF) 260, 265
Murray, Lieutenant Colonel Raymond 127
Muslims 273
Mutters Ridge, Vietnam 246

Nagasaki, Japan 36, 62
Naha, Okinawa 60, 80
Nakagawa, Colonel Kunio 43
Nakajima B5N 40
Nakajima B6N Tenzan 40
Naktong Bulge, Korea 129–130, 133–134
Naktong River, Korea 127–129, 144
Napalm 36, 60
Naples, Italy 255
Nashville, TN 27
National Defense Medal 164
Navaho code talkers 31
Navy and Marine Corps Achievement Medal 269, 276
Navy and Marine Corps Commendation Medal 281
Navy Cross 51, 151, 193, 244
NBC-TV News Department 110
Negros, Philippines 119
Nelson, Dustin 299–300
Nevada City Outposts, Korea 185–186, 192–193
New Britain 57, 65, 160, 286
New Caledonia 19, 64, 69, 94
New England 295
New Guinea 28, 48, 56–57, 64–65, 67, 160
New Hope, PA 237
New Jersey 110
New Mexico 237
New River, NC 100
New York 110, 230
New York City, NY 83

New York City College, NY 194
New York Times newspaper 299
New York University, NY 194
New Zealand 14, 19–20, 28, 38, 57, 94, 233
Newby, Jeremy 288–289
Ngesebus Island, Palau Island Group 65
Nichols, Charles 78–81
Nidetch, Jean 182
Nietzche, Friedrich 218
Nightfighters 272–279
Nimitz, Admiral Chester 28, 43
Norfolk, VA 32
North Atlantic Treaty Organization (NATO) 199, 289
North Carolina State University 32
North Korea 121, 136, 141–142, 156, 161, 165, 172, 199
North Korean People's Army (NKPA) 129, 134
North Vietnam 57
North Vietnamese Army (NVA) 205–210, 213–216, 220–222, 228, 234–236, 242
Norwood, MA 78

Oahu, Hawaii 108
Oakman, AL 68
Obata, Lieutenant General Hideyoshi 41
Obong-ni, South Korea 129
Obong-ni Ridge, South Korea 129, 133
Oceanside, CA 83
Officer Candidate School (OCC), Quantico, VA 212
Ogata, Colonel Kiyochi 34
Ohman, Joseph 149–152
Okinawa Island 11, 15, 23, 31, 39–40, 44, 48, 56–62, 66–67, 72–76, 79–80, 104, 160, 216, 233, 245, 248, 255, 259, 286, 292, 298
Oklahoma 83
Old Breed News newsletter 12, 49, 194
Omaha, NE 289
Omaha World-Herald newspaper 284
Omar, Mullah 273
Operation Allen Brook 220–225, 227–230
Operation Buffalo 205–210
Operation Chromite 287
Operation Desert Shield 15, 44, 57, 160, 260, 286, 298
Operation Desert Storm 15, 34, 44, 57, 160, 260, 272, 286
Operation Detachment 86
Operation Enduring Freedom 272, 298
Operation Iraqi Freedom 15, 260, 269, 272, 286, 298
Operation Just Cause, Panama 15
Operation Kentucky 233–234
Operation Napolean/Saline 233
Operation Restore Hope, Somalia 298
Operation Thor 233–236
Orlando, FL 76
Ortiz, Jefferson 293

Outpost Berlin, Korea 198
Outpost Carson, Korea 185–186, 192
Outpost East Berlin, Korea 198
Outpost Reno, Korea 185–186, 189, 192
Outpost Vegas, Korea 185–194, 198
Overbrook School for the Blind 25

P-47 Thunderbolts 36
Pace College 109
Pakistan 273
Palau Island Group 28, 43–49, 52–54, 56–58, 65–66, 70–72, 78–79
Palestine Liberation Group (PLO) 260
Palizzolo, William 177–179
Panama 238
Panama Canal 94
Panama City, Florida 264
Panay, Philippines 119
Panmunjon, North Korea 185, 193
Panmunjon Corridor, Korea 193
Papuan Peninsula 28
Parent's magazine 194
Pasadena, CA 19
Pasadena City College 248
Paterson, NJ 153
Pavuvu Island, Russell Island Group 44–45, 48, 52, 65–66, 69–70, 72, 78
Peabody College, TN 31
Pearl Harbor, HI 2, 8, 18, 20, 43, 56, 68, 80, 94, 100, 103, 250
Pearl Harbor Survivors 12
Pease Air Force Base, NH 80
Peleliu Island, Palau Island Group 43–49, 52–54, 56–58, 65–66, 70–72, 78–79, 104, 160, 286
Pemberton, NJ 167
Pendracki, Andrew 304
Pensacola, FL 255
Pentagon 299
PerezTorrez, Alberto 287–290
Peto, George 56–63
Philadelphia, PA 92, 94
Philippines 20, 28, 31, 36, 41, 43–44, 65, 118–121
Phoenix, AZ 153
Phu Bai 246, 286
Phu Dong (2), Vietnam 233
Pickett, Major General George 303
Pitman, Todd 296
Piva Forks Battle, Bougainville 95
Plainville, CT 295
Poland 93
Ponce, Puerto Rico 262
Porter, Jack 27–32
Portsmouth, NH 86
Post Traumatic Stress Disorder (PTSD) 237
Potomac River 19
Poughkeepsie, NY 264
Presidential Unit Citation 11, 34, 44, 62, 117, 163, 294

Prisoner of War (POW) 168–169, 182–184; Medal 169
Prominitz, Frank 147, 147
Puerta Vallarta, Mexico 248
Puller, Lieutenant General Lewis "Chesty" 51, 58, 125, 127, 145, 147, 165, 173–174, 182
"Purple Heart Express" 133
Purple Heart Medal 100, 107, 110–111, 135, 152, 155, 163, 169, 176, 240, 244, 269, 280
Purple Heart Society 12, 148
Pusan, South Korea 127–128, 133–134, 137–138, 183
Pusan Perimeter, Korea 127–128, 134–135, 137–138, 144, 183
P'yongyang, North Korea 173

Qu Nhon, Vietnam 160
Quang Nam Province, Vietnam 39, 220, 252
Quang Tri Province, Vietnam 396, 205, 286
Quantico, VA 14, 80, 216, 255
Que Son Mountains, Vietnam/Laos 220–221

Ra Al Mishb, Kuwait 57
Rabaul, New Britain Island 94–95
Ramadi, Iraq 282–283, 292–293
Razor Back, Vietnam 246
Reagan, President Ronald 307
Rearden, Corporal 87
Red Cross 20, 110, 243
Red Dragon — Faces of War II 164, 179, 199
Reed Springs, MO 160
Rendezvous with Hell 147
Reno Block, Korea 189, 193
Republic of Korea (ROK) Army 127, 162, 168, 186, 239–240
Reserve Officer Training Corps (ROTC) 38, 93, 232
Rickey, Branch 82
Ridgewood, NJ 111
Riordan, Arthur 226–231
Riverside Press Enterprise newspaper 302
Robbins, Anthony 153
Rochester, NY 306
Rocket Belt, Vietnam 220
Rockpile, Vietnam 246
Rodriquez, Anthony 267
Rogers, Warrant Officer Jeromine 288
Roi-Namur Islands 33–34
Romeau, Gregory 285
Roosevelt, President Franklin D. 43, 68, 119
Rosenthal, Joseph 107
Rupertus, Major General William H. 43
Russell Island Group 44, 69
Ryuku Island Group 31, 36, 41, 56–62, 72–76, 79–80

Sabol, Colonel Stephen 60
Sach'on, South Korea 128–129, 131
St. Louis, MO 101, 195
St. Michiel, France 44

Saipan Island 16, 23, 28–31, 33–35, 39, 41, 259, 292, 294
Saito, Lieutenant General Yoshitsugu 28, 31
Saldarriage, Katheryn 270
Salem, OR 270
Salvation Army 76
Samo, Andrew 38–42
San Antonio, TX 38
San Diego, CA 14–15, 19, 23, 76, 94, 127, 154, 246, 259, 275, 292
San Francisco, CA 25, 80, 100, 193
Santa Monica, CA 218
Santa Monica College, CA 224
Santo Domingo 213
Saratoga, FL 76
Saudi Arabia 44, 233, 286, 298
Saving Private Ryan 1
Savo Island, Guadalcanal 9
Schening, Lieutenant Colonel Richard 205–206
Schmidt, Major General Harry 34, 294
Schmuck, Lieutenant Colonel Donald 174
Schuller, Robert 113
Scout Observation Curtis Seaplane 11
Sea of Japan 128
Seattle, WA 25, 54, 80
Second Marine Division Association 25–26, 32, 101
Seider, James 43–49
Seoul, South Korea 57, 138–139, 145, 150, 155–156, 160–161, 182–184, 186, 286
Sgt. Grit 237
Shakespeare, William 27, 123
Shanghai, China 14
Shell Oil 27
Shite (Shia) 265
Shuri Castle, Okinawa 60, 62, 79
Shuri Heights, Okinawa 60, 74
Silver Star 51, 151, 215, 244
Simonsen, Robert 218–225
Simula Corporation 299
Sinatra, Frank 111
Singapore 20
Slater, Captain Al 207
Small Arms Protective Plates (SAPI 299–302
Smith, Lieutenant General Holland "Howlin Mad" Smith 28, 31, 35, 86, 89–90
Smith, Major General Julian 20
Smith, Major General Oliver P. Smith 60, 161, 165–166, 169, 173, 176
Smith, Major General Ralph 31
Smyth, George 103–112
Solomon Islands 10, 15–16, 28, 38, 78–79, 94
Somalia 44
Sosa, South Korea 145
Sousa, John Phillip 19
South China Sea 245
South Korea 127–128, 136, 141, 150, 154, 157, 161, 172, 199
Soviet Union 199, 222

Spielberg, Stephen 1
Spring, TX 300
Stagner, Mike 245–249
Stalmate II 44
Stars and Stripes 265, 270–271, 278–279, 285, 290, 302
State University of Iowa 147
Stephenson, Captain Edward 98–100
Stevens, Kenneth 82–91
Stewart, Dick 125
Strickbine, Norman 164, 169, 179
Sudong Valley, North Korea 161
Sudong-ni, North Korea 161, 163, 168
Sugar Loaf Hill, Okinawa 60
Suicide Creek, Cape Gloucester 64
Sullivan, Captain E.V. 233
Sullivan, Ed 110
Sullivan brothers 11
Sunni 282–283
Suplee, Charles 166–167
Sweeney, Major Charles 36
Syria (Syrians) 260, 265, 283, 298

Taft, Lieutenant Kenneth 188–190, 192–193
Taft, President William H. 188
Takashima, Lieutenant General Takeshi 41
Taliban 272–273
"Talon" 281
Tammim, Iraq 283
Tampa, FL 278
Tarawa Atoll 15–16, 20–22, 26, 28–29, 292
Task Force Drysdale 165, 168–169
Tempe, AZ 299
Tennessee 27, 83, 217
Tet Offensive, Vietnam 219, 227, 233
Texas 83, 111
The Texas Chainsaw Massacre 239
Third Marine Division Association 42, 90, 101, 109, 237
38th Parallel, Korea 172, 185, 187, 195
Thomas, Major General Gerald 196
Three House Island, Vietnam 253–254
Thua Thien Province, Vietnam 39
Tibbits, Colonel Paul W. 36
Tijuana, Mexico 182
Time magazine 108
Tinian Island 15–16, 23, 31, 34–37, 259, 292, 294
Tinian Town, Tinian 35
Titonka, IA 50
Tojo, Hideki 31
Tokyo, Japan 28, 70, 84
Tokyo Rose 45
Topeka, KS 118
Topsham, ME 295
Travis Air Force Base, CA 134
Treasure Island, CA 135, 193
Trilling, Diana 177
Trippler General Hospital, Oahu, HI 151
Truman, President Harry S. 36, 92, 127

Trump, Donald 286
Tucson, AZ 300
Turkish Brigade 193
Turnage, Major General Allen Hal 95
Turner, Admiral Richmond Turner 35
Tuy Loan, Vietnam 252
Twenty-nine Palms, CA 160, 233, 297–298
21 Club, New York, NY 110

Udo, General Takehido 58
Uijongbu, Korea 183
Umurbrogal Mountains, Peleliu 45, 48
United Nations (UN) 127, 145, 161, 172–173; Security Council 263; Service Medal 164
U.S. Army: 6th Army 119; 8th Army 119, 127, 129, 134, 161, 172–173; III Corps 57; X Corps 161, 172–174; XXIV Corps 58; 7th Division 58, 161, 172–173; 23rd Division 193; 24th Division 129; 25th Division 198; 27th Division 20, 28–29, 31, 58; 28th Division 282; 77th Division 41, 58; 96th Division 58; 2nd Brigade 282; 31st Regiment 165–166; 58th Regiment 92; 81st Regiment 43; 321st Regiment 45; 1st Cavalry 184; 167th Cavalry 283; Air Corps 36, 50, 250; National Guard 38, 39, 68, 125, 283; Rangers 237; Reserves 93; Special Forces 273
U.S. Civil War 148, 303
U.S. Department of Fish and Wildlife 143
U.S. Gypsum 101
U.S. Marine Corps: Fleet Marine Force 14, 82, 104, 213, 294; 1st Division 15, 43–48, 51–54, 56–62, 64–66, 69–76, 78–80, 127, 134–135, 138–141, 144–147, 149–151, 154–159, 160–199, 220–225, 286–290, 294, 297–298; 2nd Division 14–16, 20–21, 23, 27–31, 34, 57, 58, 127, 259–265, 292–294, 307; 3rd Division 34, 38–42, 82–90, 94–100, 104–107, 203–211, 213–216, 233, 245–249, 252, 272–279; 4th Division 28, 33–37, 86–87, 97, 99, 105, 294; 5th Division 86–88, 96, 105, 113–117, 218–220; 6th Division 58, 60; 1st Marine Regiment (1st Marines) 3, 44, 56–57, 60–61, 63, 144–147, 154–159, 165–166, 173–176, 186, 195, 238–244, 286–290; 3rd Marines 207, 251, 272–279; 4th Marines 118, 213–216, 266; 5th Marines 52–54, 64, 66, 69–76, 127–135, 138–141, 156, 170–171, 173–174, 180–181, 183, 186, 192–193, 300; 7th Marines 47, 149–151, 156, 160–164, 170, 173–174, 177, 183–184, 186, 193, 197, 210, 220–222, 224, 281; 8th Marines 259–265, 292–294; 9th Marines 203–211, 233–236; 10th Marines 27–28, 30, 94, 185, 193; 11th Marines 14, 78–80, 167–169, 172, 173, 185–193, 214; 12th Marines 94–100, 214, 245–249; 14th Marines 34; 19th Marines 34; 20th Marines 34; 21th Marines 38–41, 82–90, 97–100,

104–107; 22nd Marines 80; 23rd Marines 34, 105; 24th Marines 34; 25th Marines 33–36, 294–296; 26th Marines 114, 117; 27th Marines 114, 117, 210, 219–225, 227–231, 244; 28th Marines 113–117; 1st Marine Parachute Regiment 114; Regimental Combat Team-2 304; Regimental Combat Team-5 295, 297–299; Regimental Combat Team-7 270, 298, 306; Regimental Combat Team-8 266; 1st Provisional Marine Brigade 41, 127–134, 136–138, 144, 183; 1st Marine Brigade 94; 2nd Marine Brigade 14, 259; 1st Marine Expeditionary Force (MEF) 297; 7th MEF 298; 3rd Marine Amphibious Force (MAF) 213; 24th Marine Amphibious Unit (MAU) 262; Marine Aircraft Group (MAG) 33, 127; 1st Marine Aircraft Wing (MAW) 127; 3rd MAW 270; 7th Engineering Battalion 224; 8th Engineering Battalion 280; 13th Engineering Battalion 218–219, 224; 2nd Defense Battalion 93; 18th Defense Battalion 19; 40th Replacement Battalion 51, 54; Light Armored Reconnaissance (LAR) Battalion 205, 297–302; Marine Raider Battalion 113–114; Military Police 28–29, 251; 1st Pioneer Battalion 45–48; 1st Reconnaissance Battalion 239; 3rd Reconnaissance Battalion 207; 1st Tank Battalion 166; 3rd Tank Battalion 233–236; 5th Tank Battalion 232, 236–237; Battalion Landing Team (BLT) 207, 262; Marine Corps Band 19–20, 23, 25–26; Marine Corps Reserves 7, 34, 93, 101, 149, 177, 294–295; 2nd Force Service Support Group 280; Combined Action Company (CACO) 252; Combined Action Group (CAG) 252; Combined Action Platoon (CAP) 251–254

U.S. Navy: 6th Fleet 213; Corpsmen 2–3, 20, 23, 50–55, 58, 61, 68–77, 79, 88, 90, 106–108, 132–133, 140–141, 146–147, 190, 195, 197–199, 205, 209, 222, 229–230, 252–253, 259, 262, 264, 272, 275–277, 293, 300–302; Reserves 76; Seabees 36, 81, 95, 117; U.S. Naval Air Station, Jacksonville, FL 76; U.S. Naval Air Station, Memphis, TN 143; U.S. Naval Air Station, Minneapolis, MN 149; U.S. Naval Ammunition Depot, McAlester, OK 251; U.S. Naval Boot Camp, San Diego, CA 69; U.S. Naval Detention Barracks, Philadelphia, PA 25; U.S. Naval Hospital #10 108; U.S. Naval Hospital #111 107–108; U.S. Naval Hospital, Camp Lejeune, NC 109; U.S. Naval Hospital, Da Nang (First Medical Battalion), Vietnam 233; U.S. Naval Hospital, Da Nang (Naval Support Activity), Vietnam 240; U.S. Naval Hospital, Oak Knoll, CA 11, 147; U.S. Naval Hospital, Oakland, CA 134; U.S. Naval Hospital, Philadelphia, PA 80, 147; U.S. Naval Hospital, San Diego, CA 69, 197;

U.S. Naval Hospital, San Francisco, CA 108; U.S. Naval Hospital, Yokosuka, Japan 147, 157, 175; U.S. Naval Hospital Corps School, Balboa Park, CA 69; U.S. Naval Hospital Corps School, Farragut, ID 50; U.S. Naval Ordnance Test Station, Ridgecrest, CA 154; U.S. Naval Training Base, Farragut, ID 50; USS *Bolivar* 96; USS *Buckner* 154 ; USS *Colorado* 35; USS *Consolation* 134; USS *Indianapolis* 36–37; USS *Iowa* 154; USS *John Pope* 193; USS *Juneau* 11; USS *Loundes* 107; USS LST-27 100; USS LST-117 39–40; USS LST-341 94; USS *Lurline* 94; USS *Meigs* 197; USS *New Orleans* 8; USS *President Jackson* 83; USS *Rochambeau* 64; USS *San Francisco* 7–13; USS *Sanctuary* 209; USS *Santa Isabel* 100; USS *Scott* 35; USS *Springfield* 213; USS *Upshur* 251; USS *Whetstone* 248
U.S. Rubber Company 109
University of Denver, CO 237
University of Minnesota 14
University of North Carolina 32
University of Pennsylvania 25
University of Tennessee 212
University of West Florida 255
Ushijima, General Mitsuru 58, 60, 62
Utah 56, 247

Valdez, Steven 275
Valkenburg, Renald 153–159
Vallejo, CA 7
Vandergrift, Major General Alexander 15
Van Vleet, Robert 247–248
Veronee, Marvin 117
Veterans Administration (VA) 76, 178
Veterans of Foreign Wars (VFW) 90, 135, 249
Veterans of the Vietnam War 234
Viet Cong, (VC) 220, 228, 241
Vietnam 1, 19, 39, 44, 167, 199, 201–255, 280, 286, 291
Vietnam Tanker's Association 237
Vietnam Veterans of America 210, 237
Vietnam War 51, 57, 117, 177, 201–255, 272, 289, 303
Vietnamese Popular Force (PF) 252–255
Vincens, Jay 238–244

Wainwright, Major General Johnathan 119
Wake Island 134
Walker, Lieutenant General Walton 129
Walking Dead 205
Walt, General Lewis 193, 251–252
Wana Draw, Okinawa 60–62, 74
Wana Ridge, Okinawa 60
Wantagh, Long Island, NY 226
War Stories: Accounts of Minnesotans Who Defended Their Nation 17, 67, 143, 152
Wars Against Terrorism 2, 15, 34, 39, 44, 160, 205, 257–307

Index

Washington, DC 42, 255
Washington, ME 78
Wayne, John 235, 240
Wear, John, II 232–237
Weisbaden, Germany 264
Welch, Jack 172
Wellington, New Zealand 20, 28, 286
West Africa 272
Westbrook, CT 295
Western Union. 109–111
Westmoreland, General William 251
White, Kenneth 45, 47, 49
Wickman, Robert 197–199
Wilhelm, Kermit 136–143
Williams, Dewayne 242, 244
Wilson, Arthur 164, 179
Wilson, NY 182
Wisconsin 43
Wolmi-do Island, Korea 138, 150, 183
Wonson, North Korea 145, 156, 183
Woodham, Lieutenant Colonel Tullis, Jr. 227
Woodland, OR 50

World Trade Center, NY 272, 306
World War I 7, 19, 28, 38, 44, 51, 92, 113, 152, 175, 195, 303
World War II 1–3, 5–121, 125, 127, 136, 138, 144, 152–153, 160, 176, 205, 219, 238, 246, 250, 259, 272, 286, 292, 294, 303
Worry, Lieutenant Herbert 116
Worthington, OH 63

Yalu River, North Korea 156, 161, 172–173, 184
Yokoi, Shoichi 41
Yong Dong Po, South Korea 155
Yontan, Okinawa 80
Young, Captain Cassin 11
Young Men's Christian Association (YMCA) 113
Yudam-ni, North Korea 140–141, 168, 170, 173, 183–184

Zdon, Al 17, 67, 143, 152
Zucroft, Corporal Steven 221

www.ingramcontent.com/pod-product-compliance
Ingram Content Group UK Ltd.
Pitfield, Milton Keynes, MK11 3LW, UK
UKHW041922140426
5217IPUK00014B/279

9 780786 438211